CONCISE COLLEGE CASENOTES

CASES AND STATUTES

ON

LAND LAW

By

E. L. G. TYLER, M.A.(OXON)
of Lincoln's Inn, Barrister;
Barrister and Solicitor of the Supreme Court of Tasmania
and of the High Court and Federal Courts of Australia;
Professor of Law, University of Hong Kong

SECOND EDITION

LONDON
SWEET & MAXWELL
1986

First Edition 1974
Second Impression 1982
Second Edition 1986

Published by
Sweet and Maxwell Limited of
11 New Fetter Lane, London
and printed in Great Britain
by Page Bros. (Norwich) Ltd.

British Library in Cataloguing Publication Data

Tyler, E. L. G.
Cases and statutes on land law.—2nd ed.—
(Concise college casenotes)
1. Real property—England—Cases
I. Title. II. Series
344.2064′3′0264 KD828

ISBN 0–421–34350–8

CONCISE COLLEGE CA

CASES AND STATUTES
ON
LAND LAW

OTHER BOOKS IN THIS SERIES:

Cases and Statutes on Commercial Law,
by Paul L. Bradbury and Paul Dobson
Cases and Statutes on Contract, by Rodney Brazier
Cases and Statutes on Criminal Law,
by John Slater and A. P. Dobson
Cases and Statutes on Hotel and Catering Law, by David Field
Cases and Statutes on Tort, by Paul L. Bradbury

AUSTRALIA AND NEW ZEALAND
The Law Book Company Ltd.
Sydney : Melbourne : Perth

CANADA AND U.S.A.
The Carswell Company Ltd.
Agincourt, Ontario

INDIA
N. M. Tripathi Private Ltd.
Bombay
and
Eastern Law House Private Ltd.
Calcutta and Delhi
M.P.P. House
Bangalore

ISRAEL
Steimatzky's Agency Ltd.
Jerusalem : Tel Aviv : Haifa

MALAYSIA : SINGAPORE : BRUNEI
Malayan Law Journal (Pte.) Ltd.
Singapore

PAKISTAN
Pakistan Law House
Karachi

PREFACE

The first edition of this Casenotes book was published in 1974. Over the decade since, there have been many important Land Law cases, most notably in relation to rights in the matrimonial home, estoppel and restrictive covenants. In this new edition, 56 cases included in the first edition have been omitted. This does not necessarily mean that all of the omitted cases are obsolete or no longer of any importance but some omissions had to be made for new material. The second edition includes 93 new cases.

In this edition the section on co-ownership has been removed from the chapter on Settlements and Trusts for Sale, and brought forward as a new Chapter 3. This reflects the importance of the numerous recent cases on co-ownership. The section in Chapter 1 on personal and proprietary rights has been expanded to include licence and estoppel cases. Otherwise the format of the original book has been retained. The cases on the annexation of restrictive covenants have been retained despite the *Federated Homes* case.

Limitations of space have meant that some material has had to be excluded and Rent Act legislation and cases are only included where relevant to other matters. Nor has it been possible to cover some of the public law topics included in some Land Law courses. For further statutory material the student should have the current edition of Sweet & Maxwell's *Property Statutes*.

There is no substitute for the student reading the reports and legislation and making his or her own notes. However, for those without ready access to primary material, or as a preliminary guide or revision handbook, I trust this small book may be of some use.

September 1, 1985

E. L. G. TYLER
Hong Kong

CONTENTS

CHAPTER 5. MORTGAGES

CHAPTER 6. EASEMENTS

CHAPTER 7. RESTRICTIVE COVENANTS

CHAPTER 8. SETTLEMENTS AND TRUSTS FOR SALE

TABLE OF CASES

[References in **bold** type are to a consideration of the case.]

TABLE OF STATUTES

[References in **bold** type are to a consideration of the Act.]

ABBREVIATIONS

L. & T.A.	Landlord and Tenant Act
L.C.A.	Land Charges Act
L.P.A.*	Law of Property Act
L.R.A.*	Land Registration Act
S.L.A.*	Settled Land Act

* If no date is specified after the abbreviation the 1925 Act is intended.

CHAPTER 1

ESTATES AND INTERESTS IN LAND

1. LEGAL ESTATES AND EQUITABLE INTERESTS

Law of Property Act 1925, ss.1, 4, 205

"1. (1) The only estates in land which are capable of subsisting or of being conveyed or created at law are—

(*a*) An estate in fee simple absolute in possession;
(*b*) A term of years absolute.

(2) The only interests or charges in or over land which are capable of subsisting or of being conveyed or created at law are—

(*a*) An easement, right, or privilege in or over land for an interest equivalent to an estate in fee simple absolute in possession or a term of years absolute; . . .
(*c*) A charge by way of legal mortgage; . . .
(*e*) Rights of entry exercisable over or in respect of a legal term of years absolute . . .

(3) All other estates, interests, and charges in or over land take effect as equitable interests.

(6) A legal estate is not capable of subsisting or of being created in an undivided share in land or of being held by an infant.

4. (1) Interests in land validly created or arising after the commencement of this Act, which are not capable of subsisting as legal estates, shall take effect as equitable interests, and, save as otherwise expressly provided by statute, interests in land which under the Statute of Uses or otherwise could before the commencement of this Act have been created as legal interests, shall be capable of being created as equitable interests:

Provided that, after the commencement of this Act (and save as hereinafter expressly enacted), an equitable interest in land shall only be capable of being validly created in any case in which an equivalent equitable interest in property real or personal could have been validly created before such commencement."

Note: On s.4, see *E. R. Ives Investment Ltd.* v. *High* (below, p. 210).

"205. (1) In this Act unless the context otherwise requires, the following expressions have the meanings hereby assigned to them respectively, that is to say—

(ix) 'Land' includes land of any tenure, and mines and minerals, whether or not held apart from the surface, buildings or parts of buildings (whether the division is horizontal, vertical or made in any other way) and other corporeal hereditaments; also . . . a rent and other incorporeal hereditaments, and an easement, right, privilege, or benefit in, over, or derived from land; but not an undivided share in land; . . .

(xix) 'Possession' includes receipt of rents and profits or the right to receive the same, if any; and 'income' includes rents and profits . . .

(xxi) 'Purchaser' means a purchaser in good faith for valuable consideration . . . except that in Part 1 [ss.1-37] of this Act and elsewhere where so expressly provided 'purchaser' only means a person who acquires an interest in or charge on property for money or money's worth; . . . 'valuable consideration' includes marriage but does not include a nominal consideration in money; . . ."

2. Personal Rights and Proprietary Rights

Pritchard v. Briggs [1980] Ch. 338, C.A.

In 1944, Major and Mrs. L. the owners of the Pen-y-Gwryd Hotel, Beddgelert, sold the hotel. They retained adjoining land and a house and covenanted with the purchaser of the hotel and his successors in title, for themselves and their successors in title that "so long as the purchaser shall live and the vendors shall also be alive" neither they nor the survivor of them would sell or concur in selling all or any part of the retained property without giving to the purchaser the option of purchasing the retained property on specified terms. This right of pre-emption was registered under the L.C.A. 1925 as an estate contract (see the L.C.A. 1972, below, p. 18). In 1954 the hotel was conveyed to Mr. and Mrs. Briggs together with the benefit of the right of pre-emption. In 1959 Major and Mrs. L. granted a lease of the retained land to the plaintiff and an option to purchase the property retained by Major and Mrs. L. exercisable by notice to be given within three months after the death of the survivor of Major and Mrs. L. The option was repeated in a further lease in 1964 and was duly registered under the L.C.A. 1925 as an estate contract. Mrs. L. died in 1969 and in 1971 Major L.'s nephew, who had been appointed his receiver under the Mental Health Act 1959 (now 1983), contracted to sell the retained property to the Briggs, purportedly pursuant to the right of the pre-emption, but at an increased price and with an indemnity against any claims arising out of the plaintiffs' rights. Major L. died in 1973 and the contract was completed by his executors. The plaintiff exercised the option and claimed specific performance of the contract for sale consequential upon such exercise. The trial judge dismissed the claim, holding that the right of pre-emption created an interest in land which by reason of its prior registration under the L.C.A. had priority to the plaintiff's option. On appeal it was held that on the true construction of the right of pre-emption (and the case was essentially one of construction of the right), because the right of pre-emption conferred no right to call for a conveyance unless the grantor chose to fulfil the conditions on which the right could be exercised (*i.e.* sale in the lifetime of Major & Mrs. L.), it did not create any present or contingent interest in the retained property. It was a mere personal contract. According to Goff L.J. it could not subsequently become an interest in land binding on a successor in title of the grantor. But the majority (Templeman and Stephenson L.JJ.) thought that the right would become an interest in land if the grantor chose to fulfil the condition on which the grantee could exercise his right and, if registered as an estate contract, it would bind a successor in title of the grantor. In any event the condition was not fulfilled by the grant of the option, because the right of pre-emption applied to a sale or an agreement for sale by Major and Mrs. L. in their lifetime and the grant of option exercisable after (in the events that happened) the death of Major L. was not a sale by the couple in their lifetime. On the grant of the option the retained land became subject to the option and any sale by Major and Mrs. L. or the survivor of them was subject to the option. Alternatively, a majority (Goff and Stephenson L.JJ.) held that, if the right of pre-emption did create an interest in land having, by virtue of its registration, priority to the option, the 1973 sale was not, because of the additional price and terms and negotiations, made pursuant to the right of the pre-emption and therefore it was a sale subject to the option. The plaintiff was entitled to specific performance.

Note: See also the following cases in this section and below, pp. 12, 15-17, 23-25, 28-31.

D.H.N. Food Distributors Ltd. v. Tower Hamlets London Borough Council [1976] 1 W.L.R. 852, C.A.

The plaintiff company carried on a grocery business. It agreed to buy new premises. A bank agreed to finance the purchase. Terms of the loan were that the property should be purchased in the name of Bronze Investments Ltd. (Bronze), a company wholly owned by the bank, and that Bronze should a year later sell the property to the plaintiff. The property was duly transferred to

Bronze and the plaintiff went into occupation (according to the company's books of accounts paying a yearly rent to Bronze) and made alterations to the premises. Subsequently the time for the sale on from Bronze to the plaintiff was extended. In 1966 the plaintiff purchased all the shares in Bronze from the bank. Bronze never traded, but simply held the property. The plaintiff had another wholly owned subsidiary, D.H.N. Food Transport Ltd., which owned the vehicles used in the business. In 1969, the defendant made a compulsory order for the premises. The compensation for the land was assessed at £360,000. As no suitable alternative premises for the grocery business could be found, the business came to an end and the three companies were wound up. The plaintiff and the transport company claimed compensation for disturbance, on the grounds that they had either an equitable interest in the property, or an irrevocable licence or that the corporate veil should be pierced and the plaintiff treated as the real owner. The Council claimed that the plaintiff was a mere licensee and as the licence could be terminated on short notice, any compensation would be negligible. There was no doubt that if the same entity had owned both the land and the business, substantial compensation for disturbance would be payable. The Court of Appeal was prepared to pierce the corporate veil which regarded the three companies as separate legal units and treat the group as a single economic entity for the purpose of awarding compensation for disturbance. If the companies had to be treated as separate entities, then because the plaintiff had paid all the purchase money for the property and held all the shares in Bronze, it had an irrevocable licence to occupy and remain in the premises for so long as it wanted to, which (*per* Lord Denning M.R.) gave rise to a constructive trust or (*per* Goff L.J.) an equitable interest in the land or (*per* Goff and Shaw L.JJ.) Bronze held the legal title in trust initially for the bank, and then when the plaintiff purchased the Bronze shares from the bank in trust for the plaintiff. For all these reasons the plaintiff had a sufficient interest in the land for proper compensation for disturbance.

Note: And see note below, p. 82.

Bannister v. Bannister [1948] 2 All E.R. 133, C.A.

The defendant agreed to sell to her brother-in-law, the plaintiff, her cottage on the plaintiff's oral undertaking that the defendant would be allowed to live in the cottage rent free for as long as she wished. A conveyance was duly executed in 1943, but the undertaking was not put in writing. The purchase price was about half the true market value. Subsequently, with the defendant's consent, the plaintiff occupied the cottage save for the defendant's room. In 1947, the plaintiff let some strangers into occupation of the cottage as tenants and sought possession of the defendant's room. It was held that the oral undertaking amounted to a promise to create a life interest rather than a tenancy at will in the cottage in favour of the defendant, determinable on the defendant ceasing to live there. Reference was made to *Re Carne's Settled Estates* (see below, p. 273). The plaintiff held the property on a constructive trust. It was not necessary to show that the conveyance had been fraudulently obtained. "The fraud which brings the principle [of constructive trusts] into play arises as soon as the absolute character of the conveyance is set up for the purpose of defeating the beneficial interest. . . . "

Errington v. Errington and Woods [1952] 1 K.B. 290, C.A.

In 1936, a father bought a house for his son and daughter-in-law to live in. The purchase price was £750. The father paid £250 down and raised the balance with a building society mortgage. He told the daughter-in-law that the £250 was a present for them, but they were to pay the mortgage repayments, and that when the mortgage was paid off the house would be theirs and he would transfer it into their names. The son and daughter-in-law went into occupation and paid the mortgage instalments regularly, though the father paid the rates. The father died in 1945 before the mortgage had been paid off, leaving the house to his wife, the plaintiff, by his will. The son then left the daughter-in-law, the defendant. The plaintiff claimed possession from the defendant and her sister who was then living with her. It was held that the daughter-in-law was a licensee. Although the son and daughter-in-law were in exclusive possession, and a person in exclusive possession was prima facie to be considered a tenant, the circumstances might negative any intention to create a tenancy. The son and daughter-in-law were licensees with a contractual right to remain. Having acted on the father's promise that the property should belong to them, neither the father nor his widow, his successor in title, could eject them in disregard of it.

Note: This case can be treated either as illustrating a contractual licence or a licence by estoppel. The better view is that it is not a contractual licence case because the father was not bound to convey the house to the son and daughter-in-law until the mortgage had been paid off. Also there is some doubt whether a contractual licence binds a third party (but see *Binions* v. *Evans*, below, p. 16). Accordingly it is preferable to treat the case as one of licence by estoppel.

Tanner v. Tanner [1975] 1 W.L.R. 1346, C.A.

The plaintiff was a married man, who, in his own words, got fed up with his marriage and decided to have a "good time." He met the defendant. She had a protected tenancy of a flat. There was no question of marriage between them. She became pregnant by the plaintiff and gave birth to twin daughters. The plaintiff bought a house in his own name as a home for the defendant and the babies. They moved into the ground floor. The first floor was let. The defendant managed the lettings. In the meantime the plaintiff was associating with another woman. In 1973 he was divorced from his wife and he married the other woman. He offered the defendant £4,000 to leave the house. She refused this. He purported to terminate the defendant's licence and sought possession of the ground floor of the house. The county court judge ordered delivery up of possession. He rejected the defendant's claim to a beneficial interest in the house and an irrevocable licence. On the appeal (by which time the defendant had vacated the premises) it was held that the defendant had no proprietary interest in the house, but the inference to be drawn from the circumstances was that the defendant had a contractual licence to have accommodation in the house for herself and the children so long as the children were of school age and reasonably required the accommodation. Accordingly the possession order should not have been made. Two thousand pounds was awarded to the defendant for the loss of her licence (being the amount she might reasonably have obtained for the surrender of the licence).

Hardwick v. Johnson [1978] 1 W.L.R. 683, C.A.

The plaintiff bought a house in her own name for her son and the defendant (the son's second wife) to live in. (She had helped her son and his first wife buy a home and there had been complications when the first marriage had broken down.) It was agreed that the couple should pay her £28 a month. It was unclear whether this was for rent or purchase. The family agreement was loose. The couple made a few payments then stopped. The plaintiff did not demand payment. The second marriage failed and the son left home. The plaintiff wanted to sell the house. The defendant, who by then had a child by the son, refused to go. The plaintiff claimed possession. The claim was dismissed, the county court judge finding that the plaintiff had granted a joint licence to her son and the defendant and that the defendant was entitled to remain in occupation on payment of £7 a week and the arrears. On the appeal, Lord Denning M.R. held that the defendant had an equitable licence. He did not think it could be called a contractual licence, because it was difficult to say this family arrangement was a contract. Both Roskill and Browne L.JJ. thought it was a contractual licence. The court had to spell out the terms of the licence imputing an intention to the parties which they had never formed. The most fitting terms were that the licence was a joint licence to live in the house on payment of £28 per month. The plaintiff had shown by her conduct that she was prepared to postpone the payments, so the failure to pay had not given ground for terminating the licence. The licence was not given only to the son. The defendant was therefore entitled to remain. The court indicated that there might be circumstances which would terminate the licence but it was not necessary to specify them.

Chandler v. Kerley [1978] 1 W.L.R. 693, C.A.

In 1972, Mr. & Mrs. Kerley jointly purchased a house for £11,000, intending it to be the family home. The purchase was partly financed by a mortgage. In 1974 the Kerleys' marriage broke down. Mr. Kerley left, leaving Mrs. Kerley and the children in the house. Early in 1975, the Kerleys unsuccessfully tried to sell the house for £14,300. The mortgagee was threatening to foreclose. By this time Mrs. Kerley had become the plaintiff's mistress. The plaintiff agreed to buy the house for £10,000 on the understanding that Mrs. Kerley could live there until her divorce and thereafter they would live there together. When she asked the plaintiff what would happen if they parted, he replied that he could not put her out. Shortly afterwards their relationship ended. The plaintiff sought possession claiming that Mrs. Kerley was a mere licensee and her licence had been terminated. She claimed to be tenant for life or, alternatively a beneficiary under a constructive trust entitled to remain in the house with the children for as long as she wished. The county court judge found a constructive trust under which she was entitled to occupy the premises for her lifetime or as long as she wished. On appeal by the plaintiff Mrs. K was given leave to amend her counterclaim to claim that she was a licensee for life or for as long as the children remained in her custody and she did not remarry or for a period terminable only by reasonable notice. Dismissing the appeal but varying the original order, it was held that the defendant had a contractual licence terminable on reasonable notice, 12 months being reasonable notice in the circumstances. It was impossible to imply a licence to the defendant to occupy the house for her life. It would be wrong to infer, in the absence of an express promise, that the plaintiff was assuming the burden of housing another man's wife and children indefinitely and long after his relationship with her ended (*per* Lord Scarman). If the defendant could have established a licence for life, there was neither room nor need for an equitable interest for such a legal right could be protected by injunction. In such a case the role of equity is supportive and supplementary. Lord Scarman saw *Bannister* v. *Bannister* (above, p. 4), *Errington* v. *Errington* (above, p. 5) and *Binions* v. *Evans* (below, p. 16) as examples of the supportive role of equity providing a remedy to protect the legal right or supplementing a contractual right so as to give effect to the intention of the parties to the arrangement.

Note: For licences, see also below, pp. 14-18, 28, 111.

Pascoe v. Turner [1979] 1 W.L.R. 431, C.A.

In 1963, the defendant moved into the plaintiff's house as housekeeper. A year later they began cohabiting. The plaintiff offered marriage, but the defendant declined. In 1965 the plaintiff bought a new house. He took the defendant to inspect it for her approval before buying. They moved in. The plaintiff paid for the house and contents. The house was in his name. He gave the defendant a housekeeping allowance. In 1973 the plaintiff took up with another woman. On the defendant's return from a holiday the plaintiff told her about the affair but assured her that the house was hers and everything in it. He said he had put the transfer of the house into his solicitors' hands. The defendant stayed on in the house doing substantial (to her) improvements, repairs, maintenance and decoration to the house and buying new carpets and curtains, to the knowledge of the plaintiff. She still collected some rents for him. Then in 1976 they quarrelled and the plaintiff purported to terminate the defendant's licence. She refused to go and the plaintiff sued for possession in the county court. The judge held that the plaintiff had made a gift of the house and contents to the defendant and that he held the house on a constructive trust for her. On appeal it was held that any gift that had been made had not been perfected, there being no writing. Nor could a constructive trust be inferred from the circumstances of the imperfect gift. The defendant occupied the house initially after 1973 under a licence revocable at will. But the defendant's expenditure in reliance upon the plaintiff's declaration that he was giving, and later had given, the house to her gave rise to an estoppel and the minimum equity to do justice to the defendant was to compel the plaintiff to give effect to his promise by ordering him to execute a conveyance of the house in favour of the defendant. The court considered that the plaintiff was determined to evict the defendant if he could. To give her a mere licence to remain for an indefinite period would not protect her, as a licence could not be registered as a land charge and the defendant might find herself ousted by a purchaser for value without notice.

Greasley v. Cooke [1980] 1 W.L.R. 1306, C.A.

In 1938, when she was 16, the defendant went as maid to the house of Mr. Greasley, a widower with four teenage children. From 1946 she and Kenneth, one of the sons, lived together as man and wife in the house. She looked after Clarice, another of the children, who was mentally ill, and the other children until they left home. In 1948 Mr. Greasley died. He left the house to two of his sons, Howard and Kenneth. Kenneth had told the defendant that he would do the right thing by her, and another brother, Hedley, had told her she had no need to worry. Howard died intestate in 1966, his share passing to his children. Clarice and Kenneth died in 1975. Kenneth left his share to Hedley. After Kenneth's death the defendant was given notice to quit the house. The plaintiffs sued for possession. The defendant claimed to be entitled to remain in the house for the rest of her life, relying on proprietary estoppel. At the hearing the plaintiffs withdrew the claim. On the counterclaim the county court judge held that the burden of proving that she had acted to her detriment as a result of what the brothers told her rested on the defendant and as there was no such evidence to satisfy him (she might have stayed on in the house because of her relationship with Kenneth, rather than because of what she was promised) he ordered possession. On appeal it was held that, once it was shown that the defendant had relied on the assurances given to her, the burden of proving that she had acted to her detriment in staying on in the house did not rest on her. There was a presumption that she did so. The burden of proving that she had not done so rested on the plaintiffs. They had not appeared at the hearing to give any evidence and accordingly had not discharged the burden of proof on them. The court declared that the defendant was entitled to remain in the house rent free for as long as she wished. Lord Denning M.R. said that expenditure of money, though it had happened in many cases of proprietary estoppel, was not a necessary element of it. It is sufficient to raise the equity if the party to whom the assurance is given acts on the faith of it.

Note: On estoppel, see also below, pp. 14, 17, 22-23, 28-29, 78-79, 95, 119-120, 130, 186, 199 and 210.

3. The Doctrine of Notice

General note: The main difference between legal and equitable interests is illustrated by the doctrine of notice. A legal interest is enforceable against everyone (subject to registration under the

L.C.A. 1972 or L.R.A. 1925, where appropriate; and for a selling mortgagee's powers, see below, p. 191). An equitable interest is not enforceable against a bona fide purchaser of the legal estate without notice of that equitable interest. (For constructive notice and notice by registration, see below, p. 13, and 19 and 32 respectively. For overreaching, see below, pp. 51-52).

Bona Fide Purchaser for Value of the Legal Estate without Notice of Prior Equitable Interest

Pilcher v. Rawlins (1872) 7 Ch.App. 259, Court of Appeal in Chancery

In 1851 Rawlins, a solicitor, mortgaged his Whitchurch property to the trustees of Jeremiah Pilcher's settlement. The mortgage conveyance (before 1925 a legal mortgage was usually made by conveyance subject to a provision for reconveyance on repayment) to the trustees recited the trusts. In 1856 W. H. Pilcher, the surviving trustee and a solicitor, improperly reconveyed the property to Rawlins, acting in collusion with him, although only part of the mortgage moneys had been repaid. Then Rawlins remortgaged the property to Stockwell and Lamb not disclosing the 1851 mortgage and the reconveyance. The complete title deeds would have disclosed that Pilcher settlement trust moneys had been advanced to Rawlins. Pilcher and Rawlins spent the moneys advanced by Stockwell and Lamb. Subsequently, the beneficiaries under the Pilcher settlement discovered what had been going on and commenced proceedings claiming priority over Stockwell and Lamb. It was a case of which of two innocent parties was to suffer. It was held that S. and L. were bona fide purchasers for value of the legal estate without notice and took free from the trusts. They therefore had priority over the beneficiaries. Although, in order to make out their title to the legal estate S. and L. had to rely on the 1851 mortgage which disclosed the trusts and the subsequent reconveyance, they could still rely on the defence of purchaser for value without notice, because they did not have notice of those deeds at the time of their mortgage.

Cave v. Cave (1880) 15 Ch.D. 639

A trustee, a solicitor, used trust funds to purchase land which was conveyed to his brother, for whom he later acted in one legal and several equitable mortgages of the land. On the brother's bankruptcy the trust beneficiaries claimed priority over the mortgagees. Fry J. held that the legal mortgagee had priority over the beneficiaries because he was a bona fide purchaser for value of the legal estate without notice. But the beneficiaries had priority over the equitable mortgagees being prior in time.

Note: See *Wilkes* v. *Spooner* (below, p. 250).

Priority between Equitable Interests

Rice v. Rice (1853) 2 Drew. 73, V.-C.

The first defendant, Michael Rice, purchased certain leasehold property from George Rice and others. Although the assignment acknowledged receipt of the purchase-money, only one of the vendors was paid his share. Accordingly the others had an equitable lien on the property for the money due to them. Before they had been paid MR equitably mortgaged the property by deposit of deeds with Ede and Knight. MR subsequently absconded without paying the vendors or the mortgagees. The proceeds of sale of the property would not pay off both and the question was which of the equitable interests had priority. Kindersley V.-C. held that the possession of the deeds and the fact of the indorsement of the acknowledgement of receipt of the purchase-money on the assignment gave the mortgagees the better equity and therefore priority. The first in time would have priority only if the competing equitable interests were equal. In examining the relative merits of competing parties the court will direct its attention, *inter alia*, to the circumstances of the acquisition and the conduct of the parties.

Note: See *Barclays Bank Ltd.* v. *Taylor* (below, p. 41).

Equitable Interest and Mere Equity

Latec Investments Ltd. v. Hotel Terrigal Pty. Ltd.
(1965) 113 C.L.R. 265, High Court of Australia

Latec were mortgagees of land and in exercise of their power of sale sold the land to a wholly-owned subsidiary company at an undervalue, very much below the reserve price at the auction. Also the auction had been held on an unsuitable day and at short notice. There was no doubt that the mortgagor was entitled to have the sale set aside (see below, p. 188). But before the mortgagor acted the purchaser company charged the land by way of equitable mortgage under a debenture. Five years after the sale the mortgagor sought to set aside the sale. It was held that Latec and its subsidiary were guilty of fraud and the sale should be set aside. The next question was who had priority between the mortgagor and the debenture trustee. The mortgagor would probably have been estopped from claiming against the trustee because of the delay in commencing proceedings, but even if this were not so the trustee still had priority. Until the mortgagor had succeeded in its claim to have the sale set aside it had a mere equity (like the equity to rectification of a deed) and it therefore did not have an equitable interest sufficient to attract the rule that the first in time prevailed.

Note: In relation to registered land, see *Blacklocks* v. *J. B. Developments (Godalming) Ltd.* (below, p. 51).

Getting in the Legal Estate

Bailey v. Barnes [1894] 1 Ch. 25

The defendant as mortgagee sold the mortgaged property for the exact amount of the mortgage debt (£1,579). The purchaser, M., then mortgaged the property for £6,000 and sold the equity of redemption to L. for £2,500. The original mortgagor got the sale to M. set aside as a fraudulent exercise of the power of sale. When L. heard of this he paid off the £6,000 mortgage and took a reconveyance from the mortgagees. L. had no actual notice of any impropriety in the sale to M. at the time of his purchase of the equity of redemption. The mortgagor claimed to be entitled as against L. to redeem the mortgaged property as owning the prior equity of redemption. Stirling J. held that L. had no constructive notice of any impropriety in the sale. The equities were, therefore, equal. But the maxim *qui prior est tempore, potior est jure* was subject to an important qualification, that, where the equities are equal, the legal title prevails. L.'s acquisition of the legal estate gave his equity of redemption priority.

McCarthy & Stone Ltd. v. Julian S. Hodge & Co. Ltd.
[1971] 1 W.L.R. 1547, Ch. D.

On February 17, 1964, Cityfield Properties Ltd., the owners of a building site, and the plaintiffs, builders, entered into an agreement whereby the plaintiffs would develop the site and Cityfield sell it to the builders. By March 14, 1964, work had already begun on the site. On that date the defendants, a bank, which was fully aware of the arrangements and providing the finance for the development, obtained an equitable mortgage from Cityfield on the site, and on the same date Cityfield made a declaration of trust of the property in favour of the defendants and appointed the defendants its attorney to execute a legal mortgage (both usual clauses in a formal equitable mortgage). The bank's equitable mortgage was registered against Cityfield under the Companies Act 1948, s.95, on April 13, 1964. The agreement between Cityfield and the plaintiffs was registered as an estate contract under the Land Charges Act 1925, section 10(1), Class C(iv), (see now L.C.A. 1972, s.2(4), below, p. 18) on September 27, 1965. On June 21, 1967, the bank obtained a legal charge on the site under the earlier arrangements. Later that year Cityfield went into liquidation. The plaintiffs claimed priority over the bank. The bank contended, *inter alia*, that the agreement of February 17, 1964, was void against it as it had not been registered as a land charge when the bank obtained its equitable mortgage (see below, p. 19); alternatively, that by subsequently obtaining a legal charge it had precedence over the plaintiffs' equitable interest. Foster J. held that the bank, as equitable mortgagee, was not a purchaser of the legal estate in the land and, therefore, the agreement was not void against the bank for non-registration as an estate contract. Therefore, it was a case of two competing equitable interests. The bank's getting in of the legal estate would give it priority only if it had no notice of the agreement at the date of the equitable mortgage. But the bank had constructive notice of the agreement by virtue of its knowledge of the arrangements. Nor did the declaration of trust give the bank a better right to the legal estate. The agreement with the plaintiffs was a specifically enforceable agreement and therefore Cityfield was trustee of the legal estate for the plaintiffs and could not subsequently declare itself trustee thereof for the bank.

Constructive Notice under the Law of Property Act 1925, s.199(1)(ii)

"199. (1) A purchaser shall not be prejudicially affected by notice of—

(ii) any other instrument or matter or any fact or thing unless—

(*a*) it is within his own knowledge, or would have come to his knowledge if such inquiries and inspections had been made as ought reasonably to have been made by him; or

(*b*) in the same transaction with respect to which a question of notice to the purchaser arises, it has come to the knowledge of his counsel, as such, or of his solicitor or other agent, as such, or would have come to the knowledge of his solicitor or other agent, as such, if such inquiries and inspections had been made as ought reasonably to have been made by the solicitor or other agent."

Midland Bank Ltd. v. Farmpride Hatcheries Ltd.
(1981) 260 E.G. 493, C.A.

The defendant company, which was controlled by Mr & Mrs Willey, carried on a chicken hatchery business. It wished to expand the business and obtained funds from the plaintiff bank secured by a mortgage over the defendant's unregistered land and buildings thereon. Mr. W. was employed by the defendant under a service agreement, which gave him and his family a rent-free licence to occupy the house on the farm. The licence was not disclosed to the bank nor discovered by the bank when the mortgage was made, but the relevant bank official knew the family was living in the house. The defendant defaulted on the mortgage and the bank sought possession preliminary to the sale of the property. The defendants claimed, relying on section 199(1)(ii), that the bank had constructive notice of the licence and was bound by it. The case proceeded on the assumption that the licence created an equitable interest in the land (*cf. Chandler* v. *Kerley* (above, p. 7) and *London Borough of Hounslow* v. *Twickenham Garden Developments Ltd.* (below, p. 111)). The trial judge, Dillon J., after referring to *Hunt* v. *Luck* (below, p. 15) held that, because of the unusual nature of Mr. W.'s right the bank did not have constructive notice of the licence. On appeal it was held, by a majority, that the bank ought to have inquired about Mr W.'s occupation. The test is not whether it is likely or probable that an adverse interest may exist, but whether it is reasonable in the circumstances to pursue inquiry (*per* Shaw L.J.). A purchaser or mortgagee is not entitled to assume that, because an employee is living in the property, the occupation is that of the employer. The employee could be a service tenant. However Mr. W. was estopped by his own conduct, by concealing the existence of the licence, from relying on the doctrine of constructive notice. By failing to disclose the licence he had encouraged the bank to act to its detriment by advancing money. Alternatively (*per* Oliver L.J.) an agent (as Mr. W. was for the company) negotiating a sale or mortgage for his principal represents that he himself has no right adverse to the title. The bank were thus relieved from enquiry.

Rights of Persons in Occupation

Hunt v. Luck [1902] 1 Ch. 428, C.A.

The plaintiff claimed to have set aside certain conveyances purportedly made by her late husband to one Gilbert on the ground that they were forgeries. The defendant, Miss Luck, who was Gilbert's real representative, did not defend the proceedings, but several persons to whom Gilbert had mortgaged the properties did. They claimed to be bona fide purchasers for value without notice—actual or constructive. The plaintiff contended that the mortgagees' agents should have made inquiries of the tenants. It was held, affirming Farwell J., that the mortgagees were purchasers for value without notice and that their title must prevail against that of the plaintiff. A tenant's occupation of land affects a purchaser of that land with constructive notice of all the tenant's rights, but not with notice of his landlord's title or rights.

Note: The tenant's occupation is not notice of a mere equity such as a right to apply to the court to have his tenancy agreement rectified: *Smith* v. *Jones* [1954] 1 W.L.R. 1089; (but see now, *Blacklocks* v. *J. B. Developments (Godalming) Ltd.* (below, p. 51); and *Latec Investments Ltd.* v. *Hotel Terrigal Pty. Ltd.* (above, p. 11)). And note the effect now of non-registration of the agreement as a land charge (below, pp. 19, 26-27).

National Provincial Bank Ltd. v. Ainsworth [1965] A.C. 1175, H.L.

Mr. Ainsworth was the registered proprietor of a house where he lived with his wife and four infant children. He deserted his wife leaving her in occupation of the house. Later he mortgaged the house to the plaintiff bank to secure loans. The bank did not know that the husband had deserted the wife. After the wife had commenced divorce proceedings the husband formed a company (Hastings Car Mart Ltd.) to take over his business. He transferred his properties to the company and the company charged them, including the house, to the bank, the earlier mortgage being discharged. After this the bank learned that the husband had deserted the wife. The bank subsequently called in the debt and on default of payment, as mortgagee, sought possession of the house from the wife. The wife claimed a deserted wife's equity to remain in occupation of the matrimonial home and that the equity was enforceable against the bank as a purchaser of the house with notice. Cross J., at first instance, rejecting the concept of the deserted wife's equity as creating any more than a personal right, held that as the wife's right of occupation was a personal right and not a right *in rem*, it was not an overriding interest within the L.R.A. 1925, s.70(1)(*g*) (see below, p. 38), and the bank was entitled to possession. The Court of Appeal (Russell L.J. dissenting) held that the wife's right of occupation was an overriding interest, save where inquiry was made of her and her rights were not disclosed. The House of Lords unanimously rejected the wife's claim. A deserted wife's rights of occupation were personal rights not conferring any equitable interest or right of property in the land capable of enduring through different ownerships of the land according to the normal conception of title to real property. It was therefore not an overriding interest. Nor was a deserted wife a licensee of her husband. In any event, both Lord Upjohn and Lord Wilberforce (and Russell L.J. in the C.A.) doubted whether a contractual licence, whatever might be the position between licensor and licensee, is binding on third parties.

Note: This decision was quickly followed by the Matrimonial Homes Act 1967, which gave "rights of occupation" which can be protected against third parties by registration as a land charge or protection under the L.R.A., as appropriate (see now Matrimonial Homes Act 1983, below, pp. 19, 107 and 109).

Mere personal rights (as opposed to proprietary rights) do not generally bind a third party. But, in appropriate circumstances, a purchaser with actual knowledge of a personal right might be liable for the tort of interference with contractual relations (see *Swiss Bank Corpn.* v. *Lloyds Bank Ltd.*, below, p. 246).

Binions v. Evans [1972] Ch. 359, C.A.

Mr. Evans worked for the Tredegar Estate all his life. He and his wife lived in a cottage in Newport belonging to the Estate. He paid no rent or rates. After his death the defendant, his widow, stayed on. In 1968, when she was 76, the Estate made a written agreement with her. The parties were described as the "Landlords" and the "Tenant." The purpose of the agreement was expressed to be "to provide a temporary home" for her. She was thereby permitted to occupy the cottage as tenant at will free of rent for the remainder of her life, unless she determined the tenancy by four weeks' notice in writing to the Estate. In 1970, the Estate sold the cottage to Mr. and Mrs. Binions. They were supplied with a copy of the agreement and in the contract of sale the property was sold subject to the defendant's tenancy. The plaintiffs paid a reduced price because of this. Some months after completion the plaintiffs gave the defendant notice to quit. They then claimed possession on the ground that the defendant had been a tenant at will and that the tenancy having been determined she was now a trespasser. The county court judge refused to order her out. The Court of Appeal had to decide what was Mrs. Evans's interest in the cottage. The majority held that she was tenant for life under the S.L.A. 1925 (following *Bannister* v. *Bannister* (above)), and since the plaintiffs took with express notice of the agreement they were bound by it. (Alternatively, Megaw L.J. suggested that the defendant's interest was an irrevocable licence and that the plaintiffs would be guilty of the tort of interference with contract if they were to evict Mrs. Evans.) In considering the various alternatives Lord Denning M.R. ruled out a tenancy at will because for that both parties must have a right to immediate termination. Nor was any other type of tenancy possible since the agreement was not for a definite period. He rejected a tenancy for life under the S.L.A. 1925 because that would give Mrs. Evans the right to dispose of the cottage, which could not have been intended. He thought that the defendant had a licence. The effect of this was somewhat uncertain. If such a licence created an equitable interest in land then a purchaser with notice of the agreement could not turn her out in breach of the terms of the agreement. He referred to *Errington* v. *Errington* (above, p. 5). But if the licence itself did not amount to a proprietary interest (see *National Provincial Bank Ltd.* v. *Ainsworth* (above, p. 15), after the sale to the plaintiffs she had one under the constructive trust imposed on the plaintiffs which arose on the sale, because of the plaintiffs' notice of her rights and their expressly taking subject to the agreement. (The Master of the Rolls also suggested that a constructive trust could be imposed where the purchaser took implicitly subject to another's occupation, *e.g.* the *Hodgson* v. *Marks* (below, p. 48) situation.) Accordingly, the plaintiffs were not entitled to possession.

Note: And see *Lyus* v. *Prowsa Developments Ltd.*, below, p. 46. A licence may be enforceable against a third party by virtue of the principle in *Halsall* v. *Brizell* (below, p. 243) that he who takes the benefit must accept the burden. In *Hopgood* v. *Brown* [1955] 1 W.L.R. 213, C.A., a new boundary line was created by estoppel by company B. Ltd. agreeing to its neighbour, B., building part of his garage on B. Ltd.'s land. The plaintiff, a successor in title to B. Ltd., was also bound by the new line. At the same time as the garage had been built, B. had constructed a manhole and connecting drain on B. Ltd.'s land to act as a junction for the collection of water from the two plots to flow thence by a single outflow which recrossed the boundary line and through B.'s land to the main drain in the road. It was held that this drainage system conferred on the plaintiff and the defendant rights in the nature of reciprocal licences and that the plaintiff could not revoke the defendant's licence to discharge water through his drain to the manhole whilst the plaintiff was continuing to enjoy the benefit of the outflow under the defendant's land.

4. LAND CHARGES

Land Charges Act 1972, ss. 2, 3, 4, 17

"2. (4) A Class C land charge is any of the following, namely–

(i) a puisne mortgage;
(ii) a limited owner's charge;
(iii) a general equitable charge;
(iv) an estate contract;

and for this purpose–

(i) a puisne mortgage is a legal mortgage which is not protected by a deposit of documents relating to the legal estate affected;
(ii) . . .
(iii) a general equitable charge is any equitable charge which–

(*a*) is not secured by a deposit of documents relating to the legal estate affected; and
(*b*) does not arise or affect an interest arising under a trust for sale or a settlement; and
(*c*) is not a charge given by way of indemnity against rents equitably apportioned or charged exclusively on land in exoneration of other land and against the breach or non-observance of covenants or conditions; and
(*d*) is not included in any other class of land charge;

(iv) an estate contract is a contract by an estate owner or by a person entitled at the date of the contract to have a legal estate conveyed to him to convey or create a legal estate, including a contract conferring either expressly or by statutory implication a valid option to purchase, a right of pre-emption or any other like right.

(5) A Class D land charge is any of the following . . ., namely–

(i) an Inland Revenue charge;
(ii) a restrictive covenant;

(iii) an equitable easement;

and for this purpose—

(i) . . .

(ii) a restrictive covenant is a covenant or agreement (other than a covenant or agreement between a lessor and a lessee) restrictive of the user of land and entered into on or after 1st January 1926;

(iii) an equitable easement is an easement, right or privilege over or affecting land created or arising on or after 1st January 1926, and being merely an equitable interest.

(7) A Class F land charge is a charge affecting any land by virtue of the Matrimonial Homes Act [1983]."

Note: For the Matrimonial Homes Act 1983 see below, p. 107.

"3. (1) A land charge shall be registered in the name of the estate owner whose estate is intended to be affected. . . .

(7) In the case of a land charge for securing money created by a company before 1st January 1970 or so created at any time as a floating charge, registration under [the Companies Act 1948, s.95 and its predecessors] shall be sufficient in place of registration under this Act, and shall have effect as if the land charge had been registered under this Act.

4. (5) A land charge of Class B and a land charge of Class C (other than an estate contract) created or arising on or after 1st January 1926 shall be void as against a purchaser of the land charged with it, or of any interest in such land, unless the land charge is registered in the appropriate register before the completion of the purchase.

(6) An estate contract and a land charge of Class D created or entered into on or after 1st January 1926 shall be void as against a purchaser for money or money's worth of a legal estate in the land charged with it, unless the land charge is registered in the appropriate register before the completion of the purchase.

(7) . . .

(8) A land charge of Class F shall be void as against a purchaser of the land charged with it, or of any interest in such land, unless the land charge is registered in the appropriate register before the completion of the purchase."

17. (1) In this Act, unless the context otherwise requires,—

. . . "purchaser" means any person (including a mortgagee or lessee) who, for valuable consideration, takes any interest in land or in a charge on land . . .

Law of Property Act 1925, ss.198(1), 199(1)(i)

"198. (1) The registration of any instrument or matter under the provisions of the Land Charges Act 1925, or any enactment which it replaces, in any register kept at the land registry or elsewhere, shall be deemed to constitute actual notice of such instrument or matter, and of the fact of such registration, to all persons and for all purposes connected with the land affected, as from the date of registration or other prescribed date and so long as the registration continues in force.

199. (1) A purchaser shall not be prejudicially affected by notice of–

(i) any instrument or matter capable of registration under the provisions of the Land Charges Act 1925, or any enactment which it replaces, which is void or not enforceable as against him under that Act or enactment, by reason of the non-registration thereof . . ."

Note: The Land Charges Act 1925 is now considered in the L.C.A. 1972.

Estate Contract

Thomas v. Rose [1968] 1 W.L.R. 1797, Ch. D.

The plaintiff, the owner of certain freehold land known as Rhydw Tump, entered into an agreement, called a contract of agency, with the defendant whereby he appointed the defendant his sole agent to dispose of minerals on the land. The defendant was to have the right to accept or refuse all offers for sale of the land and to be paid a percentage of the moneys derived from the sale of minerals or the land. The agreement was improperly registered as an estate contract by the defendant. Megarry J. held that the only contracts which fell within Class C (iv) of the L.C.A. 1925, were those which themselves created an obligation on the estate owner or other persons entitled to convey or create a legal estate. The present contract, being one that merely provided machinery for the making of a further contract to create such an obligation did not fall within Class C (iv). Some doubt was thrown on *Turley* v. *Mackay* [1944] Ch. 37 (Uthwatt J.), where the plaintiff agreed to sell any land he might acquire in three specified counties within the next six years to any person whom the defendant-agents nominated. The defendants registered an estate contract and the plaintiff then applied to have the registration vacated. That case correctly illustrates that Class C (iv) is not confined to cases where a contracting party is to receive the legal estate. But Megarry J. doubted whether the contract fell within Class C (iv) as that requires the contract to be one "affecting land" and it was difficult to see how any registration could affect after-acquired land. Also in *Thomas* v. *Rose* there was an agreement recorded in correspondence whereby Rose and another defendant were to pay the plaintiff a specified sum, prepare the land for development and be entitled to a percentage of the proceeds of sale on any sale by the plaintiff. The second defendant registered this agreement as a general equitable charge (Class C (iii)). Megarry J. held that the agreement did not create an equitable charge affecting land. There was no loan to be charged on the land, merely a contract to divide the proceeds of sale thereof. Accordingly both registrations should be vacated.

Note: Nor is there a Class (iii) land charge where there is a charge on an undivided share in land (*Re Rayleigh Weir Stadium* [1954] 1 W.L.R. 786, Ch.D., Harman J.) because the doctrine of conversion, applicable where there is co-ownership, converts the land into personalty, *i.e.* the proceeds of sale thereof (see below, p. 75).

Beesly v. Hallwood Estates Ltd.
[1960] 1 W.L.R. 549, Ch. D.

A lease granted in 1938 contained an option to renew for a further term of 21 years. In 1948 the residue of the term was assigned to the plaintiff and the benefit of the option automatically passed to her. In 1955 the freehold reversion was conveyed to the defendant company which bought with express notice of the option. The option was not registered as a land charge. In 1958 the plaintiff purported to exercise the option, but after negotiations as to the new lease the defendant finally decided not to grant a new lease. Buckley J. held that the defendant having sealed the lease and delivered it as an escrow, on the execution of the counterpart lease by the plaintiff the company was bound. But for this the option would not have been effective against the defendant. An option of the type in question constituted an *offer* to grant a new term which the defendant was contractually precluded from withdrawing. It was, therefore, not a *contract* falling within the first limb of Class C (iv). But it fell within the second part of Class C (iv). Accordingly the option would have been void against the defendant under the L.C.A. 1925, s.13(2) (see now L.C.A. 1972, s.4 (6)), as it was not registered before the completion of the defendant-company's purchase.

Taylor Fashions Ltd. v. Liverpool Victoria Trustees Co. Ltd.[1982] Q.B.133, Ch. D.

Old & Campbell Ltd. (Olds) owned a shop, No. 22, which had been leased in 1948 to a Mr. & Mrs. Murray for 28 years with an option to renew for a further 14 years if the tenants, at their own expense, had a lift installed. The option was not registered as an estate contract under the Land Charges Act 1925 (see now Land Charges Act 1972). In 1949 the freehold was sold to the defendant. The defendant had notice of the terms of the lease and option but was not aware of the invalidity of the option for want of registration. In 1958 the Murrays assigned the lease to the plaintiff who undertook improvements to the premises, including the installation of a lift at a cost of £5,000. The defendant was aware of and acquiesced in the installation of the lift. In 1963 Olds, which was the tenant of the defendant of No. 21, subject to a break clause entitling the defendant to determine the lease if the plaintiff failed to exercise its option to renew, took a lease of No. 20 from the defendant and this lease contained an option to renew and a break clause entitling the defendant to determine the lease if the tenant of No. 22 failed to exercise its option to renew. In 1976, when the plaintiff exercised its option to renew, the defendant claimed that the option was invalid for want of registration and sought possession of No. 22 against the plaintiff and, on the basis that the option in respect of No. 22 was ineffective against it, of Nos. 20 and 21 from Olds. Oliver J., following *Beesley* v. *Hallwood Estates Ltd.* (above), held that the option to renew was void for want of registration, and then went on to consider the plaintiff's and Olds' claim that the defendant was estopped by acquiescence in the installation of the lift and the improvements to the shops from denying the validity of the option. As to whether the defendant had to be aware of the invalidity of the option for it to be estopped, Oliver J. held that the court had to ascertain whether, in particular individual circumstances, it would be unconscionable for a party to be permitted to deny that which, knowingly or unknowingly, he has allowed or encouraged another to assume to his detriment. The doctrine of estoppel could apply where, at the time when the expectation was encouraged, both parties were acting under a mistake of law as to their rights. Whether the representor knew of the true position was merely one of the relevant factors–it might even be the determining factor in certain cases–in the overall enquiry. The judge found that the defendant had not created or encouraged the plaintiff's belief that the option was valid. Nor had the plaintiff proved that the lift had been installed on the faith of its belief that it had a valid option. Accordingly, the plaintiff's claim for specific performance of the agreement to renew failed. But the defendant was estopped from asserting the invalidity of the option against Olds, because in offering leases of Nos. 20 and 21 to Olds it had represented the validity of the plaintiff's option and it had encouraged Olds to incur expenditure on the faith of the validity of that option. Accordingly the defendant was not entitled to determine the leases of Nos. 20 and 21.

Note: Also on estate contract, see *Pritchard* v. *Briggs* (above, p. 2); below, pp. 26, 27 and 66; and *E.R. Ives Investment Ltd.* v. *High* (below, p. 210).

Equitable Easement

Poster v. Slough Estates Ltd. [1969] 1 Ch. 495

In 1946 Slough Estates Ltd. granted a lease of business premises to X. for a term of 21 years expiring on March 25, 1967. The lease provided that two buildings on the demised premises were tenant's fixtures (see below, p. 77) and could be removed by the tenant at the end of the term. In 1955 X. sub-let part of the premises, including the buildings, to Capseals Ltd., for a term expiring on March 15, 1967. In 1965 X. assigned the premises demised by the 1946 lease to the plaintiffs and by a separate deed also assigned the benefit of the right to remove the buildings. When the 1946 lease expired the plaintiffs claimed the right to enter and remove the buildings. (The sub-lease, being a business tenancy, was continued under the Landlord and Tenant Act 1954, Part II.) Cross J. held that the right of removal was an equitable interest of which Capseals had constructive notice. When they took their sub-lease they should have examined the lease and if they had done so they would have discovered the right of removal. Capseals contended that the right was void against them for non-registration as an equitable easement (land charge Class D (iii)). It was held, following Lord Denning M.R. in *Ives* v. *High* (below, p. 210), that the right was not an equitable easement and therefore not registrable. (Cross J. pointed out that had the land been registered the right would not have been an overriding interest and would not have been binding on someone in Capseals' position.) However, the right was not enforceable by the plaintiffs, being excluded by the statutory continuance of Capseals' sub-tenancy and the provisions of ss.23 and 24 of the Landlord and Tenant Act 1954.

Shiloh Spinners Ltd. v. Harding [1973] A.C. 691, H.L.

The appellants were the tenants (not the original tenants) of premises including Shiloh No. 2 Mill under two leases dated 1876 and 1904 respectively. In 1961, they assigned the Mill to Thornber Brothers Ltd. In the assignment Thornber covenanted on their own behalf and that of their successors in title to observe and perform certain stipulations, *inter alia*, as to fencing and repair and to support of buildings retained by Shiloh. The assignment contained a right of re-entry (limited by reference to the rule against perpetuities) in the event of failure to perform or observe the stipulations and a provision exonerating T. from liability under the stipulations after they had assigned the Mill. Neither the stipulations nor the right of re-entry had been registered under the L.C.A. 1925. In 1965, T. assigned the Mill to the respondent. The respondent began to demolish the Mill and was in breach of the stipulations. The stipulations were not enforceable against him in so far as they were negative for lack of registration and in so far as they were positive because the burden would not bind him since he was not a party to the 1961 assignment and in any event specific performance would not lie for such stipulations. The appellants claimed possession relying on the right for re-entry. The respondent claimed that the right was not enforceable against him for lack of registration either as an equitable easement under Class D (iii) or as an estate contract under Class C (iv) of section 10 of the L.C.A. 1925. He alternatively claimed relief from forfeiture. The Vice-Chancellor of the former Chancery Court of the County Palatine of Lancaster held that the right was not registrable and, because of the respondent's conduct, refused relief from forfeiture. The Court of Appeal held that the right was registrable under Class D (iii) but (Russell L.J. dissenting) not under Class C (iv). It was held in the House of Lords (1) that a right of entry could be validly reserved on an assignment even though the assignor retained no reversion and the right was capable of subsisting in law even though the covenants themselves were not enforceable; (2) the right of entry was not a legal interest within section 1 (2) of the Law of Property Act 1925 but an equitable interest (if it had been a legal interest it would have bound the respondent whether registrable or not); (3) the right was not registrable under Class C (iv) (since it bore no similarity to options or pre-emptions which eventuate in a contract whereas the right of entry was penal and involved the revesting of the lease) nor under Class D (iii) (since the word "right" in the phrase "easement, right or privilege over or affecting land" in Class D (iii) did not have a meaning so different in quality from easement or privilege as to include a right of entry). As to the latter class it was argued that because the right was clearly not capable of being overreached (see below, p. 51) under section 2 of the L.P.A. 1925 (below, p. 303) it must be registrable under the L.C.A. But this argument depended on there being no exception to equitable rights either falling under section 2 or being registrable and was rejected because there were clearly equitable rights which were not capable of being overreached or being registered, such as the estoppel interest in *Ives* v. *High* (below, p. 210, and see the cases on pp. 28-30, below); and (4) although the case fell into the class as to which a court of equity could grant relief, because of the respondent's wilful breaches and his continuing disregard of the appellants' rights over a period of time, this case was not one for relief.

Difficulties of a Names Register

Oak Co-operative Building Society v. Blackburn
[1968] Ch. 730, C.A.

Francis David Blackburn, an estate agent, was the owner of 34 Union Street, Southport. He carried on his business under the names of "Frank D. Blackburn" and "Frank David Blackburn." He agreed to sell the property to Phyllis Cairns under an instalment sale, which agreement was registered as an estate contract (land charge Class C (iv)) against the name "Frank David Blackburn," *i.e.* an incorrect version of the vendor's true name. Later, Blackburn raised money on the property by a mortgage to the building society. Before granting the mortgage the society applied for an official search against the name "Francis Davi*s* Blackburn," *i.e.* an incorrect version of Blackburn's name, but a proper description of the property. The search was clear, but the certificate did refer to entry of an earlier mortgage which might or might not relate, namely "Blackburn, Francis David" and "26 Crescent Road, Southport." Subsequently Blackburn defaulted on the mortgage and the society sought possession. Phyllis Cairns claimed that the society was bound by her estate contract. Ungoed-Thomas J. held that she was not protected because the registration was not in the true name of the estate owner. He was reversed on appeal, the Court of Appeal holding that registration in what might fairly be described as a version of the full names of the vendor is effective against someone who fails to search at all and also against someone, like the society in the present case, who searches against the wrong names. The society was, therefore, deemed to have actual notice of the estate contract by virtue of section 198 of the L.P.A. 1925.

Diligent Finance Co. Ltd. v. Alleyne
(1972) 23 P.&C.R. 346, Ch. D.

In 1965 a house was conveyed to the defendant, Erskine Owen Alleyne, and at the same time the property was mortgaged. In 1968 a second mortgage was executed in favour of the plaintiff and duly registered as a puisne mortgage against the defendant. In 1969 the defendant deserted his wife and she registered a Class F land charge (see above, p. 19), against the defendant, but against the name "Erskine Alleyne," the name by which she knew the defendant. In 1970 the defendant negotiated a bigger loan from the plaintiff. The plaintiff made an official search under the Land Charges Act 1925 against the defendant's true names. The search certificate did not (as was to be expected) reveal the Class F charge. Accordingly, a new charge was executed and the old charge cancelled. The defendant defaulted and the plaintiff claimed possession. Foster J. held that the plaintiff was entitled to possession. The Class F charge did not rank ahead of the legal charge because the former had not been registered against the proper name of the defendant and therefore the official search was conclusive. In the absence of evidence to the contrary the proper name of a person was that in which the conveyancing documents had been taken.

Barrett v. Hilton Developments Ltd. [1975] Ch. 237, C.A.

On April 24, 1972 the plaintiff contracted to buy a plot of land from Costains for £11,000. On April 25, 1972 he contracted to sell the land to the defendant for £30,000. On May 23, 1972, the defendant registered an estate contract (Class C (iv) land charge) against the plaintiff. On May 31, 1972 the sale by Costains to the plaintiff was completed by conveyance. Subsequently the plaintiff sold and conveyed the land to Littlewoods for £30,000, telling them that his contract with the defendant was a nullity. The plaintiff sought the vacation of the defendant's land charge entry on the ground that the registration against the plaintiff, at a time when he was not the owner of a legal estate in the land, was invalid under section 3(1) of the Land Charges Act 1972. This argument was upheld by Blackett-Ord V.-C. and the Court of Appeal.

Failure to Register

Hollington Bros. Ltd. v. Rhodes [1951] 2 T.L.R. 691 Ch. D.

The defendants were lessees of a block of offices. In 1945, they agreed to grant an underlease of part to the plaintiffs, and the plaintiffs went into possession. The lease and counterpart-lease were never exchanged so the lease was never enforceable (it being the rule that where the negotiations are subject to formal lease there is no enforceable agreement until the lease and counterpart have been exchanged). The agreement for the sub-lease was never registered as an estate contract. In 1947 the defendants assigned the premises "subject to and with the benefit of such tenancies as may affect the premises." The assignees gave the plaintiffs notice to quit, and the plaintiffs were forced into negotiating a new lease at a higher rent with the assignees. The plaintiffs sued the defendants claiming the alleged underlease and damages. Harman J. held that even if the agreement for the lease had been enforceable it was void against the assignees by virtue of s.13 of the L.C.A. 1925 (now L.C.A. 1972, s.4(6)), notwithstanding that at common law they would have had constructive notice of the plaintiffs' rights by virtue of their occupation (under the rule in *Hunt* v. *Luck*, above, p. 15), and the terms of the sale to them being subject to any tenancies.

Note: However, where a person who has agreed to take a lease (but no lease is executed) goes into possession and pays rent a common law tenancy will arise (see below, pp. 115-116) which will be binding on a third party.

Midland Bank Trust Co. Ltd. v. Green [1981] A.C. 513, H.L.

In 1961, Walter Green granted his son Geoffrey an option to purchase Gravel Hill Farm exercisable within 10 years. The option was an estate contract (Class C (iv) land charge, see above) and could have been registered, but it was not. (For proceedings by Geoffrey and his executors against his solicitors, see *Midland Bank Trust Co. Ltd.* v. *Hett, Stubbs & Kemp* [1979] Ch. 384). In 1967, in order to defeat Geoffrey's option, Walter conveyed the farm to his wife, Evelyne, for £500. The farm was then worth about £40,000. When Geoffrey learned of this, he registered the option and gave notice to exercise it and then sued to enforce it. The trial judge's decision that the conveyance was not a sham and that Evelyne was a purchaser of the legal estate for money or money's worth within the L.C.A. 1925, ss.13(2) and 20(8) (see now L.C.A. 1972, ss.4(6), 17(1)) was reversed by a majority of the Court of Appeal, holding that the 1967 sale, being at a gross undervalue, was not for money or money's worth. In addition Lord Denning M.R. held that the protection of the L.C.A. was not available in a case of fraud (meaning thereby "any dishonest dealing done so as to deprive unwary innocents of their rightful dues"). The House of Lords (Lord Wilberforce) held that Evelyne was a purchaser for money and therefore the option, not having been registered prior to the conveyance to her, was void against her. The respondent bank (Geoffrey's executor) sought to introduce the element of good faith into section 13(2) on the basis that good faith was something required by Equity in addition to absence of knowledge (registration being a statutory substitute for notice) and that it appeared in other 1925 property Acts. This was rejected because "good faith" was not referred to in the L.C.A. or its antecedents and there was no reason for departing from the wording of the Act. The House also rejected the bank's other argument that the "money" referred to in section 13(2) must be interpreted in the light of the definition of "purchaser" in L.P.A. s.205(1)(xxi) (which expressly excluded nominal consideration) (see above, p. 2 to exclude nominal consideration and the £500 paid by Evelyne was nominal. It was held that section 13(2) was clear on the face of it and the L.C.A.'s own definition of "purchaser" (s.20(8), now s.17(1)) (above, p. 21) referred to valuable consideration, which was a term of art requiring no definition. In any event, Lord Wilberforce indicated that he would have great difficulty in holding that £500 was nominal and he was not prepared to equate nominal with inadequate.

Gaps in the System

General note: The L.C.A. 1925, together with the extension of the doctrine of overreaching (see below, p. 51) in the 1925 legislation, was intended to supersede the common law doctrine of notice. It did not wholly succeed in this and there remain certain equitable rights which are not registrable as land charges nor overreachable.

(i) RIGHTS OF OCCUPATION

Ramsden v. Dyson (1866) L.R. 1 H.L. 129, H.L.

A yearly tenant erected a building on the demised premises in the belief that his landlord was in honour bound to grant him a new lease for 60 years. When subsequently the landlord refused to grant the new lease the tenant claimed to be entitled in equity to such a grant. Their Lordships stated the requirements for a licence by estoppel: "If a stranger begins to build on any land supposing it to be his own, and I, perceiving his mistake, abstain from setting him right, and leave him to persevere in his error, a court of equity will not allow me afterwards to assert my title to the land on which he had expended money on the supposition that the land was his own." But the tenant did not build in the belief that he had against the landlord an absolute right to the lease he claimed, nor did the landlord know that the tenant was proceeding under that mistaken notion. Even if this had been the case there was no equity to a lease which could have been enforced since the terms of the lease had not been determined.

Note: But this requirement of certainty for the terms of the lease or conveyance did not prevent a licence by estoppel being found in *Inwards* v. *Baker*, below.

Inwards v. Baker [1965] 2 Q.B. 29, C.A.

A father owned six acres. In 1931, his son was looking around for a piece of land on which to erect a bungalow but it was too expensive. So the father said to him: "Why not put the bungalow on my land, and make the bungalow a little bigger." The son did so. The father helped him pay for some of the work. The son lived in the bungalow thereafter. The father died in 1951 and under a will he had made in 1922 most of his property, including the land on which the son's bungalow was, passed to a Miss Inwards, with whom the father had been living for many years, and his two children by her. In 1963, they took proceedings against the son for possession. They claimed that the son had, at most, a simple licence which had been revoked. The judge at first instance had held that *Errington* v. *Errington* (above, p. 5) only protected a contractual licensee and that there was no contract in the present case. The Court of Appeal, allowing the son's appeal, held that the principle in *Ramsden* v. *Dyson* (above) applied, *i.e.* if the owner of the land requests another, or allows another, to expend money on the land under the expectation created or encouraged by the landowner that he will be able to remain there, that raises an "equity" in that licensee such as to entitle him to stay (equitable estoppel). The father could not have turned the son out nor could the plaintiffs. The son could stay in the house for life or as long as he wished. *Per* Lord Denning M.R.: "I think that any purchaser who took with notice would clearly be bound by the equity."

Re Sharpe [1980] 1 W.L.R. 219, Ch. D.

In 1972, Mr. Sharpe's 75-year-old aunt sold her property, a flat in which was occupied by Mr. and Mrs. Sharpe, and all three went to live together in a rented flat, sharing the rent, the rates and telephone bills. In 1975 Mr. Sharpe purchased in his own name a leasehold shop with maisonette above for £17,000. The aunt provided £12,000 by way of a loan (though no terms of repayment were ever agreed and she knew Mr. Sharpe could not repay her without selling the property) and the balance was raised by mortgage. The three moved into the maisonette. The aunt paid about £2,000 for decoration and fittings. Later in 1975, Mr. Sharpe gave his aunt a promissory note for £15,700 at her request, because she had left her estate by her will to her three nephews and she wanted them to be treated equally. In 1978 Mr. Sharpe was made bankrupt and his trustee sold the property (after trying unsuccessfully to find out from the aunt what claim she had) and claimed vacant possession against the aunt. She claimed a right to remain in the house until she was repaid. The claim was for an equitable interest under a constructive trust based on an extension of the principle of *Ramsden* v. *Dyson* (see above, p. 28) and thus binding on the trustee and the purchaser from him. The aunt's loan was part of a wider scheme under which she was to make her home in the house acquired with the money loaned. The trustee argued that the species of constructive trust that arose in the circumstances was not a substantive right, but an equitable remedy and in the circumstances, since the aunt had not claimed prior to the sale and the purchaser was an innocent third party, it would be inequitable to grant the aunt an interest under a constructive trust. This was rejected by Browne-Wilkinson J. who held that in order to provide a remedy the court must first find a right. It cannot be said that the right arises for the first time when the court declares it exists. Here the aunt's right arose at the time she made the loan. The aunt had an irrevocable licence to remain in the property until the loan was repaid and the trustee took the property subject to her interest. The judge expressed the wish that the Court of Appeal would clarify the law as to the extent to which irrevocable licences bound third parties. He also made it clear that his decision was only in relation to the trustee and he was not deciding whether the rights of the innocent purchaser in a claim for specific performance would prevail over those of the aunt.

Note: See above, p. 16 and *Hodgson* v. *Marks* and *Williams & Glyn's Bank Ltd.* v. *Boland* (below, pp. 48-49).

(ii) EASEMENTS BY ESTOPPEL

See *E.R. Ives Investments Ltd.* v. *High* (below, p. 210); *Ward* v. *Kirkland* (below, p. 220);

(iii) OTHER MISCELLANEOUS EQUITABLE INTERESTS

See *Poster* v. *Slough Estates Ltd.* (above, p. 23) (right of removal); *Shiloh Spinners Ltd.* v. *Harding* (above, p. 24) (right of entry); *Dartstone Ltd.* v. *Cleveland Petroleum Co. Ltd.* (below, p. 251) (covenants between landlord and tenant); and the occupation licence and constructive trust cases (above, pp. 4-9, 14, 16-17).

5. REGISTERED LAND

Land Registration Act 1925, ss.3, 19(1)(2), 20(1)(4), 48(1)(2), 49, 50(1)(2)(4), 52, 54(1), 55, 58(1)(2), 59(1)(5)(6)(7),60(1), 70, 74, 86(1)(2), 101(1)(2)(3)(4), 102(2)

3. In this Act unless the context otherwise requires, the following expressions have the meanings hereby assigned to them respectively, that is to say:–

(viii) "Land" includes land of any tenure . . . and mines and minerals, whether or not held with the surface, buildings or parts of buildings (whether the division is horizontal, vertical or made in any other way) and other corporeal hereditaments; also . . . a rent and other incorporeal hereditaments, and an easement, right, privilege, or benefit in, over, or derived from land; but not an undivided share in land;

(xv) "Minor interests" mean the interests not capable of being disposed of or created by registered dispositions and capable of being overridden (whether or not a purchaser has notice thereof) by the proprietors unless protected as provided by this Act, and all rights and interests which are not registered or protected on the register and are not overriding interests, and include–

(*a*) in the case of land held on trust for sale, all interests and powers which are under the Law of Property Act 1925 capable of being overridden by the trustees for sale, whether or not such interests and powers are so protected; and

(*b*) in the case of settled land, all interests and powers which are under the Settled Land Act 1925 and the Law of Property Act 1925, or either of them, capable of being overridden by the tenant for life or statutory owner, whether or not such interests and powers are so protected as aforesaid;

(xvi) "Overriding interests" mean all the incumbrances, interests, rights and powers not entered on the register but subject to which registered dispositions are by this Act to take effect, and in regard to land registered at the commencement of this Act include the matters which are by any enactment repealed by this Act declared not to be incumbrances;

(xviii) "Possession" includes receipt of rents and profits or the right to receive the same, if any;

(xxi) "Purchaser" means a purchaser in good faith for valuable consideration and includes a lessee, mortgagee, or other person who for valuable consideration acquires any interest in land or in any charge on land;

19. (1) The transfer of the registered estate in the land or part thereof shall be completed by the registrar entering on the register the transferee as the proprietor of the estate transferred, but until such entry is made the transferor shall be deemed to remain proprietor of the registered estate; and, where part only of the land is transferred, notice thereof shall also be noted on the register.

(2) All interests transferred or created by dispositions by the proprietor, other than a transfer of the registered estate in the land, or part thereof, shall, subject to the provisions relating to mortgages, be completed by registration in the same manner and with the same effect as provided by this Act with respect to transfers of registered estates and notice thereof shall also be noted on the register:

Provided that nothing in this subsection–

(*a*) shall authorise the registration of a lease granted for a term not exceeding twenty-one years, or require the entry of a notice of such a lease if it is granted at a rent without taking a fine; or

(*b*) shall authorise the registration of a mortgage term where there is a subsisting right of redemption; or

(*c*) shall render necessary the registration of any easement, right, or privilege except as appurtenant to registered land, or the entry of notice thereof except as against the registered title of the servient land.

Every such disposition shall, when registered, take effect as a registered disposition, and a lease made by the registered proprietor under the last foregoing section which is not required to be registered or noted on the register shall nevertheless take effect as if it were a registered disposition immediately on being granted . . .

20. (1) In the case of a freehold estate registered with an absolute title, a disposition of the registered land or of a legal estate therein, including a lease thereof, for valuable consideration shall, when registered, confer on the transferee or grantee an estate in fee simple or the term of years absolute or other legal estate expressed to be created in the land dealt with, together with all rights, privileges, and appurtenances belonging or appurtenant thereto, including (subject to any entry to the contrary in the register) the appropriate rights and interest which would, under the Law of Property Act 1925, have been transferred if the land had not been registered, subject—

(*a*) to the incumbrances and other entries, if any, appearing on the register; and
(*b*) unless the contrary is expressed on the register, to the overriding interests, if any, affecting the estate transferred or created,

but free from all other estates and interests whatsoever . . . and the disposition shall operate in like manner as if the registered transferor or grantor were (subject to any entry to the contrary in the register) entitled to the registered land in fee simple in possession for his own benefit. . . .

(4) Where any such disposition is made without valuable consideration, it shall, so far as the transferee or grantee is concerned, be subject to any minor interests subject to which the transferor or grantor held the same, but, save as aforesaid, shall, when registered, in all respects, and in particular as respects any registered dealings on the part of the transferee or grantee, have the same effect as if the disposition had been made for valuable consideration.

48. (1) Any lessee or other person entitled to or interested in a lease of registered land, where the term granted is not an overriding interest, may apply to the registrar to register notice of such lease in the prescribed manner, and when so registered, every proprietor and the persons deriving title under him shall be deemed to be affected with notice of such lease, as being an incumbrance on the registered land in respect of which the notice is entered:

Provided that a proprietor of a charge or incumbrance registered or protected on the register prior to the registration of such notice shall not be deemed to be so affected by the notice unless such proprietor is, by reason of the lease having been made under a statutory or other power or by reason of his concurrence or otherwise, bound by the terms of the lease.

(2) In order to register notice of a lease, if the proprietor of the registered land affected does not concur in the registration thereof, the applicant shall obtain an order of the court authorising the registration of notice of the lease . . . ; but if the proprietor concurs in the notice being registered, notice may be entered in such manner as may be agreed upon:

Provided that, where the lease is binding on the proprietor of the land, neither the concurrence of such proprietor nor an order of the court shall be required.

49. (1) The provisions of the last foregoing section shall be extended by the rules so as to apply to the registration of notices of or of claims in respect of—

(*a*) The grant or reservation of any annuity or rentcharge in possession . . .

(*b*) The severance of any mines or minerals from the surface . . .

(*c*) Land charges until the land charge is registered as a registered charge:

(*d*) The right of any person interested in the proceeds of sale of land held on trust for sale or in land subject to a settlement to require that (unless a trust corporation is acting as trustee) there shall be at least two trustees of the disposition on trust for sale or of the settlement:

(*e*) The rights of any widow in respect of dower . . .

(*f*) Creditors' notices and any other right, interest, or claim which it may be deemed expedient to protect by notice instead of by caution, inhibition, or restriction.

(*g*) Charging orders (within the meaning of the Charging Orders Act 1979) which in the case of unregistered land may be protected by registration under the Land Charges Act 1972 and which, notwithstanding section 59 of this Act, it may be deemed expedient to protect by notice instead of by caution.

(2) A notice shall not be registered in respect of any estate, right, or interest which (independently of this Act) is capable of being overridden by the proprietor under a trust for sale or the powers of the Settled Land Act 1925, or any other statute, or of a settlement, and of being protected by a restriction in the prescribed manner:

Provided that notice of such an estate right or interest may be lodged pending the appointment of trustees of a disposition on trust for sale or a settlement, and if so lodged, shall be cancelled if and when the appointment is made and the proper restriction (if any) is entered.

(3) A notice when registered in respect of a right, interest, or claim shall not affect prejudicially—

(*a*) The powers of disposition of the personal representative of the deceased under whose will or by the operation of whose intestacy the right, interest, or claim arose; or

(*b*) The powers of disposition (independently of this Act) of a proprietor holding the registered land on trust for sale.

50. (1) Any person entitled to the benefit of a restrictive covenant or agreement (not being a covenant or agreement made between a lessor and lessee) with respect to the building on or other user of registered land may apply to the registrar to enter notice thereof on the register, and where practicable the notice shall be by reference to the instrument, if any, which contains the covenant or agreement, and a copy or abstract of such instrument shall be filed at the registry; and where any such covenant or agreement appears to exist at the time of first registration, notice thereof shall be entered on the register. In the case of registered land the notice aforesaid shall take the place of registration as a land charge.

(2) When such a notice is entered the proprietor of the land and the persons deriving title under him (except incumbrancers or other persons who at the time when the notice is entered may not be bound by the covenant or agreement) shall be deemed to be affected with notice of the covenant or agreement as being an incumbrance on the land.

(4) The notice shall, when practicable, refer to the land, whether registered or not, for the benefit of which the restriction was made.

52. (1) A disposition by the proprietor shall take effect subject to all estates, rights, and claims which are protected by way of notice on the register at the date of the registration or entry of notice of the disposition, but only if and so far as such estates, rights, and claims may be valid and are not (independently of this Act) overridden by the disposition.

(2) Where notice of a claim is entered on the register, such entry shall operate by way of notice only, and shall not operate to render the claim valid whether made adversely to or for the benefit of the registered land or charge.

54. (1) Any person interested under any unregistered instrument, or interested as a judgment creditor, or otherwise howsoever, in any land or charge registered in the name of any other person, may lodge a caution with the registrar to the effect

that no dealing with such land or charge on the part of the proprietor is to be registered until notice has been served upon the cautioner:

Provided that a person whose estate, right, interest, or claim has been registered or protected by a notice or restriction shall not be entitled (except with the consent of the registrar) to lodge a caution in respect of such estate, right, interest or claim . . .

55. (1) After any such caution against dealings has been lodged in respect of any registered land or charge, the registrar shall not, without the consent of the cautioner, register any dealing or make any entry on the register for protecting the rights acquired under a deposit of a land or charge certificate or other dealing by the proprietor with such land or charge until he has served notice on the cautioner, warning him that his caution will cease to have any effect after the expiration of the prescribed number of days next following the date at which such notice is served; and after the expiration of such time as aforesaid the caution shall cease unless an order to the contrary is made by the registrar, and upon the caution so ceasing the registered land or charge may be dealt with in the same manner as if no caution had been lodged.

(2) If before the expiration of the said period the cautioner, or some person on his behalf, appears before the registrar, and where so required by the registrar gives sufficient security to indemnify every party against any damage that may be sustained by reason of any dealing with the registered land or charge, or the making of any such entry as aforesaid, being delayed, the registrar may thereupon, if he thinks fit to do so, delay registering any dealing with the land or charge or making any such entry for such period as he thinks just.

58. (1) Where the proprietor of any registered land or charge desires to place restrictions on transferring or charging the land or on disposing of or dealing with the land or charge in any manner in which he is by this Act authorised to dispose of or deal with it, or on the deposit by way of security of any certificate, the proprietor may apply to the registrar to make an entry in the register that no transaction to which the application relates shall be effected, unless the following things, or such of them as the proprietor may determine, are done—

(*a*) unless notice of any application for the transaction is transmitted by post to such address as he may specify to the registrar;

(*b*) unless the consent of some person or persons, to be named by the proprietor, is given to the transaction;

(*c*) unless some such other matter or thing is done as may be required by the applicant and approved by the registrar:

Provided that no restriction under this section shall extend or apply to dispositions of or dealings with minor interests.

(2) The registrar shall thereupon, if satisfied of the right of the applicant to give the directions, enter the requisite restriction on the register, and no transaction to which the restriction relates shall be effected except in conformity therewith; but it shall not be the duty of the registrar to enter any such restriction, except upon such terms as to payment of fees and otherwise as may be prescribed, or to enter any restriction that the registrar may deem unreasonable or calculated to cause inconvenience.

59. (1) A writ, order, deed of arrangement, pending action, or other interest which in the case of unregistered land may be protected by registration under the Land Charges Act 1925 shall, where the land affected or the charge securing the debt affected is registered, be protected only by lodging a creditor's notice, a bankruptcy inhibition or a caution against dealings with the land or the charge.

(2) Registration of a land charge (other than a local land charge, shall, where the land affected is registered, be effected only by registering under this Act a notice caution or other prescribed entry:

Provided that before a land charge including a local land charge affecting registered land (being a charge to secure money) is realised, it shall be registered and take effect as a registered charge under this Act in the prescribed manner, without prejudice to the priority conferred by the land charge . . .

(5) The foregoing provisions of this section shall apply only to writs and orders, deeds of arrangement, pending actions and land charges which if the land were unregistered would for purposes of protection be required to be registered or re-registered after the commencement of this Act under the Land Charges Act [1972]; and for the purposes of this section a land charge does not include a puisne mortgage. . . .

(6) Subject to the provisions of this Act relating to fraud and to the title of a trustee in bankruptcy, a purchaser acquiring title under a registered disposition, shall not be concerned with any pending action, writ, order, deed of arrangement, or other document, matter, or claim (not being an overriding interest . . .) which is not protected by a caution or other entry on the register, whether he has or has not notice thereof, express, implied, or constructive.

(7) In this section references to registration under the Land Charges Act [1972] apply to any registration made under any other statute which, in the case of unregistered land, is by the Land Charges Act [1972] to have effect as if the registration had been made under that Act.

60. (1) Where a company, registered under the Companies Act [1948], is registered as proprietor of any estate or charge already registered, the registrar shall not be concerned with any mortgage, charge, debenture, debenture stock, trust deed for securing the same, or other incumbrance created or issued by the company, whether or not registered under that Act, unless the same is registered or protected by caution or otherwise under this Act.

70. (1) All registered land shall, unless under the provisions of this Act the contrary is expressed on the register, be deemed to be subject to such of the following overriding interests as may be for the time being subsisting in reference thereto, and such interests shall not be treated as incumbrances within the meaning of this Act, (that is to say):–

(*a*) Rights of common, drainage rights, customary rights (until extinguished), public rights, profits àprendre, rights of sheepwalk, rights of way, watercourses, rights of water, and other easements not being equitable easements required to be protected by notice on the register; . . .

(*f*) Subject to the provisions of this Act, rights acquired or in course of being acquired under the Limitation Acts;

(*g*) The rights of every person in actual occupation of the land or in receipt of the rents and profits thereof, save where enquiry is made of such person and the rights are not disclosed;

(*h*) In the case of a possessory, qualified or good leasehold title, all estates, rights, interests and powers excepted from the effect of registration;

(*i*) Rights under local land charges unless and until registered or protected on the register in the prescribed manner; . . .

(*k*) Leases for any term or interest not exceeding 21 years, granted at a rent without taking a fine . . . ."

(2) Where at the time of first registration any easement, right, privilege, or benefit created by an instrument and appearing on the title adversely affects the land, the registrar shall enter a note thereof on the register.

74. Subject to the provisions of this Act as to settled land, neither the registrar nor any person dealing with a registered estate or charge shall be affected with notice of a trust express implied or constructive, and references to trusts shall, so far as possible, be excluded from the register.

86. (1) Settled land shall be registered in the name of the tenant for life or statutory owner.

(2) The successive or other interests created by or arising under a settlement shall (save as regards any legal estate which cannot be overridden under the powers of the Settled Land Act 1925, or any other statute) take effect as minor interests and not otherwise; and effect shall be given thereto by the proprietor of the settled land as provided by statute with respect to the estate owner, with such adaptations, if any, as may be prescribed in the case of registered land by rules made under this Act.

101. (1) Any person, whether being the proprietor or not, having a sufficient interest or power in or over registered land, may dispose of or deal with the same, and create any interests or rights therein which are permissible in like manner and by the like modes of assurance in all respects as if the land were not registered, but subject as provided by this section.

(2) All interests and rights disposed of or created under subsection (1) of this section (whether by the proprietor or any other person) shall, subject to the provisions of this section, take effect as minor interests, and be capable of being overridden by registered dispositions for valuable consideration.

(3) Minor interests shall, subject to the express exceptions contained in this section, take effect only in equity, but may be protected by entry on the register of such notices, cautions, inhibitions and restrictions as are provided for by this Act or rules.

(4) A minor interest in registered land subsisting or capable of taking effect at the commencement of this Act, shall not fail or become invalid by reason of the same being converted into an equitable interest; but after such commencement a minor interest in registered land shall only be capable of being validly created in any case in which an equivalent equitable interest could have been validly created if the land had not been registered . . .

102. (2) Priorities as regards dealings effected after the commencement of this Act between assignees and incumbrancers of life interests, remainders, reversions and executory interests shall be regulated by the order of the priority cautions or inhibitions lodged (in a specially prescribed form) against the proprietor of the registered estate affected, but, save as aforesaid,

priorities as between persons interested in minor interests shall not be affected by the lodgment of cautions or inhibitions.

Freer v. Unwins Ltd. [1976] Ch. 288

In 1953, No. 2, one of a parade of shops, was conveyed to the plaintiff for use as a tobacconist's and sweet shop and with the benefit of a covenant that the other shops were not to be used for the sale by retail of tobacco, cigarettes, snuff, pipes, smoker's sundries, sweets and chocolates. The burden of the restrictive covenant was registered under the L.C.A. 1925 (Class D(ii)–see above, p. 18). Subsequently the servient land was registered under the L.R.A. 1925 but the covenant did not appear in the charges register. No. 11, one of the other shops, was leased for 21 years. In 1974 the lease was assigned to the defendants and the landlord consented to a change of use. The defendants were vintners and also sold tobacco, cigarettes, chocolates, etc. When they took the assignment, they had checked the registered title to ensure that there was nothing on the title to prevent them using the premises for their business. After the writ in the action had been issued, the register of the freehold title of No. 11 was rectified by the registrar pursuant to the L.R.A. s.82(3)(*c*) upon the plaintiff's application by the issue of a new edition of the title showing the covenant in the charges register. (At the trial Walton J. queried the basis on which rectification had been made, since the freeholder was in possession by the receipt of the rent (see L.R.A. ss.3(xviii), 82(3)). The plaintiff sought an injunction to restrain the defendants selling in breach of the covenant. Subject to the effect of the rectification it was conceded that the effect of the absence of any entry as to the covenant on the title of No. 11 was that the covenant was not binding on the defendants (see L.R.A. ss.20(1), 59(6)). The primary issue before the court was whether the rectification had a retrospective effect. Walton J. held that the rectification took effect from the revised edition of the title. The lease being for 21 years was not registrable, but took effect as if it were a registered disposition immediately on being granted (L.R.A. s.19(2)). Thus it was subject to the incumbrances and other entries appearing on the register and to overriding interests (L.R.A. s.20(1)). The covenant was not noted on the register at the date of the lease. Section 50 of the Act confirmed that the date of the noting of the covenant was the relevant date. The covenant had not been noted until the revised edition. Therefore the lessee of the No. 11 lease and the defendants took free from the restrictive covenant. The plaintiff had no claim to indemnity under L.R.A. s.83 because the plaintiff's loss was not occasioned by the rectification (but by the Registry's failure to note the covenant on the first registration of the servient land).

Note: It appears that compensation was paid to the plaintiff by the Land Registry (see Ruoff and Roper's *Registered Conveyancing* (4th ed.), p. 794, note 93). For L.R.A. ss.82, 83 see pp. 69, 73, below.

General note: It might have been thought that the system of registration of title would make the common law doctrine of notice redundant. But the L.R.A. 1925 does not expressly deal with all situations where questions of priority may arise (see below, p. 170 for one which is dealt with) and the courts have fallen back, perhaps improperly, on the doctrine of notice. The doctrine is also material to certain overriding interests.

Barclays Bank Ltd. v. **Taylor** [1974] Ch. 137, C.A.

Mr. and Mrs. Duxbury were registered proprietors of a house subject to a building society mortgage. In 1961, Mr. Duxbury persuaded his bank to pay what remained of their mortgage debt, a total of £1,604. In return they deposited the land certificate with the bank (see L.R.A. 1925, s.66, below, p. 171). This was to provide security not only for the Duxburys' joint overdraft (which had been debited with the £1,604), but also for the overdraft on Mr. Duxbury's trading account (he being engaged in business as a builder and contractor). The bank gave notice to the Land Registry of the deposit of the certificate with them in June 1961 (which was duly noted in the Charges Register of the property), and three months later the Duxburys signed a memorandum with the bank declaring that the certificate had been deposited to secure the two overdrafts, and undertaking to execute a legal charge when called on to do so. (It was the practice of banks to rely on notice of deposit and not take a charge at once in order to save the fee for registration of a registered charge.) In August 1962 a mortgage by way of legal charge (*i.e.* a mortgage in unregistered form) was executed by the Duxburys in favour of the bank. This took place because Mr. Duxbury had formed a company to take over his firm and the bank had agreed to allow this company overdraft facilities. An account was opened in the company's name and Mr. Duxbury's old trading account was closed. The mortgage was to secure the company's account and the Duxburys' personal account. The bank, relying on the notice of deposit of the certificate, did not register this mortgage straight away, and before it did, in February 1968, the Duxburys contracted to sell the house for £3,500 to the defendants (Mrs. Taylor being the sister of Mrs.

Duxbury). The Duxburys paid off the money due to the bank on their joint account, but not the money due on the company's account. The bank, having called in the mortgage, took steps to exercise its power of sale under the mortgage, whereupon the Taylors entered a caution against dealings. The bank thereupon lodged the legal charge of 1962 for registration under the L.R.A. 1925, s.26 (see below, p. 170). The Taylors opposed the application claiming that if it were entitled to be registered it could only take effect subject to the priority given to them by virtue of their caution. Goulding J. at first instance held that, because the bank's mortgage was not in registered charge form and registered, it took effect under the L.R.A. s.106 (see below, p. 171). This section (until it was amended by the A.J.A. 1977, see below, p. 171) provided for protection by a special mortgage caution and *in no other way* and that until so protected the legal charge was a minor interest capable of being overridden. It was therefore postponed to the defendants' estate contract. Reversing this decision the Court of Appeal upheld the bank's priority. The bank's interest, by virtue of section 106(4) (now s.106(2)(*b*)) took effect only in equity as a minor interest, but so did the defendants' estate contract (see L.R.A. s.101). The caution lodged by the Taylors had no effect whatever by itself on priorities, it simply conferred on them the right to be given notice of any dealing proposed to be registered (see section 54 of the Act). A caution has only this limited effect. The mere failure of the bank to lodge its caution was in itself insufficient reason to disturb the ordinary rules of priority: "*Qui prior est tempore, potior est jure*" (above, p. 11). In the words of Russell L.J., "In truth, the bank in respect of its mortgage, albeit taking effect as a minor interest only in equity, did not need any protection against the subsequent equitable interest of the Taylors: it only needed protection against the registration of the Taylors as proprietors (and, for this, possession of the land certificate was at least *de facto* protection), or against a subsequent mortgagee whose charge was registered or perhaps who lodged a caution in special form (although again here there would, we apprehend, be the same *de facto* protection)."

Re White Rose Cottage [1965] Ch. 940, C.A.

Kamerun Ltd., the registered proprietor of the cottage, mortgaged it to its bank, William Brandts, by an equitable mortgage made by deposit of the land certificate and an accompanying memorandum of charge under seal. The memorandum contained an undertaking to execute a legal charge when called on, and appointed the bank K.'s attorney to vest the legal estate in the cottage in any purchaser on any sale made by the bank as mortgagee. The bank gave notice of the deposit of the land certificate with it to the Registry. Subsequently, Chippendales, a firm of contractors, obtained a charging order on the property. Then Kamerun contracted to sell the cottage to Mrs. Winfield. Then C. obtained another charging order on the cottage. The charging orders were protected by a caution against dealings (see below, p. 45). After all this the bank applied to the Registry to have its mortgage noted on the register of the cottage as a land charge under the L.R.A., s.49(1). On being informed of the application by the Registry, C. claimed that their charging orders had priority. They contended that the notice of deposit was a nullity because the charge in favour of the bank was created by the memorandum, not the deposit, and application for noting of the memorandum had not been made until after their cautions. This contention was not accepted. Harman L.J. thought that even if the mortgage should have been protected as a land charge under section 49, having given notice of deposit this was notice to all the world that the land certificate was in the hands of someone as security and put a subsequent incumbrancer on inquiry. Lord Denning M.R. thought that the bank had several alternative ways of protecting its mortgage: under section 49, and this would mean that every subsequent purchaser or incumbrancer would be affected with notice (see section 52 of the L.R.A. 1925); by lodging a caution under section 54, which would give notice of its interest and entitle it to have notice and to be heard before any subsequent dealing was registered (s.55); or it could, as it did, give notice of deposit under rule 239, which operated as a caution warning all persons who looked at the register that the land certificate had been deposited with them as security. The notice took effect in priority to C.'s charges and C. could not object to the bank's application for the noting of its charge under section 49.

A further point concerned the sale to Mrs. Winfield and the application by her and her mortgagees for registration. C. claimed that any registration must be subject to their charges. If the transfer had been made by the bank as mortgagee under its power of sale, the sale would overreach all charges subsequent to its own (see L.P.A. 1925 s.104(1), below, p. 193). If the transfer was made by Kamerun it could only convey its own interest, which was subject to the charges. The court construed the transfer as one by Kamerun as beneficial owner, together with a release by the bank which received the purchase money, and, therefore, Mrs. Winfield and her mortgagee acquired only the estate Kamerun had to transfer, *i.e.* one subject to C.'s charges. The Court of Appeal agreed with Wilberforce J. that had the bank and not Kamerun been the transferors they could indeed have conveyed the legal estate, although they were only equitable mortgagees and, moreover, could have done so without (*per* Harman L.J.) first going through the formality of calling for the execution by the mortgagor of a legal mortgage.

Parkash v. Irani Finance Ltd. [1970] 1 Ch. 101

Mr. Kabra was the registered proprietor of a property in Slough. A charge on the property existed in favour of Slough Corporation, and this too was registered. In January 1967, Kabra agreed to sell the property to Parkash but no formal contract was ever signed. However, Parkash paid a deposit and went into occupation on July 2, 1967. On July 7, 1967, the defendants obtained a charging order in respect of a judgment debt owed to them by Kabra. They entered a caution in the Land Registry on July 10, 1967 (see below, p. 45). Later that month Parkash's solicitors were ready to complete with Kabra and, having applied for an official search on the register, were informed by the Land Registry that the only adverse entry was the charge in favour of Slough Corporation. Kabra transferred the property to Parkash, who contemporaneously charged it to the Abbey National Building Society, which had advanced the balance of the purchase money. The Corporation's charge was paid off out of the proceeds of sale. When the defendants were informed of the application to register the transfer to Parkash and the charge in favour of the building society, they objected and claimed that their own equitable charge had priority. Plowman J. held that they were entitled to priority. He rejected an argument that Parkash should not be bound by the caution because, through the mistake on the part of the Land Registry, he was not given notice of it and therefore he was a purchaser for value of the legal estate without notice. The judge was surprised that this doctrine should be relied on in the context of registration of title and he examined the provisions of the L.R.A. 1925. Admittedly, section 59(6) of the Act said that a purchaser shall *not* be bound by an encumbrance on the property that is *not* protected by a caution or other entry on the register, and did not say that the purchaser should necessarily be bound by one that is. Nevertheless, the judge affirmed that this corollary was "implicit in the scheme of the Act and in the subsection." In his view, the effect of the relevant provisions in the Act was: "first, that the appropriate form of protection for a charging order is a caution; secondly, that once the caution is registered, the cautioner can only lose his protection either by virtue of section 55(1) or by withdrawing his caution, or consenting to its cancellation, or by order of the Chief Land Registrar or this court; and, thirdly, that therefore he does not lose it merely because a purchaser of the property does not know of its existence, even if the purchaser's ignorance is the result of a mistake of the Land Registry, short of a failure to act on an application to register the caution in the first place." Reference was made to *Re White Rose Cottage* (above) in support of these propositions. A further point concerned the question of whether the original charge in favour of Slough Corporation could be kept alive for the benefit of the building society, who claimed that since it was they who, in effect, paid off the Corporation when the transfer to Parkash was finally executed, they should be able to step into the Corporation's shoes and "inherit" the Corporation's charge, thereby gaining priority over Irani's subsequent equitable charge. The learned judge dismissed this contention for lack of evidence; there was nothing to show that it was not Kabra himself who had paid off the Corporation (albeit with money received from the Abbey National). Accordingly the building society's argument fell victim to the rule that an original mortgagor who pays off a mortgage cannot, even by express provision, keep it alive against any other encumbrance which he has created (see *Otter* v. *Lord Vaux* (1856) 6 De G.M. & G. 638, H.L., and L.P.A. 1925, s.115(3), below, p. 201).

Note: A charging order may now be protected by notice under the L.R.A. 1925, s.49(1)(*g*) (added by the Charging Orders Act 1979, s.3(3)).

Peffer v. Rigg [1977] 1 W.L.R. 285, Ch. D.

The plaintiff and the first defendant were brothers-in-law. In 1962, they agreed to purchase the house, in which their mother-in-law was a tenant of part, to provide security for her and as an investment for themselves. The property was taken in the first defendant's name, as they thought that he was more likely to obtain a mortgage. The purchase price was £2,500 and a mortgage of £2,000 was obtained and home improvement grants. They agreed to contribute equally to expenses. The first defendant was to hold the house as trustee for the two of them as tenants in common in equal shares. But nothing was put in writing. In 1967, the defendants' marriage broke down and the second defendant, the plaintiff's sister-in-law, went to live with her mother in the mother's flat in the house. The plaintiff was concerned about his interest in the house and asked his sister-in-law to get an acknowledgment in writing from her husband as to the plaintiff's interest. This she did and they later executed a trust deed formalising the position. When the top floor in the house became vacant, the plaintiff wanted to sell the house, realising that a re-letting would be protected under the Rent Act 1968. The second defendant accused him of threatening to turn her mother out of her flat. There was a stalemate. In the course of discussions the plaintiff told the defendants that he was not prepared to spend any more money on the house until its future was resolved. As a result, the first defendant had to pay the mortgage instalments. He subsequently carried out some repairs to the top flat and re-let it without informing the plaintiff. In 1971, as part of the property settlement on the defendants' divorce, the first defendant as beneficial owner transferred the house to the second defendant for one pound. The plaintiff claimed that the second defendant held the house in trust as to one half for him and an order for sale. Graham J. found that when the first defendant transferred the house to the second defendant, she knew that it was held by the first defendant in trust and held that, as the consideration was nominal and not valuable consideration, the second defendant was not protected by section 20(1) of the L.R.A. 1925 and by virtue of section 20(4) of the Act (above, p. 33), she took the property subject to the plaintiff's minor interest. If the one pound was valuable consideration (being part of a property settlement on divorce) the first defendant still did not take free of the plaintiff's interest, because it was still necessary under sections 20 and 59(6) (above, p. 37) of the L.R.A. 1925, which were to be read together, for her to have been a purchaser in good faith (see the definition of "purchaser" in section 3 above, p. 31) and since she knew of the plaintiff's interest she was not in good faith. And if he was wrong on that point, the judge held that the second defendant, because of her knowledge, held the property on constructive trust for herself and the plaintiff.

Note: It seems clear after *Williams & Glyn's Bank* v. *Boland* (see below, p. 49) that a minor interest can only bind a purchaser in good faith for valuable consideration if protected on the register. Actual notice of the interest is immaterial (see L.R.A. 1925, s.59(6)). But for equitable interests ancillary to actual occupation, see below, pp. 49 and 50.

Lyus v. Prowsa Developments Ltd.
[1982] 1 W.L.R. 1044, Ch. D.

The plaintiffs contracted to buy a house in the course of completion from a company for £14,250. Before the house was finished the company was ordered to be wound up. The house was subject to a mortgage to a bank which had priority to the plaintiffs' contract. The bank could have sold free of the plaintiffs' interest (see below, p. 193) but decided to sell the house subject to and with the benefit of the plaintiffs' contract to the first defendant. The first defendant subsequently transferred the property to the second defendant, the contract for sale providing that the sale was subject to the plaintiffs' contract. The land was registered land. The plaintiffs' contract was not protected on the register in any way and both transfers were silent as to the plaintiffs' contract. The defendants relied on the L.R.A. 1925, ss.20 (see above, p. 33) and 34(4) (under which on a sale by a mortgagee the charge and all subsequent incumbrances and entries are cancelled). Dillon J. held, relying on *Bannister* v. *Bannister* (see above, p. 4) and *Binions* v. *Evans* (above, p. 16), that the first defendant, having accepted the land subject to the plaintiffs' contract, held it upon a constructive trust to complete the contract in favour of the plaintiffs. A similar constructive trust was imposed on the second defendant by the terms of its contract for purchase. It would be a fraud on the part of the first defendant to renege on the stipulation in favour of the plaintiffs and for the second defendant to rely on the transfer to them as freeing them from the stipulation. The L.R.A. must not be used as an engine of fraud. (The plaintiffs had also relied, unsuccessfully, on L.P.A. 1925, s.56 (see below, p. 267). The stipulations relating to the plaintiffs' contract in the contracts between the bank and the first defendant and the first defendant and the second defendant could not be construed as a grant or covenant purported to be made with the plaintiffs.) The plaintiffs were entitled to specific performance. The defendant argued that specific performance should not be decreed for want of mutuality (*i.e.* because the contract was not enforceable by them against the plaintiffs) but it was held that the principle in *Halsall* v. *Brizell* (see below, p. 243) applied, *i.e.* if the plaintiffs wanted the benefit of the contract, they had to bear the burden of it. In the event, the second defendant had to complete the house at an estimated cost of £9,600 and the plaintiffs then had a house worth £27,500.

Overriding Interests

Strand Securities Ltd. v. Caswell [1965] Ch. 958, C.A.

Mrs. Caswell, who was the registered proprietor with good leasehold title of a house in St. John's Wood, in 1949 sub-let a flat in the house to Mr. Caswell, for a term of 39¼ years. This lease could have been registered but it was not. In 1952 Mrs. C. sold the house subject to the sub-lease. The purchaser accepted rent from Mr. C. In 1962 the purchaser agreed to sell the house to the plaintiffs subject to the sub-lease. On April 5, 1962, Mr. C. applied to the Registry for registration of the sub-lease. The plaintiffs applied for registration of the transfer to them on April 24, 1962. The practice of the Registry prior to this case (based on a misinterpretation of the L.R.A. 1925, s.64) had been that the head lessor's land certificate must be produced on registration of a sub-lease and accordingly the Registry had given the plaintiffs' application precedence. This practice was held to be wrong by the Court of Appeal and Mr. C.'s application had priority. As an alternative claim Mr. C. had alleged that he had an overriding interest under the L.R.A., s.70(1)(*g*) as a person in actual occupation. The flat had been sub-let to Mr. C. for twelve years, then in 1961 he allowed his step-daughter to live there with her two children rent and rates free. But he kept a good deal of his furniture there and he and his wife used it when they came up to London from the country. It was held that Mr. C. did not have an overriding interest since it was the step-daughter, not him, in actual occupation. Lord Denning M.R. stated that section 70(1)(*g*) carried forward into registered land the doctrine of *Hunt* v. *Luck* (above, p. 15), but with the difference that not only is the actual occupier protected, but also the rights of the person in receipt of the rents. But the step-daughter was not paying rent. She was only a licensee (see below, p. 111), and her licence could be determined at any time on reasonable notice (see *Minister of Health* v. *Bellotti*, below, p. 114). The plaintiffs took subject to *her* rights by virtue of section 70(1)(*g*), but could get her out. Although occupation could be shared, he could not hold that Mr. C. was sharing with his step-daughter. Russell L.J. stated that had the step-daughter been Mr. C's caretaker he would have been in actual occupation. And a husband not in actual physical occupation could, perhaps, be a person in actual occupation through his wife who was residing on the premises (but see *Williams & Glyn's Bank* v. *Boland*, below, p. 49).

Hodgson v. Marks [1971] Ch. 929, C.A.

Mrs. Hodgson, a widow aged 80, was the registered proprietor of a house in which she lived. A lodger, Evans, also lived in the house. He exercised considerable influence over her and Mrs. Hodgson's nephew, who was in the Foreign Service, wanted her to make him leave. To prevent this, in 1960 Mrs. Hodgson voluntarily transferred the house to Evans who was duly registered as proprietor. Mrs. Hodgson's intention was that the house was to remain her house though in Evans' name. In 1964, Evans sold the house to Marks who mortgaged it to a building society to raise the purchase money. Marks did not know that the plaintiff had any interest in the property. Before the purchase he had visited the premises. He saw the plaintiff but did not ascertain who she was. He knew that one bedroom in the house was occupied by a woman. Evans had told him that he was married. Marks was registered as proprietor. The plaintiff later claimed to be entitled to a transfer from the defendant free from the mortgage. She claimed that Evans held the property on a resulting trust for her and that the defendant took subject to her interest because she was "a person in actual occupation of the land" within section 70(1)(*g*) of the Act. She failed before Ungoed-Thomas J., who held that "actual occupation" for the purposes of the Act meant occupation by an act recognisable as such and apparent to the purchaser, *i.e.* actual *and apparent* occupation, and the plaintiff's occupation did not satisfy these requirements. He said that had the land been unregistered Marks would not have had constructive notice of the plaintiff's interest, *i.e.* he would have been a bona fide purchaser for value without notice. This decision was reversed on appeal. It was held that even where a vendor was, or appeared to be, in occupation, a person other than the vendor might, in certain circumstances, be held to be in actual occupation within section 70(1)(*g*) and a purchaser, to be sure of obtaining a good title, must pay heed to anyone occupying the premises. The plaintiff was at all material times in actual occupation within the meaning of the section; she was in apparent physical occupation of the house and had the right to occupy it.

Williams & Glyn's Bank Ltd. v. Boland, Williams & Glyn's Bank Ltd. v. Brown [1981] A.C. 487, H.L.

These two cases involved registered land, being the matrimonial homes of the Bolands and Browns, which were registered in the husband's name alone. Each wife had contributed to the purchase and was entitled to a beneficial share in the house (see, *e.g.* the cases noted at pp. 83-94, below). Each husband carried on business through a private company and each charged the home to the bank to secure loans to the company. Upon default under the mortgage the bank sought possession for the purposes of sale. Mrs. Boland and Mrs. Brown each claimed that the bank took subject to her equitable interest which by her occupation of the home constituted an overriding interest. The Courts had to consider the nature of the wife's equitable interest. By virtue of the wife's contribution the husband held the property upon trust for sale for himself and his wife. As equitable owner the wife had the right to occupy the house before sale (see *Bull* v. *Bull*, below, p. 83) and, upon sale, a share in the proceeds of sale. Was the wife's equitable interest one in the land or only in the proceeds of the sale thereof? The authorities on conversion (see below, pp. 75-77) were canvassed and the wife's right was categorised as an interest in the land (*per* Lord Denning M.R. in the Court of Appeal—"When a married man and his wife buy a house, they do so to live in it . . . They do not intend to sell it . . . the court must give effect to the intention of the parties." *Per* Lord Wilberforce, approving Lord Denning's view, " . . . to describe the interests of spouses in a house jointly bought to be lived in as a matrimonial home as merely an interest in the proceeds of sale . . . is just a little unreal.") It was held that the wives were in actual occupation, meaning physical presence as opposed to some entitlement in law. The fact that the vendor or mortgagor is in occupation does not exclude the possibility of occupation of others and the wife's occupation was not a mere shadow of the husband's (*cf. Caunce* v. *Caunce* [1969] 1 W.L.R. 286). Nor did the occupation have to be inconsistent with the registered proprietor's. The wives' interests as beneficial owners were by themselves minor interests (L.R.A. s.3(xv)), but, if accompanied by actual occupation, they were overriding interests.

Webb v. Pollmount Ltd. [1966] Ch. 584

A lease of registered land, made in 1961 between the defendant's predecessor in title and the plaintiff, gave the plaintiff an option to purchase the freehold. The option was not protected by notice or caution. In 1962 the defendant acquired the freehold. The plaintiff was in occupation of the premises. Later he exercised the option, but the defendant claimed it was not binding on him. Ungoed-Thomas J. held that the option was an overriding interest. Section 70(1)(*g*) was not limited to the rights by virtue of which a person is in actual occupation but included all the rights of the person in actual occupation which affected the estate transferred (see the L.R.A. 1925, s.20, above). These rights are, *per* Russell, L.J. in the Court of Appeal in *National Provincial Bank Ltd.* v. *Ainsworth* (see above, p. 15) "rights in reference to land which have the quality of enduring through different ownerships of the land." An option was such a right. The judge also considered that in the case of unregistered land occupation by a tenant would give constructive notice of an option to purchase under the rule in *Hunt* v. *Luck* (above, p. 15).

Note: But after the Land Charges Act 1925 an option over unregistered land would require registration as a Class C (iv) land charge to be enforceable against a purchaser of the freehold. The above case, illustrates a situation where a person may be better off if the land is registered than he would be if it was unregistered. Had the land been unregistered on the above facts, the failure to protect the option by registration as a land charge would have rendered it unenforceable against the defendant. And see *Grace Rymer Investments Ltd.* v. *Waite* (below, p. 121) and *City Permanent Building Society* v. *Miller* (below, p. 121).

Blacklocks v. J.B. Developments (Godalming) Ltd. [1982] Ch. 183

The plaintiff and his uncle were joint owners of a farm. In 1968 they sold part of the farm to G. By a common mistake a triangular piece of land (the disputed land) was included in the contract and conveyance. G. was registered as proprietor of the whole of the land conveyed. After the sale the plaintiff fenced the disputed land as part of his land and later built a Dutch barn on it without objection from G., who was in occupation of his land. Judge Mervyn Davies, sitting as a High Court judge, found that the plaintiff could have obtained rectification of the register against G. (for rectification, see below, p. 69). In 1973 G. sold his land to the defendant. One of G's answers to the defendant's enquiries before contract disclosed the true boundary to G.'s land. An inspection of the land and comparison against the filed plan would have disclosed to the defendant the true extent of G.'s land. The defendant was registered as proprietor of G.'s land including the disputed land. The plaintiff claimed that his right of rectification combined with his actual occupation of the disputed land constituted an overriding interest to which the defendant took subject and sought a declaration that the defendant held the disputed land on trust for him and rectification of the register. The defendant argued that the right to rectify was a personal right—a mere equity—and, relying on *National Provincial Bank Ltd.* v. *Ainsworth* (see above, p. 15), not capable of being an overriding interest within L.R.A. s.70(1)(*g*). The judge, referring also to *Latec Investments Ltd.* v. *Hotel Terrigal Pty. Ltd.* (see above, p. 11), said the question was whether the right to rectify here was a mere naked equity or an equity ancillary to an equitable estate or interest in land. He found it was the latter. The association of the right with actual occupation constituted an overriding interest binding in the hands of the defendant. The judge added that had the land been unregistered land the right of the rectification would, in his view, have been enforceable against the defendant's legal estate. He made the declaration sought and ordered rectification.

Note: For other cases of overriding interests, see above, p. 14, and below, pp. 55, 65, 71, 75.

6. Overreaching

General note: A purchaser of land may take free from equitable interests therein, even where he has notice of them, under the doctrine of overreaching. Subject to certain conditions (the payment of the purchase-money to specified recipients—see L.P.A. 1925, s.27(2), below, pp. 106 and 303 and the cases at pp. 283-286, below) on a sale the purchaser takes free of all beneficial interests (and some legal interests) in the land. These interests (usually family interests under trusts) are said to be overreached, that is shifted from the land to the purchase-money. For the overreaching power of a mortgagee, see below, p. 193: and *Duke* v. *Robson*, below, p. 191.

CHAPTER 2

OWNERSHIP OF LAND

General note: In English law land (realty) is treated differently from chattels (personalty) in a number of ways. The absolute ownership of land in English law is in the Crown, if it is anywhere. The subject enjoys land by tenure—freehold or leasehold. He does not even hold the land as such, but rather an estate in the land. Moreover, title to land in English law is relative, not absolute. For historical and other reasons English law is more concerned with possession of land rather than ownership. This is illustrated by the possessory title (squatter's rights) and the proof of title on the sale of land. Even a registered title is not indefeasible and the register may be rectified. Finally, in some cases English law treats land as personalty (the doctrine of conversion) and chattels as land (fixtures).

1. POSSESSORY TITLE

Squatter's Rights against Third Parties

Asher v. Whitlock (1865) L.R. 1 Q.B. 1, Ct.Exch.Ch

In 1842 Williamson enclosed some manorial waste land. In 1850 he enclosed more land adjoining and built a cottage. He occupied the whole until 1860 when he died. The period of limitation at the time was 20 years so at W.'s death the title of the lord of the manor had not been extinguished. W. devised the land to his wife so long as she did not marry, with remainder to his daughter in fee. On W.'s death the widow and daughter continued to reside in the property. In 1861 the defendant married the widow and came to reside with them. In 1863 the daughter died aged 18 years and the mother died soon after. The defendant continued to occupy the property. In 1865 the daughter's heir-at-law brought ejectment against him. It was held that the plaintiff was entitled to recover the property. *Per* Cockburn C.J.: "On the simple ground that possession is good title against all but the true owner, I think the plaintiff entitled to succeed . . . the defendant . . . had no right to interfere with the testator, so he had no right against the daughter, and had she lived she could have brought ejectment . . . the same right belongs to her heir."

See also *Re Nisbet and Pott's Contract* (below, p. 250). For the rule that a tenant cannot deny the landlord's title, see below, p. 119.

Negative Effect of Limitation

Limitation Act 1980, s.17.

"Subject to—

(*a*) section 18 of this Act [Settled land and land held on trust]; and

(*b*) section 75 of the Land Registration Act 1925;

at the expiration of the period prescribed by this Act for any person to bring an action to recover land (including a redemption action) the title of that person to the land shall be extinguished."

Land Registration Act 1925, s.75

"(1) The Limitation Acts shall apply to registered land in the same manner and to the same extent as those Acts apply to land not registered, except that where, if the land were not registered, the estate of the person registered as proprietor would be extinguished, such estate shall not be extinguished but shall be deemed to be held by the proprietor for the time being in trust for the person who, by virtue of the said Acts, has acquired title against any proprietor, but without prejudice to the estates and interests of any other person interested in the land whose estate or interest is not extinguished by those Acts.

(2) Any person claiming to have acquired a title under the Limitation Acts to a registered estate in the land may apply to be registered as proprietor thereof.

(3) The registrar shall, on being satisfied as to the applicant's title, enter the applicant as proprietor either with absolute, good leasehold, qualified, or possessory title, as the case may require, but without prejudice to any estate or interest protected by any entry on the register which may not have been extinguished under the Limitation Acts, and such registration shall, subject as aforesaid, have the same effect as the registration of a first proprietor: but the proprietor or the applicant or any other person interested may apply to the court for the determination of any question arising under this section . . . "

Note: See *Young* v. *Clarey*, below, p. 198.

Tichborne v. Weir (1892) 67 L.T. 735, C.A.

In 1802 the plaintiff's predecessor in title granted a lease of a house to Baxter for 89 years. The lease contained a covenant to repair by the tenant. B. mortgaged the premises to Giraud who entered into possession and remained in possession until 1876, paying the rent payable under the lease. In 1876 G. assigned all his estate and interest in the lease to the defendant, who paid the rent until 1891 when he delivered up possession to the plaintiff on the determination of the lease. The plaintiff then sued the defendant for breach of covenant for repair. It was held that, although B.'s title had been barred under the Real Property Limitation Act 1833, the lease had not vested in G. The defendant was not liable on the covenants.

Note: Compare registered land (see the note to *Bridges* v. *Mees*, below, p. 65.

Fairweather v. St. Marylebone Property Co. Ltd.
[1963] A.C. 510, H.L.

The freehold owner of two adjoining properties, Nos. 311 and 315, built a shed in the back garden, three-quarters of the shed being on 315 and the remainder, which included the entrance, on 311. In 1893 both properties were let by separate leases for 99 years. In 1920 M., the sub-lessee of 311, repaired the shed and thereafter treated it as his own so that he had acquired title to it by adverse possession as against the tenants of 315 by 1932. In 1951 M. (sub-)sub-let 311 and the shed for 21 years. In 1958 M. bought the freehold of 311. In 1959 the respondents bought the freehold of 315 subject to the 99-year lease and shortly afterwards this lease was surrendered to them. The appellant became sub-tenant of 311 by an assignment in 1960 of the remainder of the 21-year term. The respondents claimed possession of the shed. The appellant claimed that the respondents were not entitled to possession until the 99-year lease of 315 had expired. The House of Lords held that the respondents were entitled to possession. Despite the title acquired by M. against the tenant of 315 the estate between freeholder and tenant of 315 was not destroyed. The tenant still had a right to possession against his landlord, the freeholder, and therefore something to surrender in 1959. On the surrender the tenant abandoned his right to possession against the freeholder and the lease merged in the freehold, rather than operating as an assignment of the remainder of the term. Accordingly the freeholder was entitled to possession in 1959 by virtue of his freehold estate against which the squatter could say nothing.

Note: The decision has been severely criticised principally on the ground that a landlord relying on surrender must be claiming *through the lessee* and therefore could not prejudice the squatter's right to possession until the expiry of the term, but the reasoning of Lord Denning in *Fairweather's* case had been accepted in *Tickner* v. *Buzzacott* (below). And see the note to *Bridges* v. *Mees* (below, p. 65).

Tickner v. Buzzacott [1965] Ch. 426.

In 1930 M. granted S. a lease of a house for a term of 75 years. The plaintiff's mother lived in the house with S. S. died in 1941. The mother stayed on, though she was not entitled to the lease, and paid the rent due under the lease until her death in 1960. In 1962 the defendant, the assignee of the reversion from M., forfeited the lease and re-entered the house. The premises had been empty since the mother's death and no rent paid. The defendant did not know that the mother was a squatter. The plaintiff claimed possession and relief from forfeiture. Plowman J. held that the mother was a squatter and had acquired a title by adverse possession against S. and his estate but she did not hold under the lease, and accordingly when the lease was forfeited was not entitled to apply for relief. The payment of rent by the mother did not give rise to a yearly tenancy as there was no evidence of any intention of either party to create a new relationship of landlord and tenant, especially since while the lease was on foot only a reversionary tenancy could have been granted, and it was unlikely that the parties could have intended that.

Adverse Possession

Limitation Act 1980, s.15(1), Sched. 1, Pt. I, paras. 1, 5, 8.

Section 15(1)

"15. (1) No action shall be brought by any person to recover any land after the expiration after 12 years from the date on which the right of action accrued to him or, if it first accrued to some person through whom he claims, to that person."

Sched. 1, Pt. 1

1. "Where the person bringing an action to recover land, or some person through whom he claims, has been in possession of the land, and has while entitled to the land been dispossessed or discontinued his possession, the right of action shall be treated as having accrued on the date of the dispossession or discontinuance.

5. (1) Subject to sub-paragraph (2) below, a tenancy from year to year or other period, without a lease in writing, shall for the purposes of this Act be treated as being determined at the expiration of the first year or other period; and accordingly the right of action of the person entitled to the land subject to the tenancy shall be treated as having accrued at the date on which in accordance with this sub-paragraph the tenancy is determined.

(2) Where any rent has subsequently been received in respect of the tenancy, the right of action shall be treated as having accrued on the date of the last receipt of rent.

8. (1) No right of action to recover land shall be treated as accruing unless the land is in the possession of some person in whose favour the period of limitation can run (referred to below in this paragraph as "adverse possession"); and where under the preceding provisions of this Schedule any such right of action is treated as accruing on a certain date and no person is in adverse possession on that date, the right of action shall not be treated as accruing unless and until adverse possession is taken of the land.

(2) Where a right of action to recover land has accrued and after its accrual, before the right is barred, the land ceases to be in adverse possession, the right of action shall no longer be treated as having accrued and no fresh right of action shall be treated as accruing unless and until the land is again taken into adverse possession.

(3) For the purposes of this paragraph—

(*b*) . . . receipt of rent under a lease by a person wrongfully claiming to be entitled to the land in reversion immediately expectant on the determination of the lease shall be treated as adverse possession of the land.

(4) For the purpose of determining whether a person occupying any land is in adverse possession of the land it shall not be assumed by implication of law that his occupation is by permission of the person entitled to the land merely by virtue of the fact that his occupation is not inconsistent with the latter's present or future enjoyment of the land.

This provision shall not be taken as prejudicing a finding to the effect that a person's occupation of any land is by implied permission of the person entitled to the land in any case where such a finding is justified on the actual facts of the case."

Leigh v. Jack (1879) 5 Ex.D. 264, C.A.

In 1854 Leigh conveyed to the defendant a plot of land on the south side of an intended road in Kirkdale, Liverpool, upon which the defendant built a factory. In 1857 Leigh conveyed to the Mersey Dock Trustees another plot of land to the north of the intended street and in 1872 this plot was sold to the defendant. The plots were described as bounded by the intended road. From 1854 the defendant had placed factory materials on the road so as to block it except as to foot passengers and in 1865 he enclosed a part of it. The plaintiff was tenant for life of all Leigh's land and sued to recover the site of the road. Within 20 years (the then limitation period), Leigh had repaired a gate at one end of the road. It was held that the conveyance had not granted the site of the road and the defendant did not have a possessory title. There had been no dispossession of the plaintiff and her predecessors. *Per* Bramwell L.J.: " . . . in order to defeat a title by dispossessing the former owner, acts must be done which are inconsistent with his enjoyment of the soil for the purposes for which he intended to use it . . . the intention of the plaintiff and her predecessors in title was not either to build upon or to cultivate the land but to devote it at some future time to public purposes." *Per* Cotton L.J.: " . . . there can be no discontinuance by absence of use and enjoyment where the land is not capable of use and enjoyment."

Williams Brothers Direct Supply Ltd. v. Raftery
[1958] 1 Q.B. 159

In 1937 the plaintiffs purchased a vacant site at the rear of some shops in Edmonton, London, for development. The 1939-45 war prevented development. In 1948 they had twice had the site surveyed and had applied for planning permission which was refused, but they never abandoned their intention to develop when the opportunity arose. In 1953 the plaintiffs dumped some rubbish on the land. The defendant was the tenant of a maisonette on top of one of the shops. In 1940 someone had begun to cultivate the land as part of the "dig for victory" campaign and from 1943 to 1948 the defendant did the same. In 1948 the defendant erected a shed on part of the land for breeding greyhounds. He later claimed a squatter's title to the land. The defendant admitted that he was not trying to take over the land, but exercising rights he thought he had as tenant of the maisonette. It was held that the plaintiffs had never discontinued possession and these acts of the defendant did not amount to dispossession of the plaintiffs. *Per* Hodson L.J.: "The first question . . . is whether the plaintiffs . . . had discontinued their possession . . . there was never any intention on the part of the plaintiffs to discontinue their ownership . . . the second question . . . depends on whether they had been dispossessed by . . . the defendant . . . there was no evidence on which he [the county court judge] could properly find that the defendant had dispossessed the plaintiffs . . . the defendant never even thought he was dispossessing the plaintiffs; he never claimed to do more than work the soil, as he thought he was permitted to do . . . No attempt was made by the defendant here to fence off his piece of ground so as to exclude anyone from it."

George Wimpey & Co. Ltd. v. Sohn [1967] Ch. 487, C.A.

In 1960 the plaintiffs agreed to purchase a hotel from the defendants. Included in the sale was an adjoining garden strip, part of a square, essential to the plaintiffs' proposed development. The defendants had rights to use the garden but no documentary title to the land itself. By the contract they agreed to convey such right, title and interest as they had over the garden land supported by 20 years and more undisputed possession of it. The defendants were, in fact, unable to show this and offered 12 years' adverse possession instead. It was held that the defendants did not perform their contract by offering different evidence and in any event had not proved a possessory title. Accordingly the plaintiffs could properly rescind. A right to use the garden had existed since 1833 to be enjoyed by the owners of the houses surrounding the square. Since 1930 a road through the square had been stopped up. Since then the garden strip had been used only by the inhabitants of the hotel. It was held that although the fencing of land belonging to another could often be an act of exclusion of the owner, in the present case the purpose of the fencing was equivocal, because it might have been done only for the purpose of protecting the garden rights. Reliance was placed on *Littledale* v. *Liverpool College* [1900] 1 Ch. 19, C.A. (where the plaintiffs had a right of way over a strip of land separating two fields. Both the fields and the strip belonged, on paper, to the defendants. The plaintiffs erected gates at each end of the strip and kept them locked. Then they claimed a possessory title against the defendants. It was held that the erection of the gates was equivocal and might merely have been done to protect the right of way from invasion by the public. Accordingly, the plaintiffs had not acquired title. *Per* Russell L.J.: "It must, of course, be a very exceptional case in which enclosure . . . will not demonstrate the relevant adverse possession. . . . But where there is an easement as against the landowner to use the land as a garden . . . a very clear case must be made to establish possession adverse to the landowner so long as the land continues to be used as a garden."

Wallis's Cayton Bay Holiday Camp Ltd. v. Shell Mex and B.P. Ltd. [1975] Q.B. 94, C.A.

The plaintiff owned a caravan holiday camp to the south of a main road. Next door, to the east, was a garage. Beyond that was a field, then a road leading to a farm and another field. In 1950 a strip of land parallel to the main road running across the two fields and behind the garage was conveyed by the farmer to the county council for the site of a proposed new road. The site was not fenced in or marked out in any way. In 1957 the garage owner purchased the part of the field adjoining (about 1.33 acres) between the main road and the proposed road site (the disputed land). It was assumed that he intended to extend the garage if the new road was made. In 1961 he sold the land to the defendant and it saw value in the land as an extension for the garage when the road was constructed. The land was not fenced or marked out. In 1961 a subsidiary company of the plaintiff had purchased the farm. Thereafter it treated the disputed land and the new road site as part and parcel of the farm, although originally it had permission from the council to use the road site. Cattle grazed on the land and one year the land was ploughed. In 1971 the land became used as a playing area for the holiday camp. Grass was cut and litter was collected. A football pitch was set up and the fence at the main road painted. In 1972 the council abandoned its proposal for a new road. The defendant then decided that the land was surplus to requirement and made an offer to sell by letter to the plaintiff. The plaintiff did not reply to that and subsequent letters and by the time the defendant commenced fencing off the land the 12 years period had expired. The county court judge found that the plaintiff had had *de facto* possession of the land, that the defendant and its predecessor never intended to discontinue ownership and the plaintiff did not intend to be trespassers until after receipt of the offer letter, because they thought that they were the owners of the land, albeit mistakenly. The appeal was dismissed. Lord Denning M.R. and Ormrod L.J. held that there had been no ouster of the defendant. When the owner of land intends to use the land for a particular purpose in the future, (*per* Lord Denning) the possession of the land by the squatter is to be ascribed to a licence or permission of the owner, (*per* Ormrod L.J.) trivial acts of trespass, which do not prejudice the true owner's contemplated future use of the land, will not amount to adverse possession. Stamp L.J. dissenting, held that there was no special rule for future purpose cases. The cases relied on for the supposed rule were explicable on the facts that they were either land which was waste or not enclosed or that the acts of the trespasser did not amount to dispossession.

Note: On implied licence or permission (see Lord Denning, above), see now the Limitation Act 1980, Sched. 1, Pt. 1, para. 8(4).

Williams v. Usherwood (1983) 45 P.&C.R. 235, C.A.

Two semi-detached houses (Nos. 31 and 33) were intended to share a common driveway. Two feet and six inches in width of the drive went with No. 33 and the balance to No. 31. The original conveyances of the houses granted reciprocal rights of way over the parts of the drive as access to the respective properties. The conveyance of No. 31 contained a covenant to erect and maintain a boundary fence between the two houses. No. 33 had a driveway on the No. 35 side and did not have to use the common driveway. In 1935 the owner of No. 31 erected a boundary fence in such a way as to enclose within No. 31 No. 33's part of the common drive. The owner of No. 33 did not complain, believing the land belonged to No. 31. The drive was used for parking cars. Later a garage was erected on part of it and also crazy paving was laid on part. It was held that the defendant had acquired a possessory title to the part of the drive originally part of No. 33. In 1935 the owner of No. 33 had abandoned the land. Even though, when the owner of No. 31 fenced in the land, he thought the land belonged to him this did not prevent the requisite animus possedendi. The necessary intention was evidenced from the acts of enclosure and parking. The laying of crazy paving was an assertion of exclusive possession, rather than a new claim. The eaves and gutters of No. 33 protruded above the disputed land and drains from No. 33 ran through the disputed land before linking up in a combined drain. The plaintiff claimed this prevented adverse possession being established. The argument failed, but it was held that the defendant obtained a possessory title subject to the plaintiff's rights of overhang, access for maintenance of the side wall and drainage.

Note: The plaintiff's rights could not be an easement of necessity, because this supposes a grant (see *Nickerson* v. *Barraclough*, below, p. 214). But Cumming-Bruce L.J. said that the rights arose as a matter of law independent of grant.

Tenancies

Bligh v. Martin [1968] 1 W.L.R. 804, Ch. D.

An arable field was conveyed with other land to the defendant in 1945. He did not realise the field was included in the conveyance. In 1948 the field was conveyed to a predecessor in title of the plaintiff, the vendor being under the impression that she still owned it and had not sold it in 1945. In 1966 the plaintiff claimed a possessory title to the field. From 1954 till the spring of 1960, the defendant ploughed, sowed and harvested the field under a contractual arrangement made with the plaintiff, but for four or five winter months each year he turned cattle out in the field without the plaintiff's knowledge. For periods in 1960 and 1961 the defendant occupied the land under summer grazing agreements for a rent, and, again, put cattle in the field in the winter without the plaintiff's knowledge. Pennycuick J. held that the plaintiff had established a possessory title, and the defendant's winter use did not amount to dispossession of the plaintiff. Possession can continue notwithstanding the fact that there are intervals between the acts of user. The plaintiff's receipt of rent under the grazing agreements amounted to adverse possession under the Limitation Act 1939, s.10(3) (see now L.A. 1980, Sched. 1, Pt. I, para 8(3)(*b*)) even though the defendant was at that stage still the rightful owner of the field.

Hayward v. Chaloner [1968] 1 Q.B. 107, C.A.

Some time prior to 1938 the Saville Estate let on a half-yearly oral tenancy a small piece of land of less than a quarter of an acre to the rector of Bilsthorpe for use as part of his garden. The rector paid 10s. a year rent for the land. In 1938 the Estate was sold up. Rent was last paid by the rector in 1942. The owner of the land, who had bought it as part of a farm, thereafter never asked for rent "because it was the church." Rectors came and went. The land was used as part of the gardens of some cottages belonging to the church. Subsequently it was used by the tenant of the cottages for putting motor vehicles on and later the tenant erected a Nissen hut on the land. The appellants were the present owners of the farm, the conveyance of which to them included the disputed land. The respondent, the rector, claimed a possessory title. It was held (Lord Denning dissenting on the ground that the possession was not adverse, not being inconsistent with the enjoyment of the land by the owner of the paper title (see *Williams Brothers Direct Supply Ltd.* v. *Raftery*, above, p. 58) that there having been a periodic oral tenancy to the rector he ceased to be tenant when the period covered by the last payment of rent expired (Limitation

Act 1939, s.9(2)) (see now L.A. 1980, Sched. 1, Pt. 1, para. 5(1)) and his subsequent possession became adverse. Accordingly the appellants' right of action to recover the land was barred by reason of more than 12 years' adverse possession. Cases like *Williams Brothers Direct Supply Ltd.* v. *Raftery* have no bearing on cases arising under section 9(2) of the 1939 Act. Once the period covered by the last payment of rent expires the former tenant's possession becomes adverse. "The generous indulgence of the plaintiffs having resulted in a free accretion at their expense to the lands of their church, their reward may be in the next world, but in this jurisdiction we can only qualify them for that reward by allowing the appeal": *per* Russell L.J.

Hughes v. Griffin [1969] 1 W.L.R. 23, C.A.

In 1947 Mr. G. married the defendant and they lived together in his bungalow. Mr. G. said that the defendant would have the house when he was gone. But there was no agreement in this respect and the defendant lived in the house simply because it was her husband's and not because of any claim of hers. In 1951 Mr. G. executed a conveyance of the property to his nephew, the plaintiff, expressed to be in consideration of £1,500. At first the plaintiff did not know of this but Mr. G. later told him. Later Mr. G. forgave the plaintiff the debt of £1,500. In 1959 Mr. G. gave the plaintiff the deeds and in 1960 said he would go if necessary but the plaintiff said he could stay. Mr. G. died in 1965. The plaintiff claimed possession. The defendant claimed title under the Limitation Act 1939, contending that the plaintiff's right of action must, by virtue of section 5(3) of the Act (see now L.A. 1980, Sched. 1, Pt. 1, para. 3), be deemed to have accrued at the date of the conveyance and as more than 12 years had since elapsed, the action must be statute-barred. It was held that the plaintiff was entitled to possession. The defendant's possession had never been adverse within the meaning of section 10(1) of the Act (now L.A. 1980, Sched. 1, Pt. 1, para. 8), because she was the licensee of the plaintiff. But if Mr. G.'s possession was adverse after 1951 the handing over of the deeds in 1959, or the permission to stay in 1960, created a tenancy at will which stopped time running so that adverse possession did not commence afresh until one year thereafter (see section 9 of the Act, now L.A. 1980, Sched. 1, Pt. 1, para. 5(1)) in which case the limitation period had not expired.

Heslop v. Burns [1974] 1 W.L.R. 1241, C.A.

Mr. Timms was a property owner in Lambeth. In 1951 the defendants went to London and Mrs. Burns worked for Mr. T. in his office for a short while. He formed a romantic attachment to her and, being concerned about the conditions in which she and her husband lived, bought a cottage for them to live in. He became godfather to their child and paid for her education. Subsequently they moved first to one and then in 1954 to another house bought by Mr. T. for them to live in. Mr. T. used to visit the defendants daily for meals and they went to the seaside together. No payment was made by the defendants for use of the house. Mr. T. paid the rates and maintained the premises. Mr. T. told Mrs. B. that the house would be hers after his death. He completed rent books for the house as if the defendants had paid rent and included the mythical rent in his tax return. In 1970 he died. He had not left the house to Mrs. B. by his will and his executors claimed possession. The defendants claimed to have occupied the house since 1954 as tenants at will, that by the effect of the Limitation Act 1939, s.9 (see now L.A. 1980, Sched. 1, Pt. 1, para. 5(1)) the tenancy was deemed to have determined at the expiration of one year from the commencement thereof and accordingly they had acquired a possessory title by 1967. The county court judge, influenced by the rent books and inclusion of rent in the tax returns, accepted the defendants' submissions. On appeal, it was held that, having regard to the circumstances in which the defendants were allowed to move into the house and occupy it, with no arrangements as to the terms on which they should do so, it was impossible to infer an intention to create legal relations, still less to infer an intention on the part of Mr. T. to grant the defendants an interest in the house of such a nature as would give them the right to exclude him therefrom. Accordingly the defendants had entered into occupation of the house as licensees and not tenants at will. Even if they had established exclusive possession the defendants would not necessarily have succeeded, for the court is less and less inclined to infer a tenancy at will from an exclusive occupation of indefinite duration (*per* Scarman L.J.).

Note: And see *Cobb* v. *Lane* (below, p. 115).

Hyde v. Pearce [1982] 1 W.L.R. 560, C.A.

In 1958 the plaintiff contracted to purchase No. 138 and a small piece of land adjoining. He paid a deposit and was allowed into possession before completion upon an undertaking to return the keys on demand. The Law Society's Conditions of Sale, which applied to the contract, provided that a purchaser taking possession before completion occupied the land as licensee. The vendors then discovered that they had inadvertently sold the piece of land before. They proposed a reduction of the purchase price, but after negotiations to agree a figure failed, they demanded the return of the keys and subsequently proposed arbitration. For reasons which were not explained, nothing then happened for 14 years. The plaintiff remained in possession. In 1972 the vendors sold No. 138 to the defendant, who was able to take possession in the plaintiff's temporary absence. The plaintiff claimed title by adverse possession. The trial judge held that the plaintiff's licence to occupy under the contract had been revoked by the demand for the keys and that thereafter the plaintiff had been a squatter and accordingly had acquired title by adverse possession. On appeal, it was held that while, generally, the licence under the contract could not be revoked without rescinding the contract (and the contract had never been rescinded) the condition of the contract creating the status of licensee had been varied by the undertaking to return the keys. The demand for the keys had revoked the licence. As neither party had sought to rescind the contract the plaintiff continued to occupy the property thereafter as purchaser under the contract pending completion and not as trespasser. Therefore the plaintiff's possession had never been adverse and, as the contract had not been registered as a land charge, on the 1972 sale the defendant took free from the plaintiff's equitable interest as purchaser.

Note: No. 138 appears from the report to have been registered land by the time of the 1972 sale, but there is no reference to the L.R.A. 1925 in the judgments. For a purchaser as adverse possession, see *Bridges* v. *Mees*, below. But there the purchaser had paid the purchase price.

Registered Land

Bridges v. Mees [1957] Ch. 475

In April 1939 the plaintiff, who was the registered proprietor of a house, contracted to purchase a strip of unregistered land at the back of his house and the adjoining house belonging to the defendant from the owner of the land. The plaintiff went into possession of the land and retained possession of it without interference from the owner and the next year had completed the payment of the purchase-price (which was paid by instalments). The land was never transferred to him, nor did he protect his rights by, *e.g.* a caution against first registration. In 1955 the owner conveyed the land to the defendant who was duly registered as proprietor of it. The plaintiff claimed to be the beneficial owner of the land and sought rectification of the register. Harman J. held that the defendant was trustee of the land for the plaintiff and he ought to transfer it to him or, alternatively, the register should be rectified. After receiving the full purchase-money the owner of the land became a bare trustee of the legal estate for the plaintiff and its right of action was barred under the Limitation Act 1939, s.10(1) (now L.A. 1980 Sched. 1, Pt. 1, para. 8) by the plaintiff's subsequent possession for 12 years. The title acquired by the defendant as registered proprietor was subject to the plaintiff's rights (his equitable interest under the contract and his right to specific performance) which were overriding interests within section 70(1)(*g*) of the Land Registration Act 1925. As soon as the plaintiff had paid the purchase price his possession, which originally might be referred to the owner's leave and licence, became adverse.

Note: In the case of unregistered land a purchaser who had paid the full purchase-money but not taken a conveyance and had failed to protect his contract as an estate contract (above, p. 18) would, if his possession was long enough, be able to rely on his possessory title.

In *Fairweather* v. *St. Marylebone Property Co. Ltd.* (above, p. 55) the squatter claimed that, as the lease had been registered, s.75 of the Land Registration Act 1925 applied. This provides that in a case of adverse possession the proprietor's title is not extinguished but is to be deemed to be held on trust for the squatter (see above, p. 54). The squatter contended it gave him a beneficial interest in the lease and therefore the subsequent surrender of the lease was inoperative. It was held that section 75 applied only to events occurring after 1925 and where the tenant was registered. But there was no evidence in that case that the extinguishment had taken place after registration and not before. The squatter's argument would mean that section 75 would seem to have a *positive* effect, giving the squatter an interest in the lease (*cf. Tichborne* v. *Weir*, above, p. 55) and therefore markedly different from the position of unregistered land under the Limitation Act. But neither Lord Radcliffe nor Lord Denning was satisfied that section 75 had the effect contended for.

Spectrum Investment Co. v. Holmes
[1981] 1 W.L.R. 221, Ch. D.

In 1902, a 99 years lease was granted by the owner of a house. The lease was registered. In 1939 the then proprietor of the leasehold interest granted an oral monthly sub-tenancy of the house. The lease was transferred to a Mrs. David in 1944 (see the next case where Mrs. David also featured) and the sub-tenant was told to pay the rent to the transferee's solicitors, but they would not accept it. No rent was paid by the sub-tenant to Mrs. David from 1944, though between 1947 and 1951 the local council, which had carried out work on the house, required the sub-tenant to pay rent to it. The sub-tenant died in 1951 and her daughter (the defendant) remained in occupation of the house without paying rent to anyone. The plaintiff acquired the freehold interest in 1957. In 1968 the defendant applied to the Land Registry to be registered as proprietor of the leasehold interest with possessory title. Notice of the application was given to Mrs. David's solicitors, but no action was taken. The Registry closed the registration of the original leasehold title and opened a new leasehold title under a new number with the defendant as proprietor with possessory title. In 1975 Mrs. David purported to surrender the residue of the lease to the plaintiff. The surrender was made by deed of surrender by reference to the original leasehold title number, but the deed was not submitted to the Registry. The plaintiff sought the deletion of the defendant's leasehold title from the register or, alternatively, rectification of the leasehold register reinstating Mrs. David as proprietor. Browne-Wilkinson J., after considering the effect of the *Fairweather* v. *St. Marylebone Property Co. Ltd.* (above, p. 55) in relation to unregistered land, held that the surrender was ineffective. The defendant was the registered proprietor of the lease and only she could surrender the lease. The plaintiff's first claim failed because the term was still in existence and the plaintiff therefore had no right to immediate possession. Even if Mrs. David had been the registered proprietor of the lease the surrender was not effective because it had not been registered. As to the claim for rectification (Mrs. David had been added as co-plaintiff so that the court could deal with the claim) this raised the question whether the effect of adverse possession of registered land was different from that of unregistered land. The defendant's counsel argued that the effect of adverse possession of registered land was to make the squatter the successor in title of the documentary owner by parliamentary conveyance. The plaintiff argued that the effect was the same as for unregistered land. The judge did not find it necessary to decide this point, as he was able to dismiss the claim for rectification on the wording of the L.R.A. 1925, s.75, subsection (2) of which applied to leasehold interests and subsection (3) of which made it mandatory on the Registrar to register the defendant. The judge was therefore not called upon to decide the effect of section 75(1) which dealt with the period between the date when the squatter obtained title by adverse possession and the date of the registration of title.

Jessamine Investment Co. v. Schwartz [1978] Q.B. 264, C.A.

The plaintiff was the registered proprietor of the freehold interest in No. 29 Evering Road. Nos. 29 and 31 had been leased in 1874 for 99 years by a predecessor in title of the plaintiff. In 1924 the leasehold interest was severed when No. 29 was assigned to a Mrs.

David (see *Spectrum Investment Co.* v. *Holmes*, above, for another case in which Mrs. David featured). Mrs. D. granted a weekly tenancy of No. 29 to the defendant. In 1939 the contractual tenancy ceased and the defendant became a statutory tenant protected by the Rent Act. No demand for rent was made by Mrs. D. after 1945 and the defendant did not know Mrs. D.'s whereabouts and no rent was paid. In 1973 the defendant applied to the Land Registry to be registered as proprietor with possessory title and for the first time learned of the freehold interest. The application was rejected. The 99 years lease expired in 1973 and the plaintiff claimed possession. The primary question was whether the defendant lost her statutory tenancy as against the freeholder when she acquired a possessory title to the 99 years leasehold title. It was held that the Limitation Act 1939 applied to the statutory tenancy. By virtue of section 9(2) of the Act (see now L.A. 1980, Sched. 1, Pt. 1, para. 5(1)) the weekly tenancy was deemed to have determined at the end of the first week and Mrs. D.'s right of action accrued at that date subject to the proviso to section 9(2) (now L.A. 1980, Sched. 1, Pt. 1, para. 5(2)), postponing the accruer of the right of action until the last receipt of rent. Mrs. D.'s right of action accrued at the latest by 1945 and 12 years later the defendant acquired a possessory title, with the result that Mrs. D.'s title was extinguished as against the defendant but continued to exist against the freeholder (see *Fairweather* v. *St. Marylebone Property Co. Ltd*, above, p. 55), until the lease determined by effluxion of time. But that would not protect the defendant now, if her statutory tenancy no longer existed. The county court judge had held that, by virtue of the L.R.A. s.75, Mrs. D. held the leasehold interest in trust for the defendant with the result that there was no merger of the weekly tenancy into the leasehold interest. On appeal it was held that section 75 did not assist the defendant and the county court judge was wrong in holding that it caused the statutory tenancy to continue. It was held that a statutory tenant had no interest in the land, but merely a personal right to retain the property (a status of irremovability—*per* Stephenson L.J.). By obtaining a possessory title to the leasehold interest, the defendant had not changed the character of her occupation. There was no inconsistency between the transformation by operation of law of a statutory tenancy into a possessory leasehold interest as against the mesne landlord and the continuance of a statutory tenancy as against the freeholder and the rest of the world. The defendant was therefore a protected tenant and the plaintiff was not entitled to possession.

2. Proof of Title

Law of Property Act 1925, s.44(1)

"After the commencement of this Act thirty years shall be substituted for forty years as the period of commencement of title which a purchaser of land may require; nevertheless earlier title than thirty years may be required in cases similar to those in which earlier title than forty years might immediately before the commencement of this Act be required."

Law of Property Act 1969, s.23

"Section 44(1) of the Law of Property Act 1925 (under which the period of commencement of title which may be required under a contract expressing no contrary intention is thirty years except in certain cases) shall have effect, in its application to contracts made after the commencement of this Act, as if it specified fifteen years instead of thirty years as the period of commencement of title which may be so required."

And see Law of Property Act 1925, s.199(1)(i), (ii) (above, pp. 13, 20); *Poster* v. *Slough Estates Ltd.* (above, p. 23); *Re Nisbet and Pott's Contract* (below, p. 250).

3. Registered Title

Rectification of the Register

Land Registration Act 1925, s.82(1), (3)

"(1) The register may be rectified pursuant to an order of the court or by the registrar, subject to an appeal to the court, in any of the following cases, but subject to the provisions of this section:—

> (*a*) Subject to any express provisions of this Act to the contrary, where a court of competent jurisdiction has decided that any person is entitled to any estate right or interest in or to any registered land or charge, and as a consequence of such decision such court is of opinion that a rectification of the register is required, and makes an order to that effect;
>
> . . .
>
> (*g*) Where a legal estate has been registered in the name of a person who if the land had not been registered would not have been the estate owner; and

(*h*) In any other case where, by reason of any error or omission in the register, or by reason of any entry made under a mistake, it may be deemed just to rectify the register.

(3) The register shall not be rectified, except for the purpose of giving effect to an overriding interest, so as to affect the title of the proprietor who is in possession—

(*a*) unless such proprietor is a party or privy or has caused or substantially contributed, by his act, neglect or default, to the fraud, mistake or omission in consequence of which such rectification is sought; or
(*b*) unless the immediate disposition to him was void, or the disposition to any person through whom he claims otherwise than for valuable consideration was void; or
(*c*) unless for any other reason, in any particular case, it is considered that it would be unjust not to rectify the register against him."

Note: For the 1977 amendments to sub-section (3), see below, p. 73

Re 139 High Street, Deptford
[1951] Ch. 884

Mr. Dobkins bought a small shop under a railway arch and an annexe thereto. Unknown to D. or his vendor the annexe belonged to the British Transport Commission. D. applied for first registration producing, *inter alia*, his conveyance which described the land conveyed as including the annexe, and was registered as proprietor of the land conveyed. The B.T.C. claimed rectification to exclude the annexe under paragraphs (*a*), (*b*) and (*c*) of s.82(3) of the L.R.A. 1925. D. was in possession of the annexe. Wynn-Parry J. stated that the question (on the claim under paragraph (*a*)) was whether or not D. could be said to have substantially contributed to the mistake. He considered *Chowood's* case (below, p. 75) and held that D. had substantially contributed to the mistake merely by lodging the conveyance which contained the misdescription. He went on to state also that paragraph (*b*) did not apply. This was designed to cover cases, *e.g.* where the deed was a forgery. And the judge would not have been prepared to rectify under paragraph (*c*), because the Commission had no real use for the annexe and would have been sufficiently compensated by indemnity and because D. had spent money on the annexe. Subsequently Dobkins successfully claimed an indemnity for the rectification.

Re Seaview Gardens, Claridge v. Tingey [1967] 1 W.L.R. 134, Ch. D.

In 1934 a company had conveyed the disputed plot of land to the plaintiff's predecessor in title. No memorandum of the sale was indorsed on the company's deeds. In 1964 the company sold land, including the disputed plot, to the defendant. The defendant applied for first registration of the plot, producing the transfer to her which included the plot, and she was duly registered as proprietor. The defendant later began to build on the plot and the plaintiff claimed rectification. Following the *Deptford* case, Pennycuick J. held that although the defendant was in possession of the plot, he had discretion to rectify, because the defendant had substantially contributed to the mistake on the register by submitting the transfer to her, but as there was insufficient evidence before him on which to decide whether, as a matter of discretion, rectification should be ordered, the case was adjourned. In any event rectification would not be ordered if the true owner, knowing that the registered proprietor was doing work on the land, stood by and allowed the work to be done before intervening to apply for rectification (*cf.* the cases at pp. 28-29, above).

Epps v. Esso Petroleum Co. [1973] 1 W.L.R. 1071, C.A.

Mr. Clifford owned 4 Darland Avenue, Gillingham and Darland Garage, which was next door but separated from the house by a brick wall four feet away from the house. A Mr. Jones was tenant of the Garage. In 1955, some years after Mr. Clifford's death, his personal representative conveyed to Mrs. Jones No. 4 together with an 11 foot strip of Garage land adjacent to No. 4 (the disputed land). Mrs. Jones covenanted to erect a wall so as to delineate the boundary between her property and the Garage, but this was never done. A fence was erected, but this was eventually destroyed by children. Mr. Jones claimed to have parked his car on the strip between 1935 and the end of 1968. In 1956 Mr. Jones was given a new lease of the Garage which purported to include the strip. This mistake was repeated in a conveyance in 1959 of the Garage from the personal representatives of Mr. Clifford to a Mr. Ball, subject to the lease to Mr. Jones. The title to the Garage was then registered and the strip was mistakenly included in the title. In 1964 Mr. Ball transferred the Garage to the defendant. In 1968 Mr. Jones, who had inherited No. 4 on his wife's death, conveyed No. 4 (the description including the strip) to the plaintiffs. Their title was then registered with the strip excluded. The plaintiffs sought rectification of the Register. They claimed that when Mrs. Jones was deprived of her legal estate by the registration of the Garage including the strip, she retained or acquired an equitable interest in the strip and Mr. Ball, and later the defendant, acquired the legal estate in the strip subject to this equitable interest. This principle seems to have been accepted by Templeman J. The plaintiffs claimed this equitable interest was by virtue of actual occupation of the strip (the parking of the car) an overriding interest. They claimed rectification pursuant to L.R.A. s.82(1)(*g*) (see above) and that, there being an overriding interest, the limitations in section 82(3) (see above) did not apply. According to Templeman J. the critical questions were (i) whether Mr. Jones was in actual occupation of the strip in 1964 when the defendant purchased; (ii) whether the defendant was in possession in 1968; and (iii), if those questions were decided in favour of the defendant, whether it would be unjust not to rectify against it. He considered that the discretion to rectify or not given by section 82(1) applied even if one of the conditions specified in section 82(3) was established. And where section 82(3) did not apply, there might still be circumstances to defeat the claim for rectification. He held that Mr. Jones was not in actual occupation. Even if he regularly parked on the strip (and the evidence was uncertain) the parking of a car on a strip 11 feet wide and 80 feet deep did not actually occupy the whole, or a substantial, or any defined part of the strip for the whole or any defined time. The defendant was in possession. The justice in the case lay wholly with the defendant. The wall which was four feet from No. 4 was an assertion that the Garage extended to the wall. The strip appeared as part and parcel of the Garage. Inspection of the site would have revealed to the plaintiffs the original wall and the title disclosed the obligation of Mrs. Jones to build a new boundary wall. The plaintiffs should have realised that there might be some difficulty over the boundary. As to it being unjust not to rectify, the plaintiffs claimed that the court should look at the respective indemnity positions of the parties. If rectification was not ordered, then by virtue of section 83(11) the plaintiffs would not be entitled to any compensation, since the six years limitation period ran from 1959 (see section 83(6)). The judge held that the proviso to section 83(11) would not apply to the defendant if rectification were ordered. By virtue of section 83(6)(*b*) any compensation for the defendant was to be determined at the 1973 value of the strip. However the judge thought this argument was not sufficient to justify rectification. The defendant had bought the Garage to exploit it for commercial purposes and not to lose the strip, even for a 1973 value, which in real terms would not adequately indemnify it. Accordingly he refused to order rectification of the Register.

Also on rectification, see *Bridges* v. *Mees* (above, p. 65); *Re Chowood's Registered Land* (below, p. 75).

Administration of Justice Act 1977, s.24

"In section 82(3) of the Land Registration Act 1925–

(*a*) after the word "interest," there shall be inserted the words "or an order of the court";
(*b*) the following paragraph shall be substituted for paragraph (a)–"(a) unless the proprietor has caused or substantially contributed to the error or omission by fraud or lack of proper care; or"; and
(*c*) paragraph (b) shall cease to have effect."

Indemnity

Land Registration Act 1925, s.83

"(1) . . . any person suffering loss by reason of any rectification of the register under this Act shall be entitled to be indemnified.

(5) No indemnity shall be payable under this Act in any of the following cases;–

(*a*) Where the applicant has himself caused or substantially contributed to the loss by his fraud, or derives title (otherwise than under a disposition for valuable consideration which is registered or protected on the register) from a person so committing fraud . . . .

(6) Where an indemnity is paid in respect of the loss of an estate or interest in or charge on land the amount so paid shall not exceed–

(*a*) Where the register is not rectified, the value of the estate, interest or charge at the time when the error or omission which caused the loss was made;
(*b*) Where the register is rectified, the value (if there had been no rectification) of the estate, interest or charge, immediately before the time of rectification. . . .

(11) A liability to pay indemnity under this Act shall be deemed a simple contract debt; and for the purposes of the Limitation Act [1980] the cause of action shall be deemed to arise at the time when the claimant knows, or but for his own default might have known, of the existence of his claim;

Provided that, when a claim to indemnity arises in consequence of the registration of an estate in land with an absolute or good leasehold title, the claim shall be enforceable only if made within six years from the date of such registration, except in the following cases . . . "

Land Registration Act 1966, s.1(4)

"Subsection (5)(*a*) of the said section 83 (losses wholly or partly due to fraud by the applicant for indemnity, or in certain cases, fraud by his predecessor in title) shall apply to any loss incurred after the commencement of this Act as if references in that paragraph to fraud included references to any act, neglect or default."

Land Registration and Land Charges Act 1971, s.3(1)

This substituted a new section 83(5)(*a*) to the principal Act as follows:

> "No indemnity shall be payable under the Act in any of the following cases:—
>
> (*a*) Where the applicant or a person from whom he derives title (otherwise than under a disposition for valuable consideration which is registered or protected on the register) has caused or substantially contributed to the loss by fraud or lack of proper care. . . . "

Note: Section 82(3)(*a*), prior to the 1977 amendment, had been interpreted by the courts to cover cases where the proprietor had innocently contributed to the mistake by producing a faulty transfer for first registration (see *Deptford* and *Seaview Gardens* cases, above, pp. 70, 71). But the innocent applicant was entitled to compensation under the original section 83(5)(*a*), where only fraud excluded indemnity (as in the *Deptford* case itself). This could be said to be unjustified because Dobkins had no title to the annexe before registration and in that respect had not suffered any loss. The 1966 Act equated the indemnity and rectification-against-a-person-in-possession provisions by the reference to "act, neglect or default." Pennycuick J.'s decision in the *Seaview Gardens* case was a reminder that the submission of a faulty transfer was an "act" which allowed rectification to be ordered against a person in possession. Therefore it was suggested that such submission by an innocent applicant would be an act excluding compensation. Although this was not the interpretation acted upon by the Registry, the opportunity was taken in the amendment in 1971

Act to settle fears aroused. "Lack of proper care" enables the innocent applicant to claim indemnity.

Re Chowood's Registered Land [1933] Ch. 574

Chowood Ltd. applied for first registration and was duly registered as proprietor of certain freehold land which had been conveyed to it. The land conveyed (by reference to a plan) and registered included strips of woodland to which, without the knowledge of Chowood or its vendor, Mrs. Lyall had obtained a possessory title under the Limitation Acts. Chowood sued Mrs. Lyall for trespass. She counter-claimed for rectification of the register. In *Chowood Ltd.* v. *Lyall* Luxmoor J. ordered rectification. He considered that he had power to do this under section 82(1)(*g*) and (*h*) and section 82(3)(*a*) and (*c*). As to (*a*), the plaintiff had "by its own act, that is, by the registration of a conveyance, which is by itself inoperative to pass the pieces of land in dispute, caused the mistake." On appeal, the Court of Appeal took the same view as to the application of section 82(1)(*g*) and (*h*), but held that because the registered proprietor (Chowood) was not in possession of the woodlands, section 82(3) did not come into play. By the later action Chowood sought an indemnity for the rectification. Clauson J. held that because Chowood's registration was in any event subject to the overriding rights of Mrs. Lyall under the L.R.A. 1925, s.70(1)(*f*) (above, p. 38), the rectification of the register put it in no worse position than it was in before rectification. Accordingly, Chowood had suffered no loss and were not entitled to be indemnified.

4. THE DOCTRINE OF CONVERSION

Conversion

Re Kempthorne [1930] 1 Ch. 268, C.A.

By his will made in 1911 a testator devised to his brother Charles "all my freehold . . . property." He gave his leasehold property and personal estate to be divided amongst his brothers and sisters. At his death in 1928 the testator was entitled to a two-ninths share in certain freehold property. On the coming into force of the Law of Property Act 1925 the land had become vested in trustees on the statutory trusts, *i.e.* upon a trust for sale (see below, p. 81). It was held that the testator's interest in undivided shares was converted into personal property by the trust for sale and passed under the gift of the personal estate.

Elias v. Mitchell [1972] Ch. 652

Elias and Mitchell were partners in a business of property owners in respect of a house. Mitchell was the sole registered proprietor of the house, but the partnership agreement provided that Mitchell stood possessed of the property on trust for the partners in equal shares. The partnership ended in August 1970. In October 1970 Mitchell transferred the property to the second defendant, Dar. The latter had no notice of Miss Elias' interest. Before Dar had applied for registration of the transfer to him, the plaintiff lodged a caution against dealings with the property under the Land Registration Act 1925, s.54 (see above, p. 35). Dar claimed that the plaintiff was not a person interested in land because of the trust for sale arising under the partnership agreement. Pennycuick V.-C. reviewed the cases and accepted the general view that an interest under a trust for sale is not land but personalty. However, one had to look at the particular Act. The definition of "land" in section 3(viii) of the L.R.A. excluded an undivided share in land. But section 3(xv)(*a*) (see above, p. 31) defined minor interests so as to include an undivided share in land. A minor interest was an interest in land and therefore the plaintiff could lodge a caution under section 54. In any event section 101(3) (see above, p. 39) provides for the protection of minor interests by cautions. Therefore the plaintiff must have been able to lodge a caution.

Note: In *Williams & Glyn's Bank Ltd.* v. *Boland* (above, p. 49) the equitable interest of a wife who had contributed to the purchase of a house taken in the husband's sole name was characterised as an interest in land.

Cooper v. Critchley [1955] Ch. 431, C.A.

The parties held property on trust for sale for themselves as tenants in common. The property was let to a company controlled by the parties. The defendant agreed to sell his beneficial share in the property to the plaintiff, but then refused to go on with the sale. The plaintiff sued for specific performance. It was held that there was no enforceable agreement for sale because the parties had never reached the stage of a concluded contract. The court went on to observe, *obiter*, that had there been a concluded contract the absence of writing would have been fatal to the plaintiff's claim. The Law of Property Act 1925, s.40 requires a contract for the sale of land, or of any interest in land, to be in writing or evidenced in writing. An undivided share in land was an interest in land for the purpose of section 40. Although the L.P.A. 1925, s.205(1)(ix) (above, p. 1) defined "land" to exclude an undivided share in land, the definition was subject to the qualification "unless the context otherwise requires." Jenkins L.J., giving, in effect, the sole judgment of the court, would have been disposed to hold that a share in the proceeds to arise from a sale of land was an interest in land within s.40.

Note: Prior to the Charging Orders Act 1979 a charging order could not be made against a beneficial interest under a trust for sale of land because such an interest was not "land" (see generally *First National Securities Ltd* v. *Hegerty* [1984] 3 W.L.R. 769, C.A., noted below, p. 100).

Reconversion

Re Cook [1948] Ch. 212

By virtue of section 36(1) of the L.P.A. 1925 (below, p. 82) a husband and wife held the legal estate in respect of a house as trustees (as joint tenants) upon trust for sale for themselves as beneficial joint tenants. The trust for sale automatically converted the land into personalty. The husband died in 1944 and his wife a few months later. Shortly before her death the wife had made a will giving her "personal estate" to her nephew and nieces. After her death they claimed that this gift carried the house. Harman J. held that the trust for sale affecting the house came to an end on the husband's death and the property was reconverted to land. The claimants were not entitled and the house, being undisposed of by the will, passed as on intestacy.

5. Fixtures

Holland v. Hodgson (1872) L.R. 7 C.P. 328, Exch.Ch.

A worsted mill contained looms attached to the stone floors of the mill by means of nails driven through holes in the feet of the looms, in some cases into beams which had been built into the stone, and in other cases into plugs of wood driven into holes drilled in the stone for the purpose. The looms could be quite easily removed by drawing out the nails and without serious damage to the floor. The mill owner mortgaged the mill, machinery, etc., to the plaintiffs. Later he assigned all his property to the defendants as trustees for his creditors. The plaintiffs claimed the looms back. Blackburn J. held that they were entitled to them. The looms became fixtures and the title to them passed by the mortgage to the plaintiffs as part of the realty. " . . . what is annexed to the land becomes part of the land; but it is very difficult, if not impossible, to say with precision what constitutes an annexation sufficient for this purpose. It is a question which must depend on the circumstances of each case, and mainly on two circumstances, as indicating the intention, *viz.*, the degree of annexation and the object of the annexation."

D'Eyncourt v. Gregory (1866) L.R. 3 Eq. 382, M.R.

A tenant for life of settled estates erected a new mansion-house and furnished it, *inter alia*, with tapestries, pictures in panels and frames filled with satin, all attached to the walls, and placed statues, figures, vases and stone garden seats in the grounds. It was held by Lord Romilly M.R. that all the items which were essentially part of the house or of the architectural design of the building or grounds were fixtures and passed to the next tenant for life. So statues, etc., standing by their own weight whether or not fixed with cement or brackets would be fixtures if part of the design. But other items, such as pictures not in panels, not being part of the building, could be removed and passed under the deceased life tenant's will.

Hamp v. Bygrave (1983) 266 E.G. 720, Q.B.D.

The defendants agreed to sell their house to the plaintiffs. Between the plaintiffs' viewing and completion the defendants removed a number of items of ornamental nature, including several stone urns three feet high filled with soil and flowers, a large lead trough also filled with soil and flowers, a stone ornament 21 inches high on a plinth in the pond and a statue three feet six inches high on a concrete plinth. None of these items were attached to the ground. The vendors also removed the patio lights which were fixed into the wall with screws. All the items were there when the plaintiffs viewed. They were also mentioned in the estate agents' particulars. In the negotiations there was discussion that the price could be reduced if certain items were excluded from the sale. Standard form enquiries before contract asked whether garden ornaments were included in the sale. After taking their clients' instructions the vendors' solicitors replied in the affirmative. To the question as to what fixtures and fittings were not included in the sale, the reply was "None." The answers to the requisitions on title confirmed the replies to the preliminary enquiries. The contract included a list of items which were included in the sale including some lights, but none of the disputed items were mentioned on the list. In finding that the disputed items were fixtures, Boreham J. considered the purpose of the installation as more important than the degree of annexation. Those items which were attached to the land by their own weight were prima facie chattels, but this inference could be displaced if the intention was that the items should pass with the land. Such an inference was displaced here by their inclusion in the particulars of sale, by the answer to the preliminary enquiries and by the negotiation as to the reduction of the price if any of the items were excluded. The lights were fixed to the property. Prima facie they were fixtures. The reference to the other lights in the schedule of chattels to the contract being included in the sale did not imply that the lights not listed were not included in the sale. The judge further held that even if the items were not fixtures, the vendor should have been estopped from removing them, because by the conduct referred to above, they induced the purchaser to act in the belief that the items were included in the sale and because of this they paid a higher price than they otherwise would have done.

Simmons v. Midford [1969] 2 Ch. 415

A transfer by C. to the plaintiff's predecessor in title included the grant of a right of way over a strip of C's land, a right to lay and maintain pipes and cables under the strip and the free and uninterrupted passage and running of water, soil, gas and electricity therethrough. The purchaser built a house on the land transferred and laid a drain under the strip to the public sewer. Subsequently C.'s successors in title purported to grant the defendant the right to lay a drain under their land and to connect that drain to the drain laid by the plaintiff's predecessor in title under the strip. The plaintiff brought proceedings to restrain the defendant connecting any pipes or drains to the drain in the strip. Buckley J. stated: "Where a chattel is physically attached to realty, one of three possible results may follow. The chattel may lose its character as a chattel and adhere to the realty so as to become part of it for all purposes; or the chattel may become part of the realty while it remained a chattel, without the person who owned it losing the right subsequently to detach it from the realty and repossess it as a chattel; or it may never lose its character as a chattel." In the present case on the construction of the grant and the circumstances Buckley J. held that the drain fell into this third category. It was vested in the plaintiff as appurtenant to the plaintiff's land. He did not have to determine whether it should be regarded as personalty or realty. In view of his decision there had been no power to make the grant to the defendant to connect into the plaintiff's drain. If he was wrong and the drain was annexed to the strip the defendant was still not entitled to connect with the drain, because the plaintiff was entitled to exclusive use of it.

New Zealand Government Property Corpn. v. H.M. & S. Ltd.

[1982] Q.B. 1145, C.A.

The defendant was the tenant of Her Majesty's Theatre, Haymarket, London. As business premises the tenant had security of tenure within Part II of the Landlord and Tenant Act 1954. The original lease expired in 1970, but automatically continued under the Act upon service by the tenant of a counter-notice. A new lease was negotiated with the rent for the first seven years of the term agreed. The parties could not agree the rent for the second seven year term. The problem arose whether the fixtures (seats, *etc.*) installed by the tenant and not removed during the period of the original lease had become the landlord's and therefore had to be taken into account in assessing the new rent. There was no doubt that the common law conferred upon the tenant the right to remove the tenant's fixtures. The question was for how long that right of removal lasted. Was it only as long as the tenancy existed or did it continue so long as the tenant remained in possession of the premises as tenant, even though under a new tenancy? The Court of Appeal held that the correct rule was that at common law a tenant, other than an agricultural tenant (and his position is recognised by the compensation provisions of the Agricultural Holdings Act 1948), had a right to remove tenant's fixtures so long as he was in possession as tenant, whether holding over or as a statutory tenant under the Rent Act or upon an extension of a lease of business premises under Part II of the Landlord and Tenant Act 1954.

CHAPTER 3

CO-OWNERSHIP

1. JOINT TENANCY OR TENANCY IN COMMON

Re North [1952] Ch. 397

The testator devised property to his two sons on condition that they agreed to pay in equal shares to his wife . . . the sum of 10 shillings per week. Both sons survived the testator and when one subsequently died the question arose as to whether the interest of the sons was a joint tenancy or a tenancy in common. Wynn-Parry J. held that as the effect of the condition attached to the gift was to create a personal obligation on each of the sons, the language of the condition was sufficient to indicate that the interest of the two sons in the property was a tenancy in common, and not a joint tenancy.

Note: Whether a beneficial joint tenancy or a tenancy in common is created depends on the words used. If there are no words of severance, *e.g.* "in equal shares" (and the four unities of interest, title, time and possession are present) there will be a joint tenancy. This means that, unless the joint tenancy is severed (see below, p. 96) *inter vivos* (severance cannot be effected by a will, unless all the joint tenants make mutual wills), on the death of a joint tenant the surviving joint tenants or tenant will be entitled to the property and the deceased will not have any share to pass under his will or intestacy. This right of survivorship (*jus accrescendi*) is satisfactory between husband and wife (at least, until there is a matrimonial dispute), because the deceased would usually want the survivor to take all, but not where the beneficiaries are strangers or businessmen. Accordingly, where there are no words of severance, equity nevertheless holds there to be a tenancy in common (a) where purchase money is provided in unequal shares (see *Bull* v. *Bull*, below, p. 83); (b) where money is lent by several persons on mortgage (but now the L.P.A. 1925, s.111, provides that as between the mortgagees and mortgagor they are deemed to have advanced the money jointly); and (c) where partners buy land for the partnership (*Lake* v. *Craddock* (1732) 3 P.Wms. 158). After 1925 a *legal* estate cannot be held on a tenancy in common (in undivided shares).

Statutory Trusts

Law of Property Act 1925, ss.34, 35, 36(1)

"34. (1) An undivided share in land shall not be capable of being created except as provided by the Settled Land Act 1925, or as hereinafter mentioned.

(2) Where, after the commencement of this Act, land is expressed to be conveyed to any persons in undivided shares and those persons are of full age, the conveyance shall (notwithstanding anything to the contrary in this Act) operate as if the land had been expressed to be conveyed to the grantees, or, if there are more than four grantees, to the four first named in the conveyance, as joint tenants upon the statutory trusts hereinafter mentioned and so as to give effect to the rights of the persons who would have been entitled to the shares had the conveyance operated to create those shares: . . .

35. (See below, p. 299).

36. (1) Where a legal estate (not being settled land) is beneficially limited to or held in trust for any persons as joint tenants, the same shall be held on trust for sale, in like manner as if the persons beneficially entitled were tenants in common, but not so as to sever their joint tenancy in equity."

Settled Land

Settled Land Act 1925, s.36

(See below p. 277.)

Note: After 1925 the beneficial interests of co-owners may be joint or in common (which it will be depends on the principles stated above, p. 81, and in the following cases). Where the beneficial interest is expressly declared, this declaration determines the shares (subject to the Matrimonial Proceedings and Property Act 1970, s.37, below, p. 94). Where the property is taken in joint names, but the beneficial shares are not expressed, the beneficial ownership will, generally, depend on the parties' intention as expressed, or if not expressed as evidenced by the parties' contributions to the acquisition of the property. (But see *Young* v. *Young* (1984) F.L.R. 375, C.A., where the house was taken in joint names because Mrs. Young would not have got a mortgage on her own, mortgage repayments were made for 5 months out of a joint account, but Mr. Young was held to have no interest.) In exceptional circumstances the shares may be altered by agreement or the effect of the Matrimonial Proceedings and Property Act 1970, s.37. Sometimes the conveyance is taken in the name of one of several purchasers. In this case the paper title holder will hold on a resulting trust for the contributors according to their contributions (and see above, p. 3). In the case of, for example, a spouse or *de facto* spouse whose name is not on the title, where that spouse has contributed directly or indirectly (*e.g.* by relieving the paper title owner of other expenses, so as the more easily to be able to pay the mortgage) to the purchase of the property, the court may be able to find on the facts an agreement, express or implied, that the contributor, though not a purchaser in the sense mentioned above, was to have a beneficial interest in the property. Effect will be given to such finding by imposing a (constructive) trust on the paper title owner. In the event of marriage breakdown it will often be unnecessary for the contributing spouse, usually the wife, to claim under such a constructive trust, because the court has wide powers under the Matrimonial Causes Act 1933, s.24 (see below, p. 94) to transfer the property or any interest in property of one spouse to the other spouse. Save in exceptional cases, property disputes between spouses should be dealt with under the Matrimonial Causes Act 1973, s.24 and not under the Married Women's Property Act 1882, s.17 or the L.P.A. 1925, s.30 (see *Re Holliday*, below, p. 103).

2. Beneficial Ownership

Conveyance in Sole Name of One of Several Purchasers

Bull v. Bull [1955] 1 Q.B. 234, C.A.

The plaintiff and his mother, the defendant, contributed in unequal shares to the purchase price of a house which was conveyed to the plaintiff alone. The mother's contribution was not intended to be a gift to the son and the defendant accordingly became entitled under a resulting trust to an equitable interest in the house proportionate to her contribution. Differences arose between the mother and daughter-in-law. The plaintiff gave his mother notice to quit and claimed possession. It was held that the effect of the conveyance was that the plaintiff and the defendant became beneficial tenants in common of the proceeds of sale of the property which was subjected to the statutory trust for sale. *Per* Denning L.J.: "All tenancies in common now are equitable only and take effect behind a trust for sale (see the S.L.A. 1925, s.36(4), below, p. 277) . . . until a sale takes place these equitable tenants in common have the same right to enjoy the land as legal tenants used to have . . . neither of them is entitled to evict the other . . . what is to happen when the two disagree . . . the house must then be sold? . . . The son is the legal owner and he holds it on the statutory trusts for sale. He cannot at the present moment sell the house because he cannot give a valid receipt. It needs two trustees to give a receipt. . . . The son could get over this difficulty by appointing another trustee. . . . If the trustees wished . . . to sell with vacant possession the only thing they could do would be to apply to the court under the L.P.A. 1925, s.30" (see below, p. 100).

Note: The L.P.A. 1925, s.34 does not on the face of it appear to apply when land is conveyed to one person and there is no express creation of undivided shares. Section 34(2) provides that where land is *expressed* to be conveyed, etc., and does not cover the case where the undivided shares arise, as in the above case, by implication of law. However, Denning L.J. was able to find that the statutory trusts applied relying on the S.L.A., 1925, s.36(4).

Conveyance in Joint Names—Beneficial Interests Not Expressed

Bernard v. Josephs [1982] Ch. 291, C.A.

In 1973 Miss Bernard and Mr. Josephs became engaged to be married. In 1974 they arranged to purchase a home in South East London for £11,750. The conveyance was taken in their joint names without any express declaration of trust. The whole of the purchase price was raised by a Council mortgage. B. contributed £200 to the initial expenses (legal costs, removal expenses, etc.) and J. contributed £650. Subsequently J. spent £2,000 on repairs and redecoration. Part of the premises was let. Both B. and J. were working. B. paid for the food and housekeeping, J. paid the mortgage, electricity and other bills. After 18 months B. and J. quarrelled and B. left. She subsequently sought a declaration that she was entitled to a half share in the house and proceeds of sale and an order for sale under the L.P.A. 1925, s.30 (see below, p. 100). The trial judge, Judge Mervyn Davies Q.C., held that, subject to each party receiving credit for initial contributions and J. receiving credit for the sum spent on improvements, the parties had equal shares and, since the purpose for which the house had been acquired (*i.e.* a home for the couple) was at an end, it should be sold. J. appealed, claiming that he should have the major share in the equity in the house and against the order for sale. The Court of Appeal upheld the trial judge and confirmed the view expressed in earlier cases (see, *e.g.* *Cooke* v. *Head* [1972] 1 W.L.R. 518, C.A.) that in the case of unmarried couples the shares of the beneficial interest in the property were to be ascertained according to the same principles applicable to married couples. However, since living together outside marriage may not involve the same degree of commitment as a marriage, the nature of the relationship had a bearing on the ascertainment of the parties' common intention, the assumptions to be made and the inferences to be drawn (*per* Griffiths and Kerr L.JJ.). A conveyance into joint names does not necessarily mean equal beneficial shares. The respective shares were to be ascertained according to the circumstances and the parties' respective contributions to the purchase and the joint finances of the home (see also the cases following). There was some difference between the members of the Court as to when the beneficial interest crystallises. Griffiths L.J. concurred with the trial judge that, in the absence of special circumstances, this was the time of acquisition, but he added that to ascertain this a judge must look at all the evidence, including all the contributions made by the parties. Kerr L.J. thought the time of acquisition was the starting point and both he and Lord Denning M.R. thought that, on the authorities, the court should consider the ultimate position by reference to the time of separation, but later events could be considered (*per* Kerr L.J. for the purposes of equitable accounting). The Court of Appeal held that the proper inference to be drawn in this case was that the parties intended equal shares, subject to the credits mentioned, including J., in effect, having to pay an occupation rent (see *Dennis* v. *McDonald*, below, p. 104). The purpose for which the house was bought, *i.e.* a home for both B. and J., having been exhausted on separation, the trial judge had been correct in ordering a sale. But before the Court, B. had agreed to J. buying out her interest at a sum calculated by the Court. It calculated that sum as £6,000, being one half of the vacant possession value of the house less the mortgage, and the appropriate debits and credits being made. The order for sale was confirmed, but it was not to be enforced if J. paid B. £6,000 within four months.

Note: The Law Reform (Miscellaneous Provisions) Act 1970, s.2 provides that, in the case of engaged couples, where the agreement to marry is terminated, any rule of law relating to the rights of the husbands and wives in relation to property in which either or both have a beneficial interest . . . shall apply. The plaintiff did not rely on this provision. Its extent is uncertain.

As to the consequence of the conveyance into joint names, Lord Denning M.R. held that the L.P.A. 1925, s.36(1) applied. But section 36(1) provides that where a legal estate . . . is beneficially limited to or held in trust for . . . joint tenants. It therefore applies where the beneficial joint tenancy is expressed or where a beneficial joint tenancy is found on the facts. In the above case there were no expressed beneficial shares and therefore to say that section 36(1) applied before determining the beneficial ownership (in the event a tenancy in common) was jumping the gun and was wrong (see *Bull* v. *Bull*, above, p. 83, for another gap in the legislation; and *Re Buchanan-Wollaston's Conveyance*, below, p. 101). Both Lord Denning M.R. and Griffiths L.J. confirmed the rule that if there is an express declaration as to the beneficial interests this determines the beneficial shares (but this may be subject to subsequent agreement and the effect of the Matrimonial Proceedings and Property Act 1970, s.37).

Constructive Trusts

Pettitt v. Pettitt [1970] A.C. 777, H.L.

The parties married in 1952. At first they lived in a house the wife had inherited. The husband made some improvements to the house, largely redecorating. In 1960 they bought Tinker's Cottage. The price was £3,813. It was paid for by the wife out of the proceeds of the former home. In 1965 the parties separated, the wife remaining on in the house with the two children of their marriage. They were divorced in 1967. The husband, in proceedings under the Married Women's Property Act 1882, s.17, claimed an interest in the house based on work done on Tinker's Cottage. (He made no claim in respect of the previous house, because his wife had paid off a car for him from the proceeds.) He claimed to have provided labour and materials to the value of about £723 and (he was an estate agent's negotiator) to have enhanced the value of the cottage by £1,000. The registrar declared that the husband was entitled to a beneficial interest in the cottage to the value of £300 and this was affirmed by the Court of Appeal. In the House of Lords it was held, that section 17 was a procedural provision only and did not entitle the court to vary the existing proprietary rights of the parties. Any special concept of family property or family assets was rejected. Allowing the appeal, it was held that it was impossible to impute to the parties as reasonable husband and wife any common intention that the husband's activities were to have any effect on the existing proprietary interest in the cottage. Many husbands and wives decorate and make improvements to their family home with no other intention than to indulge a hobby and to make the home more pleasant for their common use and enjoyment.

Gissing v. Gissing [1971] A.C. 886, H.L.

The parties were married in 1935 when they were both in their twenties. They lived in a flat and both worked. In 1939 they had a son. On the outbreak of war the husband was called up for the Army. The wife returned to her parents. She continued to work. In 1946 the husband was given employment by the wife's employers and in 1951 they bought a house. The price was £2,695. The property was taken in the husband's sole name. He had a mortgage for £2,150, a loan of £500 from his employer and found the balance of the price and the legal costs from his own savings. The wife spent about £220 from her savings on furniture and laying a lawn. The wife continued to work. She paid for her own clothes and the son's from her earnings and added to the housekeeping money her husband gave her. The husband paid the mortgage and other expenses. They had separate saving accounts. In 1960 the husband left the wife for another woman. At the time of the hearing the husband was paying one shilling a year nominal maintenance. The wife claimed a beneficial interest in the house. The trial judge held that she had no interest. The Court of Appeal held, by a majority, that she had a half share, the majority being of the view that the wife's indirect contributions gave her a beneficial interest. (*per* Lord Denning M.R. the inference in such circumstances being that the house is a family asset in which each is entitled to an equal share; *per* Phillimore L.J. that on the facts the purchase was a joint venture and justice between husband and wife cannot be done by applying the strict laws of contract or by a strict application of the L.P.A. 1925, s.53 or of the law affecting the creation or operation of equitable interests). The House of Lords unanimously allowed the husband's appeal. The wife had made no contribution to the acquisition of the property from which it could be inferred that it was the common intention that she should have any beneficial interest in it.

Note: Lord Reid maintained his view, expressed in *Pettitt* v. *Pettitt*, that there could be a deemed intention, where there was in fact no agreement. Lord Diplock (who with Lord Reid had formed the minority in *Pettitt* v. *Pettitt*) referred to the majority view in the earlier case, now saying that there had to be a common intention between the parties, though it may not have been expressed. In *Cowcher* v. *Cowcher*, below, Bagnall J. tried to fit this new type of constructive (or rather informal express) trust into the ordinary principles of trusts. But, as illustrated in *Re Densham*, it may not be possible to fit the new concept into traditional principles. The trust is enforced, because it is unconscionable for the legal owner to rely on legal technicalities to defeat the agreement, expressed or unexpressed, between the parties.

Cowcher v. Cowcher [1972] 1 W.L.R. 425, Fam. D.

The parties were married in 1953. There were 3 children of the marriage. They lived in rented accommodation. The plaintiff wife worked on and off during the marriage. In 1962 she inherited a legacy under her father's will. She put about £3,000 of this into her husband's business, which subsequently failed, and gave her husband about £1,300 and contributed to household expenses. In 1962, knowing the legacy was due, they bought their first house. The defendant paid £1,000 deposit. Three thousand pounds of the purchase money was obtained by overdraft on the husband's bank account, £2,000 by a loan to the husband from the wife's brother and £8,000 by mortgage to an insurance company and, as collateral, an endowment policy with that company written under the Married Women's Property Act 1882 in favour of the wife. The house was taken in the husband's sole name. The wife subsequently paid several premiums on the policy and some mortgage payments from legacies she received after 1962. The marriage was dissolved in 1971. The wife claimed a beneficial interest in the house under the Married Women's Property Act 1882, s.17. After referring to *Pettitt* and *Gissing* (above), Bagnall J. held that on an application under section 17 the ordinary principles of trusts applied; that the expression "family assets" had no legal meaning; that rights of property are not to be determined according to what is reasonable and fair ("in determining . . . property rights, the only justice that can be attained by mortals . . . is justice according to law; the justice which flows from the application of sure and settled principles to proved or admitted facts"); that trust principles were relevant at three stages—the formation of a trust, its continuance and its winding up (including the taking of equitable accounts on a sale of the property); that a trust might be express or implied—express trusts required writing (L.P.A. 1925, s.53(1)(*b*)); implied trusts might be resulting or constructive trusts; that a resulting trust arises (unless a contrary intention is proved) where a person acquires property, but has not provided the whole of the consideration for the acquisition; that the resulting trust is in proportion to the contribution, unless a contrary intention is proved; that such a contrary intention (*e.g.* that the interests shall be equal notwithstanding one has contributed more than the other or that the share should be greater or lesser than the proportion of the contribution to the whole price, or that a person should have a share when he or she has not made any contribution) must be an express trust; that an agreement that, irrespective of actual payments to a vendor or mortgagee, the money should be treated as principal in equal shares (money consensus) could be inferred from conduct antecedent, contemporaneous or subsequent, but an agreement that, irrespective of the shares in which, as between themselves, the money has been provided, the property should be held on an express trust for themselves in equal shares (interest consensus), being a contractual express trust, conduct was irrelevant. As to varying the original shares, this must involve a disposition by one of an equitable interest to the other requiring either writing under the L.P.A. 1925, s.53(1)(*c*) or a specifically enforceable oral agreement (the latter could be implied from conduct only in the most exceptional circumstances). After considering *Pettitt* and *Gissing*, Bagnall J. held that the wife's beneficial interest in the house arose under a resulting trust based on her contribution to the purchase price, unless a contrary consensus as to the proportions in which the parties were to be taken as having provided the purchase monies could be inferred from the facts. The taking out of the endowment policy in the wife's favour and the contemplation of the parties that in future the husband alone was to be the source of the family income were conclusive against such an inference. The beneficial interests could not be altered by the mere payment by one beneficial owner of a mortgage instalment properly payable by the other. The beneficial shares were therefore one-third for the wife and two-thirds for the husband based on the source of the purchase money. By consent, sale of the house was ordered. Appropriate credits and debits should be made in the accounting of the sale proceeds for payments by one party that were a joint liability.

Re Densham (A Bankrupt) [1975] 1 W.L.R. 1519, Ch. D.

The plaintiff and the bankrupt lived together as man and wife, at first in rented accommodation. Then they decided to buy a house. The plaintiff went out to work to help towards the purchase. They saved £10 a week out of her wages and housekeeping which they hid under the carpet beneath their bed. They intended to marry as soon as she was free to do so. They were married in November 1970. In October 1970 they had signed a contract to buy a house. The wife's name was originally on the contract, but was deleted. The transfer of the house was taken in the husband's sole name. The purchase price was £5,650, of which £4,800 was raised on mortgage. The balance came from the joint savings. The wife continued to work until about March 1971. A child of the marriage was born in September 1971. In 1973, £900 was raised on a second mortgage for improvements to the house and this document was originally in both names and signed by the plaintiff, though her name was subsequently deleted. In 1974 the husband was adjudicated bankrupt. The wife claimed a beneficial interest in the house. Goff J. held that there was an agreement between the parties that savings for the house should be joint and the purchase joint. He rejected the view expressed by Bagnall J. in *Cowcher* v. *Cowcher* (above) that an interest consensus was an express trust and had to be evidenced in writing. To require this would be contrary to equitable principles, because once the agreement is found it would be unconscionable for a party to set up the statute (*i.e.* L.P.A. 1925, s.53(1)(*b*)) and repudiate the agreement. In the vast majority of cases parties did not direct their minds to treating money payments as notionally other than what they were. "What they think about, if they think at all, is ownership." There was accordingly a constructive trust of the house to give effect to the agreement. But the agreement that the wife should be a joint owner, without making a joint contribution (after she had ceased to work all the expenses were met by the husband), was void under the Bankruptcy Act 1914, s.42, the settlement not being in consideration of marriage nor the wife's contribution being consideration in a commercial sense (though the consideration did not have to equal the value of the interest given up by the bankrupt). Accordingly she could not claim a half share in the property by virtue of the agreement. But she had a claim to a beneficial share in the house by virtue of her contribution to the joint savings. The wife's share was one-ninth, being the proportion of one half of the joint savings (*i.e.* £585) of the total cost of the purchase (£5,783).

Eves v. Eves [1975] 1 W.L.R. 1338, C.A.

The plaintiff and the defendant lived together as *de facto* spouses for four and a half years. They initially intended to get married as soon as the defendant was free to. They had two children. After the birth of the first child, the defendant bought a house for the family for £5,600, £3,200 of which was raised on a mortgage on the house. The defendant used the plaintiff's age (under 21) as an excuse for not taking the house in joint names. The house was in a dilapidated condition. The plaintiff did a great deal of work on the house and garden, including stripping wallpaper, painting and breaking up concrete. Then the defendant left the plaintiff. She claimed a share in the house. The house was then worth about £13,000. The trial judge (Pennycuick V.-C.) was unable to find a common intention that the beneficial ownership should be shared, with the plaintiff contributing her labour as her contribution towards the purchase, and rejected the claim. On appeal, it was held that the plaintiff was entitled to a quarter share in the house. Relying on *Gissing* v. *Gissing* (above), Lord Denning M.R. found a constructive trust because the defendant had led the plaintiff to believe that she would have an interest in the house. Browne L.J. and Brightman J. were both prepared to draw the inference (which the trial judge had felt unable to do) that the plaintiff's activities after the purchase were in pursuance of some expressed or implied arrangement and on the understanding that the plaintiff was to have an interest in the house. The defendant (who had regained possession of the house) need not pay any occupation rent, so long as he paid the mortgage instalments. There should be no order for sale of the property (the plaintiff had remarried and had a home), so long as the defendant made reasonable provision for the maintenance of the children and paid arrears of maintenance under a magistrates' court order.

Gordon v. Douce [1983] 1 W.L.R. 563, C.A.

The plaintiff lived with the defendant from 1963 to 1968 from time to time and thereafter on a permanent basis, but without marrying, until the relationship broke up in 1980. They had two children. In 1977 the defendant bought a house for £4,500, about £3,500 of which was borrowed and about £1,000 of which came from the parties' pooled savings. The house was taken in the defendant's sole name. When the house was bought, the plaintiff gave up a tenancy she had of some rooms. The plaintiff was employed for most of the relevant period. She paid for certain repairs and improvements to the house and various outgoings. At the time of the trial the house was worth about £9,250 and only about £500 remained on loan. The county court judge declared that the plaintiff had a 25 per cent. interest in the equity in the house as at the date of the termination of the relationship. He thought he was bound by authority that the date of valuation of a share was, in the case of an unmarried couple, the date of separation, unlike a married couple where the relevant date was the date of the hearing. On appeal it was held (*per* Fox L.J.) that, generally, there is no difference in the principles to be applied to spouses and other parties. The court might be influenced by the relationship in drawing inferences as to the intentions of the parties. What might be sensible between husband and wife might not be between two brothers. As to the date of valuation, there was no such rule as the county court judge had stated. It was always a matter of discretion. Fox L.J. referred to *Bernard* v. *Josephs* (above) where the mistress's share was valued at the date of the appeal and distinguished *Hall* v. *Hall* (1982) 3 F.L.R. 379, C.A., being a case of a much shorter relationship without children and where the court took the view that the purpose of the trust ended on the separation. Here the defendant always intended the house to be a home for the plaintiff and the children, they still lived in it and the defendant did not intend to seek a sale while the children lived there. Accordingly the plaintiff's 25 per cent. was to be valued at the date of the sale of the property.

Note: In *Walker* v. *Hall* [1984] F.L.R. 126, C.A., Dillon L.J. held that, although the purpose of the trust came to an end on the separation, the trust for sale imposed by the L.P.A. 1925 as a result of the transfer of the property into joint names did not come to an end, but would continue until either the property was sold in execution of the trust for sale or one party by buying out the other became solely and absolutely entitled to the property in equity.

Burns v. Burns [1984] 2 W.L.R. 582, C.A.

In 1961 the plaintiff and the defendant started living together as man and wife in rented accommodation. In 1962 the plaintiff had a child and gave up employment. In 1963, when another child was due, the defendant purchased a house in his sole name for £4,900, £4,500 of which was raised by a mortgage on the house. The defendant paid the mortgage instalments, provided the funds for rates and telephone and gave the plaintiff a generous housekeeping allowance. The plaintiff did not work while the children were young. In 1972 she started a driving tuition business and by 1975 earned a reasonable amount from this and more later. She bought some clothing for the family, some furniture and domestic equipment and wallpapered and decorated the house. She spent her money entirely as she chose; it was in no sense joint money. The conversion of the attic into a bedroom with a bathroom en suite in 1971 was paid for by the defendant. In 1980 the plaintiff left the defendant and claimed a beneficial interest in the house by reason of her contributions to the household over 17 years. At first instance and on appeal it was held that the plaintiff was not entitled to any beneficial interest in the house. Fox L.J. thought that a trust for the benefit of the plaintiff could only arise (a) by express declaration or agreement or (b) by way of resulting trust where the claimant has directly provided part of the purchase price or (c) from the common intention of the parties. He ruled out (a) and (b). He found no evidence of any intention that the plaintiff should have any beneficial interest at the time of the purchase of the house in 1963. None of the plaintiff's subsequent expenditure was referable to the acquisition of the house. This was not a case where the woman provided the house-keeping money to enable the man to pay the mortgage. May L.J. stated that, where the home is bought in the man's name alone, the payment of or contribution to the initial deposit by the woman pointed to the necessary common intention. So too if she made direct contributions to mortgage instalments or used her own money for household expenses, so as to enable the man the more easily to pay the mortgage. But if the woman makes no real or substantial financial contribution to the acquisition of the home, she is not entitled to any beneficial interest, even though over a very substantial number of years she may have worked just as hard as the man in maintaining the family, in the sense of keeping house, giving birth to and looking after and helping to bring up the children of the union. All three members of the Court were able to distinguish *Hall* v. *Hall* (1982) 3 F.L.R. 379, C.A., where a concession that the woman was entitled to an interest was made and there may have been an indirect financial contribution by the woman in pooling her earnings to make it easier for the man to pay the mortgage. Both Fox and May L.JJ. disapproved Lord Denning's dictum in *Hall* v. *Hall* that housekeeping and looking after children may be a contribution giving rise to a beneficial interest.

Hussey v. Palmer [1972] 1 W.L.R. 1286, C.A.

In 1967 the plaintiff sold her own house and went to live with her daughter and son-in-law (the defendant). As the house was too small the defendant arranged to have a bedroom built on to the house as an extension for the plaintiff's use. The extension cost £607 and was paid for by the plaintiff direct to the builder. Nothing was said about repayment by either the plaintiff or the defendant. After several months there were differences between the parties and the plaintiff left. She subsequently sued the defendant for the £607 as a loan but in the light of what was said by the registrar allowed herself to be non-suited (*i.e.* action dismissed because no cause of action) and then brought proceedings claiming the £607 on a resulting trust. The county court judge held that the £607 was a loan and that there was no case for a resulting trust. On appeal by the plaintiff, Lord Denning M.R. held there was no loan. Phillimore L.J. thought it might have been a loan and Cairns L.J. held it was a loan. The Master of the Rolls held that there was a resulting or constructive trust. The case was within the principles of the cases where one person contributed towards the purchase price of a house so that the owner held on constructive trust for the contributor. The court would look at the circumstances of each case to decide in which way the equity could be satisfied. In some by an equitable lien (see *Chalmers* v. *Pardoe* [1963] 1 W.L.R. 677, P.C.) in others by a constructive trust (see *Inwards* v. *Baker*, above, p. 29). But in either case it is because justice and good conscience so required. Accordingly the plaintiff had an interest in the property proportionate to the £607 which she had put into it. Phillimore L.J. concurred. He did not think a loan would be inconsistent with the arrangement also being or involving a resulting trust. Cairns L.J. dissented on the ground that there had been a loan.

Matrimonial Proceedings and Property Act 1970, s.37

"It is hereby declared that where a husband or wife contributes in money or money's worth to the improvement of real or personal property in which or in the proceeds of sale of which either or both of them has or have a beneficial interest, the husband or wife so contributing shall, if the contribution is of a substantial nature and subject to any agreement between them to the contrary express or implied, be treated as having then acquired by virtue of his or her contribution a share or an enlarged share, as the case may be, in that beneficial interest of such an extent as may have been then agreed or, in default of such agreement, as may seem in all the circumstances just to any court before which the question of the existence or extent of the beneficial interest of the husband or wife arises (whether in proceedings between them or in any other proceedings)."

3. Transfer of Property on Divorce

Matrimonial Property Adjustment Orders

Matrimonial Causes Act 1973, s.24

"24. (1) On granting a decree of divorce . . . or at any time thereafter . . . the court may make any one or more of the following orders, that is to say—

(*a*) an order that a party to the marriage shall transfer to the other party . . . such property as may be so specified, being property to which the first-mentioned party is entitled . . . ;

(*b*) an order that a settlement of such property as may be so specified, being property to which a party to the marriage is so entitled, be made to the satisfaction of the court for the benefit of the other party to the marriage and of the children of the family or either or any of them . . .

4. Co-Owners' Rights

Right of Occupation of Co-Owners

Jones v. Jones [1977] 1 W.L.R. 438, C.A.

The defendant was a partner with his father and other members of the family in a scrap metal business in Kingston-upon-Thames and lived there in a house belonging to his father. In 1967 the house was compulsorily acquired and the business ceased. The father, who had married the plaintiff after the death of his first wife (the defendant's mother), moved to Suffolk with the plaintiff and subsequently suggested that the defendant and his family move there too. The father found a house which the defendant and his wife liked and he bought it for £4,000. The defendant gave up his job and moved to Suffolk. He made to his father two payments of £500 each towards the cost of the house, but the father assured the defendant that the house was his as a gift. The defendant paid the rates, but paid no rent to the father. On the father's death the plaintiff claimed the house and demanded rent. The defendant refused to pay and the plaintiff took proceedings in the county court for possession. The judge made a declaration that the beneficial interest in the house was as to the defendant one quarter and as to the plaintiff three-quarters and subsequently ordered that the defendant pay to the plaintiff 75 per cent. of a rent to be fixed by a rent officer, failing which he was to vacate and the house was to be sold (under the L.P.A. 1925, s.30; below, p. 100). On appeal, as to the order for payment of rent, it was held that the parties, as tenants in common in equity, were equally entitled to occupation of the house and one of them could not claim rent from the other for occupation, even though that other occupied the whole of the house. As to the order for sale, the doctrine of proprietary estoppel (see above, p. 9) applied. The father had led the defendant to believe that he could stay in the house for the rest of his life. On that basis the defendant had given up his job and moved to Suffolk, had paid £1,000 to his father and done work on the house. Since the father would have been estopped from dispossessing the defendant, so was the plaintiff. The implied trust for sale could not be used to defeat the purposes for which the house had been acquired, *i.e.* as a home for the defendant for life. Accordingly, the defendant was entitled to remain in the house for the rest of his life and the house could not be sold without his consent. The Court refused to make any order that the defendant had a life interest in the house.

Note: Occupation rent is only payable by one co-owner to the other in cases of "ouster" (see e.g. *Dennis* v. *McDonald*, below, p. 104; and see *Eves* v. *Eves*, above, p. 90). See also on co-owners' rights *Williams & Glyn's Bank Ltd.* v. *Boland*, above, p. 49.

5. SEVERANCE

Law of Property Act 1925, s.36(2)

"(2) No severance of a joint tenancy of a legal estate, so as to create a tenancy in common in land, shall be permissible, whether by operation of law or otherwise, but this subsection does not affect the right of a joint tenant to release his interest to the other joint tenants, or the right to sever a joint tenancy in an equitable interest whether or not the legal estate is vested in the joint tenants:

Provided that, where a legal estate (not being settled land) is vested in joint tenants beneficially, and any tenant desires to sever the joint tenancy in equity, he shall give to the other joint tenants a notice in writing of such desire or do such other acts or things as would, in the case of personal estate, have been effectual to sever the tenancy in equity, and thereupon under the trust for sale affecting the land the net proceeds of sale, and the net rents and profits until sale, shall be held upon the trusts which would have been requisite for giving effect to the beneficial interests if there had been an actual severance. Nothing in this Act affects the right of a survivor of joint tenants, who is solely and beneficially interested, to deal with his legal estate as if it were not held on trust for sale."

Re Draper's Conveyance [1969] 1 Ch. 486

A husband and wife were legal and beneficial joint tenants of a dwelling-house. In November 1965 the wife obtained a decree nisi of divorce which was made absolute in March 1966. In February 1966 she commenced proceedings against the husband under the Married Women's Property Act 1882, s.17. In her affidavit in support of the section 17 summons the wife asked that the property might be sold and the proceeds distributed equally. At the hearing of the summons it was declared that the wife had a half-share in the property and an order for sale was made. The former husband died before possession had been obtained or the house sold. The former wife claimed to be entitled to the whole beneficial interest in the house on the ground that there had been no severance of the joint tenancy. Some of the children of the marriage who were entitled on their father's intestacy claimed that there had been a severance by virtue of the various court proceedings taken by the wife and the orders made. Plowman J. held that the issue of the summons and the wife's affidavit operated to cause a severance of the joint tenancy, either as evincing an intention to sever and therefore being an example of "such other acts or things as would, in the case of personal estate, have been effective to sever the tenancy in equity" or as sufficient notice in writing within the L.P.A. 1925, s.36(2).

Re 88 Berkeley Road, London, N.W.9. [1971] Ch. 648

The plaintiff and Miss G. bought a house, providing the purchase money in equal shares. The property was transferred to them as joint tenants, both legally and beneficially. Subsequently Miss G. decided to sever the beneficial joint tenancy. Her solicitors prepared a notice of severance which she signed, and her signature was witnessed. The notice and a covering letter asking the plaintiff to accept service and acknowledge receipt were sent to the plaintiff at the house by recorded delivery. The plaintiff claimed that she had never received the letter. The evidence was that Miss G. herself took the letter in and signed for it, and she claimed that she used to put letters for the plaintiff either on the table or on the mantelpiece. Plowman J. accepted the plaintiff's evidence that she had never received the letter. The L.P.A. 1925, s.36(2) (above) provides that if a joint tenant desires to sever he shall give notice to the other joint tenant in writing. The L.P.A. 1925, s.196(4) provides that a notice shall be sufficiently served if sent by post in a registered letter addressed to the person to be served and the place of abode, and if the letter is not returned undelivered. The Recorded Delivery Act 1962 equated recorded delivery with registered post. It was held that proof on the balance of probabilities of the sending by recorded delivery of a prepaid letter properly addressed containing the notice was sufficient for service and the joint tenancy was therefore severed during Miss G's lifetime.

Nielson-Jones v. Fedden [1975] Ch. 222

The plaintiff and her then husband were legal and beneficial joint tenants of the matrimonial home. The marriage broke down, the parties separated and at the time when they were contemplating divorce they signed a home-made document which stated that the husband was "to use his entire discretion and free-will to either sell the [matrimonial home] and employ the proceeds realised to his new home, if it so is desired to sell in order to provide a home of substance for his children when visiting and himself to live in and, perhaps, to work from if it be not the [matrimonial home]," to which was subsequently added at the wife's suggestion "Not applicable to domestic contents." It was clear from correspondence between their respective solicitors that the plaintiff and her husband wished to separate their financial affairs, but no agreement had been reached. The husband found a purchaser for the house. After paying for some work to the house the plaintiff and the husband each received £200 from the deposit. Before the sale was completed and before any divorce proceedings had been started the husband died. The plaintiff appointed a new trustee to complete the sale. The plaintiff claimed to be solely entitled to the proceeds of sale. Walton J. held that the memorandum did not amount to an assignment by the plaintiff of her beneficial interest to the husband, but was merely an authority for the husband to sell the house on behalf of the plaintiff and himself. Nor could it be construed as a severance of the joint beneficial interests. As to the negotiations it was impossible to say that there was an agreement to sever because no agreement had been reached. A beneficial joint tenancy could not be severed by a unilateral declaration of intention to sever. Walton J. considered that dicta of Havers J. to the contrary in *Hawkesley* v. *May* [1956] 1 Q.B. 304 based on a misunderstanding of the classic statement of Wood V.-C. (later Lord Hatherley L.C.) in *Williams* v. *Hensman* (1861) 1 John & H. 546,557 were wrong and *Re Draper's Conveyance* wrongly decided, in so far as Plowman J. had relied on the dicta of Havers J. and had held that the issue of the summons was notice in writing under section 36(2) (when the section contemplates an irrevocable notice, whilst until any order had been made the wife was *domina litis* and could have withdrawn the proceedings entirely).

Burgess v. Rawnsley [1975] Ch. 429, C.A.

In 1966 Mr. Honick, a widower aged 63, met Mrs. Rawnsley, a widow aged about 60. They got friendly. H. thought R. would marry him. Then H. had the opportunity to buy the house in which he was tenant. R. said she would go half shares. She would have the upper flat and he the lower flat. H. signed a contract to purchase for £850 and R. paid the deposit. Early in 1967 the conveyance was taken in the name of H. and R. as trustees for sale on trust for themselves as beneficial joint tenants. H. paid the balance purchase monies from his own monies. R. paid H. £425 in four instalments for her half share. When subsequently H. realised that R. would not marry him, he tried to get her to sell her share to him. The county court judge found that in July 1968 there was an oral agreement by R. to sell her share to H. for £750. However she later changed her mind and wanted more, but H. would not pay.

So nothing further was done before H.'s death in 1971. R. claimed to be solely entitled by survivorship. Mrs. Burgess, H.'s daughter and administratrix, claimed a half share on the basis, either that there was a resulting trust upon the failure of H's object in purchasing the house (*i.e.* as the matrimonial home for himself and R.) or that the beneficial joint tenancy had been severed by the oral agreement. The county court judge upheld both claims. On appeal it was held by a majority (Brown L.J. and Sir John Pennycuick) that, as there was no *common* purpose which failed, there was no resulting trust. (*Per* Lord Denning M.R. failure of different objects had the same effect as failure of a common object.) However (by the whole court), the beneficial joint tenancy had been severed by the oral agreement for sale, even though such agreement was not specifically enforceable. A severance can be effected at common law by alienation, mutual agreement and by a course of dealing evincing an intention to sever. A specifically enforceable agreement was only relevant to severance by alienation to a third party not to severance by agreement between the joint tenants. The policy of the law as it stands today, having regard particularly to the L.P.A. 1925, s.36(2), is to facilitate severance at the instance of either party (*per* Sir John Pennycuick). Lord Denning M.R. considered that *Nielson-Jones* v. *Fedden* (above) was not correctly decided. Neither of the other members of the Court were prepared to go so far.

Harris v. Goddard [1983] 1 W.L.R. 1203, C.A.

Mr. and Mrs. Harris were the joint legal and equitable owners of their matrimonial home. The marriage broke down. Mrs. Harris commenced divorce proceedings. The petition claimed, *inter alia*, a transfer of the property to her and/or other relief under the Matrimonial Causes Act 1973, s.24 (see above, p. 94). Prior to the date fixed for the hearing of the petition Mr. Harris was injured in a car accident. He was rendered unconscious and died some weeks later without regaining consciousness. While he was in this state his solicitors, acting on the instructions of Mr. Harris's accountants, purported to serve notice of severance of the beneficial joint tenancy. But the accountants had no authority to give such instructions and it was conceded that the notice was ineffective. After Mr. Harris' death the home was sold. Mr. Harris's executors (his children by his first marriage) claimed that the prayer in the divorce petition had effected a severance and that the estate was entitled to half the proceeds of sale of the home. The Court considered the meaning of the word "sever" in the L.P.A. 1925, s.36(2) (above). It was held that the prayer in the petition did not operate to sever the joint tenancy. A desire to sever within the section must evince an intention to bring about the desired result immediately, not at some time in the future. It was further held that the notice must be one which shows an intent to bring about the consequences set out in section 36(2), *i.e.* that the net proceeds of sale shall be held upon the trusts which would have been requisite for giving effect to the beneficial interests if there had been an actual severance. The relief sought in the petition did no more than invite the Court to consider at some time in the future whether to exercise its discretion under section 24 of the 1973 Act, and if it did, to do so in one or more of three ways. Orders under section 24(*a*) and (*b*) could bring co-ownership to an end by ways other than severance (*e.g.* by an order extinguishing Mr. Harris's interest in vesting the property solely in Mrs. Harris or by resettlement of the property on Mr. and Mrs. Harris successively). *Re Draper's Conveyance* (above) was accepted as correct. Lawton L.J. stated that he did not share the doubts expressed by Walton J. in *Nielson-Jones* v. *Fedden* (above) about that case (though it was not clear whether it was the issue of the summons or its service which effect the severance). Kerr L.J. agreed and Dillon L.J. contrasted the relief sought in *Re Draper's Conveyance* with that sought in the instant case.

Note: In *First National Securities Ltd.* v. *Hegerty* [1984] 3 W.L.R. 769, Q.B.D. and C.A. where a home had been conveyed to a husband and wife as joint tenants and the husband forged his wife's signature on a mortgage of the home to secure a loan to the husband, Bingham J. held that, if the husband and wife were beneficial joint tenants (the point was uncertain as they appeared to have contributed unequally to the purchase), the disposition by the husband was a sufficient act of alienation to sever the beneficial joint tenancy (but see *Thames Guaranty Ltd.* v. *Campbell*, below, p. 168).

6. Forcing a Sale

Law of Property Act 1925, s.30

"If the trustees for sale refuse to sell or to exercise any of the powers conferred by either of the last two sections, or any requisite consent cannot be obtained, any person interested may apply to the court for a vesting or other order for giving effect to the proposed transaction or for an order directing the trustees for sale to give effect thereto, and the court may make such order as it thinks fit."

Re Buchanan-Wollaston's Conveyance
[1939] Ch. 738, C.A.

Four neighbours combined to purchase a piece of land near their properties to keep as an open space to enhance their properties. The land was conveyed to them as joint tenants, the beneficial ownership not being expressed. It was held that the L.P.A. 1925, s.36(1) applied and the land was held on the statutory trusts (s.35). The parties subsequently entered into a deed of covenant in which they agreed in effect to preserve the land as an open space. One owner subsequently sold his house and wanted the land to be sold. The others objected. He then applied for an order for sale under the L.P.A. 1925, s.30. The application was refused. The court thought the proper question to ask was whether or not the person applying for execution of the trust was a person whose voice should prevail. The object of the joint tenancy was clearly expressed by the deed of covenant and that object was still alive. In the circumstances it was not right to order a sale on the application of a person who had not acted in accordance with the deed.

Re Mayo [1943] Ch. 302

By his will a testator devised his house to his executors (a son, a daughter and a third party) on trust for his widow for life and then for the son and daughter in equal shares. After the widow's death the property became held upon trust for sale pursuant to section 36 of the S.L.A. 1925. The son wanted to sell the house but his co-trustees refused to concur in a sale. The son applied for an order for sale under the L.P.A. 1925, s.30. A sale was ordered. There was no evidence that the daughter was in occupation or any other reason why a sale should not be made. "A trust for sale will prevail, unless all three trustees agree in exercising the power to postpone . . . there is no suggestion of *mala fides* on the part of the testator's son. . . . If that were established, the position would be different . . . " (*per* Simonds J.).

Re Hyde's Conveyance (1952) 102 L.J. 58, Ch. D.

Two brothers purchased land for occupation by a company in which they were both interested and for the erection of a factory thereon. The conveyance was taken in joint names. Subsequently the brothers quarrelled and one of them applied for a sale. The company was still a going concern. The applicant had refused an offer from his brother based on the full market value of the property. The application was refused, Danckwerts J. being satisfied that the applicant was acting out of spite and endeavouring to use the trust for sale to defeat the purpose for which the land had been acquired.

Stevens v. Hutchinson [1953] Ch. 299

A husband and wife held a house on trust for sale for themselves as tenants in common in equal shares. The house was the matrimonial home. A judgment creditor of the husband applied for an order for sale. The application was refused on the ground that the applicant was not a person interested within the L.P.A. 1925, s.30. Upjohn J. went on to say that the creditor had no better right than the husband and in the circumstances as they then existed (there was no matrimonial trouble between the husband and wife) the husband would not have obtained an order for sale.

Jones v. Challenger [1961] 1 Q.B. 176, C.A.

In 1956 a husband and wife purchased a leasehold house with a term of ten years to run. The property was assigned to them in trust for sale for themselves as joint tenants. In 1957 the wife left the husband who subsequently obtained a divorce on the grounds of the wife's adultery. The husband stayed on in the house. The wife applied for an order for sale under the L.P.A. 1925, s.30. It was held that the wife was entitled to have the house sold because the purpose for which the house had been bought, *viz.* as providing a matrimonial home, had ended and the trust for sale prevailed. It was not unreasonable for the wife to want to realise her share of the property. She had paid half the purchase money and the lease was a wasting asset. Even if she broke up the marriage she should not be deprived of her property rights. However, the order for sale was to be subject to the husband being given the opportunity of buying out the wife's share at an independent valuation.

Re Evers Trust [1980] 1 W.L.R. 1327, C.A.

In 1978 the plaintiff and the defendant, who were living together, purchased a cottage for £13,950. It was taken in joint names as beneficial joint tenants. The plaintiff provided £1,050 plus expenses, the defendant £2,400 and the balance was raised by a mortgage on the property. The parties had lived together since 1974. They had a child in 1976. That year the defendant's two young children by her marriage came to live with them. In 1979 the parties separated, the defendant remaining in the cottage with the children. The plaintiff sought an order for sale under the L.P.A. 1925, s.30. The application was dismissed. On an application under section 30 the court had to have regard to the underlying purpose of the trust for sale. Here the inference was that the parties had purchased the cottage as a family home for themselves and the children for an indefinite period. There was no evidence that the plaintiff had any need to realise his investment (the cottage had doubled in value), whereas a sale would put the defendant in a very difficult position because she could not raise the finance to rehouse herself and the children. The county court judge's order postponing sale until the parties' child attained 16 was varied, since unpredictable changes in circumstances might make an order for sale when the child attained 16 inappropriate. The order, as varied, was that the plaintiff's application be dismissed upon the defendant's undertaking to pay the mortgage and other outgoings and to indemnify the plaintiff against the same so long as she occupied the property, leaving it to either party to make another application if there was a change in circumstances.

Re Holliday [1981] Ch. 405, C.A.

Mr. and Mrs. H. married in 1962. They had three children, born in 1965, 1968 and 1973 respectively. In 1970 they purchased in joint names the house in question for £7,850, of which £6,580 was raised on mortgage. In 1974 Mr. H. left his wife and children and went to live with another woman. In 1975 Mrs. H. obtained a divorce. In 1976 Mr. H. was adjudicated bankrupt on his own petition shortly after Mrs. H. had given notice of intention to seek a transfer of property order. His liabilities exceed his assets. The trustee in bankruptcy sought an order for sale of the house (then worth about £26,500 net) under the L.P.A. 1925, s.30. The trial judge ordered a sale with vacant possession. On appeal it was held that, although, in general, an application for an order for a sale of a matrimonial home where a spouse was also seeking ancillary relief in divorce proceedings should be dealt with by the Family Division, where the beneficial interest of one of the parties to the marriage was vested in the trustee in bankruptcy (so that the court could not make a property adjustment order under the Matrimonial Causes Act 1973, s.24 (above, p. 94) and its powers to make financial provision orders under section 23 of the Act against a debtor were circumscribed by the fact that he was a debtor), the matter could be dealt with in the Chancery Division. If there are young children remaining in the home this does not prolong the purpose of the trust for sale, but is merely a factor to be taken into account so far as it affects the equities between the persons entitled to the beneficial interests. In the circumstances of the case, in particular the wife's inability to purchase a home for herself and the children from her own resources (nil capital) and her half of the equity in the house, the possible upsetting of the children's education (a three-bedroomed house in the same neighbourhood would cost between £20,000 and £25,000) and the fact that any postponement of sale would cause no great hardship to the principal creditors, the Court of Appeal decided that the sale of the house should be deferred until the second child attained the age of 17.

Note: Chhokar v. *Chhokar* [1983] 80 L.S. Gaz. R. 3243, C.A., the parties' matrimonial home (which was registered land) was in the husband's sole name, but the wife had contributed to the purchase. The husband sold the property to a third party (P.) at a time when the wife was in hospital giving birth. P. was aware of the wife's contribution and the intention of the sale was to defeat the wife's interest. The husband paid off the mortgage on the house from the proceeds of sale. The wife remained in the house notwithstanding P.'s harassment and subsequently the husband returned. The trial judge held that P. was trustee for sale for himself and the wife in equal shares, ordered that the property be sold in 9 months and that the wife pay an occupation rent in the meantime. On the wife's appeal against the order for sale and payment of rent, it was held, allowing her appeal, that, though where a third party was involved the court might be more inclined to order a sale, because of P.'s behaviour the wife's voice should prevail. It was immaterial that, by allowing the husband to stay with her, in effect P. was providing a home for the husband and the wife. Nor was the wife obliged to pay P. rent. P. stood no better position than the husband. However P. was to be given credit in so far as part of the purchase money paid by him had been used to pay off the mortgage.

Dennis v. McDonald [1982] Fam. 63, Ch. D and C.A.

The plaintiff and the defendant had lived together as man and wife since 1962 and they had four or five children (the paternity of the fifth was in dispute). In 1970 they bought a home for £3,200. Two thousand pounds was raised by a mortgage on the property and the parties contributed equally to the balance. They took the property as tenants in common in equal shares. In 1974 the plaintiff was finally forced to leave the house permanently, because of the defendant's violence towards her. The plaintiff sought an order for sale under the L.P.A. 1925, s.30. The trial judge refused to order a sale. Three of the children—a trainee nurse aged 18, a 16-year-old boy undergoing training and a child still at school—were in the house with the defendant. The defendant continued to pay the mortgage repayments until the mortgage was discharged in 1980. The judge found that the defendant's conduct amounted to ouster and held that the plaintiff as tenant in common was entitled to an occupation rent of one half of a fair rent valuation (under the Rent Act 1977, s.70) such rent to be assessed yearly. On appeal the defendant argued that there had been no ouster and therefore he need not pay an occupation rent, but, if he had to, the proportion was too great, because he was housing himself and the three children and the house had been acquired as a home for the parties and their children. Also he had made a capital contribution to the installation of a bathroom in the house as required by the local authority. The Court of Appeal confirmed that although the general rule was that each tenant in common had a right to occupy the property and if one voluntarily chose not to exercise that right the other was not liable to pay compensation, a tenant in common who had been excluded from occupation of the property by the other tenant in common was entitled to compensation. The nature of the payment was that of a sort of compensation for the exclusive enjoyment of the property attributable to the wrongful exclusion of the other beneficiary. The purpose to which the party remaining in the property put it was irrelevant. The judge's basis of assessment was, in principle, correct, but excluding annual assessment, the cost of which was disproportionate to the amount involved.

Note: For other cases under L.P.A. 1925, s.30 see above, p. 83 and following and below, p. 168.

Barclay v. Barclay [1970] 2 Q.B. 677, C.A.

A testator's will expressly directed that his bungalow be sold by the executor and that the proceeds should be divided in five equal shares between his sons and daughters-in-law. One of the testator's sons lived in the bungalow with his father and continued to live there after the father's death. One of the daughters-in-law obtained a grant of representation to the testator's estate and wanted to sell the bungalow. The son in occupation refused to go so the daughter-in-law took proceedings for possession. The county court judge rejected her claim because the son was a tenant in common and, as such, entitled to occupation. On appeal, it was held that since the prime object of the will was the sale and division of the proceeds of sale of the bungalow none of the beneficiaries were given any right or interest in the bungalow itself. The beneficiaries were not tenants in common of the bungalow but only of the proceeds of sale, accordingly the defendant had no right to remain in possession and as this was not a case of the refusal of any requisite consent to the sale, the L.P.A 1925, s.30 did not apply.

7. Protecting the Beneficial Interest

Note: Where the beneficiary is on the title that is protection in itself. (For cases of attempted mortgages by one of two co-owners, see below, p. 168). Where the beneficiary is not on the title, but is in occupation, such occupation may give rise to a purchaser or mortgagee having notice of the beneficiary's interest and, in the case of registered land, an overriding interest (see *Williams & Glyn's Bank Ltd.* v. *Boland*, above, p. 49). If the beneficiary acts before completion, a sale or mortgage can be stopped by injunction. A spouse's rights of occupation under the Matrimonial Homes Act 1983 can be protected by land charge (Class F) registration or notice under the L.R.A. (as appropriate). A spouse, who is not on the title, but who has a beneficial interest in the matrimonial home, may so protect her right of occupation under the Matrimonial Homes Act 1983.

Waller v. Waller [1967] 1 W.L.R. 451, Ch. D.

The legal estate in respect of a house (not registered land) was vested in the husband's sole name but the purchase price had been substantially provided by the wife so that she had a beneficial interest in the property. The husband contracted to sell the house as beneficial owner. The wife applied for an interlocutory injunction to restrain the husband completing the sale and was granted one. The purchaser had no notice of the wife's beneficial interest, nevertheless her equitable interest had priority to the purchaser's equitable interest under the contract for sale. Stamp J. stated (*obiter*): " . . . since it is the policy of the law . . . not to allow a single trustee to sell land which he is holding on trust for sale, he [the husband] could not have sold the property and given a good receipt for the proceeds, without first appointing an additional trustee." (See the L.P.A. 1925, s.23(2), below, p. 303).

Note: See *Bull* v. *Bull*, above, p. 83. However, seems to be generally accepted that, in the absence of actual or constructive notice of the trust for sale, a purchaser from a sole trustee who has completed his purchase obtains a good title notwithstanding the L.P.A. 1925, s.27(2).

8. Spouse's Occupation Rights Under Matrimonial Homes Act 1983

Matrimonial Homes Act 1983, ss.1, 2

1. (1) Where one spouse is entitled to occupy a dwelling house by virtue of a beneficial estate or interest or contract or by virtue of any enactment giving him or her the right to remain in occupation, and the other spouse is not so entitled, then, subject to the provisions of this Act, the spouse not so entitled shall have the following rights (in this Act referred to as "rights of occupation")–

(*a*) if in occupation, a right not to be evicted or excluded from the dwelling house or any part thereof by the other spouse except with the leave of the court given by an order under this section;
(*b*) if not in occupation, a right with the leave of the court so given to enter into and occupy the dwelling house.

(2) So long as one spouse has rights of occupation, either of the spouses may apply to the court for an order–

(*a*) declaring, enforcing, restricting or terminating those rights, or
(*b*) prohibiting, suspending or restricting the exercise by either spouse of the right to occupy the dwelling house, or
(*c*) requiring either spouse to permit the exercise by the other of that right . . .

(10) This Act shall not apply to a dwelling house which has at no time been a matrimonial home of the spouses in question; and a spouse's rights of occupation shall continue only so long as the marriage subsists and the other spouse is entitled as mentioned in subsection (1) above to occupy the dwelling house, except where provision is made by section 2 of this Act for those rights to be a charge on an estate or interest in the dwelling house.

(11) It is hereby declared that a spouse who has an equitable interest in a dwelling house or in the proceeds of sale thereof, not being a spouse in whom is vested (whether solely or as a joint tenant) a legal estate in fee simple or a legal term of years absolute in the dwelling house, is to be treated for the purpose only of determining whether he or she has rights of occupation under this section as not being entitled to occupy the dwelling house by virtue of that interest.

2. (1) Where, at any time during the subsistence of a marriage, one spouse is entitled to occupy a dwelling house by virtue of a beneficial estate or interest, then the other spouse's rights of occupation shall be a charge on that estate or interest, having the like priority as if it were an equitable interest created at whichever is the latest of the following dates, that is to say—

(*a*) the date when the spouse so entitled acquires the estate or interest,
(*b*) the date of the marriage, and
(*c*) the 1st January 1968 (which is the date of commencement of the Act of 1967) . . .

(4) Notwithstanding that a spouse's rights of occupation are a charge on an estate or interest in the dwelling house, those rights shall be brought to an end by—

(*a*) the death of the other spouse, or
(*b*) the termination (otherwise than by death) of the marriage,

unless in the event of a matrimonial dispute or estrangement the court sees fit to direct otherwise by an order made under section 1 above during the subsistence of the marriage.

(5) Where a spouse's rights of occupation are a charge on the estate or interest of the other spouse or of trustees for the other spouse—

(*a*) any order under section 1 above against the other spouse shall, except in so far as the contrary intention appears, have the like effect against persons deriving title under the other spouse or under the trustees and affected by the charge, and
(*b*) subsections (2) to (8) of section 1 above shall apply in relation to any person deriving title under the other spouse or under the trustees and affected by the charge as they apply in relation to the other spouse . . .

(7) Where a spouse's rights of occupation are a charge on the estate or interest of the other spouse or of trustees for the other spouse, and the other spouse—

(*a*) is adjudged bankrupt or makes a conveyance or assignment of his or her property (including that estate or interest) to trustees for the benefit of his or her creditors generally, or
(*b*) dies and his or her estate is insolvent,

then, notwithstanding that it is registered under section 2 of the Land Charges Act 1972 or subsection (8) below, the charge shall be void against the trustee in bankruptcy, the trustees under the conveyance or assignment or the personal representatives of the deceased spouse, as the case may be.

(8) Where the title to the legal estate by virtue of which a spouse is entitled to occupy a dwelling house (including any legal estate held by trustees for that spouse) is registered under the Land Registration Act 1925 or any enactment replaced by that Act—

(*a*) registration of a land charge affecting the dwelling house, by virtue of this Act shall be effected by registering a notice under that Act, and

(*b*) a spouse's right of occupation shall not be an overriding interest within the meaning of that Act affecting the dwelling house notwithstanding that the spouse is in actual occupation of the dwelling house.

(9) A spouse's rights of occupation (whether or not constituting a charge) shall not entitle that spouse to lodge a caution under section 54 of the Land Registration Act 1925.

Wroth v. Tyler [1974] Ch. 30

In 1971 the defendant was preparing for retirement from the Civil Service. He intended to sell the bungalow, of which he was registered proprietor and in which he, his wife and their grown up daughter lived, and move to another part of the country where housing was cheaper. The plaintiffs were interested in the defendant's house. They viewed it several times. The defendant's wife did not seem opposed to the sale. A contract was signed on May 27, 1971. The price was £6,050 (£6,000 for the house and the balance for chattels). The next day the defendant's wife caused an entry to be made in the charges register to the property of her rights of occupation under the Matrimonial Homes Act 1967. Some weeks later the defendant learned of his wife's action from his mortgagee building society. He was unable to persuade his wife to remove her entry. The plaintiffs claimed specific performance and in addition or alternatively damages. Megarry J. considered the nature of the rights conferred by the Act. They are not positive rights. The Act works as a shield against eviction. As the defendant owned the house at the commencement of the Act, the wife's rights were a charge on his estate. The charge is neither legal nor equitable but a pure creature of statute with a priority (although not a nature) defined by a reference to equity. It is the charge created by the Act rather than the provisions for registration (as a Class F land charge or, in the case of registered land, by notice) that makes the right binding on successors in title. The provisions for registration were essentially negative. If not duly protected by registration the right becomes void against a subsequent purchaser. Megarry J. refused to order specific performance with vacant possession, as this could mean the defendant having to sue his wife. Nor would he order specific performance subject to the rights of the wife, as this would lead to the family being split up. As to damages, the wife's right was not a defect in title for the purposes of the rule in *Bain* v. *Fothergill* (1874) L.R. 7 H.L. 158, limiting the damages payable by the inability of a vendor of property to remove a defect of title to return of the deposit and expenses but no more than nominal damages. Damages were to be assessed as at the date of the trial. In the meantime house prices had risen. The house was worth £7,500 at the date of breach (*i.e.* the date of completion) and was worth now £11,550. Damages were assessed at £5,500, the difference between the price of the house under the contract and the price of an equivalent house by the time of the trial.

CHAPTER 4

LEASES

1. LICENCES

London Borough of Hounslow v. Twickenham Garden Developments Ltd. [1971] Ch. 233

A multi-million pound building contract for a local authority housing development provided that if the contractor failed to proceed with the works regularly or diligently, the architect could give notice to remedy the fault within 14 days and on a failure to do so the borough could terminate the contract. The work was delayed by strikes and the borough eventually terminated the contract. The contractor refused to accept the termination and to vacate the site. The borough claimed that the licence given to the contractor to enter the site was a bare licence which could be revoked on reasonable notice, and was independent of the contract. Accordingly, the validity of the notices terminating the contract was immaterial to the revocation of the licence. Megarry J. (following dicta of Lord Greene M.R. in *Millennium Productions Ltd.* v. *Winter Garden Theatre (London) Ltd.* [1946] 1 All E.R. 678, C.A.), held that the licence was part of the contract and could not be revoked while the contract was running. The validity of the notices had to be decided and it was uncertain whether or not the contract still subsisted. If the contract was still running, the licence was. The judge reviewed the threefold classification of licences, *i.e.* bare licences, contractual licences and licences coupled with an interest, and the earlier authorities. The licence in question was essentially connected with the building contract and thus a contractual licence. It was not a licence coupled with an interest since such interests must normally be of a proprietary nature involving some legal or equitable interest in the land itself. The licence was by its terms irrevocable in that there was an implied obligation on the borough not to revoke it while the period of the contract was running and equity would not assist the borough to revoke the licence in breach of its contract.

Note: Compare *Midland Bank Ltd.* v. *Farmpride Hatcheries Ltd,* above, p. 14.

Lease or Licence

General note: For most practical purposes a licence to occupy premises has much the same effect as a lease. But a lease and a licence are different in nature. Transactions, which might otherwise have been expressly made as leases, have been made as licences, to avoid statutory protection for tenants. The object has not always been achieved.

Addiscombe Garden Estates Ltd. v. Crabbe
[1958] 1 Q.B. 513, C.A.

The owner of tennis courts and a club house granted a licence to the trustees of a lawn tennis club to use the premises for two years in consideration of monthly payments of "court fees." The agreement contained covenants and other provisions appropriate to a tenancy agreement or lease. After two years had expired the trustees claimed the right to new tenancy under Part II of the Landlord and Tenant Act 1954. It was held that the agreement created a tenancy and not a licence. Whatever label the parties may have put on the document the whole of the document must be looked at. The phraseology used was indicative of a tenancy and having regard to its (the document) showing an intention to confer a right to exclusive possession the relationship of landlord and tenant has been created.

Shell-Mex & B.P. Ltd. v. Manchester Garages Ltd.
[1971] 1 W.L.R. 612, C.A.

The plaintiffs owned a petrol filling station. They allowed the defendants to go into occupation under the terms of a document called a licence. The agreement was to be for a year. It was expressed to be solely for the purpose of selling the plaintiffs' fuels. Amongst the terms was one that the defendants undertook not to impede the plaintiffs' employees in the exercise by them of the plaintiffs' rights of possession and control of the premises, and to give them reasonable assistance and facilities for the alteration at any time of the layout, decorations and equipment of the premises. Differences arose between the parties. The defendants claimed a tenancy protected by the Landlord and Tenant Act 1954, Pt. II. It was held that the defendants were licensees. Exclusive possession was no longer the decisive factor. Primarily the matter depended on whether the agreement conferred a personal privilege, in which case it was a licence, or whether it granted an interest in the land, in which case it was a tenancy. The provisions of the agreement—the personal tie to deal only in Shell petrol and the fact that the plaintiffs' men could go and visit the premises when they liked—pointed to a licence and not a tenancy. The fact that the contract is not assignable is material and points to a licence, for a tenancy involves an interest in land and it is normally a characteristic of that interest that it is assignable.

Note: Lord Denning M.R. indicated that since the Landlord and Tenant Act 1954, Pt. II could be contracted out of (see L.P.A. 1969, s.5) the objection that a licence was a means of avoidance of the Act was no longer material.

Marchant v. Charters [1977] 1 W.L.R. 1181, C.A.

The plaintiff let bed-sitting rooms in a house. Each room was fully furnished and had a gas ring and grill. The bathroom and lavatory were shared. A housekeeper cleaned the rooms, changed linen weekly and, if required, cooked evening meals. The rent was inclusive of these services. The defendant had successfully sought a rent reduction from a rent officer and the plaintiff gave him notice to quit and sought possession. The county court judge held that the defendant was a tenant, but, as the rent included payments for services which were by no means minimal, he was not protected by the Rent Acts. On appeal it was held that the defendant was not a tenant but a licensee. Lord Denning M.R. stated the test of tenant or licensee as follows: "It does not depend on . . . exclusive possession . . . It does not depend on whether the room is furnished or not. It does not depend on whether the occupation is permanent or temporary. It does not depend on the label the parties put upon it . . . the answer depends on the nature and quality of the occupancy. Was it intended that the occupier should have a stake in the room or did he have only permission for himself personally to occupy the room . . . In which case he is a licensee." As a licensee the defendant had no security of tenure under the Rent Acts. The Court of Appeal took the county court judge's finding of the rent attributable to the services being no means minimal to mean that the value of the attendance formed a substantial part of the whole rent (see now Rent Act 1977, s.7), so even if the defendant had been a tenant he did not have a protected tenancy under the Rent Acts. As licensee, the defendant should have sought a reduction of rent from the rent tribunal and not, as he had done, from a rent officer (see now Rent Act 1977, s.19 and Part V).

Street v. Mountford [1985] 2 All E.R. 289, H.L.

Mrs. M. signed an agreement for exclusive possession of residential accommodation for a term at a rent. The agreement was expressed to be a licence and Mrs. M. signed a declaration at the foot of the document that she understood and accepted that a licence in the above form did not and was not intended to give her a tenancy protected under the Rent Acts. The Court of Appeal had upheld the decision of the county court judge that Mrs. M. was a licensee and not a tenant. Allowing Mrs. M.'s appeal, the House of

Lords re-affirmed the test of exclusive possession as the bench mark of a tenancy. The respondent had relied on recent authorities (see, *e.g.*, *Marchant* v. *Charters*, above; and *Somma* v. *Hazlehurst* [1978] 1 W.L.R. 1014, C.A.) as demonstrating that an occupier granted exclusive possession for a term at a rent could nevertheless be a licensee, if there was manifested the clear intention of both parties that the rights granted are to be merely those of a personal right of occupation and not those of a tenant. Referring to Lord Denning's words in *Marchant* v. *Charters* (above), Lord Templeman (with whom the other Law Lords agreed) said that, in order to ascertain the nature and quality of the occupancy and to see whether the occupier had or had not a stake in the room or only permission for himself personally, the Court had to decide whether upon its true construction the agreement conferred on the occupier exclusive possession. *Somma* v. *Hazlehurst*, above, in which there had been *separate* agreements with Mr. H. and Miss S. for the use of a double bed-sitting room, so that the C.A. held that it was impossible to construe the agreements as granting exclusive possession, was overruled. The intention was, said Lord Templeman, that H. and S. might live together in quasi-connubial bliss and if the landlord had served a notice to quit on H. and required S. to share the room with a strange man that would have been a disguised notice to quit on both. The two agreements constituted the grant to H. and S. jointly of exclusive possession and therefore constituted a tenancy. Lord Templeman said that, although the Rent Acts were not to be allowed to alter or influence the construction of an agreement, the Court should be astute to detect and frustrate sham devices and artificial transactions whose only object was to disguise the grant of a tenancy and evade the Rent Acts. (For an example of a sham, see *Walsh* v. *Griffith-Jones* (1978) 2 All E.R. 1002. Save for cases where there was no intention to create legal relations or the occupancy was referable to a contract for sale or contract of employment, where residential accommodation was offered and accepted with exclusive possession for a term at a rent, the result was a tenancy.

Packing-up Period

Minister of Health v. Bellotti [1944] K.B. 298, C.A.

The respondents were evacuees from Gibraltar and occupied a flat in a block of flats which had been requisitioned under licence from the Ministry. They paid for the accommodation and were allowed to bring in their furniture, etc. Differences arose between them and the Ministry officials and they were given a week's notice to quit. They contended that the notice was unreasonably short. It was held that a notice revoking a revocable licence must give the licensee a reasonable time to find alternative accommodation ("packing-up period"). The length of time to be given depends on the circumstances of the case and in the present case a week's notice was not long enough. However the notice became operative to determine the licence on the expiration of a reasonable time from the date of service.

Tenancy at Will or Licence

Cobb v. Lane [1952] 1 All E.R. 1199, C.A.

In 1935 the defendant wanted to buy a house. In 1936 his sister bought a house and gave possession to the defendant. He never paid his sister anything for use and occupation and, save for the first year, she paid the rates. The sister died in 1950 and her executors claimed possession alleging that the defendant was a licensee. He claimed, *inter alia*, that he was originally in occupation as a tenant at will and that under the Limitation Act 1939, s.9(1) (see now Limitation Act 1980, s.15(6), Sched. 1, Pt. I, para. 5(1) above, p. 57), that tenancy must be deemed to be determined at the end of the year from its commencement so that the plaintiffs' claim was barred 12 years later. It was held that the fact of exclusive occupation of property for an indefinite period was no longer inconsistent with the occupier being a licensee and not a tenant at will. Whether or not a relationship of landlord and tenant had been created depends on the intention of the parties, and the circumstances. Here was a case of a family arrangement. What was intended was a personal privilege and not an interest in the land. The defendant was a licensee and the plaintiffs were entitled to possession.

Note: And see *Hughes* v. *Griffin*, above, p. 63; *Helsop* v. *Burns*, above, p. 63; *Wheeler* v. *Mercer*, below, p. 125.

Implied Terms

Western Electric Ltd. v. Welsh Development Agency [1983] Q.B. 796

The plaintiff was a tenant of a factory on the defendant's industrial estate at Rhyl. In 1979 the plaintiff urgently required further accommodation. The defendant agreed to build an extension and in the meanwhile to give the plaintiff a 12 month licence (to avoid the effect of the Landlord and Tenant Act 1954) to use other premises in the course of construction. The terms of the licence, which were all to the advantage of the defendant, were set out in an offer letter dated June 21, 1979. The plaintiff did not reply to the letter, but on June 25, 1979 went into possession. In August it became apparent that the foundations of the building were inadequate to support it and by about November the building became so dangerous the plaintiff had to vacate. The plaintiff sued for damages for breach of an implied term of the licence of fitness for purpose. Judge John Newey Q.C., sitting as judge of the High Court, held that, although the plaintiff had not communicated its acceptance of the terms of the letter of June 21, 1979, the parties had by their conduct (*i.e.* the plaintiff going into occupation and the defendant permitting it) made a contract for a licence effective forthwith. Although a term that premises were suitable for their purposes was not an implied term of lease (see *Bottomley* v. *Bannister* [1932] 1 K.B. 458, C.A.), other than a lease of furnished premises (see *Smith* v. *Marrable* (1843) 11 M. & W. 5, Exch.) or under statute (see *e.g.* Housing Act 1957, s.6), such a term would be implied into a contractual licence to give business efficacy to the agreement or to complete an incomplete agreement (see *Liverpool City Council* v. *Irwin*, below, p. 131). The sole purpose of the licence was to enable the plaintiff to carry on and expand its business while the existing factory was being enlarged by the defendant. Either, on *The Moorcock* (1889) 14 P.D. 64, C.A. test or as in *Liverpool City Council* v. *Irwin* to complete the contract as the parties must clearly have intended, a warranty of soundness and suitability of purpose was to be implied in the licence.

Note: With regard to *Bottomley* v. *Bannister*, above, a landlord who designed or built premises owes a duty of care to persons who might reasonably be expected to be affected by the condition of the premises: see *Rimmer* v. *Liverpool City Council* [1985] Q.B. 1, C.A. (thin glass panel as part of inside wall, tenant put his hand through the glass and severely injured hand and wrist, Council liable).

2. Agreement for a Lease

Walsh v. Lonsdale (1882) 21 Ch.D. 9, C.A.

The defendant agreed in writing to grant the plaintiff a lease of a mill for seven years, the rent to vary according to the number of looms operated, subject to a minimum figure, and to be payable in advance if demanded. No deed was executed. The plaintiff took possession and paid rent quarterly in arrears. About three years later the plaintiff failed to pay rent and the defendant demanded a year's rent in advance. The plaintiff did not pay and the defendant levied distress. The plaintiff brought an action for illegal distress and specific performance of the agreement. He claimed that by entering into possession and paying rent by reference to a year he was a common law yearly tenant on the terms of the agreement consistent with a yearly tenancy. Payment of a year's rent *in advance* was inconsistent with the yearly tenancy and therefore the distress was illegal (because to justify distress there must be a legal tenancy). It was held that after the Judicature Act 1873 there were not two estates as there were formerly, one at common law by reason of the payment of the rent from year to year and an estate in equity under the agreement. The rules of equity prevailed. The plaintiff held under an agreement for a lease under the same terms as if the lease had been granted *i.e.*, including a term for payment of rent in advance if demanded. Therefore the plaintiff could not complain.

Note: So where there is both a specifically enforceable agreement for a lease and a legal tenancy arising from payment of rent the former prevails. See also on the Fusion of the Common Law and Equity *United Scientific Holdings Ltd.* v. *Burnley Borough Council*, below, p. 146.

Agreement Not Always as Good as a Lease

Warmington v. Miller [1973] Q.B. 877, C.A.

"The *Walsh* v. *Lonsdale* situation, where the intended lessee is treated as having the same rights as if a lease had in fact been granted to him, only applies if the lessee is entitled to specific performance," *per* Stamp L.J. The defendant was tenant under a lease for a term of 21 years containing an unqualified covenant not to assign, underlet or part with possession of part only of the demised premises. The defendant orally agreed to grant the plaintiffs an underlease of the workshop part of the premises for 12 months and thereafter until determined by 12 months' notice on either side. The plaintiffs went into possession and paid rent of £20 a week. The defendant failed to grant the underlease and the plaintiffs claimed specific performance of the oral agreement. The county court judge found the agreement proved and ordered specific performance of it. On appeal, it was held that the county court judge ought not to have ordered specific performance requiring the defendant to do that which he could not do under the terms of a lease and which, if he did, would expose him to proceedings for forfeiture.

Coatsworth v. Johnson (1886) 55 L.J.Q.B. 220, C.A.

The plaintiff went into possession of a farm under a written agreement for a lease. The terms of the lease, which were set out in a draft lease which was signed but not sealed, contained a covenant by the plaintiff to cultivate the land according to the approved course of husbandry. The plaintiff had paid no rent and had failed to cultivate the farm properly. The defendant turned him out. The plaintiff claimed damages for trespass and relief from forfeiture. It was held that the plaintiff was a tenant at will only. He could not be regarded as lessee for the term of years mentioned in the agreement. Equity would not decree specific performance of the agreement because the plaintiff would have to admit that he himself had failed to perform a material portion of the contract.

Manchester Brewery Co. v. Coombs [1901] 2 Ch. 608

A brewery company agreed in writing (but it never executed the document) to grant a yearly tenancy of an hotel to the defendant, who covenanted to buy all his beer from the brewery and their successors in business. The brewery sold their business to the plaintiffs. Shortly afterwards the defendant ceased to buy his beer from the plaintiffs. They brought an action to restrain a breach of the covenant. Farwell J. held that the plaintiffs were entitled to the benefit of the covenant. The covenant was not personal to the original brewery company but one which ran with the land. Specific performance of the agreement would be granted and the court treated it as granted. Accordingly, the plaintiffs could sue on the covenant in the same manner as they could have done if the brewery had actually executed the original agreement.

Note: That the plaintiffs were assigns of the *benefit* of the covenant, not original parties to the contract, but they could obtain specific performance. Compare the next case where it was the defendants who were the assigns of the *burden* of the covenant. As to the burden running with the land, see below, pp. 119 and 158. And see ss.141, 142 L.P.A. (below, p. 160) and *Boyer* v. *Warbey* (below, p. 160).

Purchase v. Lichfield Brewery Co.
[1915] 1 K.B. 184, K.B.D.

By an agreement in writing but not under seal the plaintiff purported to grant L. a lease of a house for a term of 15 years, subject to a covenant against assigning the term without the plaintiff's consent, such consent not to be unreasonably withheld (see below, p. 141). The next day L. assigned the house to the defendant by way of mortgage. The defendant never went into possession. L. failed to pay the rent and the plaintiff sued the defendant for it. It was held that the defendant was not liable for the rent or to other covenants in the agreement, as there was no privity of contract or estate between it and the plaintiff. The defendant never had a term vested in it because no term was created. Therefore there was never privity of estate. It never went into possession nor was recognised by the landlord. Therefore there was never privity of contract. It was impossible that specific performance of a contract could be decreed against a person with whom there is neither privity of contract nor privity of estate.

Note: A mortgage by assignment is no longer possible (see L.P.A. 1925, s.86(1), below p. 165). It has been suggested that specific performance would now be decreed on the facts of the last noted case. It was an unusual situation. The defendant never went into possession, the assignment to it was in breach of covenant and the defendant's interest was only as security.

As to the burden of covenants, generally, not running with the land, see below, p. 242. But for restrictive covenants, see below, p. 247. For the running of covenants in leases, see below, p. 158.

For another example of where an agreement is not as good as a lease, see L.P.A. 1925, s.62(1) below, p. 216 and p. 219.

Industrial Properties Ltd v. Associated Electrical Industries Ltd. [1977] Q.B. 580, C.A.

The freehold of the Barton Hill Trading Estate was owned by the trustees of the Parker family trust. In 1959 for tax purposes the trustees agreed to sell the Estate to three companies controlled by members of the Parker family. The contract was registered as a land charge but conveyances were never executed in order to save stamp duty. In 1966 the defendant was granted a new lease of factory premises on the Estate. The lessor was the plaintiff. The defendant was told that the plaintiff was the freeholder. The lease contained a covenant to repair by the defendant. The lease was terminated by the plaintiff after seven years pursuant to the break clause in the lease. The defendant vacated the premises leaving them in a very dilapidated condition. Subsequently the plaintiff sued for breach of the repairing covenant. The defendant then discovered that the plaintiff was not the paper title owner. The defendant claimed that the plaintiff was not the legal owner and as it was no longer in possession it could deny the landlord's title and, relying on the Court of Appeal's decision in *Harrison* v. *Wells* [1967] 1 Q.B. 263, the landlord could not sue on the covenant. Holding that that case was wrongly decided *per incuriam*, the Court of Appeal stated the correct rule to be that if a landlord lets a tenant into possession under a lease, then, so long as the tenant remains in possession undisturbed by any adverse claim, the tenant cannot dispute the landlord's title. This rule continued to operate after the termination of the lease unless a claim was made against the tenant by title paramount in respect of some part of the period of the lease. Since the defendant had had possession for the whole term undisturbed then or thereafter by any adverse claim or possibility thereof and since the innocent misrepresentation that the lessor was the freeholder had done no harm, the defendant was estopped from disputing the landlord's title and was liable on the repairing covenant. Even if the defendant were not estopped, the "lease" would have been effective as an agreement for a lease on the principle of *Walsh* v. *Lonsdale* (see above, p. 116). It made no difference that in this case, unlike *Walsh* v. *Lonsdale*, there was no contractual relationship between the parties (*per* Roskill L.J.).

Note: See further, on the principle that a tenant cannot deny his landlord's title, *National Westminster Bank Ltd.* v. *Hart* [1983] Q.B. 773, C.A. (where C.'s long lease expired in 1967, but the head landlord did not assert title. In 1978, the defendant sub-tenants refused to continue paying rent until the plaintiff, C.'s executor, had proved its title. The plaintiff claimed that since there was no adverse claimant to the rent and no-one claimed a better title than the bank the defendants were estopped from denying its title. It was held that there was no requirement that a third party should have claimed title before the tenant could withhold rent. The plaintiff's title had determined and the defendants were not obliged to pay rent. Nor were they estopped from relying on the determination by the payment of rent between 1967 and 1978, because they had no knowledge of the determination of the head lease).

Registration

Land Charges Act 1972, s.2(4), Class C (iv) (see above, p. 18).

Registered Land

Grace Rymer Investments Ltd. v. Waite
[1958] Ch. 831, C.A.

The defendants orally agreed to grant Mrs. H. a weekly tenancy of property they intended to acquire and Mrs. H. paid three years' rent in advance. Later the defendants signed a contract to purchase the freehold of the property. A month later Mrs. H. went into possession. The defendants completed the purchase and charged the property in favour of the plaintiff. The charge did not exclude the mortgagor's leasing powers (see below p. 184). The transfer and charge were duly registered. The defendants fell into arrears with the mortgage payments and the plaintiff sought possession. It was held that the plaintiff was not entitled to possession. When the defendants took their transfer they were estopped from denying Mrs. H.'s right to remain as tenant for the period for which she had paid rent (for tenancy by estoppel, see below, p. 130). The plaintiff was in no better position than the defendants. Its charge was not effective until registration (L.R.A. 1925, ss.19 and 20, notwithstanding s.27(3) which states that the charge "shall take effect from the date of the delivery of the deed"). Mrs. H.'s interest was an overriding interest (see above, p. 47) to which the plaintiff's charge was made subject.

City Permanent Building Society v. Miller
[1952] Ch. 840, C.A.

The defendant orally agreed to grant the second defendant, Mrs. C. a tenancy of a flat for three years and then on a weekly basis. At that time the defendant had no interest in the property. Mrs. C. paid him three years' rent in advance and he executed a short document acknowledging receipt of the payment and describing the premises and the terms of the agreement. Subsequently the defendant purchased the property, took a transfer and charged the property to the plaintiff. The transfer and charge were duly registered. Later Mrs. C. went into occupation. The defendant defaulted on the mortgage and the plaintiff claimed possession. It was held that the lease being for more than three years had to be created by deed (see L.P.A. 1925, ss.52 and 54). Mrs. C.'s interest was that of a person who had a contract for the grant of a lease and a right to obtain specific performance of the contract. Her interest was not an overriding interest within the L.R.A. 1925, s.70(1)(*k*) as a lease for a term not exceeding 21 years, since that provision required a grant and not a mere agreement.

Note: That as Mrs. C. had not taken possession by the date of the registration of the charge she could not rely on s.70(1)(*g*) (rights of person in actual occupation, see above, pp. 47-48).

3. Types of Lease or Tenancy

Periodic

Re Midland Railway Co.'s Agreement, Charles Clay & Sons Ltd. v. British Railways Board [1971] Ch. 725, C.A.

The Midland Railway Co. granted the plaintiffs a lease for six months to continue from half-year to half-year until determination on either side by three months' notice. There was a proviso that the landlords should not determine the lease until they required the premises for their own undertaking. The Board, the original landlord's successor in title, who did not need the land for their own business, gave the tenant six months' notice to quit under section 25 of the Landlord and Tenant Act 1954. The Board claimed that the lease was void for uncertainty (because it failed to satisfy the basic requirements of a lease that the duration should be certain (see *Lace* v. *Chantler* [1944] K.B. 368, C.A.)), and alternatively that the fetter on the right to determine was repugnant to the nature of the tenancy and should be set aside so as to leave a tenancy determinable on three months' notice on either side. It was held that the rule as to certainty of duration does not apply to periodic tenancies. In one sense it is uncertain at the outset of a periodic tenancy what the maximum length will be. The term grows year by year (in the case of a yearly tenancy) as a single term springing from the original grant, rather than lots of separate tenancies of a year. Its duration will depend on the time that will elapse before either party gives notice of determination. The tenancy can be made subject to a definite limit by either side giving notice. But in this case the landlord's right to determine was restricted. Did this make a difference? It was held that in the absence of any authority to prevent the court it was preferable as a matter of justice to hold parties to their clearly expressed bargain rather than to introduce for the first time in 1971 an extension of a doctrine of land law so as to deny the efficacy of their bargain. The alternative claim of the Board based on repugnancy also failed, the instinct of the court being to give effect if possible to the bargain made by the parties and there being some comparatively recent authority (*Breams Property Investment Co. Ltd.* v. *Stroulger* (below, p. 158)) where a curb for three years was upheld by the court notwithstanding some old authorities to the contrary. *Per* Russell L.J.: "It may well be that if in a periodic tenancy an attempt was made to prevent the lessor ever determining the tenancy that would be so inconsistent with the stated bargain that either a greater estate must be found to have been constituted or the attempt must be rejected as repugnant" (see the next case). It was suggested that should the Board sell the reversion to another it might be arguable that the proviso would be no longer relevant. For the above reasons the Board's notice to quit was invalid.

Centaploy Ltd. v. Matlodge Ltd. [1974] Ch. 1

The plaintiffs claimed to be tenants of certain garage premises. The terms of the tenancies had been agreed orally with the landlord's agent and were subsequently set out in short memoranda signed by him acknowledging receipt of one week's rent and stating "to continue until determined by the lessee." The plaintiffs claimed the documents provided for a tenancy from week to week unless determined by them. The defendants contended that the tenancies were void for uncertainty, the provision for determination being inconsistent with a weekly tenancy. Alternatively the defendants claimed that it was repugnant to a periodic tenancy that the right to determine should rest solely with the tenant. On the uncertainty point the defendants' case was stronger here than in *Re Midland Railway Co.'s Agreement* (above) because the landlord could not ever determine the agreement. Whitford J. felt bound by the earlier decision (though but for that decision he would have been prepared to accept the defendants' argument). On the repugnancy point (which, of course, was the very point left open in the earlier case) it was held that although the right to determine might be fettered for an uncertain period it was nevertheless basic to a tenancy that at some stage the grantor should have the right to determine. A tenancy under which the landlord would never have the right to determine was a contradiction in terms. On the evidence it was clear that the parties had intended a weekly tenancy rather than a perpetually renewable lease (which the plaintiffs claimed as an alternative). Accordingly the fetter placed on the landlord's right to determine the tenancy was void as being repugnant to the nature of the tenancy granted. Nevertheless the notice to quit which the defendants had served on the plaintiffs was bad because it was held that the plaintiffs carried on the business of letting parking and garage space at the premises, the premises were therefore business premises and any notice to quit had to satisfy the requirements of the Landlord and Tenant Act 1954, Part II. The defendants (who were anxious to obtain possession to redevelop) were not entitled to possession.

Adler v. Blackman [1953] 1 Q.B. 146, C.A.

The defendant, a weekly tenant, entered into an agreement with his landlord for a tenancy for one year at a rent of £3 a week. At the end of the year the tenant held over at the same rent. The landlord later served notice to quit on the basis that the defendant was a weekly tenant. The defendant claimed a yearly tenancy and therefore to be entitled to six months' notice to quit, his tenancy being an implied yearly tenancy on a holding over after a tenancy for one year. It was held that for such an implied tenancy to arise the rent for the one year's tenancy had to be an annual rent. In the present case the rent was expressed to be payable as a weekly rent and accordingly the defendant held over as a weekly tenant. The position would have been different if the rent had been expressed as a rent per year, though payable half-yearly, quarterly, monthly or weekly.

Tenancy at Will

Wheeler v. Mercer [1957] A.C. 416, H.L.

The respondent was the tenant of business premises which she held under a quarterly tenancy. On the termination of the tenancy negotiations for a new tenancy took place but proved inconclusive. The respondent remained in occupation meanwhile, not paying any rent. It was held that the respondent was not a licensee nor a tenant at sufferance (since she was in possession with the landlord's positive assent), but a tenant at will. *Per* Viscount Simonds: " . . . a tenant at will is regarded at law as being in possession by his own will and at the will express or implied of his landlord, he is a tenant by their mutual agreement, and the agreement may, therefore, be called a tenancy agreement. He is distinguished from a tenant at sufferance in that such a tenant is said to be in possession without either the agreement or disagreement of the landlord. I am not satisfied that a tenancy at will could be described as a tenancy created by a tenancy agreement [and is, if business premises, protected by the provisions of the Landlord and Tenant Act 1954; see the next case]. A tenancy at will, though called a tenancy, is unlike any other tenancy except a tenancy at sufferance to which it is next-of-kin. It has been properly described as a personal relation between the landlord and his tenant. It is determined by the death of either of them, or by any one of a variety of acts, even by a voluntary alienation which would not affect the subsistence of any other tenancy. It is true that, in some cases, the relation of tenant at will may be expressly created by contract, but this is an exceptional case and I do not exclude the possibility of such a contract being a 'tenancy agreement' even if a tenancy at will arising by implication of law is not."

Manfield & Sons Ltd. v. Botchin [1970] 2 Q.B. 612

The plaintiffs were the landlords of three shops. They were anxious to redevelop the site and were waiting for planning permission. They entered into a written agreement with the defendant to grant him a tenancy at will of one shop at an agreed yearly rent to be paid when demanded. The agreement was expressed not to create any periodic tenancy and to be personal to the defendant, the defendant acknowledging that his occupation should not be protected by the L. & T.A. 1954. There was no provision for re-entry. The tenant remained in possession for over four-and-a-half years paying rent on demand monthly. Later the landlords obtained planning permission and sought possession of the shop. Cooke J. held that the agreement created a tenancy at will. The express intention to create a tenancy at will in the agreement overrode the fact that rent was reserved by reference to a year and was subsequently paid monthly. The L. & T.A. 1954 did not apply to a tenancy at will created by express agreement. Section 25 of that Act dealt with tenancies determined by notice to quit or effluxion of time. Tenancies at will were not determined by either of these means.

Note: "It is of the essence of a tenancy at will that it should be determinable by either party on demand," *per* Denning L.J. in *Errington* v. *Errington and Woods* (above, p. 5). And see *Cobb* v. *Lane* (above, p. 115); *Hughes* v. *Griffin* (above, p. 63); *Heslop* v. *Burns*, above, p. 63.

Perpetually renewable

Law of Property Act 1922, s.145, Sched. 15, paras. 5, 10

"For the purpose of converting perpetually renewable leases and underleases . . . into long terms, for preventing the creation of perpetually renewable leasehold interests and for providing for the interests of the persons affected, the provisions contained in the Fifteenth Schedule to this Act shall have effect.

Fifteenth Schedule

5. A grant . . . of a term, subterm or other leasehold interest with a covenant or obligation for perpetual renewal . . . shall . . . take effect as a demise for a term of two thousand years or in the case of a subdemise for a term less in duration by one day than the term out of which it is derived, to commence from the date fixed for the

commencement of the term, subterm, or other interest, and in every case free from any obligation for renewal or for payment of any fines, fees, costs, or other money in respect of renewal.

10. (1) Every lease or underlease [so converted] shall be deemed to contain:

(i) A power (exercisable only with the consent of the persons, if any, interested in any derivative interest which might be prejudically affected) for the lessee or underlessee by giving notice in writing to the lessor at least ten days before the lease or underlease would (but for this Act) have expired if it had not been renewed . . . to determine the lease or underlease at the date on which (but for this Act) it would have expired if it had not been renewed . . . "

Parkus v. Greenwood [1950] Ch. 644, C.A.

A tenancy agreement for three years provided that the landlord would on the written request of the tenant, made three calendar months before the expiration of the term, grant to the tenant a further term of three years at the same rent and containing the like agreements and provisions as were therein contained including the present covenant for renewal. It was held (overruling Harman J.) that the provision operated to make the lease perpetually renewable and accordingly the term granted by the agreement was converted into a term for 2,000 years by the L.P.A. 1922 (see above).

Re Hopkins' Lease, Caerphilly Concrete Products Ltd. v. **Owen** [1972] 1 W.L.R. 372, C.A.

The defendant was tenant under a lease for a term of five years which provided that the landlord would, on the written request of the tenant made six months before the expiration of the term thereby created and if there should not at the time of such request be any existing breach or non-observance of any of the covenants on the part of the tenant therein contained . . . grant to him a lease of the premises for the further term of five years from the expiration of the term granted at the same rent and containing the like covenants and provisos therein contained (including an option to renew such lease for a further term of five years at the expiration thereof). The defendant did not exercise the right of renewal and the plaintiffs claimed that the lease was at an end. The defendant claimed to be entitled to a perpetually renewable lease under Sched. 15, para. 5, to the L.P.A. 1922. It was held that the express reference to the option to renew to be included in the new lease made it plain that the "like covenants and provisos" was intended to include in the new lease an option to renew and therefore the lease was a perpetually renewable lease and took effect as a lease for 2,000 years.

Marjorie Burnett Ltd. v. Barclay
(1981) 125 Sol.Jo. 199, Ch.D.

The defendant was tenant of a shop with living accommodation for a term of seven years. The lease contained an option to renew, such renewed lease to be at a new rent determined by a specified formula and to contain "a like covenant for renewal for a further term of 7 years on the expiration of the term thereby granted." The defendant claimed that the lease was perpetually renewable and took effect as a term for 2,000 years, but nevertheless exercised the option to renew in case that claim was not upheld. The plaintiff sought a declaration that the lease was not perpetually renewable, but could be renewed twice only. Nourse J. found in favour of the landlord. He said that in *Parkus* v. *Greenwood* (above) Harman J. had been overruled on the construction of the option, not on the statement of principle he had expounded that for a lease to be perpetually renewable one had to find an express covenant for perpetual renewal. The option in this case was not expressly one for perpetual renewal and Nourse J. construed it as one for renewal twice. He held that in construing such an option the Court should see what the second lease should contain if the option has been exercised and also the intention of the parties. He found that the notion of a 2,000 years term was completely inimical to a lease containing a rent review every seven years.

Note: In the two previous cases, the rent for the renewed term was to be the same as for the original term. Also the renewal provisions referred to a further lease on like terms and expressly "included" the provision for renewal within those terms. Nevertheless it is difficult to reconcile the later decision with the earlier ones.

For Lives

Law of Property Act 1925, s.149(6)(a)

"Any lease or underlease at a rent, or in consideration of a fine, for life or lives or for any term of years determinable with life or lives, or on the marriage of the lessee, or any contract therefor . . . shall take effect as a lease, underlease or contract therefor, for a

term of ninety years determinable after the death or marriage (as the case may be) of the original lessee . . . :
Provided that–

(*a*) this subsection shall not apply to any term taking effect in equity under a settlement or created out of an equitable interest under a settlement for mortgage, indemnity, or other like purposes; . . ."

Note: See *Re Catling* (below, p. 273).

Future Leases

Law of Property Act 1925, s.149(3)

"A term, at a rent or granted in consideration of a fine, limited . . . to take effect more than twenty-one years from the date of the instrument purporting to create it, shall be void, and any contract . . . to create such a term shall likewise be void. . . ."

Re Strand and Savoy Properties Ltd. [1960] Ch. 582

A lease for 35 years granted in November 1928 contained an option for renewal in the following terms: "the lessors will at the written request of the lessee made 12 months before the expiration of the term hereby created . . . grant to him a lease of the demised premises for the further term of 35 years from the expiration of the said term hereby granted at the same rent." In November 1953 the tenants gave notice exercising the option. The landlords claimed that the option was void by virtue of section 149(3). Buckley J. held that the option was good. The subsection invalidates contracts for the granting of leases which will, when granted, be reversionary leases, the postponement of the commencement of the term being for more than 21 years from the date of the lease creating such a term.

Note: It was assumed that the option was a contract. The true nature of an option is that of an irrevocable offer (see *Beesly* v. *Hallwood Estates Ltd.*, above, p. 21 and the next case).

Weg Motors Ltd. v. Hales [1962] Ch. 49, C.A.

In 1937 GRI Ltd. charged certain premises of which they were the registered proprietors by way of legal mortgage to an insurance company. In July 1938 GRI Ltd. leased the premises to the plaintiff company for 21 years. By a separate agreement made at the same time the plaintiff was given an option, exercisable at any time before December 25, 1959, to surrender the lease and take a further lease for 21 years. The parties to the agreement were defined to include their successors in title. The option was noted in the Charges Register of the property. Subsequently there were miscellaneous dealings to raise money for redevelopment by way of sale and lease back and mortgage of the freehold, and the 1937 mortgage was vacated. In 1959 the plaintiff gave notice to the defendants (successors in title of GRI Ltd.) exercising the option, but they refused to grant a new lease on the ground that the option was invalid, *inter alia*, under section 149(3) of the L.P.A. 1925 and under the rule against perpetuities. It was held that the agreement was an option to renew, an option is not a contract and therefore not such a contract as is comprehended by section 149(3). The option and the lease were a single transaction so the rights and obligations of the option were incidents of the demise and as an option for renewal fell within a long established exception to the rule against perpetuities (see *Woodall* v. *Clifton*, below, p. 321). If it was necessary to be within that exception that the obligation of the agreement should run with the reversion under section 142(1) of the L.P.A. 1925 (see below, p. 160), the obligation did fall within that provision. Although the property was subject to the legal charge at the date of the option agreement GRI Ltd. did have "power to bind the reversionary estate immediately expectant on the term granted by the lease" within section 142(1) because the charge did not have the effect under s.87(2) of the L.P.A. 1925 of vesting any term of years in the chargee (and see below, p. 167).

Estoppel

Church of England Building Society v. Piskor
[1954] Ch. 533, C.A.

In September 1946 the defendant contracted to buy a leasehold house and were allowed into possession before completion. In November they purported to grant a weekly sub-tenancy to H. and others. On November 25, 1946, their purchase was completed by an assignment of the residue of the term and at the same time they mortgaged the property by a legal charge to the plaintiffs. The charge recited that the property was vested in the defendants "free from incumbrances" and excluded the mortgagor's statutory leasing powers (see below, p. 184). H. sub-let his part of the property to X. who was entitled to the protection of the Rent Acts. The plaintiffs claimed that H.'s and therefore X.'s tenancy was not binding on them. The purported sub-tenancy to H. at a time when the defendant had no estate created a tenancy by estoppel binding only the defendants. But if the defendants got in the legal estate (by the assignment) prior to the mortgage the estoppel would have been "fed" and H's sub-tenancy would have priority to the mortgage. The plaintiffs claimed that the assignment and mortgage were one transaction and therefore the estoppel was not fed until after the mortgage so that the plaintiffs had priority. It was held that there was a "*scintilla temporis*" (moment of time) between the assignment and the mortgage (and the recital mentioned above supported this) and it followed that the estoppel created by the purported grant of the sub-tenancy was fed by the assignment vesting a legal interest in the defendants so that the sub-tenancy was paramount to the mortgage. The plaintiffs were, therefore, not entitled to possession.

Note: And see *Grace Rymer Investments Ltd.* v. *Waite*, above, p. 121.

4. Covenants in Leases

Implied Covenants

Liverpool City Council v. Irwin [1977] A.C. 239, H.L.

The Council was the owner of a 15 storey tower block in Everton. The defendants were the tenants of a maisonette on the ninth and tenth floors. Access to the maisonette was via a staircase and two lifts. There was an internal rubbish chute. The lifts continually failed to work, stairs were dangerous with no lighting and unguarded holes giving access to the chutes, and the chutes were frequently blocked. The defects were attributable to vandalism and irresponsible action by the tenants. The tenants refused to pay rent. The Council claimed possession. The tenants counterclaimed for damages for breach of the implied covenant on the part of the landlord for quiet enjoyment (see below, p. 132), breach of the implied covenant under the Housing Act 1961, s.32 (to keep in repair and proper working order the installations in a dwelling house) and breach of an implied covenant to keep the common part in repair. The county court judge (who said in his judgment that he was appalled by the general condition of the property) ordered possession, but found for the defendants on the counterclaim awarding £10 damages. The Council's appeal was allowed by the Court of Appeal. A majority (Lord Denning M.R. dissenting) held that no covenant to repair the common parts should be implied. (The Court of Appeal unanimously agreed that there was no breach of the covenant under the Housing Act and the tenants conceded there was no breach of the landlord's implied covenant of quiet enjoyment.) The House was agreed that the courts do not have power to introduce into contracts any terms which they think reasonable or to anticipate legislative recommendations of the Law Commission (as Lord Denning had held). Lord Wilberforce categorised the situations in which a term might be implied:–(i) where there is a bilateral contract (*e.g.* implied commercial useage into a commercial contract); (ii) where *The Moorcock* (1889) 14 P.D. 64 doctrine applies (*i.e.* to give business efficacy to the contract); (iii) he rejected Lord Denning's approach of the implication of reasonable terms; (iv) where the court is concerned to establish what the contract is, the parties not having themselves fully stated the terms. In the present case, since the contract of letting between the Council and the tenants as represented by the standard Conditions of Tenancy which the tenants had signed was incomplete in that its terms were of unilateral nature, it had to be established what the complete contract was. So far as the common parts were concerned, there had to be implied an easement for the tenants and their licensees to use the stairs, a right in the nature of an easement to use the lifts and an easement to use the rubbish chutes. While a servient landowner was not obliged to maintain the subject matter of an easement for the benefit of the dominant owner, where an essential means of access was retained in the landlord's occupation, then unless the obligation to maintain the means of access was placed on the tenants individually or collectively (which was not the case here), the nature of the contract and the circumstances required that it be placed on the landlord. The standard of obligation was what was necessary, having regard to the circumstances. In the circumstances of this case the obligation was to take reasonable care to keep the means of access in reasonable repair and usability. The landlord's obligation applied also to the lighting of the common parts. But there was not sufficient evidence before the court to determine whether or not the Council was in breach of its obligations in respect of the common parts. In so far as lavatory cisterns in the block either flooded or failed to flush properly the Council was in breach of the implied covenant under the Housing Act 1961, s.32, for which nominal damages in the sum of £5 were awarded.

Note: For implied terms in a licence, see above, p. 115.

Landlord's Covenant for Quiet Enjoyment

Owen v. Gadd [1956] 2 Q.B. 99, C.A.

A lock-up shop was let for ten years at a rent of £700 a year. The tenant covenanted in the lease to use the premises only for the purposes of retailing baby carriages, radio sets and accessories and toys. The lease contained a covenant by the landlords that the tenant "shall and may peaceably and quietly hold and enjoy the same premises . . . without any lawful interruption or disturbance from or by the lessors." Three days after the lease was granted the landlords' contractors erected scaffolding in front of the windows and door of the shop in order to carry out repairs to the upper part of the premises which were occupied by the landlords. The poles interfered with access to the shop windows and trade at what would otherwise have been a particularly busy season. The poles were removed after 11 days. The tenant claimed damages for breach of the covenant for quiet enjoyment and the county court judge gave judgment for the plaintiff for 40 shillings. The landlords' appeal was dismissed. Lord Evershed M.R. thought that to constitute a breach the disturbance or interruption had to be of a direct and physical character and that this was so in the present case.

Note: That it has been held not to be a breach of covenant for the landlord to carry on a business on adjoining premises in competition with the tenant (*Port* v. *Griffith* [1938] 1 All E.R. 295, Ch.D. Luxmoore J., where the wool shop was still fit for use as a wool shop even if the profits would be diminished). In *Browne* v. *Flower* [1911] 1 Ch. 219, Parker J., the tenant of a first-floor flat in a block of flats erected, with the landlords' consent, an open-work iron staircase from the garden to the flat entrance on the first floor in such a way as to seriously affect the plaintiff ground floor tenant's privacy. The covenant for quiet enjoyment was not broken. For another example of the covenant see *Aldin* v. *Latimer Clark & Co.*, below, p. 134, and *Miller* v. *Emcer Products Ltd.*, below, p. 209).

Kenny v. Preen [1963] 1 Q.B. 499, C.A.

The defendant, a landlord, gave the plaintiff notice to quit. The validity of the notice was disputed on the ground that the premises were unfurnished and protected by the Rent Acts. The plaintiff refused to go. Thereafter the defendant threatened to evict the plaintiff by letters, shouting at her, and banging on her door. The plaintiff sued the landlord for breach of his covenant for quiet enjoyment. It was held that he was liable as his conduct amounted to direct physical interference with the plaintiff's possession and enjoyment of the premises demised, or, if not, his conduct had seriously interfered with her right to possession.

Note: For the offence of harassment of residential occupiers, see Protection from Eviction Act 1977, s.1(3).

Non-derogation from Grant

Aldin v. Latimer Clark & Co. [1894] 2 Ch. 437

In 1878 M. sold his timber business and leased the premises to the plaintiff for 21 years. The lease contained an express covenant for quiet enjoyment and a covenant by the tenant to carry on the timber business throughout the term of the lease. M. retained adjoining land. In 1892 M. died and his executors sold the reversion of the lease and the freehold of the adjoining land to the defendants. The defendants started to construct an electricity supply system on the adjoining land which interfered with the flow of air to the drying sheds used in the plaintiff's business. The plaintiff claimed an injunction restraining interference. Stirling J. held that the defendants were in breach of the express covenant for quiet enjoyment. They were also under an obligation not to derogate from the grant. Where the landlord demises part of his property for carrying on a particular business, he is bound to abstain from doing anything on the remaining portion which would render the demised premises unfit for carrying on such business in the way in which it is ordinarily carried on. The judge rejected the defendants' argument that the plaintiff had no right of action for derogation from grant unless the defendants had acted maliciously. However the obligation not to derogate only applied where land is to be used for a particular purpose and does not apply if the use of the demised land is unforeseen at the time of the letting.

Note: As to easements arising under the doctrine of non-derogation from grant, see *Ward* v. *Kirkland*, below, p. 220; and note *Bryant* v. *Lefever* and *Nickerson* v. *Barraclough*, below, p. 214 and the *Sovmots* case, below, p. 218.

Tenant's Right of Set-off

British Anzani (Felixstowe) Ltd. v. International Marine Management (U.K.) Ltd. [1980] 1 Q.B. 137

The plaintiffs were tenants under a building lease from Trinity College, Cambridge. They agreed with the defendants to construct two warehouses on the land and then grant underleases to the defendants. The agreement obliged the plaintiffs to make good, at their own expense, any defects in the floors of the warehouses within two years of completion. The underleases were duly granted, but they did not include the provision about making good. There were defects in the floors which forced the defendants to evacuate the building for a while and thereafter restricted the area which could be used. The defendants refused to pay the rent. The plaintiffs sued for rent and possession. The defendants sought to set off against the plaintiffs' claim a claim for unliquidated damages for breach of the obligation to make good. The Master directed that whether they could do so should be tried as a preliminary issue. Forbes J., after reviewing the authorities from *Taylor* v. *Beal* (1591) Cro.Eliz. 222 and including Goff J. in *Lee-Parker* v. *Izzet* [1971] 1 W.L.R. 1688, held that a tenant could set-off against rent if he expended money on repairs which the landlord had covenanted to carry out but failed to do and where the tenant had paid money at the request of the landlord in respect of some obligation of the landlord connected with the land. The tenant must first have given the landlord notice of the want of repair and the set-off must be for a sum certain which has actually been paid and its amount could not really be disputed by the landlord. The right was not strictly one of set-off, which is a creature of statute, but a case where at common law the payment was regarded as payment *pro tanto* of rent. This right was not available in the present case, because the defendants had not paid anything. They claimed a right of equitable set-off. Forbes J. held that this right was one that could be effective against a claim for rent, so long as the cross-claim arose under the lease or directly from the relationship of landlord and tenant. There was such a close connection between the agreement and the lease that it was only fair and just to treat the defendants' equity as going to the very foundation of the plaintiffs' claim for rent.

Note: In *Asco Developments Ltd.* v. *Gordon* (1978) 248 E.G. 683 Sir Robert Megarry V.-C. held that the right of deduction against rent applied to arrears of rent, as well as to future rent.

Tenant's Obligation to Repair

(i) TENANT-LIKE MANNER

Warren v. Keen [1954] 1 Q.B. 15, C.A.

In an action by a landlord against a weekly tenant to recoup moneys expended on repairs to the demised premises the landlord alleged that it was an implied term of a weekly tenancy that the tenant would use the premises in a tenant-like manner (like a tenant from year to year), would keep them wind and water proof, and would make fair and reasonable repairs thereto. The landlord complained of damage to plaster and woodwork, arising out of broken rendering on external walls and leaking window sills. It was held that the defendant was not liable: the only obligation of a weekly tenant, apart from express contract, being to use the premises in a tenant-like manner, *i.e. per* Denning L.J. if he is going away for the winter, he must turn off the water and empty the boiler; he must clean the chimneys, when necessary, and also the windows; he must mend the electric light when it fuses; he must unstop the sink when it is blocked by his waste . . . In addition, he must not, of course, damage the house wilfully or negligently. . . . But, apart from such things, if the house falls into disrepair through fair wear and tear or lapse of time or for any reason not caused by him, the tenant is not liable to repair it. The higher obligation to keep the premises "wind and water tight," whatever that might mean, did not apply to a weekly tenant.

(ii) FAIR WEAR AND TEAR

Regis Property Co. Ltd. v. Dudley [1959] A.C. 370, H.L.

A tenant under a monthly tenancy of a flat covenanted to keep the interior of the flat in good and substantial repair and clean sanitary condition (fair wear and tear . . . excepted). The landlord was responsible for exterior repairs and interior repairs necessitated by fair wear and tear. In determining the rent limit for the flat it was necessary to fix the appropriate fraction (by which to multiply the gross rateable value) and this varied according to the burdens of the landlord and tenant in relation to repair. The House of Lords considered the effects of the exception for fair wear and tear. "Reasonable wear and tear means the reasonable use of the house by the tenant and the ordinary operation of natural forces. . . . It does not mean that if there is a defect originally proceeding from reasonable wear and tear the tenant is released from his obligation to keep in good repair and condition everything which it may be possible to trace ultimately to that defect. He is bound to do such repairs as may be required to prevent the consequences flowing originally from wear and tear from producing others which wear and tear would not directly produce. For example, if a tile falls off a roof, the tenant is not liable for the immediate consequences; but if he does nothing and in the result more and more water gets in, the roof and walls decay and ultimately the top floor, or the whole house, becomes uninhabitable, he cannot say that it was due to reasonable wear and tear": *per* Talbot J. in *Haskell* v. *Marlow* [1928] 2 K.B. 45, at p. 49, approved by the House of Lords.

(iii) EXPRESS COVENANT

Brew Bros. Ltd. v. Snax (Ross) Ltd. [1970] 1 Q.B. 612, C.A.

A fourteen-year lease contained a covenant by the tenant to repair uphold support maintain . . . and keep in repair the demised premises, to pay on demand a reasonable share of the expense of maintaining party walls, drains, etc., and to permit the landlords to enter to view the condition of the demised premises and to repair any want of repair due to the tenant's breach. About a year after the lease a wall of the demised premises tilted and had to be shored up temporarily. The foundations had moved because of seepage from broken drains (probably broken by wartime bomb damage). The landlords ought to have known of the dangerous state of the premises. To make the premises safe the drains had to be repaired and several walls of the house rebuilt at a cost of about £8,000, though the value of the repaired building would not be much more. The landlords and tenants were sued by the adjoining garage owner in nuisance for the obstruction caused to his forecourt by the shoring. As between landlord and tenant, it was held that because the landlords knew or ought to have known of the dangerous state of the premises they were jointly liable notwithstanding the full repairing covenant in the lease. The tenant was liable for the repairs of the drains, but the work that had to be done was more than repair. Whether work was repair was a question of degree to be approached by looking at the particular building, the state in which it was in at the date of the lease and the precise terms of the lease. It was to be determined not by looking at component parts of the work, but by asking whether the total work to be done could properly be described as repair because it was in effect renewal or replacement of defective parts, or whether it was in effect renewal or replacement of substantially the whole.

Ravenseft Properties Ltd. v. Davstone Holdings Ltd. [1980] Q.B. 12

An underlease between the plaintiff and the defendant contained a covenant by the tenant in the very widest terms "when, where and so often as occasion shall require well and sufficiently to repair renew rebuild . . . and keep the premises and every part thereof . . . and all floors, walls . . . " The demised premises were a 16 storey block of maisonettes built between 1958 and 1960. The building was constructed in concrete with an external cladding of stone. No expansion joints had been included when the building was constructed and the stone had not been tied in properly to the building. It was not engineering practice to include expansion joints at the time the building was constructed, but it had later become the practice. In 1973, as the frame of the building expanded, the stonework began to bow away from the concrete frame and there was danger of stones falling. The plaintiff required the defendant to carry out the necessary work. The defendant refused, denying that it was liable, on the ground the damage was caused by an inherent defect in the building, *i.e.* the failure to use expansion joints. Forbes J. reviewed the authorities and rejected the contention of the defendant that if it can be shown that any want of repair has been caused by an inherent defect, then that want of repair is not within the ambit of a covenant to repair. The true test was that it was always a question of degree whether that which the tenant was being asked to do could properly be described as repair, or whether on the contrary it would involve giving back to the landlord a wholly different thing from that which he demised. The proportion of the cost of repair to the value of the premises might sometimes be helpful as a guide. The total cost of the remedial work was about £55,000, of which about £5,000 could be attributed to the insertion of the expansion joints. The value of the building was about £3 million. The cost of inserting these joints was not a substantial part of the cost of repair, much less a substantial part of the value or cost of the building. The defendant was liable for reparation work. It was also a question of degree whether the remedying of an inherent defect was work of repair. Since no competent professional engineer would permit the re-erection of the cladding to be undertaken without the inclusion of expansion joints, it was the only way in which the building could be repaired. Therefore the defendant could not exclude from the cost of repair the case of inserting expansion joints.

(iv) LEAVE TO SUE

Leasehold Property (Repairs) Act 1938

[This provides that where a landlord intends to sue for damages or to enforce a forfeiture in respect of a covenant to keep or put in repair property (other than an agricultural holding) which has been let for a period of not less than seven years, of which at least 3 years remain unexpired, the landlord must serve a notice under the L.P.A. 1925, s.146 (see below, p. 152) and if the tenant serves a counter-notice, the landlord cannot proceed without the leave of the court.]

S.E.D.A.C. Investments Ltd. v. Tanner
[1982] 1 W.L.R. 1342, Ch.D.

A lease for 14 years from 1974 contained the provision (common in a tenant's repairing covenant) that if the tenant failed to repair after notice from the landlord, then the landlord could enter and repair and recover the cost from the tenant. In 1980 the stonework on the front wall of the premises (used by the local Conservative Association) was in poor condition and parts were falling off. The tenants informed the landlord. They were concerned about the insurance position if a passer-by should be hit by falling stonework. The landlord immediately arranged for the necessary repair work to be carried out. (This was not done in pursuance of the right of entry and repair mentioned above, which required notice, but as an emergency measure). The cost of the repair was about £3,000. The landlord served a notice under the L.P.A. 1925, s.146 (see below, p. 152) alleging breach of covenant by the tenants in allowing the wall to fall into disrepair, stating that the landlord had repaired and claiming the cost of repair. The tenants served a counter-notice under the Leasehold Property (Repairs) Act 1938 without prejudice to their claim that the section 146 notice was void. The plaintiff landlord issued a summons to commence proceedings against the defendant tenants. The summons was adjourned into Court. Michael Wheeler Q.C., sitting as a deputy High Court judge, dismissed the summons. The section 146 notice was ineffective, because the section contemplated that where the covenant was one capable of remedy (see below, pp. 153 and following for examples of covenants not capable of remedy) the breach had not been remedied when the notice was given. The scheme of the 1938 Act depended on an effective section 146 notice. There being none, the tenants had no right to serve a counter-notice and the court had no jurisdiction.

Note: The 1938 Act was passed to protect tenants from unscrupulous persons who bought up reversions and then brought pressure to bear on the tenants by an exaggerated list of dilapidations. The section 146 procedure is dealing with forfeiture. This case illustrates the unfortunate (in the circumstances) result of linking the procedure under the 1938 Act to the section 146 notice.

Hamilton v. Martell Securities Ltd.
[1984] C.R. 266.

A lease gave the landlord the right, in the event of the failure of the tenant to carry out repairs in compliance with the covenant to repair, to enter the premises and carry out the repairs and recover the cost from the tenant. The defendant was in breach of a covenant to repair (a road, part of the demised premises) and the plaintiff carried out the repairs, fearing liability under the Defective Premises Act 1972 if anyone was injured on the road. The Leasehold Property (Repairs) Act 1938 applied. The plaintiff landlord applied for leave to take proceedings. The Master dismissed the application on the ground that he had no jurisdiction, considering himself bound by the decision of McNeill J. in *Swallow Securities Ltd.* v. *Brand* (1983) 45 P. & C.R. 328 (where it was held that a landlord's claim in these circumstances was one for damages for breach of covenant and not a claim for debt due under the lease) and *S.E.D.A.C. Investments Ltd.* v. *Tanner* (above). Vinelott J. thought that *Swallow Securities Ltd.* v. *Brand* was wrongly decided, amongst other reasons because the judge had not been referred to either *Bader Properties Ltd.* v. *Linley Property Investments Ltd.* (1968) 19 P. & C.R. 620, Roskill J. or *Middlegate Properties Ltd.* v. *Gidlow-Jackson* (1977) 34 P. & C.R. 4, C.A. Vinelott J. held the claim was one for a debt due under the lease and not one for damages for breach of covenant and accordingly the landlord did not need leave to proceed under the Leasehold Property (Repairs) Act 1938, s.1(3). The judge also expressed the view that the *S.E.D.A.C.* case was correctly decided, though he saw force in the argument which drew a distinction between remedying a breach of covenant to repair and remedying a state of disrepair and that upon the landlord remedying the state of disrepair, the lessee's covenant (in respect of the disrepair) became of the irremediable type.

(v) MEASURE OF DAMAGES WHERE BREACH

Landlord and Tenant Act 1927, s.18(1)

"Damages for a breach of a covenant or agreement to keep or put premises in repair during the currency of a lease, or to leave or put premises in repair at the termination of a lease, whether such covenant or agreement is expressed or implied, and whether general or specific, shall in no case exceed the amount (if any) by which the value of the reversion (whether immediate or not) in the premises is diminished owing to the breach of such covenant or agreement as aforesaid; and in particular no damage[s] shall be recovered for a breach of any such covenant or agreement to leave or put premises in repair at the termination of a lease, if it is shown that the premises, in whatever state of repair they might be, would at or shortly after termination of the tenancy have been or be pulled down, or such structural alterations made therein as would render valueless the repairs covered by the covenant or agreement."

Moss' Empires Ltd. v. Olympia (Liverpool) Ltd.
[1939] A.C. 544, H.L.

A lease by the plaintiffs to the defendants' predecessor in title contained a covenant by the tenant to expend £500 a year on repairs and decoration, or to pay the lessors the difference between £500 and the amount actually expended. Between 1933 and 1935 the defendants did not spend the stipulated sum and the plaintiffs claimed damages for breach of covenant or alternatively for money due under the covenant. The defendants claimed that the covenant fell within s.18(1) of the L. & T.A. 1927 and as there was no diminution in the value of the reversion they were not liable. It was held, reversing the C.A., that the claim was not one for damages for breach of a covenant to repair within section 18(1) but an action for debt under the covenant to pay the specified sum. So the defendants were liable. The defendants had alternatively claimed that the covenant was a bare obligation to pay money not touching the thing demised (see below, p. 158) and so not binding on them as assignees of the lease. It was held that the burden of the covenant ran with the lease.

Covenant against Assignment

Landlord and Tenant Act 1927, s.19(1)(a)

"In all leases . . . containing a covenant condition or agreement against assigning, underletting, charging or parting with the possession of demised premises or any part thereof without licence or consent, such covenant condition or agreement shall, notwithstanding any express proviso to the contrary, be deemed to be subject:–

(*a*) to a proviso to the effect that such licence or consent is not to be unreasonably withheld; . . . "

Swanson v. Forton [1949] Ch. 143, C.A.

In 1937 the plaintiff had let a house to the defendant who had covenanted, *inter alia,* not to sub-let or assign without the landlord's previous consent, such consent not to be unreasonably withheld in the case of a respectable and responsible sub-tenant or assignee. In breach of covenant the defendant sub-let the house furnished to Mrs. M. In 1945 the defendant was granted a new tenancy for two years on similar terms, the breach being waived. The defendant subsequently terminated Mrs. M.'s furnished tenancy and applied to the plaintiff for consent to assign to H.E. who had gone into possession. Twelve days before the tenancy expired and without waiting for the outcome of his application for consent, the defendant assigned the premises to H.E. The plaintiff claimed possession and damages for breach of covenant on the ground that the assignment was void and her refusal to consent reasonable. The defendant, since he was not in occupation, would not have had a statutory tenancy on the termination of the contractual tenancy, whereas H.E. would (see Rent Act 1977, s.2(1), (2)). It was held that it was not unreasonable for a landlord to refuse consent to an assignment in order to prevent a statutory tenancy arising on the termination of the contractual tenancy. But no proper notice of forfeiture had been given under L.P.A. 1925, s.146 (below, p. 152) so the tenancy had not been determined before the expiration of the contractual term and a statutory tenancy arose. The plaintiff was therefore not entitled to possession. And as H.E. was respectable and no higher rent for the premises could be obtained, nor did the plaintiff wish to sell, only 40 shillings damages were awarded.

West Layton Ltd. v. Ford [1979] Q.B. 593, C.A.

A 14 year lease made in 1971 of a butcher's shop with living accommodation above contained an absolute covenant against assigning or underletting or parting with possession of any part, except a letting on a service tenancy or occupancy of the living accommodation to any employee of the tenant or on a fully furnished tenancy with the landlord's consent, such consent not to be unreasonably withheld. Subsequently the Rent Act 1974 gave protection to tenants of furnished premises. In 1976 the defendants acquired the freehold reversion. At that time the living accommodation had been unoccupied for a year. In 1977 the plaintiff (successor in title to the original tenant) sought the landlord's consent to an underletting of the living accommodation. The landlord refused consent, fearing that if the proposed assignees went into possession they would be protected by the Rent Act 1974 and there would be difficulty in regaining possession of the whole premises when the lease expired. The county court judge held that consent had been unreasonably withheld, relying on a test adopted from earlier cases as to whether the assignment was normal or abnormal and, since the lease had several more years to run this was not a "fag end" of the lease type case (see *Swanson* v. *Forton*, above). Allowing the appeal by the landlord, it was held that there was no special rule relating to cases where the proposed assignee would obtain benefits under the Rent Acts. Nor was the normal/abnormal approach correct. The right approach was to consider the purpose of the covenant. The purpose here was to give the tenant the benefit of living accommodation for his staff or no more than a furnished tenancy. The effect of the proposed assignment would be to alter the nature of the property from primarily commercial property with one tenant to property let on a multiple tenancy, namely a shop and independent living accommodation. The refusal was not unreasonable. Whether consent had been unreasonably withheld was a question of fact depending on all the circumstances of the case. Since the county court judge had wrongly thought there were special rules for the Rent Act cases and normal lettings, he had taken into account factors which he ought not to have done and Court of Appeal could interfere with his finding that the refusal was unreasonable.

Bromley Park Garden Estates Ltd. v. Moss
[1982] 1 W.L.R. 1019, C.A.

In 1978 the landlords, St. John's College Cambridge, agreed to lease a residential flat on the upper floors of a building for three years. The ground floor was a restaurant. The tenancy agreement contained a covenant against assignment, etc., without written consent of the landlords. The Landlord and Tenant Act 1927, s.19(1) (above) accordingly applied. The tenancy was subject to the Rent Acts. Later in 1978 the landlord consented to an assignment of the tenancy and subsequently the College sold the building and other properties, subject to tenancies, to the plaintiff. In 1980 the tenant wished to assign the tenancy to the defendant, a barrister. The plaintiff said it was not its policy to permit assignments of residential tenancies and shortly afterwards positively refused consent. The tenant, who was anxious to move elsewhere, took the view that the refusal to consent was unreasonable and assigned to the defendant, who moved into the flat. The plaintiff gave notice under the L.P.A. 1925, s.146 (see below, p. 152), specifying the breach of the covenant against assignment without consent and requiring the breach to be remedied. The defendant remained in the flat. The plaintiff took proceedings for possession. The defendant denied that there had been a breach of the covenant, claiming that the plaintiff had unreasonably refused consent. At the hearing before the county court judge evidence was given that the plaintiff had, since the refusal of the assignment to the defendant, been negotiating with the tenants of the Spagetti House Restaurant on the ground floor of the building for those tenants to take a lease of the whole building. The judge, relying on a statement in Woodfall, *Landlord and Tenant*, held that the plaintiff's refusal was reasonable on the grounds of proper estate management of the building as a whole. On appeal, it was held if the refusal of consent was designed to achieve some collateral purpose wholly unconnected with the terms of the lease, then it would be unreasonable, even though the purpose was in accordance with good estate management. The reason given at the trial for the refusal (*i.e.* the use of the building as a whole) was not something in the contemplation of the parties when the agreement was made and, being collateral, could not be relied on by the plaintiff for refusing consent. In any event, even assuming that the plaintiff was not confined to the reasons for refusal expressed at the time of refusal, it could only rely on reasons which did actually influence its mind at the time of refusal. There were no negotiations with the restaurant tenants going on at the time of the refusal, so that reason could not be relied on.

Bocardo S.A. v. S. & M. Hotels Ltd.
[1980] 1 W.L.R. 17, C.A.

A covenant against assignment without consent in a lease of a flat further provided that if the tenants desired to assign they should first, by irrevocable notice in writing to the landlords, offer to surrender the tenancy without any consideration. The landlord became entitled to forfeit the lease. The defendant tenant sought relief against forfeiture as it wished to assign the lease to one of its directors. It sought a declaration that the provision as to surrender was void as a contravention of the Landlord and Tenant Act 1927, s.19(1). (In *Re Smith's Lease* [1951] 1 All E.R. 346, Ch.D., there was a covenant against assignment without consent, such consent not to be unreasonably withheld, which provided that consent was not to be deemed to be unreasonably withheld by reason only that the lessor at the time of intimating any such refusal may offer to accept a surrender. It was held by Roxburgh J. that section 19 could not be curtailed by any provision in the lease stating that certain things shall not be unreasonable. In *Adler* v. *Upper Grosvenor Street Investments Ltd.* [1957] 1 W.L.R. 22, Q.B.D., the covenant against assignment without consent was subject to a proviso that should the tenant desire to assign . . . he shall before doing so offer in writing to the landlords to surrender the lease. Hilbery J. upheld the proviso. Section 19 had no application to the proviso because it was a condition precedent to, and not part of, the covenant against assignment and section 19 was immaterial because it did not apply if there was an express stipulation (as there was in *Adler*) that consent was not to be unreasonably withheld. The *Adler* formula was upheld by the High Court of Australia in *Creer* v. *P. & O. Lines of Australia Pty. Ltd.* (1971) 125

C.L.R. 84, but dicta in *Greene* v. *Church Commissioners for England* [1974] Ch. 467, C.A. (in which the Australian case was not cited) expressed some doubt as to the correctness of *Adler*). It was held, following *Adler* and the Australian decision, that the proviso was valid. Section 19 had the limited objective of providing that where a lease provided for assignment with the landlord's consent, such consent should not be unreasonably withheld. It did not prevent parties from agreeing that assignment should be prohibited altogether, nor that the tenant should first offer to surrender the lease to the landlord.

Tie Clause

Cleveland Petroleum Co. Ltd. v. Dartstone Ltd.
[1969] 1 W.L.R. 116, C.A.

S. was the owner in fee simple of the County Oak Service Station. On July 1, 1960, he leased the premises to Cleveland for 25 years for a premium of £50,000 and a rent of £10 a year. The same day Cleveland sub-let the premises to County Oak Service Station Ltd., a company in which S. had a predominant interest, for 25 years less three days at a rent of £2,000 a year. The sub-lease contained a tie clause under which the sub-tenant covenanted not to sell motor fuels other than those supplied by Cleveland. In 1968 after several intermediate assignments the sub-term was assigned to Dartstone, who claimed that the tie was void on the basis of *Esso Petroleum Co. Ltd.* v. *Harper's Garage (Stourport) Ltd.* (below, p. 182). Cleveland sought injunctions to restrain Dartstone acting in breach of the tie. In the *Esso* case a distinction had been drawn between a man who is already in possession of the land before he ties himself to an oil company and a man who is out of possession and is let into it by an oil company. It was held that when a person takes possession of premises under a lease, not having been in possession previously, and, on taking possession, enters into a restrictive covenant tying himself to take all his supplies from his lessor, prima facie, the tie is valid.

Note: See also *Alec Lobb (Garages) Ltd.* v. *Total Oil (Great Britain) Ltd.*, below, p. 163.

Rent Review

United Scientific Holdings Ltd. v. Burnley Borough Council [1978] A.C. 904, H.L.

A building lease for 999 years made in 1962 provided for a rent of £1,000 a year for the first 10 years and a rent review clause provided that during the year immediately preceding the period of the second 10 years and each subsequent 10 year period . . . the corporation and the lessee shall agree or failing agreement shall determine by arbitration the sum total of the then current rack rent (as defined therein) and that one quarter of that sum, or £1,000, whichever was the greater, would be the rent for the next 10 years. In another appeal heard together with the Burnley appeal the rent review clause contained a more detailed procedure commencing with the landlord's notice to be given between 12 and six months before the review date. In the Burnley case no rent had been agreed or determined by arbitration before the expiry of the first 10 year period and in the other case the matter had been referred to a valuer, but he refused to accept appointment because the review clause required that he notify the parties of his valuation not less than 14 days before the review date, and that had passed. The issues raised by the appeals were, first, whether the rule of equity, whereby time was not treated as being of the essence of the contract, had any application to a contract in which compliance with a stipulation as to time was expressed as a condition precedent to the accrual of a legal right and, secondly, if the equitable rule applied, whether and in what circumstances stipulations as to time in a rent review clause were deemed to be of the essence. After a general review of the development and fusion of the rules of common law and equity since 1875 (*per* Lord Diplock:– " . . . to speak of the rules of equity as being part of the law of England in 1977 is about as meaningful as to speak similarly of the Statutes of Uses or Quia Emptores . . . to perpetuate a dichotomy between the rules of equity and common law . . . is . . . erroneous . . . (T)he metaphor of two streams of jurisdiction (sc. law and equity) running in the same channel, side by side, but their waters not mingling, was deceptive"), it was held that there was nothing in either of the leases in question to displace the presumption that adherence to the time tables specified was not of the essence of the contract. Accordingly the new rents should be determined by the procedures set out in the review clauses. It was also held that when a new rent was determined it would be payable retrospectively from the review date.

5. DETERMINATION OF LEASE

Notice

Protection from Eviction Act 1977, s.5(1)

"No notice by a landlord or a tenant to quit any premises let (whether before or after the commencement of this Act) as a dwelling shall be valid unless—

(*a*) It is in writing and contains such information as may be prescribed, and
(*b*) it is given not less than 4 weeks before the date on which it is to take effect."

Forfeiture

(i) RESTRICTIONS ON RIGHTS

Protection from Eviction Act 1977, ss.2, 3(1)

"2. Where any premises are let as a dwelling on a lease which is subject to a right of re-entry or forfeiture it shall not be lawful to enforce that right otherwise than by proceedings in the court while any person is lawfully residing in the premises or part of them.

3. (1) Where any premises are let as a dwelling under a tenancy which is not a statutory protected tenancy and—

(*a*) the tenancy (in this section referred to as the former tenancy) has come to an end, but
(*b*) the occupier continues to reside in the premises or part of them,

it shall not be lawful for the owner to enforce against the occupier, otherwise than by proceedings in the court, his right to possession of the premises.

(2) In this section 'the occupier,' in relation to any premises, means any person lawfully residing in the premises or part of them at the termination of the former tenancy.

(2A) Subsections (1) and (2) above apply in relation to any restricted contract (within the meaning of the Rent Act 1977) which—

(*a*) creates a licence, and
(*b*) is entered into after the commencement of section 69 of the Housing Act 1980;

as they apply in relation to a restricted contract which creates a tenancy."

(ii) RELIEF FROM FORFEITURE

(a) Non-payment of rent

Common Law Procedure Act 1852, ss.210, 212

"In all cases between landlord and tenant, as often as it shall happen that one half year's rent shall be in arrear, and the landlord or lessor to whom the same is due, hath right by law to re-enter for the non-payment thereof, such landlord or lessor shall and may, without any formal demand or re-entry, serve a writ in ejectment for the recovery of the demised premises . . . if it shall be made appear to the court where the said action is depending . . . that half a year's rent was due before the said writ was served, and that no sufficient distress was to be found on the demised premises, countervailing the arrears then due, and that the lessor had power to re-enter, then and in every such case the lessor shall recover judgment and execution, in the same manner as if the rent in arrear had been legally demanded, and re-entry made; and in case the lessee or his assignee, or other person claiming or deriving under the said lease, shall permit and suffer judgment to be had and recovered on such trial in ejectment, and execution to be executed thereon without paying the rent and arrears, together with full costs, and without proceeding for relief in equity within six months after such execution executed, then and in such case the said lessee, his assignee, and all other persons claiming and deriving under the said lease, shall be barred and foreclosed from all relief. . . .

212. If the tenant . . . shall, at any time before the trial . . ., pay or tender to the . . . landlord . . ., or pay into . . . court . . ., all the rent and arrears, together with the costs, then . . . all further proceedings . . . shall cease and be discontinued; . . ."

Supreme Court Act 1981, s.38

"(1) In any action in the High Court for the forfeiture of a lease for non-payment of rent, the court shall have power to grant relief against forfeiture in a summary manner, and may do so subject to the same terms and conditions as to the payment of rent, costs and otherwise as could have been imposed by it in such an action immediately before the commencement of this Act.

(2) Where the lessee or a person deriving title under him is granted relief under this section, he shall hold the demised premises in accordance with the terms of the lease without the necessity for a new lease."

County Court Act 1959, s.191(1)

"Where a lessor is proceeding by action in a county court (being an action in which a county court has jurisdiction) to enforce against a lessee a right of re-entry or forfeiture in respect of any land for non-payment of rent, the following provisions shall have effect:–

(*a*) If the lessee pays into court not less than five clear days before the return day all rent in arrear and the costs of the action, the action shall cease, and the lessee shall hold the land according to the lease without any new lease;

(*b*) If the action does not cease as aforesaid, and the court at the trial is satisfied that the lessor is entitled to enforce the right of re-entry or forfeiture, the court shall order possession of the land to be given to the lessor at the expiration of such period, not being less than four weeks from the date of the order, as the court thinks fit, unless within that period the lessee pays into court all the rent in arrear and the costs of the action;

(*c*) if within the period specified in the order, the lessee pays into court all the rent in arrear and the costs of the action, he shall hold the land according to the lease without any new lease, but if the lessee does not, within the said period, pay into court all the rent in arrear and the costs of the action, the order shall be enforced in the prescribed manner, and so long as the order remains unreversed the lessee shall be barred from relief: . . . "

Note: The relief which is barred by section 191(1)(*c*) includes relief under the equitable jurisdiction of the High Court (for which see below, p. 151) so that a tenant, who had failed to pay arrears of rent specified in a conditional county court possession order and been evicted by the bailiffs, was not entitled to seek relief against forfeiture in the High Court (see *Di Palma* v. *Victoria Square Property Co. Ltd.* [1984]; on appeal, *The Times*, 7 May 1985; *cf. Jones* v. *Barnett* [1984] Ch. 500).

Standard Pattern Co. Ltd. v. Ivey [1962] Ch. 432

The defendant was tenant for a fixed term of 13¼years less three days of premises belonging to the plaintiff. The rent was payable quarterly and there was a forfeiture clause which became operative if the rent was unpaid for 14 days. The defendant failed to pay one quarter's rent and the plaintiff, claiming forfeiture, sought possession. The defendant claimed relief from forfeiture. Before the hearing, the defendant gave notice to the plaintiff of payment into court under the Common Law Procedure Act 1852, s.212, and he claimed that proceedings should be stayed under that Act. Wilberforce J. held that section 212 applied only when the rent was six months in arrear (see s.210) and the notice was therefore ineffective to bring section 212 into operation, but the defendant was entitled to relief under the Judicature Act 1925, s.46 (see now Supreme Court Act 1981, s.38) on terms of paying all rent and other sums due and costs.

Gill v. Lewis [1956] 2 Q.B. 1, C.A.

The two defendants were joint tenants of two houses leased to them under separate leases both containing a forfeiture clause for non-payment of rent. The defendants were consistently in arrears with the rent and were sued for the rent by the plaintiff. Judgment was obtained against Lewis only, the plaintiff being unable to serve the other defendant. On May 17, 1955, the plaintiff signed judgment for possession against the other defendant only, for this time she was unable to serve L., on the ground of default of appearance. On June 20, 1955, L. was convicted of indecently assaulting boys on the premises. On July 13, 1955, the defendants paid the balance of the arrears of rent, entered appearances to the plaintiff's possession action and claimed relief from forfeiture. It was held that the judgment of May 17, 1955, was not an effective judgment and therefore there had been no trial within the Common Law Procedure Act 1852, s.212, since it was obtained against only one of two joint tenants, and accordingly as the whole of the rent and costs due had been tendered all further proceedings should cease and be discontinued under section 212. Even if the judgment had been effective, relief would have been granted because in exercising its equitable jurisdiction the court would grant relief when all that was due in respect of rent and costs had been paid, save in exceptional cases. There were no exceptional circumstances here.

Belgravia Insurance Co. Ltd. v. Meah [1964] 1 Q.B. 436, C.A.

S. was granted a tenancy of a restaurant for seven years with an option to renew, subject to a covenant to repair and a forfeiture clause for non-payment of rent or breach of other covenants. S. allowed the drains to fall into disrepair but after threats from the public health authorities repaired them. Then he assigned the lease to the defendants, leaving part of the purchase money outstanding secured by mortgage of the premises made by a legal charge by the defendant in favour of S. The defendant fell into arrears with the rent and the plaintiff forfeited the lease. The premises were in disrepair but no notice under the L.P.A. 1925, s.146 (see below, p. 152) notice had been served in respect of this. The defendant being also in default under the mortgage, S. wanted to exercise his power of sale and assign the lease to N. He therefore claimed relief from forfeiture. As mortgagee, S. was in the position of underlessee (even though the legal charge did not create an actual term (see below, p. 166)). An underlessee can claim relief against forfeiture for non-payment of rent under the L.P.A. 1925, s.146(4), or under the court's general equitable jurisdiction preserved by the Judicature Act 1925, s.46 (see now Supreme Court Act 1981, s.38) or both. There was no difference between the jurisdictions. It was held that S. was entitled to relief on payment of all arrears of rent under the lease, making good breaches of other covenants and paying costs, and on these terms being fulfilled within the period specified it was ordered that the lease vest in S.

Note: See also for claims for relief by mortgagees, *Grangeside Properties Ltd.* v. *Collingwoods Securities Ltd.* (below, p. 165).

Lovelock v. Margo [1963] 2 Q.B. 786, C.A.

A lease of a lock-up fish and chip shop contained a proviso for re-entry in case of non-payment of rent and a covenant against assignment without the landlord's consent. The tenant wanted to assign and asked the landlord for her consent, producing satisfactory references of the proposed assignee. The landlord unreasonably refused consent on the ground that the area of the premises to be assigned was uncertain. Subsequently, when a few weeks' rent was in arrears, the landlord re-entered the premises by peaceably purporting to forfeit the lease for non-payment of rent, and excluded the tenant. Some months later the tenant claimed relief from forfeiture and a declaration that the landlord had unreasonably withheld her consent to the proposed assignment. It was held that (1) a tenant was entitled to relief from forfeiture even where the landlord had re-entered without legal proceedings, the court having an inherent jurisdiction to grant relief independent of statute (see also *Thatcher* v. *C.H. Pearce and Sons Contractors Ltd.* [1968] 1 W.L.R. 748, where the tenant did not bring his action until six months and four days after the landlord had resumed possession) and (2) the landlord had unreasonably refused consent. *Per* Lord Denning M.R., "The test of reasonableness is subjective. The question cannot be considered without having regard to the state of mind of the landlord."

Note: In *Re Smith's Lease* (above, p. 144) Roxburgh J. considered the test of reasonableness to be an objective one. But see *Bromley Park Garden Estates Ltd.* v. *Moss* (above, p. 143).

(b) Breach of other covenants

Law of Property Act 1925, s.146(1)(2)(4)(11)(12)

"(1) A right of re-entry or forfeiture under any proviso or stipulation in a lease for a breach of any covenant or condition in the lease shall not be enforceable, by action or otherwise, unless and until the lessor serves on the lessee a notice—

(*a*) specifying the particular breach complained of; and
(*b*) if the breach is capable of remedy, requiring the lessee to remedy the breach; and
(*c*) in any case, requiring the lessee to make compensation in money for the breach;

and the lessee fails, within a reasonable time thereafter, to remedy the breach, if it is capable of remedy, and to make reasonable compensation in money, to the satisfaction of the lessor, for the breach.

(2) Where a lessor is proceeding, by action or otherwise, to enforce such a right of re-entry or forfeiture, the lessee may, in the lessor's action, if any, or in any action brought by himself, apply to the court for relief; and the court may grant or refuse relief, as the court, having regard to the proceedings and conduct of the parties under the foregoing provisions of this section, and to all the other circumstances, thinks fit; and in case of relief may grant it on such terms, if any, as to costs, expenses, damages, compensation, penalty, or otherwise, including the granting of an injunction to restrain any like breach in the future, as the court, in the circumstances of each case, thinks fit.

(4) Where a lessor is proceeding by action or otherwise to enforce a right of re-entry or forfeiture under any covenant, proviso, or stipulation in a lease, or for non-payment of rent, the court, may, on application by any person claiming as under-lessee

any estate or interest in the property comprised in the lease or any part thereof, either in the lessor's action (if any) or in any action brought by such person for that purpose, make an order vesting, for the whole term of the lease or any less term, the property comprised in the lease or any part thereof in any person entitled as under-lessee to any estate or interest in such property upon such conditions as to execution of any deed or other document, payment of rent, costs, expenses, damages, compensation, giving security, or otherwise, as the court in the circumstances of each case may think fit, but in no case shall any such under-lessee be entitled to require a lease to be granted to him for any longer term than he had under his original sub-lease.

(11) This section does not, save as otherwise mentioned, affect the law relating to re-entry or forfeiture or relief in case of non-payment of rent.

(12) This section has effect notwithstanding any stipulation to the contrary."

Note: In relation to section 146(4), where an original sub-lease of business premises has expired by the time of the application for a vesting order, but the business tenancy has not been terminated in accordance with Part II of the L.T.A. 1954, the Court has jurisdiction to make a vesting order for a new term within the limits of the 1954 Act (see *Cadogan* v. *Dimovic* [1984] 2 All E.R. 168, C.A.).

Scala House & District Property Co. Ltd. v. Forbes
[1974] Q.B. 575, C.A.

A lease for a term expiring at the end of 1981 contained a covenant by the tenant not to assign, underlet or part with the possession of the demised premises (a cafe-restaurant in Soho) without the consent of the landlord and a proviso for re-entry on breach of covenant. The first defendant was a permitted assignee of the term. He wanted to keep the premises, but also run another business elsewhere. He entered into a management agreement with the second and third defendants (the Ds), thinking this would avoid the need for the landlord's consent. The Ds went into possession. In fact the agreement was badly drafted by the first defendant's solicitor and operated as an underletting. The first defendant denied there had been a breach of covenant. The landlord served notice under the L.P.A. 1925, s.146, asserting that the underletting was a breach of the covenant and requiring that the breach be remedied. Fourteen days later the landlord issued proceedings for forfeiture and sought summary judgment. The trial judge held that the breach of covenant (*i.e.* the underletting) was capable of remedy and that 14 days was too short a time for the defendants to remedy the breach. On appeal, it was held that breach of a covenant not to assign, etc., was not capable of remedy and therefore the 14 days between service of the notice and the writ was sufficient. However, relief against forfeiture was granted, on the grounds that an underletting had not been intended, that it did no harm to the landlord, that the landlord could not reasonably have refused consent and that it had since been terminated. Moreover forfeiture would cause a loss to the first defendant (he had recouped some of what he had paid for goodwill on the assignment to him on the underletting) and give the landlord a windfall (because the Ds would be prepared to pay it an increased rent on a new lease).

G.M.S. Syndicate Ltd. v. Gary Elliott Ltd. [1982] Ch. 1

The plaintiff was the freehold owner of 125 Queensway, London. The building comprised six floors and a basement. The upper floors were let to residential tenants. In 1969 the plaintiff leased the ground floor and basement to the defendant for a term of 12½years (but later extended). The lease contained covenants by the tenant against nuisance or using or permitting the premises to be used for any illegal or immoral purpose. The defendant sub-let the basement, with the plaintiff's consent, for use as a sauna bath, gymnasium and health club and with similar covenants to those in the headlease. The sub-tenants assigned the sub-lease to the second and third defendants who by the assignment covenanted with the defendant and the plaintiff to observe the covenants in the headlease during the residue of the term granted by the sub-lease as extended. After the expiry of the contractual term the sub-tenants held over under Part II of the Landlord and Tenant Act 1954 (protection of business tenancies). The sub-tenants permitted the basement to be used for immoral purposes (employing masseuses who "for reward committed lewd and immoral practices at the behest of customers") which caused annoyance, inconvenience or nuisance to the residential tenants and brought the premises into disrepute. The plaintiff claimed forfeiture of the ground floor and basement and damages against the second and third defendants. Nourse J. held that the second and third defendants were liable in damages for breach of covenant, construing the words "during the residue of the term granted" in the covenant in the assignment to include the extension by section 24(1) of the Landlord and Tenant Act 1954. Five hundred pounds damages were awarded to the plaintiff. As to forfeiture, the court refused to grant relief to the sub-tenants. Where the breach involves immoral use the court will not grant relief save in exceptional circumstances (see *Woolgar's* case, below, p. 156). The landlord did not want the first defendant out of the ground floor, if this was possible. The case raised the novel question whether the court had jurisdiction to grant relief in respect of part only of the property comprised in the lease. The judge, relying on *Dumpor's* case (1603) 4 Co. Rep. 119b, held that it was possible for a landlord to forfeit in respect of part of premises. Where, as here, the demised premises were physically separated into two parts, could be let and enjoyed separately and the immoral use had been confined to one part only, the court could and would grant relief.

(iii) WAIVER

Segal Securities Ltd. v. Thoseby [1963] 1 Q.B. 887

The defendant, the lady secretary of the Friends of Canterbury Cathedral, was the sub-tenant of a maisonette in Eaton Place, London, for the residue of a term of 21 years, subject, *inter alia*, to a covenant to use the premises as a private residence in the occupation of one family only. The premises were too big for the defendant herself and from time to time she took in as paying guests friends of hers or friends of friends to share the accommodation. The landlords prior to the plaintiffs had not objected to this. At the material time there were two guests, one sharing with the defendant and the other living independently on the premises. The plaintiffs, as part of a course of harassing the defendant, served a notice under the L.P.A. 1925, s.146, requiring the defendant to remedy the alleged breach (of having persons sharing with her) within 28 days. Before that period had expired, the plaintiffs' solicitors in a without prejudice letter demanded the rent which was payable in advance and due on a date before the notice expired. The rent was tendered but not accepted. When the plaintiffs later claimed possession the defendant contended that the breach had been waived. Sachs J. held that the defendant was in breach in so far as one of her guests lived independently and the breach was a continuing one. The demand for rent operated as a waiver of the breach up to the date of the service of the notice, but did not operate as a waiver of the later breach continuing between the expiry of the notice and the issue of the writ because the plaintiffs had not been shown to have knowledge at the date of the demand for rent that the breach would be continuing after the expiry of the notice. Damages for the breach were assessed at 40 shillings and the defendant was given unconditional relief from forfeiture.

Central Estates (Belgravia) Ltd. v. Woolgar (No. 2)
[1972] 1 W.L.R. 1048, C.A.

The defendant was the tenant of a house in Pimlico, London, under a lease expiring in 1993 at a ground rent of £50 a year which contained a covenant not to do anything in the premises to cause a nuisance or annoyance to the neighbours. The defendant was a pensioner from the 1914-18 War. He let furnished rooms in the house. In 1970 he was convicted of keeping a male brothel on the premises. After the plaintiffs had served their section 146 notice their managing agents instructed their employees not to accept any rent from the defendant. These instructions did not reach the clerk responsible for sending out demand notices. He sent out a demand for rent to the defendant and when the defendant paid the rent gave him an unqualified receipt. The plaintiffs and the agents did not intend to waive the forfeiture and the defendant, when he paid the rent, knew that the plaintiffs' intention to forfeit had not been changed. The defendant claimed that the payment and receipt of rent operated to waive the forfeiture. On appeal, it was held that there had been a waiver. To constitute a waiver it was sufficient if there was an unequivocal act done by the landlord which recognised the existence of the lease after having knowledge of the ground of forfeiture. The intention of the parties was irrelevant in relation to the question whether an existing lease is to continue except for deciding whether the money was received as rent or damages for trespass. Intention is material when the question is whether there is a new tenancy. In the present case the money was paid as rent and accepted by the landlords' agents with knowledge of the breach. A principal could not escape the doctrine of waiver by saying that one clerk had the knowledge, but the one who had received the rent had not. The county court judge had held that there was no waiver, but had granted relief against forfeiture. The C.A. (Buckley L.J. *dubitante*) would not in any event have interfered with the judge's decision. The county court judge had taken account of the fact that the defendant was old and sick, apart from the immoral user of the premises he was respectable, the immoral user had lasted for only a short period, the value of the house had not been diminished and the tenant stood to lose and the landlords to gain a substantial sum in the event of forfeiture.

Note: For another case where waiver was involved, see *London and County (A. and D.) Ltd.* v. *Wilfred Sportsman Ltd.* (below, p. 161).

Surrender

Jenkin R. Lewis and Son Ltd. v. Kerman
[1971] Ch. 477, C.A.

The defendant was a tenant of a farm under a tenancy granted on November 15, 1941. In 1961 he entered into an agreement with his then landlord for the increase of rent. The document was headed "Date of Tenancy Agreement 1st November 1941." In 1965 a further agreement was entered into expressed to be supplemental to the 1941 and 1961 agreements whereby the tenant surrendered a small part of the farm land. In 1968 the rent was increased by a document in the same terms as the 1961 document. The original tenant died in June 1968 and the plaintiff served notice to quit on the defendant (one of the few occasions on which a landlord of agricultural land can serve a notice to quit is within three months of the death of the tenant with whom the contract of tenancy was made, but the Agriculture (Miscellaneous Provisions) Act 1976 introduced a scheme for family succession). The defendant claimed that the 1941 tenancy had been terminated by the subsequent agreements. It was held that the notice was valid because the 1941 agreement remained in existence. On the true construction of the various agreements the parties did not intend to terminate the 1941 agreement. If a tenant accepts a new lease of the same land he is taken to have surrendered the old lease. If the length of the term is to be increased or further land is to be added and a new lease is made this may create a new tenancy. But it is possible to extend the term by a reversionary lease keeping the old lease on foot or to add further land by a new lease of that land.

Note: For the effect of a surrender on a squatter's title, see *Fairweather* v. *St. Marylebone Property Co. Ltd.* (above, p. 55).

Frustration

National Carriers Ltd. v. Panalpina (Northern) Ltd.
[1981] A.C. 675, H.L.

In 1974 a warehouse was leased by the plaintiffs to the defendant for the term of 10 years. The lease contained a covenant by the tenant not to use the demised premises otherwise than for the purpose of a warehouse and provided for the suspension of rent in the event of the premises being damaged by fire so as to be unfit for occupation. In 1979 the council closed the only vehicular access to the premises, because the warehouse opposite the demised premises was in a dangerous condition. In the events that subsequently happened the road was likely to remain closed for about 20 months. (It was still closed when the case reached the House of Lords.) The demised premises were rendered useless during this period. The landlord sued for unpaid rent and sought summary judgment. The tenant sought leave to defend the action on the ground that the lease was frustrated. Both Master Waldman and Sheen J. refused the defendant leave to defend on the basis that they were bound by the decision of the Court of Appeal in *Cricklewood Property and Investment Trust Ltd.* v. *Leighton's Investment Trust Ltd.* [1945] K.B. 493 (the House of Lords was evenly divided as to the application of the doctrine of frustration to leases [1945] A.C. 221, so the decision of the Court of Appeal stood) that a lease could not be the subject of frustration. Sheen J. granted the defendant a certificate under the Administration of Justice Act 1969, s.12 to appeal direct to the House of Lords. It was held, dismissing the appeal, that the doctrine of frustration was in principle applicable to leases, though the cases in which it could properly be applied were likely to be rare. On the facts the lease would have three more years to run after the road was re-opened. The loss was of under two years out of 10 years. Although the dislocation to the tenant was severe, the closure of the road did not so significantly change the nature of the rights and obligations under the lease from what the parties could reasonably have contemplated at the time of its execution.

6. Enforcement of Covenants

Covenants Touching and Concerning Land

Breams Property Investment Co. Ltd. v. Stroulger
[1948] 2 K.B. 1, C.A.

P. and M., two companies controlled by another company, S., were quarterly tenants of part of a building held on long lease from the Hulton Press Ltd. In the course of negotiating with S. a new quarterly tenancy for P., H. agreed that they would not give notice to quit for three years unless they required the premises for their own occupation and this was included as a covenant in the tenancy agreement. A similar provision was agreed with M. but not put in M.'s tenancy. Subsequently H. sold the reversions to the plaintiffs who gave notice to quit within the three years' period, but the tenants refused to give up possession. The defendants contended that the burden of the covenant ran with the reversion. The plaintiffs contended that the arrangement was personal to H. It was held that the provision was not repugnant to a quarterly tenancy (see above, p. 123) and that it did not run with the reversion, applying the test suggested in Cheshire's *Modern Real Property*: " . . . the proper inquiry should be whether the covenant affects either the landlord *qua* landlord or the tenant *qua* tenant. A covenant may very well have reference to the land, but, unless it is reasonably incidental to the relation of landlord and tenant it cannot be said to touch and concern the land . . . "

General note: For other cases illustrating covenants touching and concerning land, see *Manchester Brewery Co.* v. *Coombs* (above, p. 118); *Moss' Empires Ltd.* v. *Olympia (Liverpool) Ltd.* (above, p. 141); *Weg Motors Ltd.* v. *Hales* (above, p. 129); *Woodall* v. *Clifton* (below, p. 321) and cases in Chapter 7.

Assignment of Lease

Spencer's Case (1583) 5 Co. Rep. 16a, K.B.

Spencer and his wife leased land to S. for 21 years, S. covenanting for himself, his executors and administrators that he, his executors, administrators and assigns would build a brick wall on the demised premises. S. assigned the residue of the term to J., who in turn assigned it to the defendant. The wall not having been built, the plaintiff sued the defendant. It was held that the defendant was not liable. Prior to 1926, where the covenant related to something not yet in being, *i.e.* a thing *in posse*, an assignee was not bound by the covenant unless the original lessee had covenanted for himself *and his assigns*. This rule was abolished by the L.P.A. 1925, s.79(1) (see below, p. 243). The case is important because it propounds certain common law rules as to the running of covenants touching and concerning the land which still apply. As to the running of the burden of such covenants, it was stated:

"1. When the covenant extends to a thing *in esse*, parcel of the demise, the thing to be done by force of the covenant is *quodammodo* annexed and appurtenant to the thing demised, and shall go with the land, and shall bind the assignee although he be not bound by express words; . . .

4. . . . if a man makes a lease for years by this word '*concessi*' or '*demisi*,' which implies a covenant, if the assignee of the lessee being evicted, he shall have a writ of covenant: for the lessee and his assignee hath the yearly profits of the land which shall grow by his labour and industry, for an annual rent, and therefore it is reasonable, when he hath applied his labour, and employed his cost upon the land, and be evicted (whereby he loses all), that he shall take such benefit of the demise and grant as the first lessee might, and the lessor hath no other prejudice than what his especial contract with the first lessee hath bound him to."

Boyer v. Warbey [1953] 1 Q.B. 234, C.A.

A lease of a flat for three years under hand only (not sealed) contained a covenant by the tenant to pay the sum of £40 towards redecorating on the expiration of the lease. Nine days before the lease expired the tenant assigned the lease to the defendant, who became a statutory tenant under the Rent Acts on all the terms of the lease so far as they were consistent with the Acts. The landlord claimed that the covenant for payment of the £40 became a term of the statutory tenancy. *Inter alia*, the defendant claimed that because the lease was not under seal the covenant could not run with the land. It was held that nowadays the doctrine of covenants running with the land—or with the reversion—applied equally to agreements under hand as to covenants under seal. This applied to agreements for a lease of three years or less and also to agreements for a lease for more than three years where equity would perfect them, *i.e.* in the *Walsh* v. *Lonsdale* situation (above, p. 116).

Assignment of Reversion

Law of Property Act 1925, ss.141, 142(1)

"(1) Rent reserved by a lease, and the benefit of every covenant or provision therein contained, having reference to the subject-matter thereof, and on the lessee's part to be observed or performed, and every condition of re-entry and other condition therein contained, shall be annexed and incident to and shall go with the reversionary estate in the land, or in any part thereof, immediately expectant on the term granted by the lease, notwithstanding severance of that reversionary estate, and without prejudice to any liability affecting a covenantor or his estate.

(2) Any such rent, covenant or provision shall be capable of being recovered, received, enforced and taken advantage of, by the person from time to time entitled, subject to the term, to the income of the whole or any part, as the case may require, of the land leased.

142. (1) The obligation under a condition or of a covenant entered into by a lessor with reference to the subject-matter of the lease shall, if and as far as the lessor has power to bind the reversionary estate immediately expectant on the term granted by the lease, be annexed and incident to and shall go with that reversionary estate, or the several parts thereof, notwithstanding severance of that reversionary estate, and may be taken advantage of and enforced by the person in whom the term is from time to time vested by conveyance, devolution in law, or otherwise; and, if and as far as the lessor has power to bind the person from time

to time entitled to that reversionary estate, the obligation aforesaid may be taken advantage of and enforced against any person so entitled."

Re King [1963] Ch. 459, C.A.

In 1895 Edward Tagg granted a lease of land and a factory to E. who covenanted to keep the premises in repair, to insure against fire and to lay out all sums received under any fire insurance policy in rebuilding or repairing the premises. In 1907 the lease was assigned to King. In 1944 the factory was destroyed by fire but it could not be reinstated due to wartime restrictions and it was never reinstated. In 1946 the reversion was assigned to Edward Ernest Tagg who in 1960 assigned it to the London County Council after a compulsory purchase order had been made. Subsequently Edward Ernest Tagg claimed damages from King's executors for a breach of covenant to repair and reinstate prior to the assignment to the L.C.C. It was held that King's executors were not liable to Tagg. A landlord, who has assigned his reversion cannot, after the date of such assignment, sue the lessee in respect of breaches of covenant which occurred before the assignment whether or not the breaches are of a continuous nature. Lord Denning M.R. considered the historical background to the L.P.A. 1925, s.141 and held its predecessor in the Conveyancing Act 1881 to be merely declaratory of the existing law under which a breach of the covenant to pay rent caused damage only to the assignor so that he alone and not the assignee could sue for it. But a breach of the covenant to repair depreciated the property in the assignee's time so was annexed to the reversion and only the assignee could sue for the breach.

Note: The M.R.'s judgment left open the argument in *London and County (A. & D.) Ltd.* v. *Wilfred Sportsman Ltd.* (below) and his construction of s.141 as regards the effect of a breach of the covenant to pay rent was rejected.

London and County (A. & D.) Ltd. v. Wilfred Sportsman Ltd. [1971] Ch. 764, C.A.

In August 1961, the freeholders granted leases of Nos. 5 and 6 High Street, Bargoed, Glamorgan, to H. Ltd. for 21 years. The leases contained a proviso for re-entry on non-payment of rent. In September 1961, H. Ltd. assigned the leases to G. Ltd., who granted a sub-lease of No. 6 to the defendant. In 1963 G. Ltd. wanted to assign the leases to M. and licence to assign was granted by the freeholders on G. Ltd.'s guarantee to pay the rent should M. default. The leases were assigned, that of No. 6 being subject to the sub-lease, and then M. mortgaged the lease of No. 5 to the plaintiff. M. defaulted and left the premises. G. Ltd. paid the rent under the guarantee and took the rent due under the sub-lease from the defendant. In March 1965 the plaintiff as mortgagee obtained an order for possession of No. 5. The defendant then extended into No. 5 at the instigation of G. Ltd., who were negotiating new leases from the freeholders and intended to grant a new sub-lease of both premises to the defendant. New leases for a term of seven days longer than the original leases were granted in August 1965 expressed to be subject to and with the benefit of the leases of August 1961. In September 1965 the plaintiff as mortgagee claimed possession of No. 5 from the defendant. G. Ltd. was joined as third party. G. Ltd. claimed that the original lease of No. 5 had been forfeited. No rent had been paid in respect of that lease since G. Ltd. obtained the new lease. The plaintiff claimed that the payments by G. Ltd. under its guarantee were rent, in which case no occasion for forfeiture ever arose. This was rejected. The plaintiff then contended that because the new lease was subject to and with the benefit of the original lease any right of forfeiture had been waived. This too was rejected because an act of the landlord which is not communicated to a tenant or can have no impact on him cannot constitute a waiver. Then it was argued that the right of re-entry did not pass to G. Ltd. when the new lease was granted. It was claimed that G. Ltd.'s rights in respect of rent could only relate to the period after assignment and because the arrears had accrued before then no right of re-entry could arise. The plaintiff relied on an old authority to support this argument and Lord Denning M.R.'s judgment in *Re King* (above). It was held that the L.P.A. 1925, s.141 enabled an assignee of the reversion to sue and re-enter for rent in arrear at the date of the assignment even where the right of re-entry had arisen before the assignment. In the circumstances G. Ltd. had forfeited M.'s lease and had re-entered. Accordingly the plaintiff was not entitled to possession and was left with its contractual remedies against M.

Arlesford Trading Co. Ltd. v. Servan Singh
[1971] 1 W.L.R. 1080, C.A.

In 1966 D. Ltd. granted the defendant a lease of a flat for 99 years. The lease contained covenants by the tenant to pay rent, etc., with the lessor and its successors in title and provided that all obligations of the lessee and rights of the lessor thereunder should be incidental to the reversion expectant on the lease and should pass and devolve therewith. In 1968 and 1969 the defendant was in arrears with the rent. In September 1969 the defendant assigned the lease to J. To enable the transaction to go through, D. Ltd. gave a receipt for rent due in June 1969, but the judge at first instance found that there was no waiver of the rent due. There was evidence that the defendant had agreed to pay the arrears after the assignment. In October 1969 D. Ltd. conveyed the freehold reversion to the plaintiffs, who then sued the defendant for the arrears up to the date of the assignment by him. Applying *London and County* (above) it was held that by virtue of the L.P.A. 1925, s.141 an assignee of the reversion can sue for rent accrued before the assignment. Although, in the present case, there was never any privity of estate or contract between the plaintiffs and the defendant, an original lessee remains at all times liable under the lessee's covenants in the lease, unless there is some special feature absolving him. Neither D. Ltd. nor the plaintiffs could have sued the assignee because by giving the receipt to the defendant, D. Ltd. had represented to the assignee that there was no subsisting breach of covenant. But this representation did not absolve the defendant.

7. VALIDITY OF LEASE

Formalities

See the Law of Property Act 1925, ss.52, 54.

Economic Pressure

Alec Lobb (Garages) Ltd. v. Total Oil (Great Britain) Ltd.
[198] 1 W.L.R. 173, C.A.

The plaintiff owned and ran a garage and petrol filling business. It needed money to develop the site and between 1964 and 1968 mortgaged the property to the defendant three times. Each charge contained a petrol tie in favour of the defendant, the combined effect of the charges being that the tie could not be bought to an end by redeeming the security until January 1983. In 1968 and 1969 the plaintiff was under pressure from its bank and other creditors. Mr. Lobb asked the defendant for financial assistance and suggested that it took a lease of the garage forecourt for a premium and then leased back to the plaintiff. The defendant agreed to lease the premises for 51 years for a premium of £35,000 and a peppercorn rent and to lease back the premises to Mr. Lobb and his mother for 21 years at a rent of £2,250 a year (with mutual break clauses at the end of the seventh and fourteenth years), an absolute covenant against assignment and a petrol tie in favour of the defendant. The object of the leaseback to Mr. Lobb and his mother, rather than to the plaintiff, was to avoid any challenge to the validity of the tie. In 1971 the defendant permitted the underlease to be used as security for a bank overdraft and in 1976 the defendant agreed not to break the lease at the end of the fourteenth year. In 1979 the plaintiff sought to have the transaction set aside. At first instance Peter Millett Q.C., sitting as a deputy High Court judge, rejected claims that the transaction was procured by economic duress (the pressure which the plaintiff was under in 1968/69 had come from other creditors, not the defendant), and was harsh and unconscionable. However, he upheld the claim that the tie in the underlease was an unlawful restraint of trade (see the *Esso* case, below, p. 182). It had previously been thought that a lease and leaseback transaction (at least where there was a substantial reversion) was not subject to the doctrine of restraint of trade. Moreover, if the basis of invalidity of a tie was someone, who was previously free to trade, giving up the freedom, how could this apply here where the tie was in the underlease to others than the plaintiff. However the judge considered the underlease to Mr. Lobb and his mother to be a transparent device to avoid the doctrine of restraint of trade. But the tie clause and other clauses related to the supply of petrol were severable from the rest of the underlease. On the appeal, the trial judge's decision was affirmed as to severability (the main consideration moving from the plaintiff was the grant of the 51 years lease for which the market price was paid and not the restraints) and as to the transaction being neither unconscionable, coercive or oppressive (where there is unequal borrowing power, oppressive or unconscionable conduct must still be proved; her the Lobbs had had legal advice (cf. *Lloyds Bank Ltd.* v. *Bundy*, below, p. 203); and any claim by the plaintiff in equity would have been barred by laches, the delay in making the claim and allowing the defendant to spend money on the premises). However, on Total's cross-appeal while confirming that the grant of the leaseback to the Lobbs rather than the company did not preclude the application of the doctrine of restraint of trade, the Court of Appeal held that the tie clauses were reasonable and valid. The transaction was a rescue operation for the benefit of the plaintiff and the terms adopted to effect that purpose. The property was already subject to tie and as to the future the break clauses could end the lease and the tie.

CHAPTER 5

MORTGAGES

1. TYPES OF MORTGAGE

Mortgage by Demise

Law of Property Act 1925, s. 86(1)(2)

"(1) A mortgage of a term of years absolute shall only be capable of being effected at law either by a sub-demise for a term of years absolute, less by one day at least than the term vested in the mortgagor, and subject to a provision for cesser on redemption, or by a charge by deed expressed to be by way of legal mortgage; and where a licence to sub-demise by way of mortgage is required, such licence shall not be unreasonably refused: . . .

(2) Any purported assignment of a term of years absolute by way of mortgage . . . shall (to the extent of the estate of the mortgagor) operate as a sub-demise of the leasehold land to the mortgagee for a term of years absolute, but subject to cesser on redemption, in manner following, namely:–

(*a*) The term to be taken by a first or only mortgagee shall be 10 days less than the term expressed to be assigned;

(*b*) The term to be taken by a second or subsequent mortgagee shall be one day longer than the term vested in the first or other mortgagee whose security ranks immediately before that of the second or subsequent mortgagee, if the length of the last mentioned term permits, and in any case for a term less by one day at least than the term expressed to be assigned: . . ."

Note: Section 85 deals with freeholds in a similar way. The mortgage must be by demise for a term of years absolute or by a charge by way of legal mortgage. A purported mortgage by conveyance takes effect, if a first mortgage, as a term for 3,000 years, and, if a subsequent mortgage, for a term of one day longer than the term vested in the immediately prior mortgagee.

Grangeside Properties Ltd. v. Collingwoods Securities Ltd. [1964] 1 W.L.R. 139, C.A.

Eastern Trades Ltd. (who were not parties in this action) were heavily indebted to the first defendants. They purported to assign to them a lease, which they held from the plaintiffs, as security for a further loan of £3,000. The assignment was made in a "home-made" document as an apparently out-and-out assignment and not expressed to be by way of mortgage. Eastern Trades failed to inform the plaintiffs of this assignment, and to obtain their consent to it, as required by the lease. When Eastern Trades eventually went into liquidation Collingwoods gave notice of the assignment to the plaintiffs. The latter then served a notice under the L.P.A. 1925, s.146 (see above, p. 152) purporting to forfeit the lease and claimed possession. The Court of Appeal, reversing a decision of Glyn-Jones J., held that the assignment by Eastern Trades, though not expressed to be by way of mortgage, was valid and took effect as a sub-demise under the L.P.A. 1925, s.86(2). The words "by way of mortgage" in s.86(2) did not necessitate that this precise form of words should be present in the document, provided the purpose and meaning of the transaction was to effect a mortgage. *Per* Russell L.J., the use of the word "purported" in section 86(2) indicated that the assignment did not have to be expressed to be by way of mortgage. In the circumstances the defendants were entitled to relief against forfeiture by virtue of the L.P.A. 1925, s.146(4). In particular, the defendants were "mortgagees . . . responsible people who could not have been refused if they had asked their lessor in due time for a consent." Thus, subject to their paying the arrears of rent, they were entitled to an order vesting the lease in them "for the term and subject to the covenants and conditions" contained in the original lease to Eastern Trades.

Legal Charge

Law of Property Act 1925, s. 87(1)

"Where a legal mortgage of land is created by a charge by deed expressed to be by way of legal mortgage, the mortgagee shall have the same protection, powers and remedies . . . as if:—

(*a*) where the mortgage is a mortgage of an estate in fee simple, a mortgage term for 3,000 years without impeachment of waste had been thereby created in favour of the mortgagee; and

(*b*) where the mortgage is a mortgage of a term of years absolute, a sub-term less by one day than the term vested in the mortgagor had been thereby created in favour of the mortgagee."

Regent Oil Co. Ltd. v. J. A. Gregory (Hatch End) Ltd.
[1966] Ch. 402, C.A.

The defendants, Gregory, were the assignees of a lease of 21 years, with 19 years to run. The assignors, Cornwall Garage Ltd., who were the original tenants, had charged the property with the repayment of money lent to them by the plaintiffs and in the charge document entered into various covenants usually found in *solus* agreements, including a covenant to buy fuel from the plaintiffs and not to sell any other fuel. The defendants admitted that they took the property subject to this charge. Two years after the assignment they refused to accept further supplies from the plaintiffs and claimed to be free of the tie covenant. Undoubtedly, the defendants had had notice of the covenants in the charge when they took the assignment. The Court of Appeal, upholding Ungoed-Thomas J., declared the covenants binding upon the defendants on three grounds. First, the attornment clause in the mortgage executed by Cornwall (whereby Cornwall acknowledged itself to be the tenant of the plaintiffs) made Cornwall and later the defendants weekly tenant of the plaintiffs, thereby enabling the covenants to run with the land. Secondly, the court relied on the fact that the L.P.A. 1925, s.87, says that the relationship between a mortgagor by way of legal charge and his mortgagee is to be "as if" the latter were the sub-lessee of the former. This statutory similarity was not confined to powers connected solely with the charge itself. It could, as in this case, govern the passing of the burden of a restrictive covenant contained in the legal charge. In the words of Harman L.J., "the new charge by way of legal mortgage created by section 87 was intended to be a substitute in all respects for a mortgage by demise, and anything which would be good in the one is good in the other." Nor did it make any difference that in the present case the relationship of the parties appeared to be reversed from the normal situation in that it was the grantor of the sub-demise (Cornwall) who was the covenantor and not the grantee. This was an objection without substance because (i) the effect of the attornment clause was to create a weekly tenancy in the covenantor (Cornwall) and thus to complete a re-reversal of the roles of the parties, Cornwall thereby becoming tenant; and (ii) the covenant would in any event run with the land whether it was the landlord or the tenant who wished to enforce it. There was no magic in being one or the other when it came to enforcing a covenant which was in all other respects binding and enforceable; and (iii) the defendants were bound by the covenants on a simple application of the rule in *Tulk* v. *Moxhay* (below, p. 247), in that they took the land with notice of the pre-existing covenant given by their grantor. The qualification upon that decision which had been imposed in *L.C.C.* v. *Allen* (below, p. 248), that the covenantee should have retained adjoining land capable of benefiting from the covenant, does not apply to a case between lessor and lessee so long as that relationship exists. In any event, Harman L.J. was of the opinion that the mortgagee "has of necessity an interest in the land the subject-matter of the charge, which I think he is entitled to protect by covenants relating to the user of it."

Note: For other cases on the nature of a legal charge, see *Weg Motors Ltd.* v. *Hales* (above, p. 129) *Belgravia Insurance Co. Ltd.* v. *Meah* (above, p. 151); and *Cumberland Court (Brighton) Ltd.* v. *Taylor* (below, p. 202).

Equitable Mortgages—Deposit of Deeds

Russel v. Russel (1783) 1 Bro.C.C. 269, Ct. of Ch.

A debtor (who later became a bankrupt) pledged a leasehold with the plaintiff as security for a loan. This was done by a delivery of the deeds and no more. The plaintiff later claimed a sale of the leasehold and argued that he had a lien on the estate. The assignees of the bankrupt, who were the defendants, claimed in reply that to enforce the sale would be to allow land to be charged without writing, which was contrary to the Statute of Frauds. Lord Commissioner Ashhurst remarked "Where the contract is for a sale, and is admitted so to be, it is an equivocal act to be explained, whether the party was admitted as tenant or as purchaser. So here it is open to explanation upon what terms the lease was delivered." Upon the subsequent trial thus ordered the jury found that the lease was indeed deposited as security for the loan advanced by the plaintiff. The court thereupon ordered that the lease should be sold and the plaintiff paid his money. (The report also refers to the later case of *Hurford* v. *Carpenter* (1785) where Lord Thurlow held that the deposit of deeds entitled the holder to have a mortgage, and to have his lien put into effect, even though there was no special agreement to assign the property: "the deposit affords a presumption that such was the intent.")

Thames Guaranty Ltd. v. Campbell
[1984] 3 W.L.R. 109, Q.B.D. and C.A.

A husband and wife were the proprietors of the registered leasehold interest in a house. In 1972 they purchased the freehold interest. The transfer effected a merger of the leasehold in the freehold interest and was expressed to be to them both as joint tenants in law and equity. Before the transfer was registered the plaintiff agreed to lend the husband some money, the loan to be secured by a first charge on "his" property. The husband authorised his solicitors to deposit the certificate of title and pre-registration documents with the plaintiff. The plaintiff did not know of the wife's interest in the property at this stage. She did not consent to the charging of the property or the deposit. The plaintiff then gave the husband further overdraft facilities by offer-letter, the security therefor being expressed—"This facility is to be secured by a first charge on your property." The terms were accepted by the husband signing a copy of the letter and returning it to the plaintiff. In due course the certificate of title and title deeds were sent to the plaintiff and the plaintiff gave notice of deposit of the land certificate to the Land Registry. Subsequently two further loan advances were made to the husband. In each case the offer-letter indicated by its terms that the plaintiff knew that the title was registered in the names of both husband and wife and referred to the security continuing to be a first charge on the property owned by the husband and the wife. Each offer-letter was indorsed and accepted by the husband alone. The husband became bankrupt and the plaintiff claimed to have an equitable charge over the house. It did not assert an equitable mortgage or a lien by deposit under L.R.A., s.66 (below). The wife counter-claimed that, at most, there was only a contract to create a charge, in respect of which the court should not order specific performance, and that the deposit was ineffective. She also claimed rectification of the transfer to delete the words "and equity" on the ground that she had provided all the purchase money. Mann J. held that the creation of an equitable charge depended on the intention of the parties. On the facts, the first offer-letter with acceptance indorsed contained a promise by the husband to charge the property ("is to be secured" were the words used) and not an actual charge. The subsequent letters assumed the existence of a charge and did not create a charge. No charge had been created. While the court could order specific performance of the husband's promise to the extent of his actual interest in the property—the doctrine of partial performance—(*i.e.* to create an equitable charge over his equitable interest in the house) specific performance was discretionary and would not be ordered to prejudice the wife by making her vulnerable to an order for sale by the husband's trustee in bankruptcy under L.P.A., s.30 (see above, p. 100). As to the deposit, an equitable mortgage or charge by deposit could only be created if the creditor had the right to retain the deeds until the debt was paid. Since joint tenants were jointly entitled to title deeds and could only act with unanimity, the plaintiff was not entitled to retain the deeds without the wife's consent and the deposit was ineffective against the wife. Nor was there an equitable mortgage or charge by deposit of the husband's equitable interest because the husband could not unilaterally surrender custody of the documents for the purposes of charging his beneficial interest in the house. Rectification of the transfer was ordered. On the appeal on the ground that the trial judge was wrong in holding that there was not an effective charge over the husband's apparent beneficial interest, Mann J.'s decision was affirmed. The Court (*per* Slade L.J.) indicated that the mere fact that an order for partial performance in such cases would give the chargee a locus standi to apply for a sale under the L.P.A. 1925, s.30 should not, by itself, necessarily deprive an innocent chargee of the remedy of partial performance, but in the circumstances the judge had been right in refusing partial performance.

Note: For examples of other cases where an equitable charge was claimed, see *Thomas* v. *Rose*, above, p. 20; *Swiss Bank Corporation* v. *Lloyds Bank Ltd*, below, p. 246. And on a mortgage by one co-owner, see *First National Securities Ltd.* v. *Hegerty*, above, p. 100.

Land Registration Act 1925, ss.25(1) (2), 26(1), 27(1), 29, 66

"25. (1) The proprietor of any registered land may by deed:

(*a*) charge the registered land with the payment at an appointed time of any principal sum of money either with or without interest;
(*b*) charge the registered land in favour of a building society under the Building Societies Acts . . . in accordance with the rules of that society.

(2) A charge may be in any form provided that:–

(*a*) the registered land comprised in the charge is described by reference to the register or in any other manner sufficient to enable the registrar to identify the same without reference to any other document;
(*b*) the charge does not refer to any other interest or charge affecting the land which–

(i) would have priority over the same and is not registered or protected on the register,
(ii) is not an overriding interest.

26. (1) The charge shall be completed by the registrar entering on the register the person in whose favour the charge is made as the proprietor of such charge, and the particulars of the charge.

27. (1) A registered charge shall, unless made or taking effect by demise or sub-demise, and subject to any provision to the contrary contained in the charge, take effect as a charge by way of legal mortgage.

29. Subject to any entry to the contrary on the register, registered charges on the same land shall as between themselves rank according to the order in which they are entered on the register, and not according to the order in which they are created.

66. The proprietor of any registered land or charge may, subject to the overriding interests, if any, to any entry to the contrary on the register, and to any estates, interests, charges, or rights registered or protected on the register at the date of the deposit, create a lien on the registered land or charge by deposit of the land certificate or charge certificate; and such lien shall, subject as aforesaid, be equivalent to a lien created in the case of unregistered land by the deposit of documents of title or of the mortgage deed by an owner entitled for his own benefit to the registered estate, or a mortgagee beneficially entitled to the mortgage, as the case may be."

Land Registration Rules 1925, r. 239(1) (3) (4)

"(1) Any person with whom a land certificate or charge certificate is deposited as security for money may, by registered letter or otherwise, in writing give notice to the Registrar of such deposit, and of his name and address.

(3) On receipt of such notice the Registrar shall enter notice of the deposit in the Charges Register, and shall give a written acknowledgment of its receipt.

(4) Such notice shall operate as a caution under section 54 of the Act."

Land Registration Act 1925, s.106 (as amended by the Administration of Justice Act 1977, s.26)

"(1) The proprietor of any registered land may, subject to any entry to the contrary on the register, mortgage, by deed or otherwise, the land or any part of it in any manner which would have been permissible if the land had not been registered and, subject to this section, with the like effect.

(2) Unless and until the mortgage becomes a registered charge,—

(*a*) it shall take effect only in equity, and
(*b*) it shall be capable of being overridden as a minor interest unless it is protected as provided by subsection (3) below.

(3) A mortgage which is not a registered charge may be protected on the register by—

(*a*) a notice under section 49 of this Act,
(*b*) any such other notice as may be prescribed, or
(*c*) a caution under section 54 of this Act.

(4) A mortgage which is not a registered charge shall devolve and may be transferred, discharged, surrendered or otherwise dealt with by the same instruments and in the same manner as if the land had not been registered."

Note: The amendment abolished the mortgage caution. See *Barclays Bank Ltd.* v. *Taylor*, above, p. 41. See further for mortgages of registered land, above, pp. 42-45.

2. The Mortgagor's Right to Redeem

Once a Mortgage, Always a Mortgage

Samuel v. Jarrah Timber and Wood Paving Corpn. Ltd.
[1904] A.C. 323, H.L.

In return for a loan of £5,000, the defendant mortgaged debenture-stock worth £30,000 to the plaintiff. The mortgage provided, *inter alia*, that Samuel should have an option "to purchase the whole or any part of such stock at 40 per cent. at any time within 12 months." When Samuel attempted to exercise this option within the stipulated time the Corporation claimed to be able to redeem the mortgage and asked for a declaration that the option clause was void and ineffectual as being a "clog" on the equity of redemption. The House of Lords, upholding both Kekewich J. and the Court of Appeal, held that the defendants were entitled to redeem. In so doing they confirmed, and felt obliged to follow, the traditional view of a mortgage as something unique and unalterable: "Once a mortgage, always a mortgage." In other words, a transaction could not start life as a mortgage and then, *by virtue of some provision in the mortgage itself*, be converted at a later date into some other species of transaction completely foreign to the nature of security. Any provision inserted in the mortgage which fettered the mortgagor's right to redeem on performance or payment of the obligation for which the security was given was repugnant and void; and the present case exemplified the most extreme kind of fettering in that it sought to make the property *completely* irredeemable once the option was exercised. The rule against clogging the equity of redemption is a rigid rule and in the present case the House of Lords applied it with considerable regret.

Note: The House of Lords' own decision in *Reeve* v. *Lisle* [1902] A.C. 461 (where the option to purchase was created after, but independently of, the mortgage) shows that whereas an agreement embodied in a mortgage may not give the mortgagee an option to purchase the property, a separate and independent transaction to the same effect, which would be equally effective in depriving the mortgagor of his equity of redemption, is not tainted with the invalidity of being a clog on the equity of redemption. (But see *Lewis* v. *Frank Love Ltd.*, below). A right of first refusal is unobjectionable (see *Re Petrol Filling Station, Vauxhall Bridge, London. Rosemex Service Station* v. *Shell Mex and B.P. Ltd.* (1969) 20 P. & C.R. 1, Ch.D. (noted in the previous edition), because the mortgagor cannot be compelled to sell.

Lewis v. Frank Love Ltd. [1961] 1 W.L.R. 261, Ch.D.

Here the principle enunciated in the *Jarrah* case (above) was applied to a transfer of a mortgage. The transaction took the form of two separate documents. In the first the personal representatives of a deceased mortgagee transferred the benefit of the mortgage to the defendants, the latter paying off to the mortgagee's personal representatives the sum due to them. In a second document of the same date the mortgagor gave the defendants an option to purchase part of the mortgaged property in return for the defendants' promise not to insist upon repayment of the mortgage debt for two years. Plowman J., holding that "the loan (*i.e.* that which the defendant has agreed to make to the plaintiff and which was about £500 more than the sum paid to the personal representatives) . . . and the grant of the option were all part and parcel of one transaction," granted the mortgagor a declaration that the option was void and unenforceable. The rule against clogging the equity of redemption may thus apply not only to the creation but also to the transfer of a mortgage; and it may bind not only the mortgagee, but anyone to whom he later assigns his rights and who then seeks to superimpose a repugnant condition upon the mortgagor's right to redeem.

Postponing the Right to Redeem

Knightsbridge Estates Trust Ltd. v. Byrne
[1939] Ch. 441, C.A.

The plaintiff, a property company, had mortgaged a large and valuable block of properties in London at 6½per cent. interest. By the terms of the mortgage the loan was liable to be called in at any time. It was a period of falling interest rates, so the plaintiff arranged a loan from the respondents, who were the trustees of the Royal Liver Friendly Society, to pay off the existing mortgage. The new mortgage with the respondents was for £310,000 at 5¼per cent. The plaintiff covenanted to repay the loan by 80 half-yearly instalments. The mortgage deed further provided that in the event of a default on any one instalment the whole of the principal sum with interest to date should thereupon become repayable to the mortgagees. It was additionally agreed that if the mortgagor duly repaid the sum, with interest to date, by the appointed instalments or within 14 days of the appointed day for each instalment (not being otherwise in breach of the agreement in any way) this method of payment would be accepted by the mortgagees who would not require the principal money to be repaid in any other way. Four years later the plaintiff, having found another source of finance at an even lower rate of interest, gave the mortgagees notice of its intention to repay the mortgage debt within six months. The mortgagees refused to accept early repayment and the mortgagors sought a declaration releasing them from the time clause. Luxmoore J. held that the forty-year postponement was a clear infringement of the rule against clogging the equity of redemption. His decision was reversed, however, by the Court of Appeal, who declined to agree with the respondent-mortgagors that a postponement of the contractual right to redeem for forty years was so unreasonable in the present case as to merit being struck down by equity (they had not attempted to argue that such a period, or indeed any period, is *necessarily* void, but only if it fails to fulfil the requirement of reasonableness). Sir Wilfrid Greene M.R. pointed out that to release the respondents from the forty-year clause would mean "that an agreement made between two competent parties, acting under expert advice and presumably knowing their own business best, is one which the law forbids them to make on the ground that it is not 'reasonable' . . . A decision to that effect would, in our view, involve an unjustified interference with the freedom of businessmen to enter into agreements best suited to their interests and would impose upon them a test of 'reasonableness' laid down by the Courts without reference to the business realities of the case." And, after a long review of the authorities, the M.R. concluded that in all the circumstances of the present case the mortgagors had failed to discharge their burden of proving that the redemption date was an unreasonable one. Furthermore, he expressed the view that even had they done so, that alone would not have been enough. When one is dealing with the *contractual* right of redemption, as opposed to the *equitable* right to redeem, there is no rule that the postponement of such a right must be limited to a reasonable time at all: all that is necessary is that it should not subsist for so long as to make the equity of redemption illusory. On the other hand, he acknowledged "equity may give relief against contractual terms if they are oppressive or unconscionable" and in deciding this issue the length of the postponement may be an important consideration. But this represents extreme situations, and equity will not as a matter of generality "reform mortgage transactions because they are unreasonable." Something considerably more than mere unreasonableness is required.

Note: Luxmoore J. had also held that the forty-year period was not void under the perpetuity rule. He was upheld by the Court of Appeal on this point, they being of the opinion that as "the rule has never been applied to mortgages . . . it would not be right now for the first time to hold . . . " that it was thus applicable. Luxmoore J. had further held that the mortgage deed was not a "debenture" within sections 74 and 380 of the Companies Act 1929. The C.A. did not consider this point, but the House of Lords subsequently held ([1940] A.C. 613) that the deed was a debenture and not invalid, by virtue of section 74 of the 1929 Act (see now Companies Act 1948, s.89, below), because of the postponement.

Companies Act 1948, s.89

"A condition contained in any debentures or in any deed for securing any debentures . . . shall not be invalid by reason only that the debentures are thereby made irredeemable or redeemable only on the happening of a contingency, however remote, or on the expiration of a period, however long, any rule of equity to the contrary notwithstanding."

Fairclough v. Swan Brewery Co. Ltd. [1912] A.C. 565, P.C.

In this case it was argued that a provision in the mortgage of a lease with 17½years left to run, which precluded the mortgagor from redeeming at any time earlier than six weeks before the lease was due to expire, was ineffective and illegal as being a clog on the lessee's equity of redemption. The mortgage also contained a clause restricting the mortgagor-lessee to buying the mortgagees' beer for sale on the mortgaged premises. The mortgagor claimed the right to redeem the mortgage before the stipulated time and thence to be free to buy his beer elsewhere. The Privy Council upheld his claim and declared the purported restriction upon his right to redeem to be completely inoperative. In the words of Lord Macnaghten "is there any difference between [the mortgagee] forbidding redemption and permitting it, if the permission be a mere pretence? . . . For all practical purposes this mortgage is irredeemable. It was obviously meant to be irredeemable. It was made irredeemable in and by the mortgage itself."

Note: (1) And see *Davis* v. *Symons* [1934] Ch. 442, Eve J., where a postponement in two mortgages of insurance policies until after the policies matured was void for in effect making the policies irredeemable; (2) for "*solus*" agreements and restraint of trade see below, p. 182.

Collateral Advantages

Kreglinger v. New Patagonia Meat and Cold Storage Co. Ltd. [1914] A.C. 25, H.L.

The appellants, a firm of wool-brokers, agreed to lend the respondents £10,000 secured by a floating charge on the respondents' premises and other assets. The loan was not to be called in by the lenders for five years, provided interest was duly paid and other covenants observed, but the respondents could redeem at any time. In addition the respondents gave the appellants the option to purchase any sheepskins produced by the respondents, for which the appellants were to pay the best price offered by any other person. In the event of the respondents failing to offer the skins to the appellants a commission based on the value of the skins sold elsewhere was to be paid to the appellants by the respondents. This option was to last for a period of five years. Accordingly, if the respondents redeemed the mortgage during the five-year period the situation would result whereby part of the obligations entered into under the mortgage agreement would survive the redemption of the mortgage. After about two years the respondents repaid the loan and claimed to be discharged from the option clause. The appellants sought an interlocutory injunction restraining them from disregarding the agreement. This was refused by Swinfen Eady J. and the Court of Appeal, but eventually allowed by the House of Lords. The House was strongly of the opinion that the old rule, developed in completely different economic circumstances from those then prevalent, that any stipulation in a mortgage agreement other than a stipulation for repayment should be ineffective, was outdated and should be modified in so far as it could be done without permitting unconscionable bargains or reducing the mortgagor's equity of redemption to a mere shadow. In the opinion of Lord Mersey the doctrine against clogging the equity of redemption is "like an unruly dog, which, if not securely chained to its own kennel, is prone to wander into places where it ought not to be. Its introduction into the present case would give effect to no equity and would defeat justice." Such statements of law as that in

Jennings v. *Ward* (1705) 2 Vern. 520, that "a man shall not have interest for his money and a collateral advantage besides for the loan of it," no longer represented the law (the repeal of the usury laws had changed the position). Such collateral advantages were permissible unless, *per* Lord Parker of Waddington: "(1) They were unfair and unconscionable; or (2) in the nature of a penalty clogging the equity of redemption; or (3) inconsistent with or repugnant to the contractual and equitable right to redeem. . . . " These special rules do not apply where the stipulation is independent of the mortgage, being either in a separate transaction or, although in the mortgage deed, independent of the mortgage.

Note: The result might have been different if the appellants had not been required to pay the "best price" for the skins. The character and bargaining power of the parties, the circumstances of the loan, the nature of the security and the nature and duration of any restriction are some of the relevant considerations.

Biggs v. Hoddinott [1898] 2 Ch. 307, C.A.

Hoddinott owned an hotel which he mortgaged to Biggs, a brewer, as security for a loan. The mortgage was to continue for five years, Biggs promising not to call in the debt, and Hoddinott promising not to insist upon his right to redeem the property, during that time. In addition, Hoddinott covenanted to sell only the mortgagee's beer for as long as any money remained due on the mortgage. After two years he claimed, however, to be able to redeem the mortgage and thus to be released from the "*solus*" agreement. This contention was rejected both by Romer J. and by the Court of Appeal. Romer J. refused to strike down the provision delaying redemption for five years, holding that this was a reasonable postponement of the contractual right to redeem. From this decision Hoddinott did not appeal. The Court of Appeal upheld the clause tying the hotel to Biggs' brewery for the currency of the debt. This was not an unconscionable bargain, induced by fraud or undue influence, nor was it one which fettered the mortgagor's right to redeem. It was no longer true that a mortgagee could stipulate only for repayment of principal, interest and costs, and that all collateral advantages inserted for his benefit were universally and necessarily void. The present "*solus*" agreement should be upheld since to attempt to stigmatise it as unconscionable would "shock any businessman" and, furthermore, it did not purport to bind the mortgagor after redemption.

Note: See *Esso Petroleum Co. Ltd.* v. *Harper's Garage* (*Stourport*) *Ltd.* (below, p. 182).

Santley v. Wilde [1899] 2 Ch. 474, C.A.

Miss Santley was the lessee of a theatre, the lease still having 10 years to run. Wishing to borrow £2,000 for the purpose of carrying on the theatre she approached the defendant, Wilde. He realised that if Miss Santley simply mortgaged the lease to him to secure an advance the security would be inadequate. So it was agreed that in addition to Miss Santley repaying the loan over five years she would pay him a third of any rents received by her from under-lettings during the residue of the lease. In other words, as Lindley M.R. described it, his security depended "not only on the solvency of the lady, but also on the success of the theatre." Was this profit-sharing provision, as Miss Santley later alleged, a clog on her equity of redemption and, as such, void? The Court of Appeal unanimously decided that it was not. In the leading judgment, Lindley M.R. distinguished those conditions, designed to secure an additional advantage to the mortgagee, which were repugnant to the idea of security (such as a promise not to redeem) and those that were not. In his opinion the present agreement fell in the latter category. Equity will insist on a mortgagor's right to redeem; but only "on the performance of the obligation for which it is given." In the present case the disputed arrangement was not impeachable for fraud or undue influence; nor was it inconsistent with the nature of security since it in no way clogged Miss Santley's right to redeem her security once she had performed her obligation (*i.e.* repaid the £2,000 and the share of the profits) for which that security had originally been given. The law, in the court's view, had hitherto become rather confused by dicta which suggested that a mortgagee could not stipulate for any collateral advantage (*i.e.* other than repayment of the loan with interest), *at all.* The true position was that such an advantage could be stipulated for, and enforced, provided it did not purport to take away, or severely impair, the mortgagor's right to redeem; assuming, even though it did not thus fetter him, that it was not oppressive and unconscionable. Furthermore, there was no general rule that the collateral advantage contained in a mortgage is *presumed* to be oppressive and must be shown by the mortgagee not to be so before it can be enforced (Romer L.J.).

Note: This decision is difficult to reconcile with others on the same subject and was criticised in *Noakes* v. *Rice* (below). It has been suggested that it is best regarded as dealing with a transaction which "was not in essence one of mortgage, but a partnership agreement to share in the profits of the theatre."

Noakes & Co. Ltd. v. Rice [1902] A.C. 24, H.L.

Rice purchased a 26-year lease on a "free" public house and granted Noakes & Co. a mortgage of the lease in return for their advancing him part of the purchase-money. A clause in the mortgage agreement committed him and all persons deriving title under him to buy all his malt liquor from the mortgagees *for the duration of the lease, whether he had already repaid the mortgage-debt or not* (*cf. Biggs* v. *Hoddinott*, above, whether the tie was to last only as long as the mortgage). Rice sought a declaration to the effect that once he had repaid the loan and interest the property should re-vest in him completely free from the latter obligation. Cozens-Hardy J. and the Court of Appeal granted this declaration; the mortgagees then appealed to the House of Lords. They claimed that a collateral advantage which is not oppressive will be enforced, and that the whole question was one of the reasonableness of the transaction. Provided the equity of redemption was not clogged, conditions could be added which either increased what was to be paid by the mortgagor, or (as in the present case) subtracted from what the mortgagee restored to the mortgagor at the end of the day. The mortgagor denied this and claimed that the disputed clause was "unconscionable in the extreme" since he had purchased a "free" house and would get back a "tied" one; furthermore, no other brewery would ever lend him money on the security of a house that was tied elsewhere. The House of Lords preferred the latter view. They held that the clause did constitute a clog on the equity of redemption and that repayment of the debt would release the mortgagor from the "*solus*" agreement. Lord Halsbury L.C. sought to explain away the decision in *Santley* v. *Wilde* (above) as turning on its own particular facts. Lord Macnaghten, on the other hand, clearly thought the decision was contrary to principle and wrong, since the profit-sharing clause effectually rendered redemption impossible. Lord Davey, who was of the opinion that collateral advantages are only void if they clog the equity of redemption or are unfair or oppressive between the parties, clearly thought that the profit-sharing clause offended the first of these two conditions. Lord Lindley regarded the decision as perfectly consistent with the outcome in the present case, in which he concurred, and as good law.

Bradley v. Carritt [1903] A.C. 253, H.L.

Bradley mortgaged to Carritt (a tea-broker) the shares which gave Bradley a controlling interest in a tea company. One of the terms of the mortgage was if the mortgagor defaulted the mortgagee could take over the shares in satisfaction of the debt. This was a clog on the equity to redeem and therefore bad. Another clause provided that the mortgagee should always remain broker to the company thereafter and the mortgagor covenanted to use his best endeavours to secure that the mortgagee or his firm should have the sale of the mortgagor's teas and to reimburse Carritt to the extent of any lost commission if the company used any other broker. It was held by the House of Lords (Lords Lindley and Shand dissenting) that once the mortgagor had paid off the mortgage he should be released from the covenant, even though the covenant was not of such a type as could in any circumstances "run" with the mortgaged property. To the majority, the degree of deterrent which this clause provided against redemption was sufficient to constitute a fetter upon the power to redeem, Lord Macnaghten explaining that since to enforce the promise the mortgagor would have to retain control of the shares after redemption, this indirectly impeded him from recovering them free from the mortgage. Both he and Lord Davey expressed the view that since collateral advantages are only another form of interest they must *ex hypothesi* cease when the debt is discharged.

Note: See, however, the *Kreglinger* case (above, p. 176). It is not easy to reconcile the two cases (save perhaps on the ground that the covenant in *Bradley* v. *Carritt* bound all the mortgaged property and reduced its value after redemption, while in *Kreglinger* the option affected only a part of the mortgaged property and the price for the skins was not less than the borrower could get elsewhere). *Bradley* v. *Carritt* is the high-water mark of a judicial attitude which was already changing by the time of *Biggs* v. *Hoddinott*. The new attitude was fully expressed in *Kreglinger*.

Cityland and Property (Holdings) Ltd. v. Dabrah
[1968] Ch. 166

Mr. Dabrah purchased a house from the plaintiffs for £3,500. Since he could raise only £600 the plaintiffs agreed that if he would mortgage the house to them for the sum of £4,553 and "repay" this sum to them in monthly instalments spread over six years, they would advance him the remaining £2,900 needed to raise the price. A legal charge was duly executed. After a year D. fell into arrears and the company took out a summons claiming payment of all moneys due with interest at 5 per cent. (the original agreement having made no stipulation as to interest). D. claimed that as the document he signed did not contain the words "by way of legal charge" it could not constitute a legal mortgage of the property charged. The property was registered land. D.'s contention was, however, abandoned by his counsel and specifically rejected by Goff J., referring to the L.R.A. 1925, s.27(1) (above, p. 171). There is no need *in the case of registered land* for the words "by way of legal charge" to appear in the deed. (The same has been held to apply in a case in respect of *unregistered* land (see *Sopher* v. *Mercer* [1967] C.L.Y. 2543).) D. also alleged that the "premium" demanded by the plaintiffs (*i.e.* the difference between the £2,900 they had advanced him and the £4,553 he had bound himself to repay) was unconscionable and oppressive. (The premium amounted to 57 per cent. of the loan and had it represented interest the rate would be 19 per cent., or 38 per cent. taking into account that, on default, the balance became payable forthwith.) Goff J. held that the premium was oppressive and unreasonable, particularly since the whole balance of both it and the loan became instantly repayable on default: he further held that the excessive nature of the premium destroyed the equity of redemption by ensuring that nothing would be left over if and when the property were sold and the mortgage-debt discharged. He emphasised the fact that the case was not one between two large commercial concerns, but involved a man of limited means buying his own house. Accordingly, he declared that on their money claim the plaintiff-mortgagees were entitled only to repayment of their £2,900 with interest at 7 per cent. per annum from the date of the advance minus those repayments already made by Mr. Dabrah. An order for possession was also made.

Multiservice Bookbinding Ltd. v. Marden
[1978] Ch. 84

In 1966 the plaintiff needed £36,000 to finance the purchase of new premises. The defendant, who had recently sold his business and wished to invest some £40,000 in real property for his retirement, agreed to lend £36,000 to the plaintiff secured by mortgage on the new premises. The mortgage provided for repayment of principal by instalments, for payment of interest at 2 per cent. above bank rate on £36,000 notwithstanding any repayments, for arrears of interest to be capitalised after 21 days and themselves to bear interest, that the loan could not be either called in or redeemed for the first 10 years and for the amount of the principal and interest to be linked to the rate of exchange of the Swiss franc to the pound sterling. In 1966 the rate of exchange was 12 Swiss francs to the pound. In 1976 (the earliest redemption date possible under the mortgage) the plaintiff gave notice to redeem. It subsequently commenced a redemption action claiming that the Swiss franc "uplift clause" was contrary to public policy and other clauses in the mortgage, taken as a whole, were unreasonable. By 1976 the rate of exchange was about 4 Swiss francs to the pound. About £24,355 of the principal had been repaid, but after adding the Swiss franc uplift a further £63,202 principal was due. Interest payable under the mortgage totalled £45,380 made up as to £31,051 basic interest plus £14,329 uplift. The average rate of interest over 10 years was 16.01 per cent. or, 33.33 per cent. if all the uplift was treated as an interest charge for the £36,000. On the other hand the premises were shown in the plaintiff's books at a value of £93,075 and the business had done well. In the judge's view there was not much difference between the rate of capital growth of the premises and of the loan. Browne-Wilkinson J. held that an index-linked money obligation was not contrary to public policy. As to the other terms there was no general rule that collateral advantages in a mortgage had to be reasonable. The correct test was whether a term was unfair and unconscionable, not one of reasonableness. The judge did not think that Goff J. by his reference to "unreasonable" in the *Cityland* case (above) had intended to cut down the effect of the *Kreglinger* and *Knightsbridge Estates* cases. (The judge thought the combination of uplift and 2 per cent. above bank rate was unreasonable. But the test was not unreasonableness). The Swiss franc uplift was not a premium or collateral advantage. It was no more than a stipulation for the repayment of principal. Generally, there was no great inequality of bargaining power between the parties. The plaintiff was advised by solicitors. The terms of mortgage were not unfair, oppressive or morally reprehensible. The court could not rewrite the mortgage which was unobjectionable when entered into, merely because hardship would be caused to the plaintiff by the dramatic fall in the value of the pound not foreseen in 1966.

Restraint of Trade

Esso Petroleum Co. Ltd. v. Harper's Garage (Stourport) Ltd. [1968] A.C. 269, H.L.

Harper owned two garages and had entered into two "*solus*" agreements with the plaintiff, one in respect of each garage. The first agreement bound Harper to selling only Esso petrols and oils for a period of four years and five months at the garage to which it applied. The second agreement imposed a similar obligation but was for 21 years and was supported by two subsequent and interdependent transactions–a loan agreement whereby Esso agreed to lend Harper £7,000 and he promised again to buy all his motor fuel requirements from them until both loan and interest were repaid and to execute a mortgage in their favour securing the loan, and the mortgage referred to, executed four months later, which provided for repayment by way of instalments and postponed Harper's contractual right of redemption for a period of 21 years. Accordingly, not only was Harper bound to keep the mortgage alive for 21 years, but he was also committed to maintaining the "*solus*" agreement on the second garage for the same period. Both "*solus*" agreements granted Harper a rebate of 1 ¼d. on each gallon of Esso sold and, *inter alia*, bound him to remain open at reasonable hours. When cut-price petrol appeared Harper changed to different suppliers. Esso then sought to enforce the agreements and mortgage. H. claimed that the ties in the agreements and the mortgage were in restraint of trade and, therefore, unlawful. The House of Lords held that "*solus*" agreements were just as susceptible to the doctrine of restraint of trade as vendor-purchaser or master-servant agreements. They distinguished the "tied house" cases by pointing out that there the person restrained (usually the mortgagor of a newly acquired public-house) was not giving up any right he previously had and thus in no way had his rights of trading restrained or impaired. "Restraint of trade appears to me to imply that a man contracts to give up some freedom which otherwise he would have had. A person buying or leasing land has no previous right to be there at all, let alone to trade there, and when he takes possession of that land subject to a negative restrictive covenant he gives up no right or freedom which he previously had. I think that the tied house cases might be explained in this way, apart from *Biggs* v. *Hoddinott* (above, p. 177) . . . [where] . . . restraint of trade was not pleaded. If it had been, the restraint would probably have been held to be reasonable." (*Per* Lord Reid; followed in *Cleveland Petroleum Co. Ltd.* v. *Dartstone Ltd*, above, p. 145). Nor did the fact that one of the agreements was linked to a mortgage of premises in any way operate to exclude the doctrine. It can apply equally to covenants in mortgages as to those contained in ordinary contracts. The House of Lords held that in view of the various relevant criteria (stability of Esso's distribution system, corporate efficiency and economy, and, primarily, according to Lord Hodson, the public interest) the four-year agreement was not unduly long and could be upheld. However, Esso had failed to show that the 21-year agreement did not go beyond what was necessary and reasonable to provide them with adequate protection for their interests and to sustain the requirements of public interest. Therefore, both the agreements relating to the mortgaged garage were void and the mortgage itself could be redeemed, since "the '*solus*' agreement, the loan agreement and the mortgage can be linked together as incidents of one transaction."

Note: In *Texaco Ltd.* v. *Mulberry Filling Station Ltd.* [1972] 1 W.L.R. 814, Ch.D., Ungoed-Thomas J. held that a tie in a mortgage for a period of four years and seven months was enforceable. He laid some emphasis on the fact that in these cases the garage is getting a loan at a low rate of interest. See also *Alec Lobb (Garages) Ltd.* v. *Total Oil (Great Britain) Ltd*, above, p. 163.

3. LEASES BY THE MORTGAGOR

Law of Property Act 1925, s.99

"(1) A mortgagor of land while in possession shall, as against every incumbrancer, have power to make from time to time any such lease of the mortgaged land, or any part thereof, as is by this section authorised.

(3) The leases which this section authorises are:

(i) agricultural or occupation leases for any term not exceeding twenty-one years, or, in the case of a mortgage made after the commencement of this Act, fifty years; and

(ii) building leases for any term not exceeding ninety-nine years, or, in the case of a mortgage made after the commencement of this Act, nine hundred and ninety-nine years

(7) Every such lease shall contain a covenant by the lessee for payment of the rent, and a condition of re-entry on the rent not being paid within a time therein specified not exceeding thirty days.

(11) In case of a lease by the mortgagor, he shall, within one month after making the lease, deliver to the mortgagee, or, where there are more than one, to the mortgagee first in priority, a counterpart of the lease duly executed by the lessee, but the lessee shall not be concerned to see that this provision is complied with.

(13) This section applies only if and as far as a contrary intention is not expressed by the mortgagor and mortgagee in the mortgage deed, or otherwise in writing, and has effect subject to the terms of the mortgage deed or of any such writing and to the provisions therein contained.

(14) The mortgagor and mortgagee may, by agreement in writing, whether or not contained in the mortgage deed, reserve to or confer on the mortgagor or the mortgagee, or both, any further or other powers of leasing or having reference to leasing; and any

further or other powers so reserved or conferred shall be exercisable, as far as may be, as if they were conferred by this Act, and with all the like incidents, effects, and consequences: . . .

(17) The provisions of this section referring to a lease shall be construed to extend and apply, as far as circumstances admit, to any letting, and to an agreement, whether in writing or not, for leasing or letting."

Note: In *Rhodes* v. *Dalby* [1971] 1 W.L.R. 1325, Ch.D., Goff J. held that section 99(7), (11) did not apply to oral tenancies. And see *Pawson* v. *Revell* [1958] 2 Q.B. 360, C.A., for the application of the L.P.A. 1925, s.152 (below, p. 282) to validate an oral tenancy without a provision for re-entry.

Taylor v. Ellis [1960] Ch. 368

Albert and William John Ellis were the personal representatives of William Ellis, deceased. In 1924 they mortgaged a property, part of the deceased's estate, to Taylor to secure a loan of £250. The mortgage expressly forbade the mortgagors from leasing the property without first obtaining the mortgagee's written consent. Sixteen years later (William John Ellis having died) Albert Ellis leased the property to one Hayler. The tenancy was terminable by one month's notice on either side. Albert died three years later and by 1950 only one of his own personal representatives (Lionel Ellis) was left alive. It was in this year that Taylor was last paid any interest due to him under the mortgage. Taylor died in 1957. His personal representatives then sued Lionel Ellis (as the person entitled to redeem the mortgage) and the tenant Hayler (who still occupied the premises) for possession. Counsel for Hayler argued (a) that the burden should be upon the mortgagee, as plaintiff, to prove that his consent to the tenancy was never given; (b) that whether consent was actually given or not, a mortgagee must be taken to have waived a provision in the mortgage against leasing when, as here, the tenancy had subsisted *with the knowledge of the mortgagee* for 19 years. Cross J. rejected these contentions and granted the plaintiffs an order for possession. He held that in the absence of any evidence that the mortgagee *did* consent in writing, the court was bound to conclude that he did not. Secondly, he expressed the view that the present case did not fall within the same category as those, for instance, where the mortgagee serves notice on the tenant to pay the rent to him in future and not to the mortgagor. In such a case a mortgagee would be bound by the tenancy he had thus recognised: here he was not.

Lever Finance Ltd. v. Needlemans' Trustee and Kreutzer
[1956] 1 Ch. 375

"It is clear law that a mortgagee is not concerned, in a case where he wishes to take possession, with persons he may find upon the premises unless they are there in some way with his consent, because he is concerned only with the mortgagor." The mortgage made by Harry and Leslie Needleman excluded the power of leasing conferred on a mortgagor by the L.P.A. 1925, s.99 unless the mortgagors first obtained the mortgagees' consent and went on to provide that not only need this consent not be recited in the lease itself but "nor shall any lessee be concerned to see that any such consent has been given." The Needlemans had sub-let the premises for 21 years to L. without consent. L. had later assigned the sub-lease to Mrs. Kreutzer and her daughter. The plaintiffs (who were transferees of the original mortgagees) sought to eject the Kreutzers on the ground that the lease assigned to them had been granted without the mortgagees' consent. The first defendant (the Needlemans' trustee in bankruptcy) did not oppose the action, but Mrs. Kreutzer claimed that the words in the mortgage which absolved a lessee from being concerned to see whether the consent had been given protected her. The failure to obtain consent was a matter purely between mortgagor and mortgagee and did not affect her tenancy. Harman J. upheld this defence. The words relied on by Mrs. Kreutzer created an estoppel against the mortgagees, since they represented that she need not inquire into whether consent had been given. Moreover, she could properly claim to have entered into possession in reliance on that representation and thus was entitled to say: "I am in under a lease for 21 years which you may not deny was granted with your consent."

Note: Although the judge declared the above reason to be the basis of his decision, he went on to remark *obiter* that the receipt of rent from the Kreutzers by a properly appointed receiver (who had been appointed by the plaintiffs shortly after the transfer of the mortgage to them) did not, *semble*, constitute a recognition of any tenancy enjoyed by the Kreutzers, as by virtue of the L.P.A. 1925, s.109 (below, p. 199) such receiver was to be regarded as the agent of the mortgagor and not of the mortgagee. In fact, the plaintiffs lacked in the present case the authority to appoint a receiver since they had not at the time been registered as proprietors of the legal charge. Thus the receiver remained the plaintiffs' agent and the receipt of rent by him from the Kreutzers constituted a recognition by the plaintiffs that some tenancy existed.

4. MORTGAGEE'S RIGHTS AND REMEDIES

Sale

(i) STATUTORY PROVISIONS

Law of Property Act 1925, ss.101(1)(3)(4), 103

"101. (1) A mortgagee, where the mortgage is made by deed, shall, by virtue of this Act, have the following powers, to the like extent as if they had been in terms conferred by the mortgage deed, but not further (namely):

(i) A power, when the mortgage money has become due, to sell . . . the mortgaged property . . .

(3) The provisions of this Act relating to the foregoing powers, comprised either in this section, or in any other section regulating the exercise of those powers, may be varied or extended by the mortgage deed . . .

(4) This section applies only if and as far as a contrary intention is not expressed in the mortgage deed, and has effect subject to the terms of the mortgage deed and to the provisions therein contained.

103. A mortgagee shall not exercise the power of sale conferred by this Act unless and until:–

(i) Notice requiring payment of the mortgage money has been served on the mortgagor or one of two or more mortgagors, and default has been made in payment of the mortgage money, or of part thereof, for three months after such service; or

(ii) Some interest under the mortgage is in arrear and unpaid for two months after becoming due; or

(iii) There has been a breach of some provision contained in the mortgage deed or in this Act, or in an enactment replaced by this Act, and on the part of the mortgagor, or of some person concurring in making the mortgage, to be observed or performed, other than and besides a covenant for payment of the mortgage money or interest thereon.".

Land Registration Act 1925, s.34(1)

"Subject to any entry on the register to the contrary, the proprietor of a charge shall have and may exercise all the powers conferred by law as the owner of a legal mortgage."

Note: For sale by an equitable mortgagee, see *Re White Rose Cottage* (above, p. 42).

(ii) MORTGAGEE'S DUTY

Cuckmere Brick Co. Ltd. v. Mutual Finance Ltd.
[1971] Ch. 949, C.A.

The plaintiffs, a development company, borrowed £50,000 from the defendant bank on the security of a building site of about 2.65 acres on the outskirts of Maidstone. The defendants also agreed to advance further sums, up to £50,000, on the same security. There was planning permission to build 100 flats on the site. The plaintiffs, being short of capital, were unable to start work on the flats and it was proposed to build 33 houses on part of the site instead of the flats. The mortgage provided that flats should be erected, but the defendants agreed to the change of plan. Planning permission was obtained for the erection of houses. But five years after the mortgage the plaintiffs had still not commenced work, so the defendants called in the mortgage. The plaintiffs could not pay, the defendants took possession and put the site up for sale. The defendants and their agents were aware of both planning permissions and that flat development was more profitable. In advertising the site for sale no mention was made of the permission for flat development. The plaintiffs pointed this out to the defendants and asked them to postpone the auction, but they paid no regard. The defendants' agents advised them that the site would probably fetch about £35,000 or more for flat development, but they were against such development because of the position and sales resistance to flats as compared with houses. But another firm of agents, who gave valuations for the defendants for mortgage purposes, considered the site to be worth upwards of £50,000 or, perhaps, £70,000 for flat development or £50,000 for house development. Two agents for the plaintiff considered the site to be suitable for flats and valued it at £65,000 and £75,000 respectively on that basis. The defendants were aware of the various valuations but they still failed to refer to the permission for flats in advertisements. Accordingly flat developers were not present at the auction when this permission was mentioned before the site was sold for £44,000. The plaintiff and its guarantor claimed that the defendants had failed to take reasonable precautions in the exercise of their power of sale and an account on the basis that the defendants should be debited with the price that could and should have obtained for the site. Plowman J. held that the defendants had failed in their duty by ignoring the permission for flats and in refusing to postpone the sale. Referring to Lindley L.J.'s test in *Kennedy* v. *De Trafford* [1896] 1 Ch. 762, C.A.; affd. [1897] A.C. 180, H.L., that the duty of a selling mortgagee is not fraudulently, wilfully or recklessly to sacrifice the interests of the mortgagor, he found the defendants guilty of recklessness (which he equated with gross negligence). The defendants appealed. The court reviewed the earlier authorities, some of which were difficult to reconcile. They confirmed that the selling mortgagee is not a trustee for the mortgagor. Subject to this, there was a conflict between some earlier authorities, on the one hand that the mortgagee merely has to act in good faith, *i.e.* not fraudulently, wilfully or recklessly (see *Kennedy* v. *De Trafford*, mentioned above), and on the other that the mortgagee has a duty to take reasonable care to obtain whatever is the true market value of the property at the moment he chooses to sell (see *Tomlin* v. *Luce* (1889) 43 Ch.D. 191, C.A., where a mortgagee had misdescribed the property and had to make an allowance to the purchaser off the price and was held liable to the mortgagor for the difference, and *Wolff* v. *Vanderzee* (1869) 20 L.T. 350, where Stuart V.-C. held that a mortgagee was accountable to the mortgagor for the loss in purchase price occasioned by the negligence of the auctioneer employed for the sale who had stated that the property was let at a rent lower than the rent in fact paid, neither of which was cited in *Kennedy* v. *De Trafford*). The court preferred the latter line of cases. *Per* Salmon L.J.: " . . . a mortgagee, in exercising his power of sale, does owe a duty to take reasonable precaution to obtain the true market value of the mortgaged property at the date on which he decides to sell." Cairns L.J. described the duty as one "to take reasonable care to obtain a proper price for the land in the interest of the mortgagors." Salmon and Cairns L.JJ. held that the defendants and their agents had been negligent. Cross L.J. held that they had merely been guilty of an error of judgment. The defendants further contended that they had discharged their duty by going to reputable agents. Salmon and Cairns L.JJ. held that it was not open to the defendants to argue this point as it had not been taken at first instance, but Cross L.J. held that a mortgagee was liable to the mortgagor for any damage suffered by reason of negligence of the mortgagee's agent.

Standard Chartered Bank Ltd. v. Walker
[1982] 1 W.L.R. 1410, C.A.

Johnny Walker controlled a company which dealt in secondhand metal presses and moulding machines. The business was international. The bank had a debenture with a floating charge over the company's assets and Johnny and his wife had guaranteed the company's indebtedness to the bank to a limit of £75,000. The company was unable to reduce its overdraft and in November 1980 the bank appointed a receiver (see below, p. 199). He appointed reputable valuers to sell the stock. They estimated a value of about £90,000. The amount due to the bank was about £80,000. An auction sale was fixed for the end of January 1981. Mr. Walker managed to get it postponed, but only until early February. Many of his customers were from overseas, but most of those attending were local people and there was only one overseas buyer at the auction. The day was bitterly cold. The heaters made such a noise that the auctioneer could not be heard. The heaters were turned off. Many people left. Only £42,864 was realised and the expenses of the sale were almost as much. The bank sued the guarantors and obtained summary judgment, despite the guarantors' claim that the sale was at a gross undervalue, had been held at the wrong time of year and had been insufficiently advertised and poorly organised. They appealed. Bristow J. held that, since the receiver was not the bank's agent (under the debenture he was expressed to be an agent of the company), the bank owed no duty of care to the guarantors. On appeal it was held that a receiver realising assets under a debenture owed a duty to the borrower and to a guarantor to take reasonable care to obtain the best price that the circumstances permitted. This duty included using reasonable care in choosing the time of the sale. Although the receiver was deemed to be the company's agent, the bank might be held responsible for the receiver's actions if, as here, it had interfered with his conduct of the receivership. (It was alleged that the bank had pressed the receiver for an early sale). Accordingly there was a triable issue and the defendant should have leave to defend.

Tse Kwong Lam v. Wong Chit Sen
[1983] 1 W.L.R. 1349, P.C.

The appellant borrower, who in 1966 had mortgaged his building in Kowloon to the respondent, shortly afterwards defaulted and the respondent mortgagee exercised his power of sale. The auction sale was put in the hands of reputable agents and properly advertised. The respondent reserved the right to bid generally by himself or his agents. Prior to the auction the directors of the respondent's family company, *i.e.* himself, his wife and their eldest son, resolved that the wife should bid at the auction on behalf of the company up to $1.2 million. The shares in the company were held by the respondent, his wife and their children and the company financed by the respondent. The respondent fixed the reserve at $1.2 million on his own initiative. There were 30 to 40 persons at the auction. The wife made the only bid at $1.2 million and the property was knocked down to her. The respondent lent the company the purchase price and the Crown lease in the property was duly assigned to the company. When the respondent claimed the deficiency of $400,000 on the mortgage the appellant sought to have the sale set aside on the grounds, first, of sale at an undervalue and, secondly, that the sale by a mortgagee to a company in which he had an interest would only be upheld if the sale was at arm's length and the mortgagee played no part in the decision of the company to buy or in the implementation of that decision. In 1979 the trial judge held that the sale was at an undervalue, but refused to set aside the sale after 13 years and awarded damages in excess of $1 million. The Court of Appeal of Hong Kong reversed that decision. The advice of the Privy Council was that the borrower's appeal be allowed. Although there was no fixed rule that a mortgagee exercising his power of sale might not sell the mortgaged property to a company in which he was interested, in order to resist a borrower's application to set aside such sale, the mortgagee had to show that he had made the sale in good faith and had taken reasonable precautions to obtain the best price reasonably obtainable at the time. On the facts the respondent was in such a close relationship with the purchasing company and had been subject to such a conflict of duty and interest as to make it necessary to show that he had taken reasonable precautions to obtain the best price. The respondent had not so shown. Sale by auction does not necessarily prove the validity of a transaction. Alternatives to auction had not been considered. There was a period of only 15 days between the first advertisement and the auction. No independent valuer had fixed the reserve. The purchasing company, through the respondent, knew all about the property and the reserve. No expert advice as to the method of sale was obtained. The respondent had not discharged the burden that he had taken all reasonable steps. While the general rule is to set aside a sale in such circumstances, because of the delay the borrower was left with his remedy in damages (the case being remitted to Hong Kong for assessment of damages, the evidence upon which the assessment was made at the trial being, in the circumstances, unsatisfactory).

Note: For another example of delay in having the sale set aside, see *Latec Investments Ltd.* v. *Terrigal Pty. Ltd.*, above, p. 11.

(iii) CONTRACT FOR SALE

Duke v. Robson [1973] 1 W.L.R. 267, C.A.

Mr. and Mrs. Robson had mortgaged their house by way of legal charge to the Windsor Life Assurance Co. Ltd. In 1971 the Assurance Co. obtained an order for possession, the Robsons having defaulted in their payments. The order was eventually enforced in September 1972. In March 1972, however, Mr. Robson had contracted to sell his interest in the house to Mrs. Robson for £25,000 and she had contracted the following day to sell the house for the same price to Duke and the other three plaintiffs, making no reference to the mortgages. In October 1972 the plaintiffs registered their estate contract as a Class C (iv) land charge, but less than a month later the Assurance Co., rejecting an offer by the plaintiffs to place the amount due on the mortgage in the joint names of their solicitors, exercised their power of sale and contracted to sell the house to a Mr. Collins. The plaintiffs then brought an action against the Robsons, the Assurance Co. and Mr. Collins, claiming specific performance of their contract, damages for breach of contract, and an injunction to restrain the Assurance Co. from completing the sale to Mr. Collins. Their claim for an injunction was advanced on two grounds. First, bad faith on the part of the mortgagees. But Plowman J. could find no evidence of improper motive on the part of the mortgagees, and he rejected a contention, based upon the decision of Crossman J. in *Lord Waring* v. *London and Manchester Assurance Co. Ltd.* [1935] Ch. 310 that the plaintiffs' offer to deposit the sum owing in the joint names of solicitors entitled them to restrain the mortgagees from exercising their power of sale. Crossman J. had been speaking of the situation where the plaintiff had *tendered* the principal with interest and costs, or had paid it into court. The present offer was "a very different thing." Secondly, the plaintiffs claimed that the registration of their estate contract affected the fourth defendant (Mr. Collins) with notice of the contract under the Land Charges Act 1925. Plowman J. rejected this argument on the grounds that Mr. and Mrs. Robson's agreement to sell could only possibly relate to their equity of redemption, and that was "over-ridden under the overriding powers of a mortgagee contained in the L.P.A. 1925" (see section 104, below). He summarised the effect as follows: "A sale by a mortgagee under a charge by way of legal mortgage over-reaches the equity of redemption and all rights subsisting in that equity, including the right of a purchaser from the mortgagor, and notwithstanding that he may have registered an estate contract in respect of his contract for sale." (On overreaching see above, p. 51.) On appeal, the Court of Appeal unanimously upheld this decision. As regards the court's power to restrain a sale by a mortgagee, the extension of the mortgagee's duty in *Cuckmere Brick Co. Ltd.* v. *Mutual Finance Ltd.* (above) could not assist the plaintiffs in the present case where the mortgagees were seeking to realise on their sale £45,000 and the plaintiffs were seeking to enforce a sale of £25,000.

Effect of Sale

Law of Property Act 1925, ss.104, 105

"104.(1) A mortgagee exercising the power of sale conferred by this Act shall have power, by deed, to convey the property sold, for such estate and interest therein as he is by this Act authorised to sell or convey or may be the subject of the mortgage, freed from all estates, interests, and rights to which the mortgage has priority, but subject to all estates, interests, and rights which have priority to the mortgage.

(2) Where a conveyance is made in exercise of the power of sale conferred by this Act, or any enactment replaced by this Act, the title of the purchaser shall not be impeachable on the ground—

(*a*) that no case had arisen to authorise the sale; or
(*b*) that due notice was not given; or
(*c*) where the mortgage is made after the commencement of this Act, that leave of the court, when so required, was not obtained; or
(*d*) whether the mortgage was made before or after such commencement, that the power was otherwise improperly or irregularly exercised;

and a purchaser is not, either before or on conveyance, concerned to see or inquire whether a case has arisen to authorise the sale, or due notice has been given, or the power is otherwise properly and regularly exercised; but any person damnified by an unauthorised, or improper, or irregular exercise of the power shall have his remedy in damages against the person exercising the power.

105. The money which is received by the mortgagee, arising from the sale, after discharge of prior incumbrances to which the sale is not made subject, if any, or after payment into court under this Act of a sum to meet any prior incumbrance, shall be held by him in trust to be applied by him, first, in payment of all costs, charges, and expenses properly incurred by him as incident to the sale or any attempted sale, or otherwise; and secondly, in discharge of the mortgage money, interest, and costs, and other money, if any, due under the mortgage; and the residue of the money so received shall be paid to the person entitled to the mortgaged property, or authorised to give receipts for the proceeds of the sale thereof."

For sale by equitable mortgagee, see *Re White Rose Cottage*, above, p. 42.

Possession

(i) RIGHT TO POSSESSION

General note: The power of sale in itself is usually not enough, as the mortgagor will not voluntarily give up possession and the mortgagee will want to sell with vacant possession. Accordingly an order for possession is usually necessary. Formerly the mortgagee was entitled to possession as a matter of course. "The mortgagee may go into possession before the ink is dry," *per* Harman J. in *Four-Maids Ltd.* v. *Dudley Marshall (Properties) Ltd.* [1957] Ch. 317 at p. 320; and see *Birmingham Citizens Permanent Benefit Building Society* v. *Caunt* [1962] Ch. 883, Russell J. The provisions mentioned below have restricted the right to possession of a dwelling-house. An order for possession of a dwelling-house will not be made or, if made, will be suspended if the mortgagor is likely to be able within a reasonable period to pay the moneys due under the mortgage (in the case of an instalment mortgage this means arrears of instalments even though, as will usually be the case, the principal is due).

Mobil Oil Co. Ltd. v. Rawlinson
(1982) 43 P. & C.R. 221, Ch.D.

A legal charge of the defendant's garage in favour of the plaintiff secured, in addition to principal and interest, all monies at any time due under a petrol and oil supply agreement. The defendant defaulted and the plaintiff sought possession. The defendant claimed to be entitled to set off against the plaintiff's claim an unliquidated claim for damages for breaches of the supply agreement by the plaintiff. The Master made an order for possession, but with the proviso that it was not to be enforced if the defendant paid into court within 14 days a sum calculated to represent the difference between the monies due under the mortgage and the loss alleged by the defendant. On the plaintiff's application to have the proviso deleted from the order, Nourse J. held that the right to possession was an inherent part of the mortgagee's legal estate (see *Birmingham Citizens Permanent Benefit Building Society* (above) and that a mortgagor cannot resist a claim to possession by unilaterally appropriating in discharge of the mortgage debt a liquidated claim which he has against the mortgagor, even if it is equal to or more than the mortgage debt in amount; *a fortiori* an unliquidated claim (see *Samuel Keller (Holdings) Ltd.* v. *Martins Bank Ltd.* [1971] 1 W.L.R. 43, C.A.). The court might refuse to order possession if there was a substantial question as to the existence or enforcement of the mortgage.

Note: In *Quennell* v. *Maltby* [1979] 1 W.L.R. 318, C.A., an order for possession was refused. There the mortgagor had, in breach of covenant, let the mortgaged property to a tenant who became a statutory tenant protected by the Rent Acts and whose tenancy was binding on the mortgagor, but not the mortgagee bank (see above, p. 185). The mortgagor wanted to sell the property with vacant possession and he asked the bank to obtain possession from the tenant. The bank had no cause to want to sell (and therefore no need for possession) and refused to assist the mortgagor in his scheme. Accordingly the mortgagor's wife took a transfer of the mortgage from the bank and sought possession. Her claim was rejected as not being bona fide to enforce payment of the mortgage monies or to protect her security, but with the ulterior motive of assisting her husband to defeat the tenant's statutory protection.

Administration of Justice Act 1970, s.36

"(1) Where the mortgagee under a mortgage of land which consists of or includes a dwelling-house brings an action in which he claims possession of the mortgaged property . . . the court may exercise any of the powers conferred on it by subsection (2) below if it appears to the court that in the event of its exercising the power the mortgagor is likely to be able within a reasonable period to pay any sums due under the mortgage or to remedy a default consisting of a breach of any other obligation arising under or by virtue of the mortgage.

(2) The court:—

- (*a*) may adjourn the proceedings, or
- (*b*) on giving judgment, or making an order, for delivery of possession of the mortgaged property, or at any time before the execution of such judgment or order, may—
  - (i) stay or suspend execution of the judgment or order, or
  - (ii) postpone the date for delivery of possession, for such period or periods as the court thinks reasonable

(3) Any such adjournment, stay, suspension or postponement as is referred to in subsection (2) above may be made subject to such conditions with regard to payment by the mortgagor of any sum secured by the mortgage or the remedying of any default as the court thinks fit."

Administration of Justice Act 1973, s.8(1)

"Where by a mortgage of land which consists of or includes a dwelling-house, or by any agreement between the mortgagee under such a mortgage and the mortgagor, the mortgagor is entitled or is to be permitted to pay the principal sum secured by instalments or otherwise to defer payment of it in whole or in part, but provision is also made for earlier payment in the event of any default by the mortgagor or of a demand by the mortgagee or otherwise, then for purposes of section 36 of the Administration of Justice Act 1970 . . . a court may treat as due under the mortgage on account of the principal sum secured and of interest on it only such amounts as the mortgagor would have expected to be required to pay if there had been no such provision for earlier payment."

Note: This section was passed to nullify the effect of *Halifax Building Society* v. *Clark* [1973] Ch. 307, a case concerning default under an instalment mortgage, where Pennycuick V.-C. held that "any sums due under the mortgage" in section 36(1) of the 1970 Act was not limited to the arrears but meant the whole redemption moneys which had become due on default. The mortgagor might have been able to pay the arrears but clearly could not pay the whole of the moneys due and, therefore, was not entitled to relief.

Habib Bank Ltd. v. **Tailor** [1982] 1 W.L.R. 1218, C.A.

In 1978 the bank gave the defendant overdraft facilities secured by a legal charge on the defendant's home. The legal charge contained a covenant by the defendant with the bank that he would on demand in writing pay the bank the balance due and owing on the account. The bank required the defendant to reduce his overdraft. He failed to do so. The bank made demand in writing for the amount due and owing on the defendant's account (principal and interest). The defendant failed to pay. The bank sought possession in the county court. The deputy registrar made an order for possession within eight weeks, taking the view that the defendant could not pay the whole of the overdraft within a reasonable time and therefore he ought not to exercise his discretion to postpone possession under the Administration of Justice Act 1970, s.36 (see above). On appeal to the county court judge, he held that the Administration of Justice Act 1973, s.8 (above) applied and remitted the matter to the registrar to consider what period the defendant should be given to pay the outstanding interest. On appeal by the bank from that decision, it was held that s.8 did not apply. The words of the section "where . . . the mortgagor is to be permitted . . . otherwise to defer payment" pre-supposed an existing legal liability to pay which was deferred by the terms of the mortgage or the covenant. In the present case there was no provision in the agreement between the parties or in the legal charge, which permitted the mortgagor to defer payment of the principal sum until after it had become due, because under the terms of the legal charge the principal did not become due and could not be sued for by the bank until a written demand had been made. Nor was there any provision for earlier repayment in the event of any default. Repayment was not due until the demand was made and there was no provision for any payment earlier than that. It was the demand itself that made the payment due. The decision of the deputy registrar was restored.

Note: Cf. Centrax Trustees Ltd. v. *Ross* [1979] 2 All E.R. 952, Ch.D., where the mortgage was in the classic form with a repayment in six months ahead of the date of the mortgage, but it was clearly envisaged from other provisions in the mortgage, notably the provision for the payment of interest, that the mortgagor would be entitled to defer repayment of the principal beyond the date so fixed so long as he paid interest. Goulding J. suspended the order for possession. In *Bank of Scotland* v. *Grimes* [1985] 2 All E.R. 254, C.A., it was held that the A.J.A. 1973, s.8, applied where a bank mortgage provided for payment on demand, but a loan agreement expressed the period of the loan at 25 years and included other terms, *e.g.* the payment of the proceeds of an endowment policy to the bank, indicating that, subject to default in the payment of interest, etc., repayment was not required before the end of the stated period.

(ii) LIABILITY OF MORTGAGEE IN POSSESSION

White v. City of London Brewery Co.
(1889) 42 Ch.D. 237, C.A.

White mortgaged a leasehold public house on the Isle of Dogs to secure a loan of £700 from the brewery and such further sums as they might advance. Under the mortgage, he agreed to take all his beer from the brewery for the currency of the mortgage. White defaulted and the brewery went into possession, first through a manager and then through two successive tenants, from each of whom the brewery extracted an undertaking to buy beer only from the brewery. Both tenants found it impossible to operate the hostelry as a going concern and ten years after going into possession the brewery sold it for £2,650. White brought an action for an account. North J. held that the brewery could not be charged with the profits made by them on beer supplied to the two tenants, but could be charged such rent as might have been obtained if the premises had been let without a tie. He assessed this at £20 extra per annum for the last five years preceding the sale. This decision was unanimously upheld by the Court of Appeal.

(iii) POSSESSION AND LIMITATION

Limitation Act 1980, s.16

"When a mortgagee of land has been in possession of any of the mortgaged land for a period of twelve years, no action to redeem the land of which the mortgagee has been so in possession shall thereafter be brought after the end of that period by the mortgagor or any person claiming through him."

Young v. Clarey [1948] Ch. 191

Harry Brown executed two mortgages on his farm within three years. The first, in 1923, was in favour of Charles Clarey and was to secure a loan of £300. The second, in 1926, was in favour of Arthur Young and secured a loan of £500. Charles Clarey died in 1931. His personal representatives (who were the defendants in this action) went into possession of the farm in 1933. From the October of that year until March 1947 they received no principal or interest under the first mortgage, nor did they acknowledge the title of the mortgagor. In March 1947 they agreed to sell the farm for £3,900. Young claimed to be entitled to any surplus after Clarey's estate had recouped its principal, interest and costs. He acknowledged, as he was bound to do, that section 12 of the Limitation Act 1939 (see now the Limitation Act 1980, s.16) barred the right of a mortgagor or of a puisne mortgage to sue for redemption when a mortgagee of land has been in possession for a period of twelve years; and that the title of a mortgagor or puisne mortgagee would thereupon be extinguished (see now Limitation Act 1980, s.17, above, p. 54). Nevertheless, he contended that since the personal representatives had sold in exercise of their statutory power as mortgagees and not as beneficial owners they held the proceeds upon the trusts created by the L.P.A. 1925, s.105 (above, p. 193). Young argued that a puisne mortgagee whose title had been extinguished by limitation still qualified as "a person entitled to the mortgaged property, or authorised to give receipts for the proceeds of the sale thereof." Harman J. rejected this contention. He assumed for the purposes of his decision that the defendants had indeed sold the farm as mortgagees, and agreed that in this event the trusts created by section 105 came into operation. However, in his view a second mortgagee whose right to redeem had been extinguished by limitation could not possibly be a person "entitled to the mortgaged property, or authorised to give receipts for the proceeds of the sale thereof," because under the

L.A. 1939, ss.12 and 16 (now L.A. 1980, ss.16 and 17) all his title had been extinguished and he has no interest in the property.

Receiver

Law of Property Act 1925, ss.101(1)(iii), 109(1)–(3)

"101. (1) . . . (iii) A power, when the mortgage money has become due, to appoint a receiver of the income of the mortgaged property, or any part thereof; or, if the mortgaged property consists of an interest in income, or of a rentcharge or an annual or other periodical sum, a receiver of that property or any part thereof.

109. (1) A mortgagee entitled to appoint a receiver under the power in that behalf conferred by this Act shall not appoint a receiver until he has become entitled to exercise the power of sale conferred by this Act, but may then, by writing under his hand, appoint such person as he thinks fit to be receiver.

(2) A receiver appointed under the powers conferred by this Act . . . shall be deemed to be the agent of the mortgagor; and the mortgagor shall be solely responsible for the receiver's acts or defaults unless the mortgage deed otherwise provides.

(3) The receiver shall have power to demand and recover all the income of which he is appointed receiver . . . and to give effectual receipts accordingly for the same. . . ."

Chatsworth Properties Ltd. v. Effiom
[1971] 1 W.L.R. 144, C.A.

Mr. and Mrs. Lamptey were the assignees of the residue of a term of 99 years. They mortgaged their interest by way of legal charge to the plaintiffs, covenanting, *inter alia*, not to sublet the premises. The Lampteys defaulted in their repayments and, after the plaintiffs had obtained a possession order, but before they had sought to enforce it, purported to grant the defendant a weekly tenancy of part of the premises. The plaintiffs appointed a receiver and their solicitors wrote instructing Effiom not to pay "any sums to your former landlords Mr. and Mrs. Lamptey but to Mr. Richardson" the receiver. The letter did not, however, mention the mortgage. After the receiver had collected rent from Effiom for about fourteen months, the plaintiffs again claimed possession of the premises and Effiom raised the defence that they were estopped from denying him to be their tenant. This defence succeeded both in the county court and in the Court of Appeal. It was acknowledged in the latter court, following dicta of Harman J. in *Lever Finance Ltd.* v. *Needlemans' Trustee and Kreutzer* (above,

p. 186), that the receipt of rent by a receiver does not, without more, create a tenancy by estoppel against the mortgagee. However, as Salmon L.J. pointed out, there were additional factors here inducing Effiom to assume that he was paying the rent to Richardson (the receiver) as agent for the new landlords, *i.e.* the plaintiffs. The letter from the solicitors clearly gave that impression, particularly perhaps by describing the Lampteys as Effiom's "*former landlord*." Having given that impression, which was reasonably relied upon by Effiom, it was not now open to the plaintiffs to deny it and thus deprive Effiom of the tenancy which he imagined he enjoyed as a result of the representation. Accordingly, the facts of the case displaced the effect of the L.P.A. 1925, s.109(2), whereby a receiver is deemed to be the agent of the mortgagor.

Foreclosure

General note: The court is usually reluctant to order foreclosure of land, especially if this will result in a windfall profit for the lender. The powers in the Administration of Justice Act 1970, s.36 (above, p. 195) apply to a claim for possession in a foreclosure action where the mortgage is one to which the Administration of Justice Act 1973, s.8(1) (above, p. 196) applies: A.J.A. 1973, s.8(3).

Twentieth Century Banking Corporation Ltd. v. Wilkinson [1977] Ch. 99

A charge by way of legal mortgage of a guest house in Cornwall by the defendants to the plaintiff made in 1973 provided for repayment of the principal sum of £19,000 on October 31, 1988, and for interest in monthly instalments. A clause in the deed provided that for the purposes of the L.P.A. 1925 the mortgage money should become due on October 31, 1988. A further clause provided for repayment of instalments of capital beginning in the fifth year so long as interest had been paid. There was no express proviso for redemption. The defendants defaulted on interest payments. Templeman J. held that the power of sale under the L.P.A. 1925, s.101(1) did not arise until 1988. However the court had power to order the sale under the L.P.A. 1925, s.91(2) if the plaintiff had a right of foreclosure (such order for sale being in lieu of foreclosure). There being no express proviso for redemption, the defendant had only an equitable right to redeem. That right could be terminated by an order for foreclosure where, as here, the defendants were in breach of the covenant to pay interest. Sale was ordered on terms that, although by the terms of the mortgage principal was not repayable until 1988, the net proceeds of sale should be applied in *pro tanto* discharge of the mortgage.

5. Termination of Mortgage

Law of Property Act 1925, s.115(1)–(3)

"(1) A receipt endorsed on, written at the foot of, or annexed to, a mortgage for all money thereby secured, which states the name of the person who pays the money and is executed by the chargee by way of legal mortgage or the person in whom the mortgaged property is vested and who is legally entitled to give a receipt for the mortgage money shall operate, without any reconveyance, surrender, or release:–

(*a*) Where a mortgage takes effect by demise or sub-demise, as a surrender of the term, so as to determine the term or merge the same in the reversion immediately expectant thereon;

(*b*) Where the mortgage does not take effect by demise or sub-demise as a reconveyance thereof to the extent of the interest which is the subject-matter of the mortgage, to the person who immediately before the execution of the receipt was entitled to the equity of redemption;

and in either case, as a discharge of the mortgaged property from all principal money and interest secured by, and from all claims under the mortgage, but without prejudice to any term or other interest which is paramount to the estate or interest of the mortgagee or other person in whom the mortgaged property was vested.

(2) Provided that, where by the receipt the money appears to have been paid by a person who is not entitled to the immediate equity of redemption, the receipt shall operate as if the benefit of the mortgage had by deed been transferred to him; unless–

(*a*) it is otherwise expressly provided; or

(*b*) the mortgage is paid off out of capital money, or other money in the hands of a personal representative or trustee properly applicable for the discharge of the mortgage, and it is not expressly provided that the receipt is to operate as a transfer.

(3) Nothing in this section confers on a mortgagor a right to keep alive a mortgage paid off by him, so as to affect prejudicially any subsequent incumbrancer; and where there is no right to keep the mortgage alive, the receipt does not operate as a transfer."

Cumberland Court (Brighton) Ltd. v. Taylor
[1964] 1 Ch.9

Taylor agreed to buy from the plaintiffs the Cumberland Court Hotel, Brighton, but failed to complete after notice to complete had been given, alleging that the title was defective. A legal charge had been made by a previous owner encumbering the property. When he had come to convey to a purchaser on May 22, 1950, he failed (contrary to what he had intended) to convey free from the legal charge, because the charge was not paid off until two days later, and the receipt dated May 24, 1950. Taylor claimed (a) that this receipt (being two days after the conveyance) did not operate to free the property from the charge. Instead it operated as a transfer to the then vendor of the benefit of the charge by virtue of the L.P.A. 1925, s.115. It took effect thus because it was the 1950 vendor who paid off the debt secured by the charge; and s.115(2) provides that where the money appears to have been paid by one not entitled to the immediate equity of redemption (and the vendor clearly was not, having already sold the property) then "the receipt shall operate as if the benefit of the mortgage had by deed been transferred to him"; (b) thus the transfer of this benefit left a legal estate outstanding in the 1950 vendor which still subsisted. It gave him a legal estate because section 87 of the L.P.A. gives a legal chargee (and thus any transferee of his interest) "the same protection, powers and remedies" as if a legal term had been created in his favour. So the plaintiffs could not claim to be in a position to convey the whole legal estate to him. Ungoed-Thomas J. accepted only the first stage of this argument. Moreover, the words in the L.P.A. 1925, s.115(3) (that "where there is no right to keep the mortgage alive, the receipt does not operate as a transfer") did not assist the plaintiffs because they were not of general application but were subsidiary to, and confined within, the ambit of the earlier part of the subsection, and, clearly, the 1950 vendor was not "the mortgagor" after his sale. However, what was transferred to the 1950 vendor was *not* a legal estate. Section 87(1) does not vest a term of years in the mortgagee, but merely gives him the same remedies, etc., as if he had one. Since *he* has no legal term of years a transferee of his benefit can have no legal term of years either (see above, p. 166). Accordingly, there was no legal estate residing anywhere else but in the plaintiffs.

Note: And see *Parkash* v. *Irani Finance Ltd.*(above, p. 44).

6. Setting the Mortgage Aside

Undue Influence, Breach of Fiduciary Duty, Etc.

Lloyds Bank Ltd. v. Bundy [1975] Q.B. 326, C.A.

The defendant's family had owned Yew Tree Farm for generations. The defendant, who still farmed, was elderly and in poor health and had little understanding of business matters. He and his only son had been customers of the bank for many years. In 1966 he guaranteed his son's overdraft and mortgaged the farm to the bank for £1,500. In 1969 he gave a further guarantee and further charge for £6,000, after taking his solicitor's advice at the suggestion of the bank. The farm was worth £10,000 and the defendant's only asset. The son's financial situation got progressively worse during 1969. The son told the new manager that his father would give further security if necessary. On December 17, 1969, they went to see the father. The bank manager did not fully explain the financial position of the son's company to the defendant, nor that he thought the trouble deep seated. He knew the farm was the defendant's only asset. He realised that the defendant was relying on him. He told the defendant that the bank would support the company on certain terms. The father agreed to guarantee the company's account to £11,000 and he gave a further guarantee to that amount and a further charge for £3,500, bringing the total charged to £11,000. The manager had brought the documents with him already prepared. The manager did not (as on the previous occasion) leave the documents with the defendant to consider them and take independent advice. The manager witnessed the defendant's signatures on the document. The bank knew the defendant had his own solicitor. In May 1970 the son's company ceased to trade. The bank agreed to sell the farm as mortgagee for £9,500. The defendant claimed this price was undervalue. The bank sought possession. The county court judge held that the mortgages were valid and the sale proper and he ordered possession. On the appeal, it was held that there was such a relationship of confidentiality between the bank and the defendant (*per* Sir Eric Sachs, the bank being akin to "a man of affairs"), based upon the longstanding relations between the Bundy family and the bank and the defendant's reliance on the manager for advice, that the court could intervene if that position were abused. The bank had a conflict of interest between protecting its own position and the position of the defendant who might lose his only asset and be left penniless by signing the documents of December 17, 1969. The bank was in breach of its fiduciary duty in not advising the defendant to seek independent advice and in letting him commit himself to his possible ruin. The documents of December 17, 1969 should be set aside. Sir Eric Sachs and Cairns L.J. based their reasoning on that class of undue influence where the court interferes, not on the ground of any wrongful act, but on the ground of public policy. Lord Denning M.R. considered the various categories where the court will intervene where there has been inequality of bargaining power and found in them a single thread (principle) of inequality of bargaining power.

Note: For "economic duress" as an example of the single thread, see *Alec Lobb (Garages) Ltd.* v. *Total Oil (Great Britain) Ltd.*, above, p. 163.

CHAPTER 6

EASEMENTS

1. GENERAL CHARACTERISTICS

Re Ellenborough Park [1956] Ch. 134, C.A.

When the White Cross Estate, which included Ellenborough Park, had been developed in the mid-nineteenth century, the conveyance of plots surrounding the Park had contained a grant of full enjoyment at all times of the Park in common with the other persons entitled thereto subject to the payment of a fair proportion of the cost of upkeep of the Park. During the Second World War the Park was requisitioned and on de-requisition after the war compensation became payable. If the owners of the houses surrounding the Park enjoyed easements over the Park they would be entitled to compensation. It was argued, *inter alia*, that the right was too wide and vague to be an easement. It was held that the right was an easement and the four characteristics of an easement formulated in Cheshire's *Modern Real Property* were accepted, *i.e.* (1) there must be a dominant and a servient tenement; (2) an easement must "accommodate" the dominant tenement; (3) dominant and servient owners must be different persons; and (4) the right claimed must be capable of forming the subject-matter of a grant.

Phipps v. Pears [1965] 1 Q.B. 76, C.A.

Nos. 14 and 16 Market Street, Warwick, were adjoining houses owned by the same person. No. 16 was rebuilt with its flank wall flat up against the wall of No. 14. The wall of No. 16 was not in itself water-proof, but protection from the weather was provided for it by the wall of No. 14; No. 16 was sold off in 1931. Later No. 14 was sold to the Governors of Lord Leycester Hospital who demolished it leaving the wall of No. 16 exposed to the weather. The wall was damaged by frost. The plaintiffs, then the owners of No. 16, claimed damages. They claimed an easement for the protection of the wall from the weather, which, it was claimed, passed under the L.P.A. 1925, s.62 (below, p. 216) on the 1931 conveyance or, alternatively, was to be implied on the severance of the premises in 1931. It was held there was no such easement known to the law. Lord Denning M.R., stated that there were two kinds of easement known to the law: positive easements, such as a right of way, which give the owner of land a right himself to do something on or to his neighbour's land, and negative easements, such as a right of light, which gives him a right to stop his neighbour doing something on his (the neighbour's) land. The right of support did not fit neatly into either category but was more a positive than negative easement since it involved exerting a thrust on the servient land. The law was chary of creating any new negative easements. The right to protection from the weather (if it existed, which it did not) was entirely negative. It was a right to stop your neighbour pulling down his house.

Note: But see *Blackburn* v. *Lindsay*, below, p. 238.

Accommodate the Dominant Land

Hill v. Tupper (1863) 2 H. & C. 121, Exch.

The proprietors of the Basingstoke Canal Navigation leased premises on the bank of the canal to the plaintiff together with the sole and exclusive right or liberty to put or use the boats on the canal, and let the same for hire for the purpose of pleasure only. The landlord of the inn adjoining the canal let out boats for hire on the canal. The plaintiff sued him claiming disturbance of his exclusive right which he claimed to be an easement. It was held that the right was merely a licence, binding only between the plaintiff and the proprietors of the canal. It is not competent to create easements unconnected with the use and enjoyment of land. In the present case the land was ancillary to the exclusive right, rather than the right accommodating the land.

Note: That the right to do things to promote one's *business*, *e.g.* to put advertisements for one's business on neighbouring land, may be an easement (see *Moody* v. *Steggles*, below).

Moody v. Steggles (1879) 12 Ch.D. 261

A public house and an adjoining dwelling-house were previously in common ownership. The dwelling-house was conveyed away to the defendants' predecessor in title first. The plaintiffs, who owned the pub, claimed a right to keep a signboard on the defendants' house. There was no reservation of this right in the conveyance of the house. It was not known whether, and could not be assumed that, the sign had been first placed on the house during the common ownership, but it had been there for upwards of 40 years. Fry J. held that the right claimed was capable of being an easement notwithstanding the advertisement related to the *business* carried on in the pub rather than to the *land* itself (the public house could only be used by an occupant and the occupant only used the house for the business which he pursued, and therefore in some manner the right was more or less connected with the mode in which the occupant of the house used it) and a grant of easement by the defendants' predecessor in title to the plaintiffs' predecessor in title must be assumed under the doctrine of lost modern grant.

Note: To be an easement (rather than a licence) there must be a connection between the advertisements and the dominant land. So a right to use the flank walls of the adjoining premises for advertising purposes generally and not restricted to advertisements of the business carried on on the dominant tenement was a licence and not an easement (see *Clapman* v. *Edwards* [1938] 2 All E.R. 507, Ch.D., Bennett J.; *cf. Re Webb's Lease* (below, p. 212) where the Bryant and May advert had no connection with the business carried on on the ground floor of the building).

Fencing

Crow v. Wood [1971] 1 Q.B. 77, C.A.

The owner of a moor and adjoining farms let off the farms together with the right for each tenant to stray (graze) sheep on the moor but subject to the duty to keep the fences and walls of the farm in good repair. It was the custom of the moor for each farmer adjoining the moor to fence his farm against moorland sheep. The farms were subsequently sold off together with the right to stray sheep on the moor. The plaintiff, the purchaser of one of the farms, allowed her walls and fences to fall into disrepair so that the defendant's sheep got into her farm from the moor. She sued the defendant for damages for cattle trespass. It was held that the right to have one's neighbour keep up his fences is a right in the nature of an easement. Accordingly, on the conveyance of the defendant's farm which preceded the plaintiff's conveyance, there passed with the defendant's farm by virtue of the L.P.A. 1925, s.62 (below, p. 216) the right to have the walls and fences on the plaintiff's land adjoining the moors kept up. The plaintiff was in breach of her duty and was not entitled to complain of cattle trespass by the defendant's sheep.

Note: That a fencing easement is unique in that it may involve expenditure by the owner of the servient tenement. There may be an agreement between adjoining landowners to keep a hedge or fence in repair but this, being a positive convenant, binds only the parties to the agreement (see below, p. 239), unless *Halsall* v. *Brizell* (see below, p. 243) can be applied. A right to have a fence repaired may be acquired by prescription, but it is necessary to prove that the repairs have been consistently carried out by the alleged servient owner as a matter of obligation, or by presumption of lost grant (see *Jones* v. *Price* [1965] 2 Q.B. 618, C.A., where there was no evidence to support the claim on either ground).

Right Exercised as Easement

Att.-Gen. of Southern Nigeria v. John Holt & Co. [1915] A.C. 599, P.C.

The respondents owned land near the shore at Lagos. They carried out reclamation works to protect their land from the sea and under the local law the reclaimed land vested in the Crown. The respondents built walls and jetties on part of the land and stored casks on another part. They thought the reclaimed land was their own, not being aware of the local law. When they discovered it was not theirs they claimed rights over the land. The judge at first instance found that they occupied the land under an irrevocable licence from the Crown, the latter having acquiesced in the respondents' acts over many years. The local court of appeal held that the respondents had an easement over the reclaimed land. Reversing the appeal court, the J.C.P.C. thought that the right of storing goods on the land of another could exist as an easement, but they held that there would be no easement over a tenement which the owner of the dominant tenement claimed as his own.

Note: Nor where he exercises the right as co-owner (see *Copeland* v. *Greenhalf*, below).

Joint and Exclusive User

Copeland v. Greenhalf [1952] Ch. 488

The plaintiff owned a strip of land which gave access from the road to his orchard. The defendant, who lived opposite, and his father before him, carried on business as a wheelwright and for about 50 years had kept vehicles, wheels, etc., on the strip, but in such a way as to leave room for the then owners or tenants of the strip to pass. The plaintiff claimed an injunction to restrain the defendant placing things on his land. Upjohn J. held that, while it was of no objection to the alleged easement that it related only to matters of trade and business (see also *Moody* v. *Steggles*, above, p. 206), the defendant's claim really amounted to a claim to joint user with the plaintiff of the strip and was of too wide and ill-defined a nature as to constitute an easement. It should be noted that the judge specifically restricted his remarks to prescriptive easements.

Note: In *Grigsby* v. *Melville* [1974] 1 W.L.R. 80, C.A., it was held that a claim to an easement of storage in the cellar of the adjoining house, if supported (which it was not), would be tantamount to a grant of exclusive user so extensive as to be incapable of constituting an easement in law (see *Copeland* v. *Greenhalf*, above).

Miller v. Emcer Products Ltd. [1956] Ch. 304, C.A.

The defendants sub-let office premises to the plaintiff together with the right to use two W.Cs. on upper floors which were occupied by tenants of the head landlord. The sub-lease contained a covenant for quiet enjoyment (see above, p. 132) without interruption by the defendants or any person rightfully claiming under them. The tenants of the upper floors prevented the plaintiff from using the W.Cs. This was not a breach of the express covenant for quiet enjoyment since these tenants did not derive title under the defendants. The plaintiff therefore sued for breach of the implied covenants of title to grant the right to use the W.Cs. and give possession of them. It was held that the express covenant excluded any implied covenants. It was only necessary to consider the covenants for title if the right to use the W.Cs. was part of the demised property, *i.e.* it was an easement. *Per* Romer L.J.: "In my judgment the right had all the requisite characteristics of an easement. There is no doubt as to what were intended to be the dominant and servient tenements respectively, and the right was appurtenant to the former and calculated to enhance its beneficial use and enjoyment. It is true that during the times when the dominant owner exercised the right, the owner of the servient tenement would be excluded, but this in greater or lesser degree is a common feature of many easements (for example, rights of way) and does not amount to such an ouster of the servient owner's rights as was held by Upjohn J. to be incompatible with a legal easement in *Copeland* v. *Greenhalf*" (above, p. 208) and see *Wright* v. *Macadam* (below, p. 217).

2. Legal and Equitable Easements

Legal Estates and Equitable Interests

Law of Property Act 1925, ss.1 and 4 (see above, p. 1).

Equitable Easements as Land Charges

Land Charges Act 1972, s.2, Classes C (iv), D (iii) (see above, p. 18).

E. R. Ives Investment Ltd. v. High [1967] 2 Q.B. 379, C.A.

When building a block of flats the plaintiff company's predecessor in title had encroached with the foundations of the building onto the defendant's land. It was agreed that the foundations should be allowed to remain and in exchange the defendant was to have a right of way for his car over the yard of the block of flats. On that basis the defendant built a garage from and to which access by car could only be obtained over the yard. This agreement was never registered as a land charge Class C (iv) or D (iii) (above, pp. 18-19). The defendant exercised the right of way and contributed to the cost of surfacing the yard. The plaintiff bought the flats expressly subject to the right of way, but later sued the defendant for trespass, claiming that if the defendant was entitled to an equitable easement it was void against it for want of registration. It was held that the plaintiff could not object to the right of way, which was enforceable against it on the principle that he who takes the benefit must accept the burden (see *Halsall* v. *Brizell*, below, p. 243). Further, the right of way could not be prevented so long as the block of flats had its foundations in the defendant's land by virtue of the doctrine of estoppel. The plaintiff's predecessor had stood by and allowed the defendant to build his garage knowing that he believed he had a right of way over the yard. That gave rise to an equity arising out of acquiescence available against the original owner of the flats and the plaintiff. Such right was not registrable as an estate contract (land charge Class C (iv)) because there was no contract to convey a legal estate of any kind. Nor was it registrable as an equitable easement under Class D (iii) because an "equitable easement" is a proprietary interest in land such as would, before 1926, have been recognised as capable of being conveyed or created at law, but which since 1926 only takes effect as an equitable interest (see L.P.A. 1925, s.4, above, p. 1), and the defendant's right was an interest which before 1926 only subsisted in equity. But the plaintiff had purchased expressly subject to the right of way.

Note: See *Ward* v. *Kirkland* (below, p. 220) and *Crabb* v. *Arun District Council* (below, p. 230).

3. ACQUISITION

Express Grant or Reservation

Law of Property Act 1925, s.65(1)

"A reservation of a legal estate shall operate at law without any execution of the coveyance by the grantee of the legal estate out of which the reservation is made, or any regrant by him, so as to create the legal estate reserved, and so as to vest the same in possession in the person (whether being the grantor or not) for whose benefit the reservation is made."

Johnstone v. Holdway [1963] 1 Q.B. 601, C.A.

In 1936 J. agreed to sell certain land to T. Co., but no conveyance was executed. In 1948 T. Co. sold part of the land to B., J. and T. Co. conveying as trustee (being the legal owner) and beneficial owner (being the equitable owner) respectively. The conveyance contained a reservation of a right of way at all times and for all purposes (including quarrying) in favour of T. Co. The conveyance did not specify the dominant tenement for the right of way, but the quarry was marked on the plan annexed to the conveyance. The question was whether the conveyance effectively reserved a legal easement in favour of T. Co. to which the plaintiffs were successors in title. It was held that extrinsic evidence was admissible to identify the dominant land. The defendant claimed that the easement was only an equitable one because T. Co. was only the equitable owner. If so, it required registration as a land charge Class D (iii) (above, p. 19). But it had not been registered and as the defendant was a purchaser for value of the legal estate in the servient land for money's worth, he claimed to take free of the right. It was held that the L.P.A. 1925, s.65 operates as a regrant, *i.e.* a grant by B., so T. Co.'s position was irrelevant, and on the question of construction it was clear that the parties intended a legal easement.

Note: In *St. Edmundsbury and Ipswich Diocesan Board of Finance* v. *Clark* (*No.* 2) [1975] 1 W.L.R. 468, the Court of Appeal (*per* Sir John Pennycuick, in the judgment of the court) said that the effect of section 65 was merely as to formalities, rather than substance. The so-called reservation is still deemed to be a grant by the purchaser. At first instance, Megarry J. had confirmed his view, expressed previously in *Cordwell* v. *Second Clanfield Properties Ltd.* [1969] 2 Ch. 9 (in which *Johnstone* v. *Holdway* was not referred to) that section 65 had a substantive effect, so that in the case of ambiguity and for the purposes of the application of the *contra proferentem* rule of construction, the grantor was the vendor in whose favour the reservation was made. Megarry J.'s views were rejected *per curiam*, the Court of Appeal affirming his decision on other grounds (*i.e.* the reservation of a right of way to the church was to be construed, from the surrounding circumstances, as limited to pedestrian use only and there was no need to rely on the *contra proferentem* rule).

Implied Grant or Reservation

(i) ON SEVERANCE OF LAND PREVIOUSLY IN COMMON OWNERSHIP

Wheeldon v. Burrows (1879) 12 Ch.D. 31, C.A.

In January 1876 T. sold a piece of land to Mr. Wheeldon, the plaintiff's deceased husband. In February 1876 T. sold the adjoining land with a workshop on part of it to the defendant. The workshop had three windows, all of which overlooked the plaintiff's land. In 1878 the plaintiff erected hoardings on her land facing the workshop and obstructing the defendant's light. He claimed a right to light, but his claim was rejected. Thesiger L.J. stated two general rules. First (and this is now generally known as the doctrine of *Wheeldon* v. *Burrows*), on the grant by the owner of the tenement or part of that tenement as it is then used and enjoyed, there will pass to the grantee all those continuous and apparent quasi-easements, or, in other words, all those easements which are necessary to the reasonable enjoyment of the property granted and which have been and are at the time of the grant used by the owner of the entirety for the benefit of the part granted. Secondly, if the grantor intends to reserve any right over the tenement granted, it is his duty to reserve it expressly in the grant. There are certain exceptions to the second rule, *i.e.* ways of necessity and reciprocal easements of support, etc.

(ii) COMMON INTENTION

Re Webb's Lease [1951] Ch. 808, C.A.

The defendant was tenant of a three-storey building. He occupied the ground floor for the purposes of his business as a butcher. In 1939 he sub-let the other floors to the plaintiff. At that date there was on one wall of the building above ground floor level an advertisement for the defendant's business and on another wall one for Bryant and May's matches. The advertisements covered almost the whole of the walls. In 1949 the defendant granted the plaintiff a new sub-lease of the upper floors. Neither sub-lease reserved to the defendant the right to maintain the advertisements on the walls. In 1950 the plaintiff challenged the defendant's right to do so. Danckwerts J. held that it was common sense to imply an intention to the two parties that the advertisements were to remain and found for the defendant. The Court of Appeal reversed his judgment. There were certain exceptions to the general rule that a grantor of part of premises in his ownership cannot claim an easement over the part granted for the benefit of the part retained unless it is expressly reserved out of the grant, *e.g.* easements of necessity, and mutual easements such as rights of support between adjacent buildings. Also a grant or reservation will readily be implied as may be necessary to give effect to the common intention of the parties. The onus was on the defendant to prove the common intention that the land granted was to be used in some definite and particular manner. The mere fact that the plaintiff knew of the advertisements was not enough to raise an inference of a common intention that the landlord reserved to himself the right to maintain the advertisements throughout the 21 years' term granted.

Note: On advertisements, see above, p. 206.

Kwiatkowski v. Cox (1969) 213 Estates Gazette 34, Ch.D.

P. and D.'s land was previously in common ownership. P.'s house was built right up to the boundary of D.'s land in such a way that a gutter and downpipe overhung D.'s land. D.'s land was sold off first, the conveyance containing no reservation of any right of entry onto D.'s land for repair, etc., of the gutter and pipe. P. claimed a right of entry for such purposes and maintaining the flank wall of his house. Goff J. held that there was no such right, P. having failed to establish a common intention by the vendor and purchaser on the sale of D.'s land that such a right was to be reserved.

Wong v. Beaumont Property Trust Ltd.
[1965] 1 Q.B. 173, C.A.

A lease of cellar premises contained a covenant by the tenant to use the demised premises as a restaurant, to use his best endeavours to develop the business, to control and eliminate all smells, and to comply with the health regulations for the time being in force. At the time of the lease the existing ventilation system did not satisfy the current Food Hygiene Regulations, but the parties did not appreciate this. Some years later the plaintiff acquired the residue of the lease and in order to comply with the regulations desired to fix a duct on the outside of the building. The defendant company, successor in title of the original lessors, refused to allow this. It was held that an easement to carry a duct up the wall was to be implied.

Note: That although in the judgment of the court the right was referred to as an easement of necessity, the better view is that this is really a case of intended easement, notwithstanding that the parties to the lease were not aware of the need for better ventilation. The case also illustrates that the right to a flow of air through a defined channel is capable of being an easement, but the flow of air generally, not in a defined channel, cannot be an easement (see *Bryant* v. *Lefever* (1879) 4 C.P.D. 172, C.A., where the plaintiff unsuccessfully claimed that his right to a general flow of air to his chimneys had been obstructed by the defendant stacking timber on the roof of his adjoining house and above, p. 134).

Nickerson v. Barraclough [1981] CR. 426, C.A.

In 1973 the plaintiff became the owner of a field which was landlocked save for the defendants' lane which ran adjacent to the easterly boundary of the field northwards to the public highway. Access to the land had in the past been obtained through a gate in the north-east corner of the field and over a bridge spanning a ditch. The field had been used for agriculture and amateur sports from about 1921 until access was obstructed in 1973. The field originally formed part of an estate laid out at the beginning of the century and sold as building plots. The auction particulars showed proposed new roads to the north and east of the field, but stated that the vendors did not undertake to make any new roads. The original conveyance in 1906 of land including the southerly portion of the field (Plot 78A) contained a provision that the vendor did not undertake to make any of the proposed new roads nor did he give any rights of way over the same until the same should (if ever) be made. Plot 78A was not landlocked in 1906, as the purchaser owned other plots on the estate, and did not become landlocked until 1973 when it was conveyed to the plaintiff's predecessor in title. In 1922 the site of the part of the proposed east-west road adjacent to the north of Plot 78A was conveyed to the owner of the plot. It was held by Megarry V.-C. that by virtue of the 1922 conveyance the L.P.A. 1925, s.62 (see below p. 216) created a right of way for agricultural and sporting purposes over the lane to the bridge and across it on to the road site and from the road site onto Plot 78A. The V.-C. also held that the plaintiff had a right of way for all purposes of Plot 78A based upon implication from the common intention of the parties to the 1906 conveyance. Such implication appeared to be negatived by the above mentioned provision in the 1906 conveyance. But did public policy prevent the creation of such a way being negatived by an express term in the grant? He thought it did. He relied also on the doctrine of derogation of grant (see, in relation to leases, above, p. 134). On appeal, it was held that the right of way deemed by section 62 applied to the land conveyed by the 1922 conveyance, *i.e.* the road site only (see *Bracewell* v. *Appleby*, below, p. 235), and that considerations of public policy had no application to ways of necessity, which depended upon implication from the circumstances. It was well established that a way of necessity was never found to exist except in association with a grant of land (see *Williams* v. *Usherwood*, above, p. 61). In any event there was no question of a way of necessity here as the field was not landlocked in 1906. The court had to ascertain the intention of the parties. Public policy could not assist in this task. On its true construction the 1906 conveyance negatived any right over the proposed roads until made and accordingly granted no right of way over the land by implication.

Note: This case is not one of a way of necessity (though ways of necessity are often referred to in the report), but one of implication by common intention. Accordingly the views of the Court of Appeal on the non-application of public policy to easements of necessity are *obiter*. See also on implied easements *Liverpool City Council* v. *Irwin*, above, p. 131.

(iii) WAY OF NECESSITY

Barry v. Hasseldine [1952] Ch. 835

In 1947 the defendant sold to the plaintiff's predecessor in title a plot of land enclosed on one side by land belonging to the defendant and on three sides by land of third parties over whose land there was no right of way. The plot was sold for building, the conveyance containing a covenant not to use it other than for the erection of a single dwelling-house. Before the sale the purchaser agreed not to make use of any legal right of way over the defendant's land so long as he was allowed to exercise a licence to cross an adjoining disused airfield and to abandon any right over the defendant's land if he succeeded in obtaining a legal right of way over the airfield. The licence over the airfield was withdrawn and the plaintiff claimed a way of necessity over the defendant's land. Danckwerts J. held that the law would imply a way of necessity on the conveyance and this had not been abandoned.

Statutory Grant

(i) ON SEVERANCE OF LAND PREVIOUSLY IN COMMON OWNERSHIP

Law of Property Act 1925, ss.62(1), (2), 205(1)(ii)

"62.—(1) A conveyance of land shall be deemed to include and shall by virtue of this Act operate to convey, with the land, all buildings, erections, fixtures, commons, hedges, ditches, fences, ways, waters, watercourses, liberties, privileges, easements, rights, and advantages whatsoever, appertaining or reputed to appertain to the land or any part thereof, or, at the time of conveyance, demised, occupied, or enjoyed with, or reputed or known as part or parcel of or appurtenant to the land or any part thereof.

(2) A conveyance of land, having houses or other buildings thereon, shall be deemed to include and shall by virtue of this Act operate to convey, with the land, houses, or other buildings, all outhouses, erections, fixtures, cellars, areas, courts, courtyards, cisterns, sewers, gutters, drains, ways, passages, lights, watercourses, liberties, privileges, easements, rights, and advantages whatsoever, appertaining or reputed to appertain to the land, houses, or other buildings conveyed, or any of them, or any part thereof, or, at the time of conveyance, demised, occupied, or enjoyed with, or reputed or known as part or parcel of or appurtenant to, the land, houses, or other buildings conveyed, or any of them, or any part thereof.

205. (1) In this Act unless the context otherwise requires, the following expressions have the meanings hereby assigned to them . . . . . .

(ii) 'Conveyance' includes a mortgage, charge, lease, assent, vesting declaration, vesting instrument, disclaimer, release and every other assurance of property or of an interest therein by any instrument except a will. . . . "

Note: As to section 62(1) and the assignment of the benefit of restrictive covenants, see the *Federated Homes* case at first instance (below, p. 251) and *Roake* v. *Chadha* (below, p. 253).

(ii) USE AT TIME OF CONVEYANCE

International Tea Stores Co. v. Hobbs [1903] 2 Ch. 165

A landlord permitted the company, his tenants, to use a roadway on adjoining property retained by him at certain times and for certain purposes. Subsequently the landlord sold the demised premises to the company. There was no reference in the conveyance to any right of way over the road. The company claimed that, by virtue of the Conveyancing Act 1881, s.6 (now the L.P.A. 1925, s.62), it had an easement equal in extent to the previous user. The claim was upheld by Farwell J. It was irrelevant that the user had been permissive. The single question that had to be considered was the question of use in fact.

Wright v. Macadam [1949] 2 K.B. 744, C.A.

In 1940 Mrs. Wright became the weekly tenant of two rooms on the top floor of the defendant's house. In 1941 the defendant gave the plaintiff permission to use a coal shed in his garden. It is not clear from the reports whether Mrs. Wright had exclusive use of the shed or not (and for this reason the case was rather cavalierly dealt with in *Grigsby* v. *Melville* (above, p. 208)). In 1943 the defendant granted Mrs. Wright and her daughter a new tenancy of the two rooms and another room for one year but no reference was made to the coal shed in the tenancy agreement. The plaintiffs remained in occupation after the year. They continued to use the coal shed until 1947 when the defendant stopped them using it and pulled it down. It was held that the right to use the coal shed passed to the plaintiffs as an easement under the L.P.A. 1925, s.62. Although the right was enjoyed by permission it could pass under section 62 (see *International Tea Stores Co.* v. *Hobbs* (above, p. 216)). For section 62 to apply the right claimed had to be one recognised by the law, one which could be included in a lease or conveyance by the insertion of appropriate words, *i.e.* a right capable of being an easement (*cf. Green* v. *Ashco Horticulturist Ltd*, see below) and the permission given not intended to be temporary. These conditions were satisfied here.

Green v. Ashco Horticulturist Ltd.
[1966] 1 W.L.R. 889, Ch.D.

The defendants were the owners of a shop and adjoining premises. The shop had been let for many years under several leases to the plaintiff. There was a passage at the side of the shop but on the defendant's premises leading to a yard at the back and from this yard there was access to the back part of the shop premises. For most of the material period there were wooden gates at the High Street end of the passage. The gates were kept closed out of business hours. The plaintiff made use of the passage for getting goods to the shop. This use was by consent of the landlords and subject to the exigencies of their own business and to the requirements of their other tenants. When the plaintiff used the passage after business hours he had to ask an employee of the landlords to open the gates. The plaintiff was exercising the right of passage at the time of the most recent lease and he claimed that section 62 operated to give him an easement equivalent to his actual enjoyment. Cross J. held that the intermittent consensual privilege enjoyed by the plaintiff was not user that could have been the subject of a grant of a legal right and was therefore not converted by section 62 into a legal easement. A purported grant of a right of way for such periods as the servient owner might permit one to use it would not confer any legal right. It was impossible to word an express grant of the right claimed by the plaintiff without giving the plaintiff a larger easement than the privilege he was in fact enjoying.

(iii) DIVERSITY OF OWNERSHIP OR OCCUPATION

Long v. Gowlett [1923] 2 Ch. 177

The common owner of riverside properties, Whiteacre and Blackacre, used to pass over Blackacre from Whiteacre in order to repair the river bank and cut weeds on Blackacre. There was no sign of a path on Blackacre. The properties were subsequently sold off separately to two purchasers. The purchaser of Whiteacre claimed a right to enter Blackacre to repair the river bank and cut weeds in the same manner as the common vendor had done. The right was claimed under the Conveyancing Act 1881, s.6 (now the L.P.A. 1925, s.62). Sargant J. held that he had no such right. There must be diversity of ownership or occupation of the alleged dominant and servient land so that the acts relied on are not merely the general rights of the occupying owner of both properties, but refer to some advantage or privilege attaching to the owner or occupier of Whiteacre as such and *de facto* exercised over Blackacre.

Note: That this requirement of diversity of occupation does not apply to claims under *Wheeldon* v. *Burrows* (above, p. 212).

Sovmots Investments Ltd. v. The Secretary of State for the Environment [1979] A.C. 144, H.L.

In 1960 the Greater London Council granted a long lease of a site in St. Giles Circus, London, to the plaintiff. In 1967 the plaintiff had a multi-storey building, known as Centre Point, built on the site. On the upper six floors of the east wing were 36 residential maisonettes intended as pieds-à-terre for executives working in the offices in the building. None of these were let prior to 1974. In 1972 the London Borough of Camden made a compulsory purchase order in respect of the maisonettes, stairs, lifts and other accesses. Camden Council thought it would obtain certain ancillary rights (including a right of support from the building below and the right of passage for water, soil, electricity, gas and other services through pipes which served the maisonettes) on the conveyance of the acquired property. In short, the question in dispute was whether on a compulsory acquisition the acquiring authority could *create* easements. The House of Lords, allowing the plaintiff's appeal, held that the ancillary rights did not pass under the first rule in *Wheeldon* v. *Burrows* (above), because that rule related to voluntary conveyances and contracts for the sale of land and was founded on the principle that a grantor could not derogate from his own grant (see *Ward* v. *Kirkland*, below) and thus of no application to compulsory purchase. Nor did the ancillary rights pass under the L.P.A. 1925, s.62, because that section could not operate unless there had been diversity of ownership or occupation of the quasi-dominant and quasi-servient tenements prior to the conveyance. *Long* v. *Gowlett* (above) was approved. Nor did the ancillary rights pass under the Housing Act 1957, s.189.

Note: The Local Government (Miscellaneous Provisions) Act 1976, s.13 and Schedule I empowers local authorities acquiring land to acquire compulsorily, on payment of compensation, such new rights over the land as are specified in the order.

(iv) CONVEYANCE AND CONTRACT

Borman v. Griffith [1930] 1 Ch. 493

In 1923 the owner of a mansion (The Hall) and a house (The Gardens) in a park agreed in writing to let the house to the plaintiff for seven years. The house was approached by a drive which ran from the main road to The Hall. Subsequently the owner began to construct an alternative access to The Gardens, but this was impracticable for the plaintiff's trade as a poultry dealer and the plaintiff continued to use the drive. In 1926 The Hall was let to the defendant who obstructed the plaintiff's use of the drive. The plaintiff claimed a right of way over the drive, relying on the L.P.A. 1925, s.62. Maugham J. held that the agreement for the lease was not an "assurance" within the L.P.A. 1925, s.205(1)(ii), and therefore section 62 did not apply. But the plaintiff, being entitled to specific performance of the agreement, was entitled to all such rights of way, etc., as, according to the doctrine of implied grants, would pass upon a conveyance or demise. *Wheeldon* v. *Burrows* applied, the drive being plainly visible and necessary for the reasonable enjoyment of The Gardens.

Note: That at the time of the agreement the properties were in common ownership and both vacant. Diversity of occupation is not a necessary requirement for a *Wheeldon* v. *Burrows* claim. Note also that in those cases where writing alone (without a deed) is sufficient to pass the legal estate (see L.P.A. 1925, ss.52 and 54) a written agreement suffices for section 62 (see *Wright* v. *Macadam*, above p. 217).

(v) CLAIMS BASED ON EXPRESS, IMPLIED OR STATUTORY GRANT

Hansford v. Jago [1921] 1 Ch. 322

In 1911 the owner of a piece of land built four cottages on it, leaving at the rear a strip of land which was open at the road end. The cottages were then let and the tenants used the strip as a means of access to the backs of their cottages. In 1919 the cottages were sold off separately, the plaintiff and the defendants being some of the purchasers. The conveyances covered the respective parts of the strip and included the words "with the garden, outbuildings and appurtenances," but made no reference to any right of way over the strip. The defendants claimed rights of way over the plaintiff's part of the strip which was nearest the road. At the time of the sale the strip had not been made up as a road, but it was marked with rough tracks so as to make it apparent that it was used as a back approach to the cottages. Russell J. held that (1) the rights over the strip passed by way of express grant under the word "appurtenances"; (2) alternatively, the rights passed under the Conveyancing Act 1881, s.6 (now section 62 of the L.P.A. 1925); and (3) alternatively, they passed under the rule in *Wheeldon* v. *Burrows,* there being *indicia*, the tracks, etc., which made it apparent that the rights were being openly enjoyed.

Ward v. Kirkland [1967] Ch. 194

For many years prior to 1928 the plaintiff's cottage and the defendant's farmhouse were both owned by the church but both were occupied by different persons from time to time. In 1928 the cottage was sold to the plaintiff's predecessors in title together with a right to use a yard on the adjoining farmhouse property for unloading coal into the cottage. In 1942 the defendant became tenant of the farmhouse. From 1942 to 1954 the plaintiff's predecessors in title entered on the farmyard in order to maintain a wall of the cottage with the defendant's permission. There was no other way of maintaining the wall. The plaintiff bought the cottage in 1954 and converted it. The rector gave permission to the plaintiff to lay a drain-pipe under the yard and to drain bath-water. He did not give express permission to drain the W.Cs. through the pipe, though he knew these were being put into the cottage. The permission he gave was unlimited in time. The defendant had also consented to the drains being put in. Between 1954 and 1958 the plaintiff entered on to the yard to repair the wall without the defendant's permission. In 1958 the defendant bought the farmhouse and thereafter refused the plaintiff entry to maintain the wall. Ungoed-Thomas J. held that (1) the right to enter to maintain a wall was capable of existing as an easement and would not be defeated on the ground that it amounted to possession or joint possession of the defendant's property (it was claimed by the defendant that the right would prevent him from using his land right up to the boundary, but in the case of a right of way the owner of the servient land is prevented from exercising his property rights in such a way as to defeat the easement); (2) the easement in the present case did not arise under the *Wheeldon* v. *Burrows* (above, p. 212) principle since the right was not continuous and apparent; (3) it did arise under the L.P.A. 1925, s.62 on the 1928 conveyance. At that time the cottage and the farmhouse were in separate occupation (*cf. Long* v. *Gowlett*, above, p. 218) and the right had been enjoyed probably without permission for some time; (4) there was no prescriptive right owing to the permission between 1942 and 1954; (5) the plaintiff's claim based on non-derogation from grant (see above, pp. 131 and 218), *i.e.* on the ground that the cottage had been sold as a dwelling-house and it could not be properly or reasonably enjoyed as a house with means of maintaining it as such, had substance, but the judge preferred to rely on section 62; (6) the plaintiff was entitled to an injunction to restrain the defendant from interfering with the passage of bath-water (but not sewerage) by reason of the expense incurred in laying the drain in the belief that the fee simple owner (the rector) had granted permission for the drain to be there for an indefinite time and by reason of the rector's knowledge and assent. This gave rise to an equity of a permanent nature (see *Inwards* v. *Baker*, above, p. 29). The defendant was not entitled to an injunction to restrain the drainage from the W.Cs., since it made no difference whether the drains conveyed bath-water only or bath-water and effluent from the W.Cs. The trespass (if any) was trivial and in any event the defendant had consented to the drains.

Prescription

Prescription Act 1832, ss.1-4, 7, 8

"1. No claim which may be lawfully made at the common law, by custom, prescription, or grant, to any right of common or other profit or benefit to be taken and enjoyed from or upon any land

. . . shall, where such right, profit or benefit shall have been actually taken and enjoyed by any person claiming right thereto without interruption for the full period of thirty years, be defeated or destroyed by showing only that such right, profit, or benefit was first taken or enjoyed at any time prior to such period of thirty years, but nevertheless such claim may be defeated in any other way by which the same is now liable to be defeated; and when such right, profit, or benefit shall have been so taken and enjoyed as aforesaid for the full period of sixty years, the right thereto shall be deemed absolute and indefeasible, unless it shall appear that the same was taken and enjoyed by some consent or agreement expressly made or given for that purpose by deed or writing.

2. [This makes identical provision for 'any way or other easement or any watercourse or the use of any water' (this applies to all easements, not just rights of way and water: see *Dalton* v. *Angus*, below, p. 228) except that the periods are twenty and forty years respectively instead of thirty and sixty.]

3. When the access and use of light to and for any dwelling-house, workshop, or other building shall have been actually enjoyed therewith for the full period of twenty years without interruption, the right thereto shall be deemed absolute and indefeasible, any local usage or custom to the contrary notwithstanding, unless it shall appear that the same was enjoyed by some consent or agreement expressly made or given for that purpose by deed or writing.

4. Each of the respective periods of years hereinbefore mentioned shall be deemed and taken to be the period next before some suit or action wherein the claim or matter to which such period may relate shall have been or shall be brought into question; and . . . no act or other matter shall be deemed to be an interruption within the meaning of this statute, unless the same shall have been or shall be submitted to or acquiesced in for one year after the party interrupted shall have had or shall have notice thereof, and of the person making or authorising the same to be made.

7. Provided also, that the time during which any person otherwise capable of resisting any claim to any of the matters before mentioned shall have been or shall be an infant, idiot, non compos mentis, or tenant for life, or during which any action or suit shall have been pending, and which shall have been diligently prosecuted, until abated by the death of any party or parties thereto, shall be excluded only in cases where the right to claim is hereby declared to be absolute and indefeasible.

8. Provided always, . . . that when any land or water upon, over or from which any such way or other convenient watercourse or use of water shall have been or shall be enjoyed or derived hath been or shall be held under or by virtue of any term of life, or any term of years exceeding three years from the granting thereof, the time of the enjoyment of any such way or other matter as herein last before mentioned, during the continuance of such term, shall be excluded in the computation of the said period of forty years, in case the claim shall within three years next after the end or sooner determination of such term be resisted by any person entitled to any reversion expectant on the determination thereof." [S.8 is not restricted to ways and watercourses. "Convenient" is probably a misprint for "easement": *Laird* v. *Briggs* (1881) 19 Ch.D. 22, 33.]

(i) USER AS OF RIGHT

Gardner v. Hodgson's Kingston Brewery Co.
[1903] A.C. 229, H.L.

For 70 or 80 years the owners of the appellant's house had exercised a cartway from their own stables over the adjoining yard of the respondents' inn, but for more than 40 years the sum of 15 shillings a year had been paid to the respondents. There was no agreement in writing nor any conclusive evidence as to the nature or origin of the payment. The appellant claimed that the payment was in respect of an easement; the respondents claimed it was rent for a licence. It was held that the inference was that the payment was made in consideration of permission to use the way. The onus was on the appellant to prove user "as of right" and this he had failed to do. Therefore there could be no right under the Prescription Act 1832, s.2 nor was there any ground for presuming a lost grant.

Healey v. Hawkins [1968] 1 W.L.R. 1967, Ch.D.

The plaintiff and the defendant were neighbours. The plaintiff's property was called Nil Desperandum. In about 1935 a predecessor in title of the defendant had obtained the plaintiff's permission to use the plaintiff's driveway in wet weather only for access for his car. In 1938 he acquired a larger car and then he used the plaintiff's driveway regularly without permission. This regular use by the occupiers of the defendant's property continued until August 1966. In March 1967 the plaintiff commenced proceedings for an injunction to restrain the defendant from using his drive. Goff J. held that once permission has been given the user must remain permissive and so not capable of ripening into an easement (save where the permission is oral and the user has continued for 40 or 60 years) unless and until, having been given for a limited period only, it expires, or being general it is revoked or there is a change in the circumstances from which revocation may fairly be implied. In this case, the user, although permissive in origin, changed its character in 1938 and more than 20 years user next before the issue of the writ had been proved. Accordingly, the defendant has an easement by prescription over the plaintiff's drive.

Note: It is clear that a permission of any sort during the statutory periods or, in the case of common law prescription or lost modern grant the material period, will be fatal to a claim. Where permission is given at the beginning of the statutory period and is not renewed, then, if the permission is written, it will defeat a claim under either of the two periods but if it is oral it will only defeat a claim under the 20-year period. As the above case shows a permission given before the period and not renewed does not necessarily extend over the whole period, but may expire so that thereafter user will be as of right.

Diment v. N.H. Foot Ltd. [1974] 1 W.L.R. 1427, Ch.D.

The plaintiff was registered as proprietor of Sanctions Farm in 1936. She was continuously away from the Farm, sometimes abroad, until 1967. The Farm was let during this period to various tenants, the lettings being made by a firm of chartered surveyors retained by the plaintiff. The defendant, and before it the Foot family, carried on a family business on the adjoining farm to the east since about 1920. In the far north-west corner of the defendant's farm a tongue of land (a pan handle) stuck out into the plaintiff's field No. 415. From about 1936 the Foot family had vehicular access from a road bounding field No. 415 across the field to the pan handle. The slope on the pan handle meant the only vehicular access to the lower part of it was across the plaintiff's field. At the lower part there was a drinking pool. The access was used about six to ten times a year. The plaintiff first learned of the use in 1967 from her last tenant. In 1970, after the use had left deep indentations in the turf, the plaintiff issued proceedings and sought an injunction to restrain the defendant's use of the access. The defendant claimed a prescriptive easement based on 40 or, alternatively, 20 years' use. Pennycuick V.-C. relied on the statement of principle of Fry J. in *Dalton* v. *Angus* (below, p. 228) as to the 5 ingredients for a prescriptive easement:—(1) the doing of some act by one man upon the land of another; (2) the absence of right to do that act in the person doing it; (3) the knowledge of the person affected by it that the act is done; (4) the power of the person affected by the act to prevent such an act; and (5) the abstinence by him from any such interference. The presumption arising from long user of an alleged right of way, that the owner of the allegedly servient owner had knowledge or means of knowledge of such user, did not extend to the owner's agents. The plaintiff did not have actual knowledge of the user, and the defendant had failed to prove affirmatively that the plaintiff's agents had such knowledge or means of such knowledge. The plaintiff was entitled to the injunction sought. Even if the plaintiff had knowledge it might be that she had no power to prevent the use. The property was let and the tenants alone could have brought proceedings in trespass.

(ii) USER AGAINST FEE SIMPLE

Kilgour v. Gaddes [1904] 1 K.B. 457, C.A.

The defendant claimed a prescriptive right based on more than 40 years' user to use a pump on the adjoining property occupied by the plaintiff. Both parties were tenants of the same landlord. It was held that the defendant did not have a prescriptive right. With regard to easements, other than the right to light, one tenant cannot acquire an easement over land in the occupation of another tenant of the same owner because such user is not "as of right." The essential nature of an easement (other than light) is that it is a right acquired by the fee simple owner of the dominant tenement against the fee simple owner of the servient tenement.

Note: Where two adjoining properties are held by different tenants under the same landlord and one tenant has enjoyed the access and use of light in respect of his property over the other property for a period of 20 years without interruption, he acquires, by virtue of the Prescription Act 1832, s.3, an absolute and indefeasible right to light as against that other tenant and this right enures in favour of the first tenant and his successors in title not only as against the adjoining tenant and his successors in title, but as against the common landlord and his successors in title. Light is thus an exception to the rule that user must be against the fee simple (see *Morgan* v. *Fear* [1907] A.C. 425, H.L.).

Pugh v. Savage [1970] 2 Q.B. 373, C.A.

The defendant claimed a right of way with vehicles from the main road, along a lane and then over the plaintiff's field (O.S. No. 457) and another field (O.S. No. 547) to Bentley's Field. There was evidence of user by the tenants of Bentley's Field from 1932.

Between 1940 and 1950 field 457 had been tenanted by the freeholder's son. The user over field 547 had been with the consent of the tenant of that field. In 1966 the freehold owner of field 547 bought Bentley's Field and let both to the defendant. In 1968 the plaintiff, who had purchased field 457 in 1950, disputed the defendant's right over that field. The defendant relied on the user from 1932 to 1968. The fact that the user was all by tenants of the dominant land did not affect the claim, for user by a tenant will gain a prescriptive right in fee simple which the tenant can use while he is tenant and which his landlord can enjoy or grant to subsequent tenants. It was argued for the plaintiff that because the user over field 547 had been permissive there was no right over that field and therefore the owner of Bentley's Field would have no right (as opposed to permission) to get to the right of way on field 457, *i.e.* the presence of intervening land prevented an easement being acquired. But in *Todrick* v. *Western National Omnibus Co. Ltd.* [1934] Ch. 561, C.A., it was clearly established there might be a right of way as long as the servient land, if not adjacent, was sufficiently close to the dominant land to be sensibly described as appurtenant to and for the benefit of the dominant land. Nor did the purchase of Bentley's Field in 1966 by the owner of field 547 destroy the right over field 457, notwithstanding that, because of the unity of ownership, the dominant owner could get to the right of way on field 457 over his own land. It was held that the existence of the tenancy of field 457 between 1940 and 1950 was not necessarily fatal to the defendant's claim since the user began against the fee simple in or about 1932. If the defendant relied on the 20-year period under the Prescription Act 1832, s.2 it might be that the court could only look at the condition of affairs at the beginning of that period, so that here as there was a tenancy in existence in 1948 the defendant could not claim user against the fee simple. However, although the defendant had relied only on the Prescription Act in the pleadings he was not prevented from relying on other modes of prescription. The long use in the present case ought to be supported and, in the absence of evidence to the contrary, it was to be presumed that the owners of field 457 between 1932 and 1950 when the plaintiff bought it knew of the user. Therefore it was competent for the defendant to rely on the doctrine of lost modern grant.

(iii) NINETEEN YEARS AND A FRACTION

Reilly v. Orange [1955] 2 Q.B. 112, C.A.

In 1934 the plaintiff and the defendant, who were adjoining landowners, agreed that the defendant should have a right of way over the plaintiff's land until the defendant had constructed a new means of access on his own land. In 1953 the defendant constructed the new access and in December of that year the plaintiff purported to terminate the defendant's right under the agreement. On July 1, 1954, the plaintiff commenced proceedings. The defendant claimed a prescriptive right larger than the permissive right granted by the agreement. He alleged that the agreement was made in September 1934 so he could not prove 20 years' actual user down to July 1954. However, he relied on the Prescription Act 1832, s.4. He claimed that as there had been user for 19 years and several months down to the commencement of the action, and the 20-year period would expire before the interruption effected by the action could have lasted a year, his title was complete when the action was brought. It was held that what had to be shown by a person claiming a prescriptive easement was 20 years' actual user down to the date of action brought. Therefore the defendant's argument failed.

Note: The difference between the owner of the servient land obstructing more than 19 but less than 20 years' user by (1) issuing a writ claiming there is no easement, as in the above case, and (2) a mere physical obstruction. In the latter case, when the 20-year period has elapsed the owner of the dominant land will issue his writ claiming an easement and the obstruction (even though acquiesced in) being for less than a year will not be an interruption within section 4, so that the dominant owner will be able to prove 20 years' user before action brought. In the former case, if the servient owner pursues his action there will not be 20 years. In the "19 years and a fraction cases" therefore it is crucial whether the "interruption" is the issue of a writ by the owner of the servient land or a physical obstruction.

(iv) INTERRUPTION

Davies v. Du Paver [1953] 1 Q.B. 184, C.A.

The plaintiff and his predecessor in title had enjoyed rights of sheep pasturage over land of the defendant for at least 60 years. The defendant bought the servient land in 1949 and in May 1950 he began to erect fencing. The plaintiff's solicitors wrote to the defendant objecting to the fencing on July 6, 1950. The defendant's solicitors rejected the complaint. Further complaints were made by correspondence. The plaintiff's solicitors' last letter was dated August 1, 1950, and the defendant's solicitors' reply dated August 2, 1950, stated that if the plaintiff took certain steps to assert his alleged rights the defendant would be compelled to take action to protect his rights. The fencing was completed on August 9, 1950. No other step was taken by way of verbal or other protest by or on behalf of the plaintiff until the summons was issued on September 27, 1951. The defendant claimed that the plaintiff had acquiesced in the interruption of his rights for over a year. It was held by a majority (Singleton L.J. dissenting) that there had not been any acquiescence. Silence and inaction could be interpreted as submission or acquiescence. But on the facts of the case there had not been submission or acquiescence by September 27, 1950, and therefore there was not a period of submission or acquiescence for a year and therefore no interruption within the Prescription Act 1832, s.4. However, because there was no evidence that the defendant or his predecessors were aware of the user of their land (the land having been tenanted prior to 1949) the user was not "as of right" and accordingly the plaintiff had not proved prescription under the Act or at common law.

Rights of Light Act 1959, ss.2(1), 3(1)(2)

[This provides a procedure by way of notice to the local authority to prevent a right to light arising]

Lost Modern Grant

Dalton v. Angus & Co. (1881) 6 App.Cas. 740, H.L.

The plaintiffs' and the defendants' buildings adjoined and each gave and received lateral support to and from the other. The buildings had stood for upwards of 100 years. The plaintiffs then converted their building into a factory, removing the inside walls and increasing the pressure on the defendants' land. Twenty-seven years later, when the defendants pulled down their house and excavated, the factory collapsed. The plaintiffs claimed a prescriptive easement of support for their building. The House of Lords held such an easement had been acquired under the doctrine of lost modern grant. The right to support for land with a building on it is an easement. The right to support for land alone is a natural right. There was some uncertainty as to whether the Prescription Act 1832, s.2 applied or whether that section was limited to rights of way and water only, but finally (the case was argued before three judges in the Q.B.D., three judges in the Court of Appeal, and twice in the House of Lords, on the second occasion the House being advised by seven judges) it was decided that the section applied. But the main argument was on the application of the doctrine of lost modern grant. Some of the judges held that the prescription was rebuttable. The various views were considered in *Tehidy Minerals Ltd.* v. *Norman* (below), where it was held that *Dalton* v. *Angus* decided that, where there has been upward of 20 years' uninterrupted enjoyment of an easement, such enjoyment having the necessary qualities to fulfil the requirement of prescription, then unless, for some reason such as incapacity on the part of the person or persons who might at some time before the commencement of the 20-year period have made the grant, the existence of such grant is impossible, the law will adopt a legal fiction that such a grant was made, in spite of any direct evidence that no such grant was in fact made. Nor is the fiction displaced by circumstantial evidence leading to the same conclusion.

Note: In *Oakley* v. *Boston* [1976] Q.B. 270, C.A., a grant could not be presumed, so as to give rise to a right of way over former glebe land, because the approval of the Ecclesiastical Commissioners to a grant by an incumbent was necessary. Unlike the Prescription Act 1832 the doctrine of lost modern grant does not require the period of user to have been next before action brought.

Tehidy Minerals Ltd. v. **Norman** [1971] 2 Q.B. 528, C.A.

The owners of seven farms claimed common rights of grazing on a down. In the case of three of the farms user was proved from the late 19th century until 1941 when the down had been requisitioned by the Ministry of Agriculture and fenced off and ploughed up. Thereafter until 1954 grazing rights could not be exercised. The four other farms and the down had been in common ownership until January 1920, but the occupants of these farms had exercised grazing rights from 1920 until 1941. Between 1954 and 1960 the farm owners had exercised their grazing rights by licence of the Ministry. The down was de-requisitioned in 1960. Thereafter the grazing was managed by the commoners' association and the fence was retained with the agreement of the owners of the down. The owners of the down sold it in 1966 and the purchaser wanted to cultivate it. The commoners took proceedings to establish their rights. It was held that in the case of the three farms there were rights of grazing by common law prescription or under the doctrine of lost modern grant. In the case of the four farms because of the common ownership with the downs there could be no common law prescriptive rights, but under the doctrine of lost modern grant a grant would be presumed to have been made between January 1920 and October 1921. *Dalton* v. *Angus* (above) was fully considered and on the facts of the present case notwithstanding circumstantial evidence against any such rights *Dalton* v. *Angus* required the presumption of a lost grant to be made. Twenty years' user gave rise to the presumption of lost grant for easements and, although under the Prescription Act 1832 a longer period of prescription was required for a profit, it did not follow by analogy that a longer period than 20 years was required to establish the presumption of lost grant in respect of a profit. Accordingly, 20 years' user sufficed to give rise to the presumption of lost grant in respect of a profit. In the absence of any evidence of intention to abandon the rights the requisitioning of the down and the subsequent temporary arrangements with the owner following de-requisitioning, the rights were merely suspended not extinguished. Abandonment of an easement or profit can only be treated as having taken place when the person entitled to it has demonstrated a fixed intention never at any time thereafter to assert the right himself or to attempt to transmit it to anyone else.

Note: The farm owners could not claim under the Prescription Act 1832, s.1, not because the requisition was an interruption but because section 4 required the 30 years of user to be next before action brought. The co-existence of three separate methods of prescribing (common law, lost modern grant and statutory) was criticised by the court who hoped that the legislature would effect a long-overdue simplification of this branch of the law (see the recommendations of the Law Reform Committee report on prescription (1966)).

Estoppel

Crabb v. Arun District Council [1976] Ch. 179, C.A.

Mr. A., the owner of five and a half acres to the south of Hook Lane, developed the easterly portion into a front and rear lot of one acre each. He retained the land. There was access from the rear lot to Hook Lane via the front lot. After his death his executors obtained planning permission for the development of the westerly portion as a housing estate. The proposal included a road on the boundary adjoining the existing two acre development with an access onto this road from the front lot only (point A). Subsequently A.'s executors sold the two acre development to the plaintiff and the three and a half acres to the Council. The conveyance to the plaintiff granted a right of way to the proposed new road at point A and the conveyance to the Council was subject to this right. Under the terms of the conveyances the Council was to fence the boundary with the plaintiff's land. The plaintiff decided to sell his two lots separately and approached the Council informing them of this intention and seeking a grant of access onto the proposed new road from his rear lot (point B). A site meeting was held between the plaintiff, his architect and a representative of the Council and it was agreed in principle that the plaintiff should have the right of way he sought. Some months later the Council fenced the boundary, leaving gaps, and subsequently gates, at points A and B. At a meeting between the plaintiff and officers of the Council when the fence was substantially in place no indication was given to the plaintiff that he would not be given the right he sought. Believing his rear lot had access to the estate road at point B, the plaintiff sold the front lot without reserving any access over it for the rear lot. Subsequently the Council shut up the access at point B, leaving the rear lot land locked. The plaintiff claimed a right of way at point B and over the estate road based on proprietary estoppel. The trial judge (Pennycuick V.-C.) dismissed the action on the grounds that there was not a sufficiently relevant relationship between the parties to allow the plaintiff to rely on estoppel, that the defendant did not have knowledge of the sale of the front lot without access (so as to be able to correct the plaintiff's false belief of his rights), that the Council's representative did not have authority to grant the interest and the leaving of gaps and the gates did not create an estoppel as the plaintiff had previously asked for the right of way at point B. On appeal it was held that the Council representative did have authority and the Council had led the plaintiff to believe he would be granted access at point B. This was confirmed by leaving the gaps and then putting in the gate at point B. It was not necessary for the Council to know that the plaintiff was selling the front lot without reserving a right of way for the rear lot. It was sufficient that they knew of his intention to sell the lots separately. By selling the front lot without reserving access the plaintiff had acted to his detriment. Scarman L.J. relied on the five elements for equitable estoppel stated by Fry J. in *Willmot* v. *Barber* (1880) 15 Ch. 96, namely–

1. The plaintiff must have made a mistake as to his legal rights.
2. The plaintiff must have expended money or must have done some act on the faith of his mistaken belief.

3. The defendant must know of the existence of his own right which is inconsistent with the right claimed by the plaintiff.
4. The defendant must know of the plaintiff's mistaken belief of his rights.
5. The defendant must have encouraged the plaintiff in his expenditure of money or in the other acts which he has done, either directly or by abstaining from asserting his legal right.

And see *Ward* v. *Kirkland*, above, p. 220, and *E.R. Ives Investments Ltd.* v. *High*, above, p. 210.

4. EXTENT OF EASEMENTS

British Railways Board v. Glass [1965] Ch. 538, C.A.

In 1847 a strip of land, which was part of a farm, was conveyed to a railway company, a predecessor in title to the Board, for the purposes of a railway track, reserving to the vendor, the defendant's predecessors, a right of crossing the railway to the extent of 12 feet in width on the level (crossing) with all manner of cattle. Prior to the 1939-45 War part of the farm had been used as a caravan site for three caravans and a tent. There were six permanent and five temporary caravans after the Admiralty moved to Bath and several more after Bath was first bombed. The number of caravans increased after the War, until there were 29 by the time of the proceedings. The Board complained of this number. It was held (Lord Denning M.R. dissenting) that the words of exception in the 1847 conveyance conferred a general right not limited to agricultural or domestic use, and not limited to user contemplated when the grant was made. Accordingly, the Board were not entitled to restrain the user of the crossing for 29 caravans. The defendant had alternatively claimed a prescriptive right for the dominant tenement as a caravan site and the Board admitted that the dominant land was a caravan site and that there was a prescriptive right appurtenant to the caravan site (this was a dangerous admission—it should merely have admitted a prescriptive right appurtenant to the dominant land or a right for a specified number of caravans). Whatever the number of caravans the caravan site would still be a caravan site and the intensification of user was not excessive. The site could not be used for a factory (relying on a prescriptive right) but a mere increase in numbers was not excessive user. If there was a radical change in the character of the dominant tenement, *e.g.* change from a small dwelling-house to a large hotel, then the prescriptive right would not extend to it in its changed character. Lord Denning, dissenting, held that when you acquire a right of way by prescription, you are not entitled to change the character of your land so as substantially to increase or alter the burden upon the servient land. This rule is not confined to change of character but extends also to the intensity of user. He held that a prescriptive right for six caravans did not entitle the defendant to a right for 30 caravans. He rejected the point about the Board's admission as special pleading of the worst description.

Note: Mr. Megarry (as he then was) has suggested as a test the difference is between a change in quantity and change in quality. Usually a change in quantity will not be excessive user, but such a change may be so vast as to amount to a change in quality.

Jelbert v. Davis [1968] 1 W.L.R. 589, C.A.

A conveyance of the plaintiff's land in 1961 included a grant of a right of way at all times and for all purposes over the driveway on the vendor's land in common with all other persons having the like right. At the time of the conveyance the plaintiff's land was agricultural land and the driveway had a metalled surface, was 10 feet wide at the entrance, then widened out to 14 feet and was flanked by trees throughout its length. In 1966 the plaintiff obtained planning permission for a tourist caravan site for not more than 200 caravans or tents. The first defendant lived in a cottage close to the drive and used the drive for access. The second defendant lived in the lodge at the end of the drive and farmed land further up the drive. The defendants owned part of the drive and had rights over other parts of it. They objected to the use of the drive by caravans and cars and put up a notice stating that there was no entry for campers or caravans. It was held that the words of the grant were wide enough to entitle the plaintiff to use his land for a different purpose, *viz.* a caravan and camp site, but not so as to interfere unreasonably with the enjoyment of the like right by others entitled to it. Two hundred caravans was excessive. The court would not say how many would be permissible. It was stated that the extent of a right of way was limited by what was reasonably contemplated at the time of the grant and that the situation of the parties and the land could be taken into consideration (*cf. Keefe* v. *Amor*, below).

Woodhouse & Co. Ltd. v. Kirkland (Derby) Ltd.
[1970] 1 W.L.R. 1185, Ch.D.

From 1925 to 1963 the plaintiffs, who were plumbers' merchants, and their customers used the defendants' passageway as an alternative route to the plaintiffs' yard. The gate between the yard and the passage was generally kept locked by the plaintiffs. After 1963 business increased and much more use was made of the passageway, the gate being kept open during business hours. In 1965 the plaintiffs bought a small piece of the passage to improve the access to the yard and erected new gates. The defendants later objected to the plaintiffs' customers using the passage and in 1967 they erected two steel posts just within their own boundary to make access to the plaintiffs' yard more difficult and obstructed the passage in other ways. The plaintiffs claimed a declaration that they had a right of way and an injunction to restrain the obstructions. Plowman J. held that the plaintiffs had a prescriptive right of way for business purposes. The right extended to the plaintiffs' customers, because once both plaintiffs had established a right of way for their reasonable business purposes the identity of the persons using it was immaterial. The increase in the number of customers was not excessive user, being a mere increase in user rather than user of a different kind or for a different purpose. The erection of the steel posts by the defendants amounted to a derogation from grant. The 1965 conveyance did not operate an implied grant of an extended right of way even though the defendants knew the object of the purchase. The doctrine of non-derogation from grant does not operate to create positive rights such as rights of way.

Note: On non-derogation from grant, see also above, p. 221.

Keefe v. Amor [1965] 1 Q.B. 334, C.A.

A transfer of the plaintiff's house granted a right of way over a strip of land on the defendant's adjoining property and shown coloured brown on the plan. The brown colouring showed a piece of land 20 feet wide and 130 feet long. The actual features on the ground were different. The access to the strip at the plaintiff's house end was through a three-foot doorway. At the road end there was a 4 foot 6 inch gateway. There was a wall between the properties which formed one of the extremities of the brown strip. The wall belonged to the defendant but the transfer imposed liability on the plaintiff to contribute to the upkeep. Only part of the strip was gravelled to a width somewhat wider than the gap at the front gates, the rest being garden beds. The defendant widened the front gates to 7 feet 6 inches and claimed to limit the plaintiff's right of way to a 4 foot 6 inch strip of the brown land. It was held that in the circumstances (*i.e.* the contribution to the upkeep of the boundary wall) and on the terms of the transfer the right of way was a right of way over the whole 20 foot width of the brown strip. An unambiguous grant of right of way cannot be restricted by topographical features. The court stressed, however, the point that the grantee of a right of way cannot complain of every obstacle on every part of his right of way but only such obstacles as substantially interfere with the exercise of the right.

Bracewell v. Appleby [1975] Ch. 408

Six houses in a cul-de-sac each had a right of way expressed to be of the fullest description over the cul-de-sac, the appropriate parts of which were included in the transfers of the houses. The defendant owned No. 3. He subsequently bought a plot of land at the back of No. 3. The only access to the plot was through No. 3 or through the properties on the other side. The defendant built a house partly on No. 3 and partly on the plot. The new house had almost been completed before proceedings were brought by owners of two of the other houses in the cul-de-sac for an injunction. An interlocutory injunction was refused. At the trial Graham J. held that the defendant, as the owner of No. 3, had no right to extend the grant of easement appurtenant to No. 3 to the plot adjoining. However he too refused to grant an injunction because of the delay and because an injunction would render an almost completed house uninhabitable. The plaintiffs were entitled to damages under the Chancery Amendment Act 1858 (Lord Cairns' Act) (see now Supreme Court Act 1981, s.50). Damages were assessed on the basis that the potential profit on the new house was £5,000, that the defendant (who by the trial had sold No. 3 and lived in the new house) would have been prepared to pay £2,000 to the owner of the five other houses in the cul-de-sac for a right of way and accordingly each plaintiff owner was entitled to £400, *i.e.* one-fifth of £2,000.

See also *Nickerson* v. *Barraclough*, above, p. 214.

Note: The principle that an easement appurtenant to one piece of land cannot be enjoyed for the benefit of another piece of land was succinctly expressed by Romer L.J. in *Harris* v. *Flower* (1904) 91 L.J. Ch. 127, C.A. at p. 130: "If a right of way be granted for the enjoyment of Close A, the grantee, because he owns or acquires Close B, cannot use the way in substance for passing over Close A to Close B." In *Graham* v. *Philcox* [1984] 1 Q.B. 747, C.A., it was held that a conveyance of a converted coach house operated under L.P.A., s.62(2) (see above, p. 216) to convey a right of way then enjoyed by the first floor flat in the coach house and the subsequent alteration of the coach house into one dwelling did not affect the existence of the right of way. There was no evidence that the current or anticipated use was or would be excessive.

Light

Ough v. King [1967] 1 W.L.R. 1547, C.A.

The plaintiff and the defendant owned adjoining houses with a six-foot passageway between them. The plaintiff was entitled to prescriptive rights of light in respect of her main ground-floor room which she used as a living-room and office. The defendant converted his house into flats and as a result of an extension at the back the amount of light to the plaintiffs' room was reduced by about one-fifth. The plaintiff claimed an injunction and damages for interference with her right to light. The county court judge refused the injunction but awarded £300 damages. He rejected a test, established in the 1920s, for measuring the sufficiency of light put forward by the defendant's expert witness (a test which had been accepted as late as 1954 in a case relating to an office in the City of London), *i.e.* that as long as half the room remained adequately lit there was no actionable interference. He thought that the standard of lighting which people expected had gone up since the 1920s and that he was entitled to take account of the locality (*i.e.* in the City one might have to put up with less light than in Gravesend). On appeal the decision of the county court judge was upheld. "It is not every diminution of light which gives an action. It is only when it is so diminished as to be a nuisance. It means that the defendant was not allowed to build next door in such a way as to deprive the plaintiff of the light coming to her room so as to make it uncomfortable according to the ordinary notions of mankind": *per* Lord Denning M.R.

Allen v. Greenwood [1980] Ch. 119, C.A.

There had been a greenhouse in the back garden at the plaintiff's house since about 1940 and it had been used for the ordinary purposes of a greenhouse for at least 20 years before action brought. The greenhouse was close to the boundary with the defendants' house. In 1974 the defendants applied for planning permission for a two-storey extension at the back of their house. The plaintiffs objected because it would seriously diminish the access of light to the greenhouse and reduce the light to their sitting-room. The proposed building did not proceed, but soon afterwards the defendants parked a caravan alongside the greenhouse. They later put in a boundary fence close to the greenhouse. The defendants' garden was some two feet higher than the plaintiffs' and part of the fence stood nine feet above the ground level of the greenhouse about 18 inches above its eaves and substantially cut out the light to the greenhouse. Judge Blackett-Ord, Vice-Chancellor of the County Palatine of Lancaster, rejected the plaintiffs' claim for an injunction on the basis that there was plenty of light left in the greenhouse to see by and that no claim to a right by prescription for an extraordinary amount of light lies when the servient owner is unaware of the special use being made of the dominant tenement. The V.-C. found that a greenhouse was a special use, that it could still be used for other purposes and there was no evidence that the defendants knew of the special use. Allowing the appeal, it was held that the measure of light to which right was acquired under the Prescription Act 1832, s.3, was the light required for the beneficial use of the building for the ordinary purpose for which it was adapted. In the case of a greenhouse the measure of light was the high degree of light required for its normal use as such. In any event, a right to a specially high degree of light was capable of being acquired by prescription by enjoyment for 20 years to the knowledge of the servient owners. The defendants did have such knowledge. The plaintiffs had acquired a right to light not restricted to light for illumination only but to all the benefits of the light including the rays of the sun. However the court conceded that it might be necessary in some other circumstances (*e.g.* solar heating) to separate the heat or some other property of the sun from its light property. But Goff J. agreed that there would be no claim if, *e.g.* there was an interference with access of light to a swimming pool fortuitously warmed by sunlight coming through a south window, so long as adequate light was left for the pool to be used as such.

General note: The servient landowner is not generally obliged to maintain the subject matter of the easement for the benefit of the dominant owner (see *Liverpool City Council* v. *Irwin*, above p. 131).

Holden v. White [1982] Q.B. 679, C.A.

The access to Nos. 4, 6, 8, 10 and 12 Lion Lane was on foot over a pathway from the main road. The title to the pathway was vested in the defendant, who also owned Nos. 6 and 8 (where she and her husband lived) and No. 4 (which was let). The plaintiff was a milkman. When delivering milk to No. 10 he trod on a defective manhole cover in the pathway in front of No. 10 and the cover broke, causing the plaintiff to injure his foot. He sued the defendant claiming damages, *inter alia*, for the breach of the common duty of care owed by the occupier under the Occupiers'

Liability Act 1957, s.2. The trial judge found the defendant liable under the Act. On appeal it was held that the owner of land, over which there was a right of way, owed no duty of care at common law to those using the right of way; that the Act did not extend the common law duties of an occupier; (it being conceded by counsel for the defendant that she was the occupier of the pathway) that the defendant's liability under the Act was restricted to her visitors and as the plaintiff was not the defendant's visitor, she was not liable.

Note: It has been suggested that, though the plaintiff was not visiting the defendant's *house*, he was visiting the defendant's land (i.e. the pathway) and, as she conceded that she was occupier of the pathway, the plaintiff was the defendant's visitor. See now Occupiers' Liability Act 1984.

Blackburn v. Lindsay [1983] 2 All E.R. 408, Ch.D.

Nos. 53 and 55 were built as a unit, with a dividing wall (two bricks' thickness) between them (not carried up into the roof space). The houses were in common ownership until 1919 when one was sold off, the conveyance containing a declaration that the dividing wall was a party wall belonging to and repairable by the respective owners in equal shares. (By virtue of the L.P.A. 1925, Sched. 1, Pt. V, para. 1, the party wall was divided medially between the two owners with cross rights of support). The defendant allowed No. 53 to get into a derelict condition. It was also suffering extensively from dry rot which spread through the party wall and the plaintiffs had to get in Rentokil to treat it. The council made a demolition order and, with the defendant's consent, demolished No. 53, leaving the dividing wall unsupported. The plaintiffs sued the defendant in negligence and nuisance for failing to keep No. 53 in repair, in permitting the dry rot to spread through to No. 55 and failing to provide proper support and protection to No. 55. The defendant conceded that No. 55 enjoyed a right of support from No. 53 by virtue of *Wheeldon* v. *Burrows* (see above, p. 212). The question was the extent of the duty of the defendant to provide support. The defendant argued that she was not bound to repair No. 53, only not to do anything by her own act to remove the support. Judge Blackett-Ord, Vice-Chancellor of the County of Palatine of Lancaster, held that the defendant should reasonably have appreciated the danger to No. 55 from the rot and lack of repair, there were steps that she could reasonably have taken to prevent the damage occurring, that she owed a duty of care to the plaintiffs and was in breach of that duty. It was no answer that it was the council and not her which had demolished No. 53 or that the plaintiffs could have entered onto No. 53 to abate the nuisance. The plaintiffs were entitled to five buttresses to support the wall and rendering and a cement wash on the wall itself. Referring to *Phipps* v. *Pears* (above, p. 205) which had been relied on by the defendant as to there being no right to protection from weather, the V.-C. said that in that case there was no question of support or party walls. The plaintiffs were entitled to have the supporting work done to a reasonable specification so as to make good, within reason, the damage caused by the defendant's neglect.

5. EXTINGUISHMENT OF EASEMENT

Moore v. Rawson (1824) 3 B. & C. 332, K.B.

There had formerly been an old building on the plaintiff's land, windows to which enjoyed an easement of light. The plaintiff's predecessor in title pulled the building down about 17 years prior to the action and built a stable on the site which had a blank wall on the side where the windows had been in the old building. Three years before the action the defendant had erected a building on his own land near to the stable. The plaintiff then made a window in the wall of the stable and then claimed that the defendant's building was an obstruction of his ancient lights. Littledale J. held that a right acquired by enjoyment (*i.e.* a prescriptive easement) might be lost by discontinuance of the enjoyment unless an intention to resume the enjoyment within a reasonable time is shown. In this case, by erecting the blank wall the plaintiff's predecessor had not only ceased to enjoy the light, but had evinced an intention never to resume the enjoyment. The right to light was therefore extinguished.

Swan v. Sinclair [1925] A.C. 227, H.L.

In 1871 houses and shops in Essex Road, Islington, were sold off in eleven lots on terms that a strip of land at the rear of all of them was to be made into a roadway and each lot was sold subject to and with the benefit of a right of way over the roadway. The roadway was never made and the appropriate part of the strip was fenced off as part of the gardens of the various properties. The plaintiff was the freeholder of lots 2 and 3 and the tenant of lot 1, which was the nearest to the main road. The various conveyances and leases had continued to refer to a right of way over the proposed roadway, notwithstanding it was physically impossible to exercise any such right because of the fences, etc. The previous tenant of lot 1, the plaintiff's father, had in 1883 levelled up part of the lot so as to cause a six-foot drop between lots 1 and 2. Just before the plaintiff's lease of lot 1 expired he began to take steps to enable him to drive from lot 2 over lot 1 to the main road and when the lease expired he claimed a right of way over the part of the strip included in lot 1. It was held that, although mere non-user was not conclusive evidence of abandonment, having regard to the conduct of the plaintiff and his predecessor in title there was evidence of abandonment of the right of way claimed.

Gotobed v. Pridmore (1971) 115 S.J. 78, C.A.

The plaintiff claimed a right of way over a lane on the defendant's land by virtue of an enclosure award in 1819. The plaintiff's land at his end of the lane had been ploughed by his predecessors in title from 1919 to 1964 and there had been a dyke and a post and rail fence between this ploughed land and the lane during that period. The lane itself had been cultivated by the defendants between 1942 and 1946 and surrounded by a barbed-wire fence since 1948 when it had been used for chickens and grazing. The judge at first instance (Foster J.) held that the right of way had been abandoned. The plaintiff appealed and the appeal was allowed. "There was ample authority to show that the benefit of an easement might be impliedly released where the conduct of the owner was such as to manifest an intention to abandon the benefit. Mere abstinence from the use of an easement such as a right of way was insufficient to establish such an intention. To establish abandonment the conduct of the dominant owner must have been such as to make it clear that he had at the relevant time a firm intention that neither he nor any successor in title should thereafter make use of the easement. The circumstances might be that he was estopped from denying such an intention. Abandonment was not to be lightly inferred. Owners of property did not normally wish to divest themselves of it unless it was to their advantage notwithstanding that they might have no present use for it" (*per* Buckley L.J.). The ploughing was not inconsistent with an intention to retain the right of way. The cultivation of the lane had been mostly during the War when an objection to such use might have been unpatriotic. The fence around the lane was of an insubstantial kind. The failure to object to it would be a very slight ground for inferring any intention to abandon. The failure to maintain an earth bridge across the dyke and the maintenance of the fence on the plaintiff's land were not proper matters from which to infer a resolution to abandon. The physical state of affairs could easily be altered so as to restore the use of the right of way.

Note: And see *Tehidy Minerals Ltd.* v. *Norman*, above, p. 229.

CHAPTER 7

RESTRICTIVE COVENANTS

1. AT LAW: POSITIVE AND RESTRICTIVE COVENANTS

The Benefit

Shayler v. Woolf [1946] Ch. 320, C.A.

In 1938 the defendant, Mrs. Woolf, sold Mrs. Lawton a plot of land on which Mrs. Lawton was to build a bungalow called Pear Tree Cottage. By a separate agreement made at the time of the purchase Mrs. Woolf was to supply water to the bungalow from a pump on her retained land and she covenanted to do all things as might be necessary to insure a constant supply of water. In 1944 the plaintiff purchased the Cottage and Mrs. L. assigned to him, so far as it was assignable, the benefit of the agreement as to the water supply. The defendant was in breach of the agreement and the plaintiff sued. The defendant claimed that the plaintiff as a successor in title of the original covenantee did not have the benefit of the covenant which was in any event personal to Mrs. L. It was held that the right to the supply was not personal to Mrs. L. and, since it was clearly established that at common law the *benefit* of covenants, whether positive or negative, which were not personal and which touched and concerned the land of the covenantee, ran with that land, the plaintiff was entitled to sue on the agreement.

Note: For covenants touching and concerning land (and not personal), see above, p. 158, and many of the cases following in this chapter.

Law of Property Act 1925, s.78(1)

"A covenant relating to any land of the covenantee shall be deemed to be made with the covenantee and his successors in title and the persons deriving title under him or them, and shall have effect as if such successors and other persons were expressed.

For the purposes of this subsection in connection with covenants restrictive of the user of land 'successors in title' shall be deemed to include the owners and occupiers for the time being of the land of the covenantee intended to be benefited."

Smith and Snipes Hall Farm Ltd. v. River Douglas Catchment Board [1949] 2 K.B. 500, C.A.

The Board covenanted under seal with certain landowners that, in consideration of the landowners contributing to the cost, it would repair and maintain the banks of the Eller Brook which flowed into the River Douglas. One of the original covenantees conveyed her land together with the benefit of the covenant to the plaintiff, Smith, who subsequently granted a yearly tenancy of the land to his company Snipes Hall Farm Ltd. The Eller Brook burst its banks due to the Board's failure to maintain them properly and the plaintiff's land was flooded. It was held that the covenant touched and concerned the plaintiffs' land as affecting the value of the land *per se*, converting it from flooded meadows into agricultural land. Although at common law if a successor in title of the original covenantee were to be able to sue he had to have the same estate as the original owner, section 78 removed this restriction. The covenant by the Board related to land of the covenantee and by the section it was therefore deemed to be made, not only with the original owner, but also with the purchasers of the land and their tenants as if they were expressed. The plaintiffs were entitled to damages.

Note: And see *Federated Homes Ltd.* v. *Mill Lodge Properties Ltd.*, below, p. 251.

The Burden

Austerberry v. Oldham Corporation
(1885) 29 Ch.D. 750, C.A.

Certain landowners conveyed land to trustees for a company which had been formed for the purpose of building a toll road. One of these landowners was a John Elliott. In the conveyance by him the trustees covenanted with him, his heirs and assigns to build the road and thereafter maintain it. Subsequently the plaintiff bought land adjoining the road from John Elliott. Later the road was taken over by the Corporation and it sought to make the frontagers liable for the cost of making up the road. The plaintiff argued that the Corporation had taken the road from the trustees with notice of the covenant by them to maintain it and it was therefore bound to meet the cost of making up itself. As successor in title to the original covenantee he had to show that he had the benefit of the covenant. This meant proving that the covenant touched and concerned his land. It was held that it did not, but rather conferred a benefit on the public. As regards the burden of the covenant it was stated (though of course, this was *obiter*) that, apart from the case of landlord and tenant, the burden of a positive covenant can never run with the land of the covenantor at law.

Note: That in *E. & G.C. Ltd.* v. *Bate* (1935) 19 L.J.News. 203, Ch.D., Macnaghten J. held that the burden of a positive covenant does not run with the covenantor's land. In that case A. conveyed a strip of land to X., an adjoining landowner, covenanting to construct a road on part of it when required by X. to do so. Thereafter A. owned land one side of the strip and X. owned the strip and land on the other side of it. It was held that the covenant touched and concerned X.'s land. Later X. sold the land to the plaintiff and A. died and the defendant became entitled to A.'s land under A.'s will. The plaintiff required the defendant to construct the road. He refused. It was held that the covenant did not bind the defendant.

Law of Property Act 1925, s.79

"(1) A covenant relating to any land of a covenantor or capable of being bound by him, shall, unless a contrary intention is expressed, be deemed to be made by the covenantor on behalf of himself his successors in title and the persons deriving title under him or them, and, subject as aforesaid, shall have effect as if such successors and other persons were expressed.

This subsection extends to a covenant to do some act relating to the land, notwithstanding that the subject-matter may not be in existence when the covenant is made.

(2) For the purposes of this section in connection with covenants restrictive of the user of land 'successors in title' shall be deemed to include owners and occupiers for the time being of such land."

Note: See *Tophams Ltd.* v. *Earl of Sefton*, below, p. 249.

Halsall v. Brizell [1957] Ch. 169

In 1851 O. and J. purchased 40 acres of land in Liverpool now known as Cressington Park. Subsequently the land was sold off in 174 plots. After the sales only the Park roads and a promenade along a sea wall remained vested in O. and J. They entered into a deed with many of the purchasers of the plots the object of which was, *inter alia*, to declare the trusts on which the roads and promenade were to be held and to provide for payment for their maintenance and that of the sewers underneath them. The vendors declared that they held the roads, etc., on trust for the purchasers and the latter covenanted to contribute towards their upkeep and observe all rules and regulations which should from time to time

be made by the owners of the plots of land at any meeting in relation to the contribution to be made by a plot owner. The covenants by the purchasers were expressed to be for themselves, their heirs executors and assigns with O. and J., their heirs and assigns. Annual calls were made for contributions to defray the expenses of upkeep. In 1931 F. purchased one of the houses in the Park subject to the covenants in the 1851 deed. Subsequently he let the house to five separate tenants. In 1950 at the annual meeting of the owners of the houses in the Park it was decided to require an additional contribution from any owner who had divided his house into two or more dwellings. F.'s executors refused to pay and denied the validity of the decision. Upjohn J. held (1) the defendants were bound to accept the burden of the covenant for contribution in the 1851 deed because they desired to take its benefits. "First, in so far as the deed of 1851 purports to make the successors of the original contracting parties liable to pay calls, is it valid and enforceable at all? I think that this much is plain:
that the defendants could not be sued on the covenants in the deed. . . . First, a positive covenant . . . does not run with the land. . . . But it is conceded that it is ancient law that a man cannot take a benefit under a deed without subscribing to the obligations thereunder. . . . If the defendants did not desire to take the benefit of this deed for the reasons that I have given they could not be under any liability to pay the obligations thereunder. They do desire, however, to take the benefit of their deed. The defendants cannot rely on any way of necessity nor on any right by prescription . . . the defendants . . . cannot, if they desire to use their house, as they do, take advantage of the trusts concerning the user of the roads contained in the deed and the other benefits created by it without undertaking the obligations thereunder"; (2) the 1950 resolution was invalid because it purported to authorise contributions based on user of plots and on the true construction of the deed of 1851 the contribution to be computed was an amount in respect of a plot, not an amount in respect of user of the plot.

Tito v. Waddell (No. 2) [1977] Ch. 106

From 1900 phosphate had been mined on Ocean Island in the Pacific under licence from the Crown. In 1913 an agreement was made between the native (Banaban) land owners and the mining company whereby mining rights were granted to the company on terms that all worked-out land should be returned to the owners replanted with coconuts and other food-bearing trees. Pursuant to this agreement many Banaban landowners executed deeds granting the company the right to remove the phosphate and trees from their land and containing a provision that the company should replant the land. In 1927 the British Phosphate Commissioners wished to acquire further land on Ocean Island for mining. The Banabans opposed their acquisition. In 1931 the additional land was compulsorily acquired and leased to the Commissioners with royalties being paid into a fund for the Banaban landowners. In 1942 the Japanese occupied Ocean Island and killed or deported the Banabans. In 1945 the surviving Banabans were collected together on Rabi, an island in the Fiji group. In 1947 the Commissioners acquired mining rights from the Banabans over the balance of the phosphate area, but the royalty arrangements did not provide for inflation. The Banabans sued the Commissioners and the Attorney-General in 1971, claiming that the Crown had been under a trust or fiduciary duty to obtain proper royalty rates and had failed to do so. This claim failed. The Banabans also claimed for specific performance of the replanting covenant or alternatively damages for breach. Megarry V.-C. reviewed the law of benefit and burden (see *Halsall* v. *Brizell*, above, p. 243, and *E.R. Ives Investments Ltd.* v. *High*, above, p. 210). In the 1913 agreement and the deeds the benefit, conferred thereby had not been made conditional upon bearing the burdens. But there was an independent doctrine of the pure principle of benefit and burden (*i.e.* without any element of condition). Though the Commissioners had not sufficiently taken any benefit under the 1913 agreement they had under the deeds, which were to be treated on a global basis, not individually. The current Commissioners were subject to the whole of the replanting liability. The benefit of the obligation ran with the land both at law and in equity. Therefore the plaintiffs (who were not the original contracting parties) could sue. The court's jurisdiction was not excluded merely because the land was foreign land. Specific performance of the replanting obligation was possible (even though it would require supervision), but not appropriate in the circumstances, as only a few of the landowners were parties to the litigation. Damages were the appropriate remedy.

Note: For the damages award, see [1977] 3 W.L.R. 972, Ch.D. The wide doctrine of benefit and burden, illustrated in this case and emanating from the ex tempore judgment of Upjohn J. in *Halsall* v. *Brizell*, which was itself based on a concession of counsel, has been criticised as rendering irrelevant the whole body of law of restrictive covenants built up over the years. Also on *Halsall* v. *Brizell*, see *Lyus* v. *Prowsa Developments Ltd.*, above, p. 46.

Note on Positive Covenants

It will be seen from the above that the general rule is that a covenant is not enforceable against the successor in title of the original covenantor. Equity provided a major exception to the general rule as regards certain negative covenants in the development of the rule in *Tulk* v. *Moxhay* (below). But this general rule remains good for positive covenants. Save for cases where it is possible to apply *Halsall* v. *Brizell* and certain other well-known devices referred to in the textbooks, the *burden* of positive covenants does not run with the land. This causes difficulty in, *e.g.* multi-storey developments where mutual positive covenants for repair, etc., may be required but such covenants may become ineffective when the units change hands. For proposals for reform see the Law Commission Report on the Law of Positive and Restrictive Covenants (1984).

Swiss Bank Corporation v. Lloyds Bank Ltd.
[1982] A.C. 584, H.L.

The plaintiff agreed to lend 10.5 million Swiss francs to I.F.T. to enable it to acquire shares in F.I.B.I., a new Israeli bank. Exchange control conditions required, amongst other things, that the shares should be held in a separate account by the authorised depositary, initially Triumph (an indirect holding company of I.F.T.) and repayment of the borrowing was to be made from the proceeds of the sale of shares. The loan was made on terms (including clause 3(*b*) that exchange control conditions would be observed). The documentation contained an express charge as a continuing security over sterling cash deposits with the plaintiff. The shares were purchased and the certificates deposited with Triumph. I.F.T. then purported to grant an equitable charge over the shares to Lloyds and Triumph delivered the certificates to Lloyds. No exchange control consent was obtained for the transaction. At the time Lloyds did not have notice of the terms of the exchange control conditions. Subsequently Lloyds learned of the conditions. I.F.T. sold the shares with the approval and co-operation of Lloyds. The monies were held by Lloyds, who had sold the U.S. dollars obtained for the shares for sterling. The plaintiff claimed to have an equitable interest, by way of charge or trust, over the shares in priority of the defendant's equitable interest. Alternatively, the plaintiff claimed that if it had no proprietary interest in the shares, the defendant took its charge with notice of the contract between the plaintiff and I.F.T. which required the shares to be used for the servicing and the repayment of the plaintiff's loan. The trial judge (Browne-Wilkinson J.) held that if a contract bound a person to pay a debt out of specific property, such contract was specifically enforceable and created an equitable charge or interest in the property. As to the alternative claim, he held that where a person took a charge on property with actual knowledge of a contractual obligation in relation to the property in favour of another, he could be restrained by injunction from interfering with the performance of that contractual obligation (see *De Mattos* v. *Gibson* (1858) 4 De G.&J. 276). Here the charge was illegal, Bank of England exchange control consent not having been obtained, and the defendant, not having shown or pleaded that it had any honest doubt whether or not the sale of the dollars for sterling would interfere with the plaintiff's contractual rights, was liable in damages for interfering with the plaintiff's contractual rights. On appeal, it was held that, on its true construction, the documentation did not confer on the plaintiff any specifically enforceable right to have the loan repaid out of the F.I.B.I. shares or that the shares should be made available as security for repayment of the loan. There was thus no equitable mortgage or charge. On that construction there was no substance in the *De Mattos* v. *Gibson* point, because it was of no value to the plaintiff unless the obligation to repay the plaintiff out of the fruits of the borrowing was specifically enforceable. If it were specifically enforceable, then the plaintiff would have a mortgage or charge and would not need to rely on the claim of interference with contract. As it was, there was no specifically enforceable obligation to be binding on the defendant. On the construction of the exchange control requirements, the charge to the defendant was valid. The defendant therefore succeeded. On the plaintiff's appeal to the House of Lords, the decision of the Court of Appeal was affirmed. The exchange control negative conditions emanated from the Bank of England, not a party to the loan contract and the existence of the express charge in the documentation argued strongly against any intention that clause 3(*b*) was intended to create a charge (*per* Lord Wilberforce).

2. In Equity: Restrictive Covenants

The Burden

Tulk v. Moxhay (1848) 2 Ph. 774, Lord Cottenham L.C.

The plaintiff was the owner of vacant land in Leicester Square and of houses which formed the square. In 1808 he sold the vacant land to Elms. The conveyance contained a covenant by E. for himself, his heirs and assigns with the plaintiff, his heirs and assigns to keep and maintain the said piece or parcel of ground and square garden . . . in its present form, and in sufficient and proper repair, as a square garden and pleasure ground, in an open state and uncovered with any buildings, in a neat and ornamental order. The land passed through several hands to the defendant whose conveyance did not contain any similar covenant, but the defendant admitted that he had notice of the original covenant in the conveyance to E. The defendant threatened to build on the land. An injunction was granted restraining the defendant from acting in breach of the covenant.

Note: That the decision was in effect a policy one, in order to get over the common law rule that the burden of a covenant did not run with freehold land. The basis of the decision was that the defendant had notice of the covenant, but the enforceability of restrictive covenants now depends on general equitable principles. The shift in emphasis away from notice was required by conditions in the latter part of the nineteenth century with towns developing rapidly and no public planning control. Note also that a restrictive covenant, as in the case itself, may be positive in form so long as it is negative in substance.

(i) DOMINANT LAND

London County Council v. Allen [1914] 3 K.B. 642, C.A.

The defendant obtained permission from the plaintiffs to develop land which he had an option to purchase. He entered into a deed with the plaintiffs whereby he covenanted "for himself, his heirs and assigns, and other the persons claiming under him, and so far as practicable to bind the land and hereditaments herein mentioned into whosesoever hands the same may come" not to build on land which lay across the end of a proposed street on the site. Subsequently the *whole* of the plaintiffs' land was conveyed to the defendant. Later he conveyed the part of the land subject to the covenant to his wife who (with knowledge of the covenant) built three houses on it and then mortgaged it. The plaintiffs sued the defendant, his wife and the mortgagee. The latter two claimed that there was no cause of action against them. Their claim succeeded. It was held that the fact of the wife's notice was irrelevant. The benefit of the covenant "can only be asserted against an assign of the land burdened, if the covenant was made for the benefit of certain land, all or some of which remains in the possession of the covenantee or his assigns."

Formby v. Barker [1903] 2 Ch. 539, C.A.

Formby sold *all* the land he owned in Formby near Liverpool to Mutual Land Company Ltd. and the conveyance contained covenants by the purchaser restricting the user of the land. The defendant was a successor in title of the company of part of the land and took with notice of the covenants. He began to build some shops which were alleged to be in breach of covenant. Formby's personal representative sought to enforce the covenants. It was held that, even if the building of the shops were a breach of covenant, the plaintiff, having no land capable of benefiting from the covenants, was unable to enforce them.

Note: That the retention of a road leading to the land sold subject to restrictive covenants may be sufficient to enable the covenantee to enforce the covenants, see *Re Gadd's Land Transfer* [1966] Ch. 56, Ch.D., Buckley J. And note *Regent Oil Co. Ltd.* v. *J. A. Gregory (Hatch End) Ltd.*, above, p. 167.

(ii) NOT PERSONAL

Tophams Ltd. v. Earl of Sefton [1967] 1 A.C. 50, H.L.

When Tophams purchased Aintree Racecourse in 1949 they covenanted not to cause or permit the land to be used otherwise than for horse racing, but they were not to remain liable for a breach of covenant occurring after they had parted with their interest in the land. The covenant was not expressed to be for the benefit of any retained land of the Earl who did not own any land immediately adjoining the racecourse. In 1964 Tophams contracted with Capital and Counties Property Co. Ltd. to sell the racecourse for housing development (the contract was conditional on planning permission). Lord Sefton claimed an injunction against Tophams and the development company restraining them from carrying the agreement into effect. The injunction was granted at first instance and confirmed by the Court of Appeal. On appeal to the House of Lords it was held that to sell the land with knowledge that the purchaser intended to use it for a purpose other than horse racing was not of itself to "permit" such use; one did not permit what one could not control. Accordingly Tophams were not in breach. As regards the question whether the covenant was binding on purchasers from Tophams, *semble*, on the construction of the covenant it was not intended that the burden of the covenant should run with the land. On section 79 of the L.P.A. 1925 (see above, p. 243) it was indicated that this was merely a word-saving provision.

(iii) ON WHOM COVENANT BINDING

Re Nisbet and Potts' Contract [1906] 1 Ch. 386, C.A.

In 1867 and 1872 land was conveyed to K. who covenanted, *inter alia*, not to use any building on the land otherwise than as a private dwelling-house. In 1878 H. wrongfully took possession of the land and in 1890 he sold it to X. and Y. offering a possessory title based on adverse possession for over 12 years (see above, p. 53). In 1901 X. and Y. sold the land to Nisbet. Nisbet agreed to accept a title commencing in 1878. He did not know of the restrictive covenants, but would have discovered them if he had insisted on the then statutory length of title of 40 years (see above, p. 69. Accordingly he had constructive notice of the covenants. Nisbet contracted to sell the land to Potts, who discovered the existence of the covenants and refused to accept the title. Potts sought a declaration that Nisbet had failed to produce a good title. It was held that H., who was not a purchaser for value of the land, was therefore bound by the covenants and Nisbet had constructive notice. Accordingly a good title had not been shown.

Wilkes v. Spooner [1911] 2 K.B. 473, C.A.

X. was tenant of 137 High Street where he carried on business as a pork butcher. The lease contained a covenant not to use the premises for any trade other than that of a pork butcher. He was also tenant under a different landlord of 170 High Street where he carried on business as a general butcher. X. assigned the lease of 170 to Wilkes and in the assignment X. covenanted not to carry on the trade of a general butcher at 137. Later X. surrendered the lease of 137 to his landlord who had no notice of the covenant made by X. with Wilkes. The landlord granted a new lease of 137 to Spooner who knew of the covenant. S. set up business as a general butcher at 137 and W. claimed an injunction to restrain him. It was held, reversing the trial judge, that the covenant was not binding. The landlord was a bona fide purchaser for value without notice. Therefore he was free to deal with the land and to demise it free from the covenant, even to a person who had notice of the covenant.

(iv) LAND CHARGE REGISTRATION

Land Charges Act 1972

For Class D (ii) land charge, see above, p. 18.

Dartstone Ltd. v. Cleveland Petroleum Co. Ltd.
[1969] 1 W.L.R. 1807, Ch.D.

S. was the fee simple estate owner of the County Oak Service Station. On July 1, 1960, he leased the premises to Cleveland. The lease contained a covenant by S. not to use or permit others to use his adjoining land as a petrol filling station, unless it was developed in agreement with the lessees, which expression was defined so as to include Cleveland's successors in title. Cleveland sub-let the premises to County Oak Service Station Ltd. (see above, p. 145). After several intermediate assignments the sub-lease was assigned to Dartstone. Dartstone also purchased the freehold reversion in the premises and adjoining land. D. wanted to develop the adjoining land for a service station and claimed that it was not bound by the lessor's covenant in the 1960 lease because the covenant had not been registered as a land charge Class D (ii). Covenants made between landlord and tenant are excluded from Class D (ii) and are not registrable as land charges. Pennycuick J. held that, although the burden of the covenant was not annexed to the reversion of the demised premises, the benefit was annexed to the leasehold interest therein and the covenant was accordingly made between a lessor and a lessee within Class D (ii). D. as purchaser of the land burdened with the covenant was bound by it and C. was granted an injunction restraining D. from acting in breach of covenant.

(v) REGISTERED LAND

Land Registration Act 1925, s.50

See above, p.50.

The Benefit

(i) ANNEXATION

Law of Property Act 1925, s.78(1)

See above, p. 241.

Federated Homes Ltd. v. Mill Lodge Properties Ltd.
[1980] 1 W.L.R. 594, C.A.

In 1970 Mackenzie Hill Ltd. was granted outline planning permission in respect of four acres of land (the red, green, pink and blue land) for the erection of approximately 1,250 private residential dwellings. The permission was expressed to enure for the benefit of Mackenzie and its subsidiaries. The same day

Mackenzie entered into a "phasing agreement" with the council dealing with the rate of development so that it would be completed by 1980. The agreement provided for the assignment of the benefit and burden of the agreement and its disclosure on a sale of the land. In 1971 Mackenzie sold the blue land to the defendant expressly subject to the phasing agreement. By clause 5(iv) of the conveyance the purchaser covenanted with the vendor (no mention was made of assigns) that in carrying out the development of the blue land the purchaser should not build at a greater density than a total of 300 dwellings so as not to reduce the number of units which the vendor might eventually erect on the retained land under the existing planning consent. The retained land was described in the conveyance. Subsequently the red and green land was conveyed to B. Ltd., who subsequently conveyed the green land to the plaintiff. Both conveyances contained express assignments of the benefit of the covenant in the defendant's conveyance. The purchaser of the red land then sold that land to the plaintiff, but the transfer did not contain any express assignment of the benefit of the covenant. The outline planning permission lapsed in 1973. The defendant carried out development under new planning permissions for a total of 300 dwellings. When the plaintiff applied for planning permission in 1977 it learned that the defendant had in 1975 obtained planning permission for a further 32 dwellings on the blue land. The dwellings had not yet been built, but the permission might affect the number of dwellings the plaintiff was allowed to construct on its land. In any event the plaintiff claimed that the additional dwellings would be in breach of the covenant and sought an injunction restraining the defendant from building on the blue land at a greater density than 300 dwellings. John Mills Q.C., sitting as deputy High Court Judge, held that the plaintiff was entitled to enforce the covenant. As the owner of the green land, the plaintiff had the benefit of the covenant by virtue of a chain of assignments and as owner of the red land the L.P.A. 1925, s.62 (see above, p. 216, and *Roake* v. *Chadha*, below, p. 253) operated to assign the benefit of the covenant, even though the covenant was not expressly mentioned in the transfer to the plaintiff. The judge rejected claims to annexation. He rejected the claim that the L.P.A. 1925, s.78 had the effect of annexing the benefit of the covenant. It was simply a statutory shorthand for the shortening of conveyances. He also rejected the claim that upon an assignment of the benefit of a covenant thereafter it became annexed to the land. (On this point, see also *Stilwell* v. *Blackman*, below, p. 261). The judge's decision was affirmed, but on different grounds. The Court of Appeal held that the L.P.A. 1925, s.78, did have the effect, where the covenant related to the land of the covenantee in the sense of touching and concerning the land, of annexing the benefit of the covenant to the land. They rejected the orthodox view that the section was merely a statutory shorthand. "If, as the language of the section implies, a covenant relating to land which is restrictive of the user thereof is enforceable at the suit of (1) a successor in title of the covenantee, (2) a person deriving title under the covenantee or under his successors in title and (3) the owner or occupier of the land intended to be benefited by the covenant, it must, in my view, follow that the covenant runs with the land, because *ex hypothesi* every successor in title to the land, every derivative proprietor of the land and every other owner or occupier has a right by statute to the covenant" (*per* Brightman L.J.). The views expressed in *Tophams Ltd.* v. *Earl of Sefton*, see above, p. 249) on section 79 did not provide an analogy, because section 79 involved quite different considerations. As to the argument that if the benefit of covenant was annexed, it was annexed to the whole and not each and every part, Brightman L.J. said that he found the idea a difficult conception to grasp. He would have thought that if the benefit of a covenant was annexed to land, prima facie it was annexed to every part thereof unless the contrary clearly appears.

Roake v. Chadha [1984] 1 W.L.R. 40, Ch.D.

In 1934 a plot of land on the Sudbury Court Estate was transferred to the defendant's predecessor in title subject to restrictive covenants restricting building. The covenant was expressed to be made with the vendors, but so that the benefit of the covenant should not enure for the benefit of any owner or subsequent purchaser of any part of the vendor's Estate unless the benefit of the covenant should have been expressly assigned. The plaintiffs, successors in title of purchasers of other plots on the Estate, sought an injunction to prevent the defendants building in breach of the covenant. The benefit of the covenant had never been assigned. The plaintiffs claimed, relying on the *Federated Homes* case (above), that the benefit of the covenant was annexed to their land by the L.P.A. 1925, s.78 and that the effect of section 78 could not be excluded by the expression of a contrary intention. (Note that section 79 is expressed to be subject to contrary intention, but section 78 is silent on this.) Judge Paul Baker Q.C., sitting as a judge of the High Court, held that, even if one accepts that section 78 is not subject to a contrary intention (which he doubted) one still has to construe the benefit of the covenant as a whole to see whether the benefit of the covenant is annexed. One may not be able to exclude the operation of the section in extending the range of covenantees, but one has to consider the covenant as a whole to determine its true effect. One could not ignore the express words of the covenant requiring express assignment of the benefit of the covenant and accordingly there was no annexation. Nor did the L.P.A. 1925, s.62 (above, p. 216) assist the plaintiffs. The judge doubted whether the benefit of a covenant not annexed could ever pass under section 62 (see *Rogers* v. *Hosegood* (below). But in any event the benefit could not be a right appertaining or reputed to appertain to land when the terms of the covenant precluded the benefit passing unless it was expressly assigned.

Note: In *Bridges* v. *Harrow L.B.C.* (1981) 260 E.G. 284, Q.B.D. Stuart-Smith J. expressed the view obiter that section 78 would not effect an annexation where the land to be benefited was not sufficiently identified in the document creating the covenant.

General note: The principle of automatic annexation expressed in the *Federated Homes* case (above, p. 251) renders obsolete the law of annexation and assignment, illustrated below. That decision, given in an unreserved judgment by a predominantly common law bench, has been much criticised. Accordingly it is too early to jettison the knowledge of annexation and assignment illustrated below.

(a) Proper words of annexation

Rogers v. Hosegood [1900] 2 Ch. 388, C.A.

In 1869 a plot of land at Palace Gate, Kensington, was sold to the then Duke of Bedford who covenanted in the conveyance with the intent that the covenant might enure to the benefit of the vendors, their heirs and assigns, and others claiming under them to all or any of their lands adjoining or near to the said premises that not more than one dwelling-house should at any time stand on the plot. In 1872 an adjoining plot was sold off and in 1873 this was acquired by the painter Sir John Millais who did not know of the covenant made by the Duke. Subsequent purchasers of the plot sold to the Duke proposed to build a block of flats on the plot in breach of covenant. It was held that the benefit of the covenant had been annexed to the original vendors' retained land and was therefore enforceable by the plaintiffs against the defendant.

Renals v. Cowlishaw (1878) 9 Ch.D. 125

In 1845 two plots of land adjoining the Mill Hill Estate were sold to Shaw who covenanted for himself, his heirs, executors and administrators, with the vendors, their heirs, executors, administrators and assigns, not to build on the land conveyed beyond a certain line and not to use any house for any trade or business but as a private dwelling-house only. The plots were subsequently sold by S. to the defendants who took with notice of the covenants. The plaintiffs were the successors in title of the original owners of the Estate. There was no express assignment of the benefit of the covenants in the conveyances of the dominant land. The defendants were carrying on a trade on the servient land, and the plaintiffs claimed an injunction to stop them. Hall V.-C. held that the covenant was not enforceable. There was no indication in the conveyance that the burden of the restrictive covenant was imposed for the benefit of the land reserved. The word "assign" was not sufficient for this purpose, as it might refer to assigns only of the benefit of the covenant and therefore not mean assigns of the land.

(b) Land must be capable of benefiting

Re Ballard's Conveyance [1937] Ch. 473

Here the purchaser of some 18 acres, part of the 1,700 acre Childwickbury Estate, covenanted with the vendor, her heirs and assigns and successors for the benefit of the owners for the time being of the Estate that he, his heirs and assigns would perform and observe certain covenants. Successors in title of the vendor claimed an injunction to restrain a threatened breach of the covenant. Clauson J. held that the covenant could not possibly benefit the whole estate and therefore the attempted annexation was ineffective and the covenants not enforceable by the plaintiffs.

Note: That the decision has been criticised on the grounds that (1) an injury to part of an estate must necessarily be an injury to the whole; and (2) the covenant should have been severed and the annexation held to be effective as to those parts of the estate which the covenant did in fact benefit. But the decision was accepted as good in *Russell* v. *Archdale* (below, p. 261).

Wrotham Park Estate Co. Ltd. v. Parkside Homes Ltd.
[1974] 1 W.L.R. 798, Ch.D.

A conveyance of land (part of which Parkside subsequently purchased) in 1935 by the Earl of Strafford, owner of the Wrotham Park Estate, contained a covenant by the purchaser with the vendor and his assigns the owner or owners for the time being of the vendor's Wrotham Park Estate using that term in its broad and popular sense . . . and to the intent that the restrictions therein contained should run with the land and be for the benefit of the vendor's said Estate that the purchaser and all persons deriving title under him the owner and occupiers for the time being of the property thereby conveyed . . . not to develop the said land for building purposes except in strict accordance with a lay-out plan to be first submitted to and approved in writing by the vendor or his surveyors, such plan to indicate thereon the roads, sewers and drains to be constructed. The covenant was duly registered as a Class D (ii) land charge. The plaintiff owned the balance of the Wrotham Park Estate. Most of the land conveyed was developed, lay-out plans being approved. There remained a central triangular area undeveloped but capable of development for 14 houses. Parkside paid £90,000 for the site and, knowing of the covenant, commenced building works, believing the covenant to be unenforceable. The plaintiff issued a writ for an injunction restraining building other than in accordance with an approved lay-out plan and a mandatory injunction for the demolition of any building in breach of the covenant. Interlocutory relief was not sought. By the time the case came to trial all 14 houses were sold to other defendants (they being protected by insurance and indemnity from Parkside). Brightman J. rejected the defendant's contention that the only purpose of the covenant was to facilitate the development of adjoining areas by leading to a co-ordinated system of roads and drainage and that the covenant was to be construed in a narrow sense. It was a prohibition against development without prior approval of a lay-out plan showing building lots as well as roads and the line of sewers and drains. As to the benefit of the covenant it was held that the benefit was annexed to the plaintiff's land. The covenant was entered into for the benefit of the Wrotham Park Estate, which was sufficiently identifiable as an agricultural estate, and it was originally, and still was, capable of benefiting the Estate. The covenant was, as a matter of construction, annexed to the whole, rather than each and every part, of the Estate. As to the capability of the covenant benefiting the Estate, between the obvious extremes in the middle area where reasonable persons can have divergent views reasonably held, it is not for the court to pronounce which is the correct view, but to decide whether a particular view is one which can reasonably be held. The covenant was enforceable by the plaintiff. Since the demolition would involve an unpardonable waste of much needed houses, a mandatory injunction was not appropriate. Damages in lieu pursuant to the Chancery Amendment Act 1858 (Lord Cairn's Act) (see now Supreme Court Act 1981, s.50) of £2,500 (5 per cent. of Parkside's profit on the development) were awarded, payable equally by Parkside and the individual house owners (in the event payable by Parkside under its indemnity to the purchasers).

(c) Each and every part

Zetland (Marquess of) v. Driver [1939] Ch. 1, C.A.

A conveyance of a shop in Redcar, part of a large estate of settled land, contained a covenant by the purchaser to the intent and so as to bind so far as practicable the property thereby conveyed into whosesoever hands it might come and to benefit and protect such part or parts of the settled land as should for the time being remain unsold or as should have been sold by the vendor or his successors in title with the express benefit of the covenant, *inter alia*, that no act or thing should be done or permitted on the land conveyed which might be a nuisance or prejudicial to the vendor and the owners or occupiers of any adjoining property or to the neighbourhood. Certain parts of the unsold lands were adjoining but other parts were more than a mile away. The respondent, a successor in title to the original covenantor, purchased the shop with notice of the covenant. He opened a fish and chip shop. The appellant, the tenant for life of the unsold settled land, sought an injunction and was granted one. It was held that the benefit of the covenant was annexed to each part of the estate, so that severance was possible. *Re Ballard's Conveyance* was distinguishable if only on the ground that in that case the covenant was expressed to run with the whole estate, whereas in the present case the covenant is expressed to be for the benefit of the whole or any part or parts of the unsold settled property.

Note: See also *Russell* v. *Archdale*, below, p. 261; and the *Federated Homes* case, above, p. 251.

(ii) ASSIGNMENT

Re Union of London and Smith's Bank Ltd.'s Conveyance, Miles v. Easter [1933] Ch. 611, C.A.

In 1908 a plot of land was conveyed to X. The conveyance contained two sets of covenants. First, the vendors covenanted with the purchasers, their heirs and assigns or other the owners or owner for the time being of the pink land (the land sold) to observe certain covenants. These were properly annexed. Secondly, X. entered into another restrictive covenant with the vendors, their successors and assigns only. There was no language of annexation. The plaintiff became the owner of part of the pink land and the defendants became the owners of part of the retained land. The conveyance to the defendants did not expressly assign the benefit of the second covenant, but two later deeds purported to assign the benefit of it. It was held by Bennett J., affirmed by the Court of Appeal, (1) that the defendants could not enforce the second covenant because the 1908 conveyance did not define the land for the benefit of which the covenant was made (*cf.* the *Newton Abbot* case, below); (2) the purported assignments made at a time when the assignor no longer retained any land capable of being benefited by the covenant were ineffective, for at the date of the assignment the covenant had ceased to be enforceable at the instance of the covenantee and he could not confer any greater rights on the assignee than he himself possessed.

Newton Abbot Co-operative Society Ltd. v. Williamson and Treadgold Ltd. [1952] Ch. 286.

Mrs. Mardon owned premises known as Devonia in Fore Street, Bovey Tracey, where she carried on an ironmongery business, and other premises opposite Devonia known as 25 and 27 Fore Street. In 1923 she sold these other premises to George Mardon & Sons who covenanted with the vendor that they the purchasers and the persons deriving title under them would not carry on the business of ironmongery on the property conveyed. Mrs. Mardon died in 1944 and her son Leonard became entitled to Devonia as residuary devisee under her will. Her executors assented in his favour. There was no reference to the covenant in the assent. He assigned the ironmongery business, together with the benefit of the covenant, to a co-operative society and granted the society a 21-year lease of Devonia. The society was later amalgamated with the plaintiff. The defendants became the owners of the other premises and started to sell ironmongery in their shop. The plaintiff claimed an injunction. The defendants contended that the plaintiff could not enforce the covenant. Upjohn J. held that the benefit of the covenant had not been annexed since the land for the benefit of which the covenant was taken was not sufficiently identified by the conveyance. The defendants further contended that there was no effective assignment, because (1) the covenant was not taken for the benefit of land, but for the benefit of Mrs. Mardon's business and (2) the land to be benefited had to be referred to or defined in the conveyance. It was held (1) the covenant enhanced the value of the land and there was nothing in the conveyance to limit the benefit to the business only; (2) for assignment, the land to be benefited need not be defined in the conveyance, but the existence and situation of the land must be indicated in the deed or otherwise shown with reasonable certainty; (3) although the benefit of the covenant had not been assigned to Leonard by his mother's executors, they held it as bare trustees for him and he was entitled to assign it in equity on the assignment of the business to the plaintiff's predecessors.

Marten v. Flight Refuelling Ltd. [1962] Ch. 115

The Crichel Estate in Dorset was an estate of about 7,500 acres and a recognisable and recognised agricultural unit. In 1943 the special executors of the former tenant for life of the estate (which was settled land) conveyed C. farm to H., a tenant farmer, and he covenanted with the vendor (a trust company) and its successors in title that no part of the land conveyed nor any building or erection thereon would at any time thereafter be used for any purpose other than agricultural purposes without the previous consent of the vendor or its agents. The covenant was registered as a Class D (ii) land charge. During the war, part of C. farm was requisitioned by the Air Ministry for use as an aerodrome. After the war the Air Ministry allowed the defendants to use the land as licensees. The defendants, *inter alia*, designed and developed flight refuelling equipment. In 1950 the first plaintiff attained her majority and disentailed, thus becoming the absolute owner of the estate, and the trust company assented in her favour. There was no assignment of the benefit of the covenant in this assent. In 1958 H.'s executors conveyed the greater part of the requisitioned land to the Air Ministry (who had compulsorily acquired the land after the war) subject to the covenants. In 1959 the plaintiff commenced proceedings against the defendant company and the Air Ministry for breach of covenant. Wilberforce J. held (1) that, where there was no annexation and the plaintiff was relying on assignment of the benefit of the covenant, he must show that the covenant was taken for the benefit of defined land which (or part of which) he holds, but the intention need not be expressly stated, nor need the land to be benefited be specifically identified in the conveyance if the intention can be shown by extrinsic evidence; (2) the Crichel Estate as a whole was capable of being benefited by the easement (*cf. Re Ballard's Conveyance*, above, p. 255); (3) notwithstanding that there was no assignment of the benefit of the covenant, the first plaintiff could enforce the covenant as she was the person, as the infant equitable owner of the estate, for whose benefit in equity the covenant was made, *i.e.* this was *not* a case of a successor in title of the covenantee trying to enforce the covenant but of someone who was in effect the covenantee and therefore assignment was immaterial; (4) the court could not interfere with the use of the servient land as an aerodrome or for any of the statutory purposes for which it had been compulsorily acquired; (5) in determining whether or not to grant an injunction to stop the other uses and the scope of any injunction the court could take into account the fact that the plaintiff had not drawn the defendant company's attention to the existence of the covenant, even though it had been registered.

Leicester (Earl of) v. Wells Urban District Council [1973] Ch. 110

In 1948 the fourth Earl of Leicester, the life tenant of settled land (the Holkham Estate of 32,000 acres) sold about 19 acres of it to Wells-next-the-Sea U.D.C. for use as allotments. In the conveyance the U.D.C. covenanted not to use or permit the use of the property . . . for any other purpose than small-holdings and allotments. The plaintiff succeeded to the title in 1949 on his father's death. A grant of probate limited to settled land was obtained by the settlement trustees as special executors and in 1951 they executed a vesting assent vesting the properties and other incorporeal hereditaments within the settlement in the plaintiff (the assent did not include any express assignment of the benefit of the covenant). During the 1960s the demand for allotments declined and in 1971 the council obtained consent from the Minister of Agriculture to appropriate the land for housing purposes and were granted planning permission for 53 houses. They then proposed to sell the land under the Housing Act 1957, s.105, whereby the purchaser was bound to develop the land for housing in accordance with the planning permission. The plaintiff sought, *inter alia*, an injunction to restrain the council from breach of the covenant. The council claimed (1) that the plaintiff had no title to sue on the covenant because there had been no express assignment of the benefit of the covenant to him; (2) that the covenant was ineffective as it was not capable of benefiting the whole of the Holkham Estate; (3) that the proposal to sell did not contravene the covenant not to "permit" the land to be used other than as allotments; (4) that the covenant was personal to the council and was binding only so long as they were the owners of the land; (5) that to have entered into the covenant was *ultra vires* the council's powers; and (6) that the court in its discretion should not grant the injunction, because where there was a conflict between private right and public need, public need should prevail. Plowman J. held (1) on the assumption that the vesting assent was not effective to pass the benefit of the covenant (*i.e.* under the L.P.A. 1925, s.62(1) (see above, p. 216); *cf.* the *Federated Homes* case at first instance (above, p. 251)), nevertheless the special executors held the benefit of the covenant as bare trustees for the plaintiff and he did not have to join them as parties to the action; (2) on the unrefuted evidence that the Holkham Estate was a single entity, the covenant did benefit the entire estate (see *Marten* v. *Flight Refuelling Ltd*, above); (3) the conditions of sale expressly bound the purchaser to housing development; if they required it, then, *a fortiori*, they "permitted" it (*cf. Tophams Ltd.* v. *Earl of Sefton*, above, p. 249); (4) the covenant was not personal since it contemplated the use of the land by persons other than the council; (5) the covenant was not *ultra vires*; (6) there was no reason why the council should not be held to the bargain into which they had freely entered.

Note: That the council might have applied for the modification or discharge of the covenant under section 84 (1) (aa) of the L.P.A. 1925 (below, p. 269). Alternatively, it might have been able to override the covenant by virtue of its statutory powers on payment of compensation.

Russell v. Archdale [1964] Ch. 38, affd. *The Times*, December 1, 1962, C.A.

W. Co. owned the Hedgerley Park Estate and the Bulstrode Park Estate near Stoke Poges. In 1938 the company sold a plot of land surrounded mostly by other land on the H.P. Estate but also by land of the B.P. Estate to the predecessor in title of the defendant, who covenanted to the intent so as to bind the land conveyed into whosesoever hands the same might come and to benefit the vendor's adjoining and neighbouring land that no trade or business should be carried on on the land and that no part of it should be used for the storage of building materials or lumber. In 1958 the company sold the part of the H.P. Estate still retained by it to the plaintiffs and the conveyance was expressed to be together with the full benefit of the covenants entered into for the benefit of the H.P. Estate so far as they affected the land conveyed, *i.e.* there was an express assignment of the benefit of the covenants. The defendant used her property in breach of covenant and the plaintiffs sought an injunction to restrain her. It was held that (1) the benefit of the covenants was annexed to the whole of the company's land and not each and every part of it and as the plaintiffs had acquired a part only of it, they could not rely on annexation; but (2) by virtue of the assignment of the benefit of the covenants they could enforce them.

Stilwell v. Blackman [1968] Ch. 508

In 1955 a piece of land was conveyed to the defendant's predecessor in title, the purchaser covenanting with intent and so as to bind (so far as applicable) the property thereby conveyed into whosesoever hands the same might come and to benefit and protect the adjoining property of the vendor to observe and perform certain covenants, including one not to use the land for any purpose whatsoever except as a private garden. The covenant was held to have been annexed to the retained land as a whole and not each and every part thereof. In 1957 the vendor's retained land was conveyed to the plaintiff. That conveyance expressly assigned the benefit of the covenants to the plaintiff. In 1964 the plaintiff conveyed part of this land to X. who in turn sold to the defendant who was also the owner of part of the land sold by the 1955 conveyance. He used the latter in breach of covenant. The plaintiff sought an injunction. The defendant claimed that as the covenants were taken for the benefit of the whole of the retained land they were not enforceable after the sale off of part of that land in 1964. Ungoed-Thomas J. held that (1) it was a question of construction of the words of covenant used whether express assignment was excluded by annexation. In the present case it was not; (2) express assignment of the benefit of the covenant did not automatically operate as an annexation of the covenant; (3) annexation to the whole did not prevent assignment of the benefit of the covenants on a sale of part; (4) the benefit of the express assignment was not lost by the 1964 sale of part of the plaintiff's land. Accordingly, the plaintiff was entitled to enforce the covenant.

(iii) SCHEME OF DEVELOPMENT

Elliston v. Reacher [1908] Ch. 665, C.A.

The owners of a large area of land who intended to sell off the land for development had an estate plan prepared which showed the estate divided into numbered plots. The conditions of sale on which plots were to be sold were also printed on the plan. The vendors conveyed two plots to predecessors in title of the defendant and another two plots to predecessors in title of the plaintiffs. All four conveyances were on printed forms in similar terms. The defendants began to use buildings on their land as an hotel in breach of covenant. It was held that the plaintiffs were entitled to enforce the covenants and an injunction to restrain the breach. The conditions for a scheme of development were formulated by Parker J. at first instance, as follows: "It must be proved (1) that both the plaintiffs and defendants derive title under a common vendor; (2) that previously to selling the lands to which the plaintiffs and defendants are respectively entitled, the vendor laid out his estate, or a defined portion thereof (including the lands purchased by the plaintiffs and defendants respectively), for sale in lots subject to restrictions intended to be imposed on all the lots, and which, though varying in details as to particular lots, are consistent and consistent only with some general scheme of development; (3) that these restrictions were intended by the common vendor to be and were for the benefit of all the lots intended to be sold, whether or not they were also intended to be and were for the benefit of other land retained by the vendor; and (4) that both the plaintiffs and the defendants, or their predecessors in title, purchased their lots from the common vendor upon the footing that the restrictions subject to which the purchases were made were to enure for the benefit of the other lots included in the general scheme whether or not they were also to enure for the benefit of other lands retained by the vendors."

Note: In *Reid* v. *Bickerstaffe* [1909] 2 Ch. 305, C.A., a fifth condition was added, namely that the area of the scheme must be clearly defined. In that case the trustees of F. sold off in plots an estate of about 64 acres in Liverpool in the 1830s and 1840s. Although these were similar covenants in the respective conveyances there was no reference in the conveyances to the covenants on earlier sales off, nor was there any defined area within which any scheme was to operate. *Per* Cozens-Hardy M.R.: "A building scheme is not created by the mere fact that the owner of an estate sells it in lots and takes varying covenants from various purchasers. There must be notice to the various purchasers of what I may venture to call the local law imposed by the vendors upon a definite area."

Re Pinewood Estate, Farnborough [1958] Ch. 280

The owner of the Pinewood Estate laid it out in plots and in 1899 conveyed them to four purchasers subject to certain restrictive covenants. There was, at this stage, a scheme of development. Subsequently the four purchasers entered into a deed of covenant by which they released each other from the covenants in the conveyances and entered into new restrictive covenants. The deed did not annex the benefit of the covenants to any land. The applicants were successors in title of one of the plots. Another plot was conveyed to a purchaser together with the benefit of the covenants and was later conveyed to the respondents, but without any reference to the benefit of the covenants. The applicants sought a declaration under the L.P.A. 1925, s.84(2) (see below, p. 269) that the covenants were not enforceable against them. Wynn-Parry J. held that the covenants were not enforceable against the applicants because the deed brought the building scheme to an end and it did not create a new building scheme because there was not a common vendor. There was no annexation nor was there a complete chain of assignments.

Note: It has been suggested (based on older authorities) that a chain of assignments is not necessary and that an express assignment operates to *annex* the benefit of the covenant to the land. But the above case, *Stilwell* v. *Blackman* (above, p. 261) and the *Federated Homes* case at first instance are against this view.

Baxter v. Four Oaks Properties Ltd. [1965] Ch. 876

By a conveyance in 1891 Lord C., the owner of an estate of some 288 acres at Sutton Coldfield known as the Four Oaks Estate, sold part to H. The conveyance contained a covenant by H. with Lord C. that he, his heirs and assigns and all persons deriving title under him would perform and observe certain covenants as to building on and user of the land conveyed. By a deed of the same date as this conveyance and expressed to be made between Lord C., H. and all other persons who might thereafter purchase lands forming part of the Estate, H. and all such other persons, their heirs, assigns and persons deriving title under them covenanted to observe and perform certain covenants and conditions set out in the schedule to the deed including a covenant that no dwelling-house should be used otherwise than as a private dwelling-house. It was also provided that the covenants would be enforceable by any other person entitled for the time being to any other land forming part of the Estate in the event of breach. Subsequent purchasers took conveyances containing covenants in substantially the same terms as those in the conveyance to H. and also executed the deed of covenant. There was no evidence that Lord C. had laid out the Estate in plots before beginning to sell it and the plots sold were of varying sizes. The plaintiffs and the defendant company were successors in title of original purchasers of plots. The defendant erected a block of flats which was in breach of covenant if the covenant was enforceable. The plaintiffs relied on a scheme of development (although in the case of some of them it was conceded at the hearing that the benefit of the covenant by the defendant's predecessor in title had been annexed to their land). The defendant denied the existence of a scheme on the ground that the Estate had not been laid out in plots. Cross J. held that the court was satisfied that it was the intention of the parties that the various purchasers from a common vendor of parts of a defined area of land should have rights *inter se*; the court would give effect to that intention and the fact that the common vendor did not lay out the defined area in lots did not, as a matter of law, preclude sufficient proof of that intention. On the facts the plaintiffs proved a scheme. The defendants failed to make out a defence based on the change in the character of the neighbourhood. An injunction was not granted, but the first three plaintiffs whose houses were nearest the flats were granted £500, £100 and £150 respectively. The fourth and fifth plaintiffs were adequately safeguarded by the declaration as to the enforceability of the covenants.

Re Dolphin's Conveyance [1970] Ch. 654

Robert Dolphin, a Birmingham solicitor, was the owner of Selly Hill Estate near Birmingham consisting of some 30 acres. After R.D.'s death in 1870 the bulk of the estate was sold off by nine conveyances. All the conveyances, except the last, were in identical form, recited the title of the vendors to the Selly Hill Estate and contained covenants by the purchasers for themselves, their heirs and assigns with the vendors, their heirs, executors, administrators and assigns to the effect that every house built on the land conveyed had to cost at least £400, be detached, have at least a quarter of an acre of ground and be not less than 21 feet from the road. The vendors covenanted that on a sale or lease of any other part of the Estate it should be sold or leased subject to the same stipulations and with covenants to the like effect. Successors in title of one of the original purchasers of one of the plots sought a declaration that the covenants entered into by the original purchaser were not enforceable against them. There was no annexation or assignment and the only way in which the covenants could be enforced was if there was a scheme of development. Stamp J. held that the covenants contained in the conveyances were imposed for the common benefit of the vendors and the other purchasers who all had a common interest in their enforcement and there was an equity in the owner of each parcel of land to enforce the covenants against the owners of the other parcels of land arising out of the common interest and common intentions expressed in the conveyances which were to be equated with mutual covenants. *Baxter* v. *Four Oaks Properties Ltd.* (above, p. 264) was followed. "It is trite law that if one finds conveyances of the several parts of an estate all containing the same or similar restrictive covenants with the vendor, that is not enough to impute an intention on the part of that vendor that the restrictions should be for the common benefit of the vendor and the several purchasers *inter se.* For it is at least as likely that he imposed them for the benefit of himself and of the unsold parts of the estate alone. That is not this case. . . . For what possible reason does a vendor of part of an estate, who has extracted restrictive covenants from a purchaser, covenant with that purchaser that the other parts of the estate, when sold, shall contain the same restrictions, unless it be with the intention that the purchaser with whom he covenants as well as himself shall have the benefit of the restrictions when imposed. . . . As a matter of construction of the conveyances, I find that what was intended, by the vendors as well as the several purchasers, was to lay down what has been referred to as a local law for the estate for the common benefit of all several purchasers of it. . . . To hold that only where one finds the necessary concomitants of a building scheme or a deed of mutual covenants can one give effect to the common intention found in the conveyances themselves, would . . . be to ignore the wider principle on which building scheme cases can be founded and fly in the face of other authority of which the clearest and most recent case is *Baxter* v. *Four Oaks Properties Ltd.*" (above, p. 264).

Sub-scheme

Brunner v. Greenslade [1971] Ch. 993

In 1926 Sir Coles Child sold off the greater part of his Bromley Palace Estate to Bromley Park Gardens Estates Ltd. subject to certain restrictive covenants (to the intent that the restrictions might enure for the benefit of owners of the land capable of deriving benefit from it) including a covenant against building other than private houses and only eight per acre of such houses (the grandparent covenants). In 1928 B.P.G.E. Ltd. sold off 0.7 of an acre to Stanfords (Builders) Ltd., who covenanted by way of indemnity only to perform and observe the grandparent covenants and also entered into direct covenants expressed to be with the vendors for the benefit of the vendors' Bromley Park Gardens Estate (of which the land conveyed formed part) and the present and future owners lessees and tenants from time to time of the Estate or any part thereof to observe certain restrictive covenants including one that no more than one house would be erected on each building plot (the parent covenants). The vendors reserved the right to alter the plotting or general scheme of development of any remaining land on the Estate. Stanfords divided their land into five plots, built a house on each and sold them subject (at least as regards the parties' land) to the covenants contained or referred to in the 1928 conveyance, and the purchasers covenanted, by way of indemnity only, to observe the said restrictions (the children covenants). Megarry J. held (1) there was no sub-scheme but (2) the purchasers of the five plots were bound by the head scheme. "Where there is a head scheme, any sub-purchasers are bound *inter se* by the covenants of that head scheme even though they have entered into no covenants with the sub-vendor or with each other. What binds the sub-purchaser *inter se* is not any covenant of their own making (for there is none) but an equity independent of any contractual obligation entered into by them, and arising from the circumstances of the existence of the head scheme, the process of division into sub-lots and the disposal of those lots. If on the disposal the common intention was that the local law created by the head scheme should apply within the sub-area, then apply it would. It would be remarkable if the restrictions of the head scheme were to be reciprocally enforceable between the owner of a sub-lot and a plot elsewhere on the estate, however distant, and yet unenforceable as between neighbouring owners of sub-lots." The plaintiffs having established a strong prima facie case for the existence of a right to the benefit of the covenants, an interlocutory injunction was granted.

(iv) LAW OF PROPERTY ACT 1925, s.56(1)

"A person may take an immediate or other interest in land or other property, or the benefit of any condition, right of entry, covenant or agreement over or respecting land or other property, although he may not be named as a party to the conveyance or other instrument."

Re Ecclesiastical Commissioners for England's Conveyance
[1936] Ch. 430

In 1887 G. purchased the subject property from the Commissioners and in the conveyance thereof entered into certain restrictive covenants with the Commissioners and their successors in such terms as to annex the benefit of the covenant to the Commissioners' retained land and also, as a separate covenant, purported to enter into the same covenants with their assigns, owners for the time being of land adjoining or adjacent to the land conveyed. Various plots situated near the subject property had been sold off by the Commissioners prior to 1877. The main question on an application by the owners of the subject site, successors in title of G., under the L.P.A. 1925, s.84(2) (see below, p. 269) was whether the defendants, as successors in title of those who had purchased their plots before 1887, could enforce the covenants. Luxmoore J. held that such of them as owned land adjoining or adjacent to the subject site could enforce the covenants by virtue of the L.P.A. 1925, s.56(1). The 1887 deed described their predecessors as covenantees and the covenants were expressed to affect the land such predecessors had purchased, so that the benefit of the covenant was annexed to the land and was enforceable by their successors, the defendants.

White v. Bijou Mansions Ltd.
[1938] Ch. 351, C.A.

In 1886 an estate was sold for development, the vendors undertaking with the developers to grant leases or conveyances of plots to purchasers of them as the houses were built and when requested by the developers. The leases or conveyances were to contain covenants restricting the use of the houses to private residences. F. purchased a plot and the conveyance to him by the vendors and the developers contained, *inter alia*, a covenant by F. to use the house only as a private residence and a covenant by the vendors that every lease or conveyance of plots on the estate should contain similar covenants, subject to a power of modification, that similar restrictions would apply to any land retained by the vendors and that at F.'s request the vendors would enforce the covenants against future lessees and purchasers. Subsequently N. purchased another plot. He entered into a covenant with the vendors and the developers their heirs and assigns for himself his heirs, executors, administrators and assigns to use his house only as a private residence. Unlike the conveyance to F. there was no covenant by the vendors or the developers. The plaintiff was a successor in title of F. The defendants were tenants of the house N. had bought. Their landlord, a successor in title of N., was the registered proprietor of that property and the covenants entered into by N. were registered in the Charges Register of the title. The defendants took their lease without express notice of the covenants. The plaintiffs sought an injunction to restrain the defendants from using their house as flatlets. They claimed that since they did not have express notice of the covenants they took free from them. It was held that the plaintiff did not have the benefit of the covenants. There was no evidence of any intention to create a building scheme and there was no annexation or assignment. The plaintiff could not rely on section 56(1), as the assigns referred to in N.'s conveyance were those taking plots thereafter not those, such as F., who had already taken.

Note: That restrictive covenants often appear on the Charges Register of titles registered under the L.R.A. 1925, but this does not, of itself, mean that the covenants are enforceable. Covenants appearing to affect the title are automatically entered on first registration of the title without any consideration of their validity. The same applies to covenants registered under the Land Charges Act, the registration again being a purely administrative process without consideration of the validity of the charge.

For another case where s.56 was relied on, see *Lyus* v. *Prowsa Developments Ltd.*, above, p. 46.

3. Enforceability of Covenants

General note: For example, a developer may want to build a block of flats or a number of houses on the site of a large old house which is subject to a restrictive covenant, imposed by an old conveyance, permitting one private dwelling-house only. It is often doubtful whether such a covenant is enforceable. There is usually no doubt that the land is subject to the burden of the covenant, but it may be uncertain whether anyone has the benefit of the covenant to be able to enforce it. The benefit may not have been properly annexed (though if the *Federated Homes* case, above, p. 251, is correct, this will no longer be a problem in many cases). The chances of an effective chain of assignments is usually remote. In the more recent cases the courts have indicated a greater willingness to find a building scheme in appropriate circumstances. If the developer is uncertain whether the covenant is enforceable he can either (a) take the risk that no one will object or that the covenant is unenforceable; (b) protect himself by indemnity insurance against breach (see the *Wrotham Park Estate* case, above, p. 255); (c) apply to the court (Chancery Division) under the L.P.A. 1925, s.84(2) for a declaration as to whether or not the land is affected by the covenant or the covenant is enforceable; (d) assume that the covenant is enforceable and apply to the Lands Tribunal under the L.P.A. 1925, s.84(1) to have it modified or discharged.

4. Extinguishment of Covenants

Unity of Seisin

Re Tiltwood, Sussex [1978] Ch. 269

In 1951 the Tiltwood Estate was broken up. The purchaser of four parcels of agricultural land surrounding the mansion house covenanted with the vendor to use the land for agricultural purposes only and not permit the erection of any houses thereon. (The covenant was to protect the view to the south of the mansion). In 1952 Mrs. Spence bought the mansion with an express assignment of the benefit of the covenants. She sold off the west part without any express assignment of the benefit of the covenants. She then purchased three of the four parcels of agricultural land subject to the covenants. The remaining part of the mansion and the land was then divided into six lots. Four of the lots, including the rest of the house, were sold to the defendant with an express assignment of the benefit of the covenant. Then the remaining two lots (part of the land sold in 1951) were sold to the plaintiff. The plaintiff obtained planning permission to build eight houses to the acre on her land. She sought a declaration that she was not bound by the 1951 covenants, because they were extinguished when the burdened land came into common ownership with the benefited land. Foster J., applying by analogy the rule with regard to easements that unity of seisin of the dominant and servient tenements destroys all easements, held that where the fee simple of the benefited land and the burdened land is vested in one person, the restrictive covenants are extinguished unless the common owner recreates them. The judge said that different considerations applied to building schemes (see above, p. 262), referring to the *Texaco* case (below).

Note: The analogy between restrictive covenants and easements is not exact, for easements are the creature of common law, where merger occurs irrespective of intention. In *Texaco Antilles Ltd.* v. *Kernochan* [1973] A.C. 609, P.C., it was argued that a covenant not to build a public garage (construed by the trial judge and the Court of Appeal of the Bahamas as in 1925 including a service station) imposed in a building scheme had been extinguished when the burdened and benefited land came into one ownership, so that after the severance of the common ownership the covenant was no longer enforceable. The opinion of the Privy Council was that in the case of a building scheme unity of seisin did not extinguish the covenant and that upon the severance of the common ownership, the covenant will apply as between the owners of the lots previously in common ownership unless the conveyance on severance provides that the restriction shall no longer apply. A building scheme is not simply a matter of covenant between two people, but creates a "local law" (see above, pp. 262,263).

CHAPTER 8

SETTLEMENTS AND TRUSTS FOR SALE

I. STRICT SETTLEMENTS

1. DEFINITION OF SETTLED LAND

Settled Land Act 1925, s.1(1)(7)

"(1) Any deed, will, agreement for a settlement or other agreement, Act of Parliament, or other instrument, or any number of instruments . . . by virtue of which . . . any land . . . stands for the time being:–

(i) limited in trust for any persons by way of succession; or

(ii) limited in trust for any person in possession:–

(*a*) for an entailed interest whether or not capable of being barred or defeated;

(*b*) for an estate in fee simple or for a term of years absolute subject to an executory limitation, gift, or disposition over on failure of his issue or in any other event; . . .

(*d*) being an infant, for an estate in fee simple or for a term of years absolute; or

(iii) limited in trust for any person for an estate in fee simple or for a term of years absolute contingently on the happening of any event; or . . .

(v) charged, whether voluntarily or in consideration of marriage or by way of family arrangement, and whether immediately or after an interval, with the payment of any rentcharge for the life of any person, or any less period, or of any capital, annual or periodical sums for the portions, advancement, maintenance, or otherwise for the benefit of any persons, with or without any term of years for securing or raising the same;

creates or is for the purposes of this Act a settlement. . . .

(7) This section does not apply to land held upon trust for sale."

2. Tenant for Life

Settled Land Act 1925, ss.19, 20(1), 117(1)(xxviii)

"19. (1) The person of full age who is for the time being beneficially entitled under a settlement to possession of settled land for his life is for the purposes of this Act the tenant for life of that land and the tenant for life under that settlement.

(2) If in any case there are two or more persons of full age so entitled as joint tenants, they together constitute the tenant for life for the purposes of this Act.

20. (1) Each of the following persons being of full age shall, when his estate or interest is in possession, have the powers of a tenant for life under this Act, (namely):—

(i) A tenant in tail . . . ;

(ii) A person entitled to land for an estate in fee simple or for a term of years absolute with or subject to, in any of such cases, an executory limitation, gift, or disposition over on failure of his issue or in any other event; . . .

(iv) A tenant for years determinable on life, not holding merely under a lease at a rent;

(v) A tenant for the life of another, not holding merely under a lease at a rent;

(vi) A tenant for his own or any other life, or for years determinable on life, whose estate is liable to cease in any event during that life, whether by expiration of the estate, or by conditional limitation, or otherwise, or to be defeated by an executory limitation, gift, or disposition over, or is subject to a trust for accumulation of income for any purpose; . . .

(viii) A person entitled to the income of land under a trust or direction for payment thereof to him during his own or any other life, whether or not subject to expenses of management or to a trust for accumulation of income for any purpose, or until sale of the land, or until forfeiture, cesser or determination by any means of his interest therein, unless the land is subject to an immediate binding trust for sale;

(ix) A person beneficially entitled to land for an estate in fee simple or for a term of years absolute subject to any estates, interests, charges, or powers of charging, subsisting or capable of being exercised under a settlement.

117. (1) . . . (xxviii) 'Tenant for life' includes a person (not being a statutory owner) who has the powers of a tenant for life under this Act, and also (where the context requires) one of two or more persons who together constitute the tenant for life, or have the powers of a tenant for life; . . ."

Re Catling [1931] 2 Ch. 359

A testator devised a house to trustees on trust to grant a lease thereof to his widow at the rent of £1 a year, the tenancy not to be determined while the widow made the house her principal residence and performed the covenants under the lease. The widow claimed that these provisions of the will made her tenant for life of settled land within section 20(1)(vi) or (viii) of the S.L.A. 1925. She claimed that because the rent was nominal and other provisions, *e.g.* that she was to receive the rent from any letting of the house, indicated that she was a S.L.A. tenant for life. Bennett J. held that section 20(1)(iv) indicated that a person who was a tenant under a lease at a rent was excluded from the class of tenants for life under section 20. As a matter of construction the widow was tenant under a lease at a rent.

Note: Re Waleran Settled Estates [1927] 1 Ch. 522, Clauson J. Immediately before January 1, 1926, land was vested in trustees for a term of 99 years if A. should live so long on trust to pay the income to A. during her life and subject thereto to Lord Waleran for his life with remainders over. Mrs. A. claimed to be tenant for life. It was held that she was a tenant for life within section 20(1)(viii) of the S.L.A. 1925. It was not necessary to slavishly follow the form of trust in paragraph (viii). By virtue of the trusts of the settlement Mrs. A. was a person entitled to the income of the land until the determination of her interest by means of the term expiring during her lifetime. Accordingly she was entitled to have a vesting deed executed in her favour.

Re Carne's Settled Estates [1899] 1 Ch. 324

By a settlement a house was vested in trustees upon trust to allow the plaintiff to occupy it rent free for so long as she wished with remainders over in favour, *inter alia*, of one of the defendants. The question arose whether the plaintiff was tenant for life within the S.L.A. 1882 and entitled to exercise the statutory powers thereunder, including a power of sale. North J. held that the plaintiff was tenant for life. The gift amounted to a gift to the plaintiff of an estate for life. The trustees of the term were not trustees for the purposes of the Act and such trustees must be appointed.

Note: See *Bannister* v. *Bannister* (above, p. 4); *Binions* v. *Evans* (above, p. 16).

Re Frewen [1926] Ch. 580

Land was given to trustees to pay two-thirds of the net income to A. for life and to hold the remaining one-third for accumulation upon trust after the death of A. for his first and other sons in tail. The settlement declared that the trustees should during A.'s life have all the powers conferred by the S.L.A. 1925 on a tenant for life in possession of settled land. Lawrence J. held that A. was not entitled to the income of the settled estate within section 20(1)(viii) of the S.L.A. 1925 and the trustees had the powers of a tenant for life by virtue of the terms of the settlement and section 23 of the Act.

Note: And see *Re Jefferys*, below, p. 286.

Re Gallenga Will Trusts [1938] 1 All E.R. 106, Ch.D.

A testatrix by her will gave land to trustees upon trust during the lifetime of her son to take the rents and profits thereof with powers of management and, after payment of certain annuities, to pay all or any part of the net rents and profits unto, or apply the same for the maintenance or benefit of, all or any one of a number of persons, of whom the son was one. There followed a power to allow any of the class referred to to occupy any freehold properties and remainders over with a power of appointment and in default of appointment for the son's heirs. The son claimed to be tenant for life. Bennett J. held that his interest was too insubstantial to be the tenant for life of the settlement and accordingly the powers of the tenant for life were exercisable by the trustees of the settlement.

Statutory Owners

Settled Land Act 1925, ss.23(1), 26(1), 117(1)(xxvi)

"23. (1) Where under a settlement there is no tenant for life nor, independently of this section, a person having by virtue of this Act the powers of a tenant for life then—

(*a*) any person of full age on whom such powers are by the settlement expressed to be conferred; and
(*b*) in any other case the trustees of the settlement;

shall have the powers of a tenant for life under this Act.

26. (1) Where an infant is beneficially entitled in possession to land for an estate in fee simple or for a term of years absolute or would if of full age be a tenant for life of or have the powers of a tenant for life over settled land, then, during the minority of the infant–

(*a*) if the settled land is vested in a personal representative, the personal representative, until a principal vesting instrument has been executed pursuant to the provisions of this Act; and
(*b*) in every other case, the trustees of the settlement;

shall have, in reference to the settled land and capital money, all the powers conferred by this Act and the settlement on a tenant for life, and on the trustees of the settlement.

117. (1) . . . (xxvi) 'Statutory owner' means the trustees of the settlement or other persons who, during a minority, or at any other time when there is no tenant for life, have the powers of a tenant for life under this Act, but does not include the trustees of the settlement, where by virtue of an order of the court or otherwise the trustees have power to convey the settled land in the name of the tenant for life; . . ."

Re Craven Settled Estates [1926] Ch. 985

The Earl of Craven was entitled to a protected life interest in the rents and profits of the Craven Estates, with remainders over. He was not a tenant for life proper within the S.L.A. nor a limited owner having the powers of a tenant for life under the Act, but under the terms of the 1919 resettlement he was given the same powers as if he were a tenant for life in possession. He wished to allow the trustees of the settlement to exercise the powers. Astbury J. held that the Earl was a statutory owner within section 117(1)(xxvi) with a life-tenant's powers within section 23(1)(*a*) and that although a tenant for life or limited owner with the powers of a tenant for life could not release his statutory powers (see S.L.A. 1925, s.104 (below, 289)), a statutory owner could do so and that, on a release being executed, the trustees could act under section 23(1)(*b*).

3. SETTLED LAND ACT TRUSTEES

See Settled Land Act 1925, ss.30, 35.

4. Duration of Settlement

See Settled Land Act 1925, s.3 (see below, p. 295).

5. Documentation

See Settled Land Act 1925, ss.4, 5, 6.

6. The Paralysing Section

Settled Land Act 1925, s.13

"Where a tenant for life or statutory owner has become entitled to have a principal vesting deed or a vesting assent executed in his favour, then until a vesting instrument is executed or made pursuant to this Act in respect of the settled land, any purported disposition thereof *inter vivos* by any person, other than a personal representative (not being a disposition which he has power to make in right of his equitable interests or powers under a trust instrument), shall not take effect except in favour of a purchaser of a legal estate without notice of such tenant for life or statutory owner having become so entitled as aforesaid, but, save as aforesaid, shall operate only as a contract for valuable consideration to carry out the transaction after the requisite vesting instrument has been executed or made, and a purchaser of a legal estate shall not be concerned with such disposition unless the contract is registered as a land charge."

Re Alefounder's Will Trusts [1927] 1 Ch. 360

On December 16, 1925, A. became legal tenant for life in tail in possession of settled land, with remainders over but without any overriding trusts or incumbrances. On January 1, 1926, he automatically became estate owner, holding the legal estate in land in trust for himself as equitable tenant for life, with remainders over and entitled to a vesting deed. A. wanted to bar the entail and dispose of the land without the execution of a vesting deed. Astbury J. held that section 13 of the S.L.A. 1925 applied only to dispositions made under that Act. In any event on the disentail the land would cease to be settled land, so section 13 would not apply.

7. Devolution on Death of Tenant for Life

Settled Land Act 1925, ss.7(1)(2)(4)(5), 36(1)(2)(4)

"7. (1) If, on the death of a tenant for life or statutory owner, or of the survivor of two or more tenants for life or statutory owners, in whom the settled land was vested, the land remains settled land, his personal representatives shall hold the settled land on trust, if and when required so to do, to convey it to the person who under the trust instrument or by virtue of this Act becomes the tenant for life or statutory owner and, if more than one, as joint tenants.

(2) If a person by reason of attaining full age becomes a tenant for life for the purposes of this Act of settled land, he shall be entitled to require the trustees of the settlement, personal representatives, or other persons in whom the settled land is vested, to convey the land to him.

(3) . . .

(4) If by reason of forfeiture, surrender, or otherwise the estate owner of any settled land ceases to have the statutory powers of a tenant for life and the land remains settled land, he shall be bound forthwith to convey the settled land to the person who under the trust instrument, or by virtue of this Act, becomes the tenant for life or statutory owner and, if more than one, as joint tenants.

(5) If any person of full age becomes absolutely entitled to the settled land (whether beneficially, or as personal representatives, or as trustee for sale or otherwise) free from all limitations, powers and charges taking effect under the settlement, he shall be entitled to require the trustees of the settlement, personal representatives, or other persons in whom the settled land is vested, to convey the land to him, and if more persons than one being of full age become so entitled to the settled land they shall be entitled to require such persons as aforesaid to convey the land to them as joint tenants.

36. (1) If and when, after the commencement of this Act, settled land is held in trust for persons entitled in possession under a trust instrument in undivided shares, the trustees of the settlement (if the settled land is not already vested in them) may require the estate owner in whom the settled land is vested (but in the case of a personal representative subject to his rights and powers for purposes of administration), at the cost of the trust estate, to convey the land to them or assent to the land vesting in them as joint tenants, and in the meantime the land shall be held on the same trusts as would have been applicable thereto if it has been so conveyed to or vested in the trustees.

(2) If and when the settled land so held in trust in undivided shares is or becomes vested in the trustees of the settlement, the

land shall be held by them (subject to any incumbrances affecting the settled land which are secured by a legal mortgage, but freed from any incumbrances affecting the undivided shares or not secured as aforesaid, and from any interests, powers and charges subsisting under the trust instrument which have priority to the trust for the persons entitled to the undivided shares) upon the statutory trusts. . . .

(4) An undivided share in land shall not be capable of being created except under a trust instrument or under the Law of Property Act 1925 and shall then only take effect behind a trust for sale." (See above, p. 82.)

Administration of Estates Act 1925, s.22(1)

"A testator may appoint, and in default of such express appointment shall be deemed to have appointed, as his special executors in regard to settled land, the persons, if any, who are at his death the trustees of the settlement thereof, and probate may be granted to such trustees specially limited to the settled land.

In this subsection 'settled land' means land vested in the testator which was settled previously to his death and not by his will."

Re Bridgett and Hayes' Contract [1928] Ch. 163

Mrs. Thornley, a tenant for life of settled land, appointed Bridgett to be the sole executor of her will. On her death the settlement came to an end. B. contracted to sell part of the land to Hayes as Mrs. Thornley's ordinary personal representative. Hayes objected and claimed that title should have been made by the sole surviving trustee of the settlement as Mrs. Thornley's special personal representative. Romer J. held that section 22(1) of the A.E.A. 1925 did not apply where the settlement came to an end on the life tenant's death and a special grant of probate limited to settled land could not have been made in favour of the trustee.

Re Cugny's Will Trusts [1931] 1 Ch. 305

Land was settled on A. for life, remainder to her children in equal shares. A. died in 1929, having by her will appointed the trustees of the settlement to be her executors. The question arose whether they should as executors of A. execute a vesting assent in favour of themselves as trustees of the will containing the settlement upon the statutory trusts for sale, or whether they should apply for a special grant limited to the land subject to the settlement as special personal representatives. Maugham J. held that section 36 of the S.L.A. 1925 applied, the land was now held on the statutory trusts and A.'s executors should execute an assent in favour of themselves as trustees of the will to hold upon the statutory trusts.

Note: The settlement notionally continues under section 36. The section requires the trustees of the settlement (which no longer exists) to call upon the deceased life tenant's ordinary personal representatives to convey the land to them. If the trustees and the personal representatives are the same persons they should execute an assent in favour of themselves. The assent should be an ordinary assent and not a vesting assent, as the settlement has come to an end, despite the reference to a vesting assent in the above case.

8. Determination of Settlement

Settled Land Act 1925, s.17(1)(3)

"(1) Where the estate owner of any settled land holds the land free from all equitable interests and powers under a trust instrument . . . the trustees of the settlement . . . shall . . . be bound to execute, at the cost of the trust estate, a deed declaring that they are discharged from the trust so far as regards that land. . . .

(3) Where a deed . . . of discharge contains no statement to the contrary, a purchaser of a legal estate in the land to which the deed . . . relates shall be entitled to assume that the land has ceased to be settled land, and is not subject to any trust for sale."

9. Powers and Duties of Tenant for Life

Tenant for Life as Trustee

Settled Land Act 1925, s.107 (1)

"A tenant for life or statutory owner shall, in exercising any power under this Act, have regard to the interests of all parties entitled under the settlement, and shall, in relation to the exercise thereof by him, be deemed to be in the position and to have the duties and liabilities of a trustee for those parties."

Power of Sale

Settled Land Act 1925, s.38(i)

"A tenant for life:–

(i) May sell the settled land, or any part thereof. . . ."

Re Marquess of Ailesbury's Settled Estates

affd. *sub nom.* **Lord Henry Bruce v. Marquess of Ailesbury** [1892] A.C. 356, H.L.

An old family mansion was vested in the tenant for life of a settlement, an impecunious young man who had mortgaged his life estate to a moneylender who was foreclosing. The tenant for life could not afford to keep up the house and grounds and had contracted to sell the estate. He applied to the court to sanction the sale. The remainderman opposed the application desiring that the house and grounds should stay in the family. The court considered the purpose of the S.L.A. 1882 to be to prevent the decay of agricultural and other interests occasioned by the deterioration of lands and buildings in the possession of impecunious life tenants. It was not for the good of the estate that an incumbered proprietor should be compelled to continue in a position in which he could do no good either to himself or anybody else. The court was bound to take into consideration not only the relative interests of the beneficiaries but the interests of the estate itself. The main purpose of the Act was not to be frustrated by too nice a regard for the interests of the persons entitled under the settlement.

Wheelwright v. Walker (No. 1) (1883) 23 Ch.D. 752

Land was settled on the testator's grandson, the defendant, for life and after his death on trust for sale for the defendant's daughter. The defendant was aged about 70 and a widower and his daughter was his only child. The daughter sold her reversion to the plaintiff. After the S.L.A. 1882 came into operation the defendant contracted to sell the settled land. The plaintiff sought an injunction to restrain the sale on the grounds that he wanted to occupy the estate on the defendant's death and that no S.L.A. trustees had been appointed. Pearson J. held that the defendant had power to sell. There was nothing in the Act which gave the remainderman any power to interfere with the power of sale. The proceeds of sale would be substituted for the land itself. (In subsequent proceedings (*No. 2*) (1883) 31 W.R. 912, Ch.D., Kay J. granted the plaintiff an injunction restraining the defendant from selling at a price lower than that which the plaintiff was prepared to pay.) But because there were no S.L.A. trustees to whom the defendant could give notice of sale an injunction was granted restraining the defendant from selling until S.L.A. trustees had been appointed.

Re 90 Thornhill Road, Tolworth, Surrey [1970] Ch. 261

A testator settled his house and furniture and effects on his widow for life and then for his two daughters, G. and E. for their joint lives and for the life of the survivor of them, and subject thereto for his grandson absolutely. After the widow's death the trustees of the will executed a vesting assent in favour of the daughters. They became joint tenants for life within section 19(2) of the S.L.A. 1925 (above, p. 272). Subsequently E. wished to sell but G. would not agree as she wanted to live in the house. E. sought an order for sale under section 93 of the S.L.A. 1925. Foster J. held that section 38(i) gave a power of sale and did not create a trust for sale. Where a joint power was not being exercised the court would not interfere and order the power to be exercised unless mala fides was found, because no question arose or doubt was entertained within section 93. ("If a question arises or a doubt is entertained (*a*) respecting the exercise or intended exercise of any of the powers conferred by this Act . . . the tenant for life . . . or any other person interested under the settlement may apply to the court and the court may make such order or give such directions . . . as the court thinks fit.") G. was not acting mala fides and the summons was dismissed.

Note: cf. L.P.A. 1925, s.30 (below, p. 100).

Power to Lease

Settled Land Act 1925, ss.41, 42(1)

"41. A tenant for life may lease the settled land, or any part thereof . . . for any term not exceeding:–

(i) in case of a building lease, nine hundred and ninety-nine years;
(ii) in case of a mining lease, one hundred years;
(iii) in case of a forestry lease, nine hundred and ninety-nine years;
(iv) in case of any other lease, fifty years.

42. (1) Save as hereinafter provided, every lease:–

(i) shall be by deed, and be made to take effect in possession not later than twelve months after its date, or in reversion after an existing lease having not more than seven years to run at the date of the new lease;
(ii) shall reserve the best rent that can reasonably be obtained, regard being had to any fine taken, and to any money laid out or to be laid out for the benefit of the

settled land, and generally to the circumstances of the case;

(iii) shall contain a covenant by the lessee for payment of the rent, and a condition of re-entry on the rent not being paid within a time therein specified not exceeding thirty days."

Law of Property Act 1925, s.152(1)

"Where in the intended exercise of any power of leasing, whether conferred by an Act of Parliament or any other instrument, a lease (in this section referred to as an invalid lease) is granted, which by reason of any failure to comply with the terms of the power is invalid, then

(*a*) as against the person entitled after the determination of the interest of the grantor to the reversion; or

(*b*) as against any other person who, subject to any lease properly granted under the power, would have been entitled to the land comprised in the lease;

the lease, if it was made in good faith, and the lessee has entered thereunder, shall take effect in equity as a contract for the grant, at the request of the lessee, of a valid lease under the power, of like effect as the invalid lease, subject to such variations as may be necessary in order to comply with the terms of the power: . . ."

Position of Purchaser

Settled Land Act 1925, ss.110(1), 18, 112(2)

"110. (1) On a sale, exchange, lease, mortgage, charge or other disposition, a purchaser dealing in good faith with a tenant for life or statutory owner shall, as against all parties entitled under the settlement, be conclusively taken to have given the best price, consideration, or rent, as the case may require, that could reasonably be obtained by the tenant for life or statutory owner, and to have complied with all the requisitions of this Act.

18. (1) Where land is the subject of a vesting instrument and the trustees of the settlement have not been discharged under this Act, then:–

(*a*) any disposition by the tenant for life or statutory owner of the land, other than a disposition authorised by this Act or any other statute, or made in pursuance of any additional or larger powers mentioned in the vesting instrument, shall be void, except for the purpose of conveying or creating such equitable interests as he has power, in right of his equitable interests and powers under the trust instrument, to convey or create; and

(*b*) if any capital money is payable in respect of a transaction, a conveyance to a purchaser of the land shall only take effect under this Act if the capital money is paid to or by the direction of the trustees of the settlement or into court; and

(*c*) notwithstanding anything to the contrary in the vesting instrument, or the trust instrument, capital money shall not, except where the trustee is a trust corporation, be paid to or by the direction of fewer persons than two as trustees of the settlement.

(2) The restrictions imposed by this section do not affect:—

(*a*) the right of a personal representative in whom the settled land may be vested to convey or deal with the land for the purposes of administration;

(*b*) the right of a person of full age who has become absolutely entitled (whether beneficially or as trustee for sale or personal representative or otherwise) to the settled land, free from all limitations, powers, and charges taking effect under the trust instrument, to require the land to be conveyed to him. . . .

112. . . . (2) Where any provision in this Act refers to sale . . . or other disposition or dealing, or to any power . . . it shall (unless the contrary appears) be construed as extending only to sales . . . dispositions . . . powers . . . under this Act."

Davies v. Hall [1954] 1 W.L.R. 855, C.A.

A tenant for life of settled land granted the defendant a weekly tenancy of premises to which the Rent Acts applied. After the death of the tenant for life the plaintiff, the sole surviving trustee of the settlement, claimed possession from the defendant. He claimed that the tenancy was invalid because (1) no vesting deed had ever been executed in favour of the tenant for life; (2) the best rent had not been reserved; and (3) there was no provision for re-entry. It was held that (1) the tenancy took effect as an agreement for a tenancy binding the settlement; and (2) the point about not reserving the best rent had not been pleaded so the plaintiff could not raise it in argument. But even if the point was open the burden of proving that the best rent had not been reserved was on the plaintiff and no evidence on the point had been given. The defendant, having acted in good faith, could rely on section 110(1) of the S.L.A. 1925. Romer L.J. was inclined to take the view that section 42(5) provided a comprehensive code for short leases with the result that the requirement in section 42(1)(iii) as to a provision for re-entry did not apply. If not, this defect was cured by section 152 of the L.P.A. 1925 (above, p. 282) which converts invalid leases into contracts to grant them on the required terms.

Note: But if there is a defect on the face of the lease, as in *Kisch* v. *Hawes Brothers Ltd.* [1935] Ch. 102, Farwell J., where the lease did not take effect in possession within 12 months after its date, the tenant cannot rely on section 110 (1) unless, perhaps, he has acted in good faith. It has been suggested that the tenant may have acted in good faith even where there are defects on the face of the lease, and, of course, section 152 of the L.P.A. 1925 may cure such defects.

Re Handman and Wilcox's Contract [1902] 1 Ch. 599

A tenant for life, purporting to act under the S.L.A. powers, granted a building lease at less than the best rent that might reasonably be obtained, the rent being reduced in consideration of the waiver by the lessee of a claim for damages against the tenant for life. The tenant became bankrupt and his trustee in bankruptcy sold the lease. The purchaser, H., had no knowledge of the arrangement between the tenant for life and the lessee. H. later contracted to sell the lease to W., who objected that the lease was of doubtful validity because the best rent had not been obtained. H. claimed that as he was a purchaser for value without notice he could make a good title. Buckley J. held that as the lease did not comply with the statutory requirements as to obtaining the best rent and the lessee had not acted in good faith it was bad and could be set aside even against a purchaser for value without notice. Section 110 applies only to the grant of a lease and has no application to the time when a subsequent transfer is made.

Weston v. Henshaw [1950] Ch. 510

In 1921 the plaintiff's grandfather conveyed property to the plaintiff's father in fee simple absolutely. In 1927 the father conveyed the property back to the grandfather. In 1931 the grandfather settled his property by will in trust for the father for life with a contingent remainder to the plaintiff at 21. After the grandfather's death his executors executed a vesting assent in favour of the father as tenant for life and they handed over the deeds of the property to the father. In 1944 the father, suppressing the deeds subsequent to 1921 and pretending to be absolute owner mortgaged the property in favour of the defendant. He subsequently mortgaged the property several times to secure further advances. In 1946 the father died and then it was discovered what he had done. The plaintiff claimed that the mortgages were void against him. The defendant relied on section 110 of the S.L.A. 1925. Danckwerts J. held that section 110 applied only to a person dealing with a tenant for life as such and who knew him to be a limited owner and therefore the defendant was not protected by it. By virtue of section 18(1)(*a*) and (*b*) the charges were void as against the plaintiff. That section was not to be read subject to the provisions of section 112(2) of the Act and accordingly was not subject to the limitation that it should apply only to dispositions made, or purporting to be made, by a tenant for life as such.

Note: This decision was doubted in the next case.

Re Morgan's Lease [1972] Ch. 1

In 1960 M., a tenant for life of settled land, purported as absolute owner to grant a lease to the plaintiffs for seven years with an option to renew for a further seven years on the same terms, with the exception of the covenant for renewal. The plaintiffs believed M. to be the absolute owner. M. died and in due course the plaintiffs gave notice to the defendants, M.'s successors in title, exercising the option. The defendants refused to grant the new lease, claiming that the original lease was void because (1) relying on *Weston* v. *Henshaw* (above), M. was tenant for life; (2) the lease was not by deed as required by section 42(1); and (3) the rent was inadequate. It was common ground that the 1960 document was void as a lease because it was not a deed but operated as an agreement for a lease and that on the exercise of the option an executory contract arose. The question was whether the plaintiffs could bring themselves within section 110(1) as they had dealt with M. as absolute owner. Ungoed-Thomas J. held that they were entitled to rely on section 110(1) irrespective of the fact that they were unaware that M. was a tenant for life, provided that they had acted in good faith. Danckwerts J.'s observation in *Weston* v. *Henshaw* was inconsistent with *Mogridge* v. *Clapp* (below), where it was treated as self-evident that a person dealing with a life tenant without knowing that he was a life tenant would be entitled to rely on the provision in the S.L.A. 1882 equivalent to section 110(1) of the S.L.A. 1925. Accordingly, there being no evidence of bad faith, the option was valid and had been validly exercised.

Note: Section 110(1) can be relied on even where there are defects in the transaction apart from the insufficiency of rent. Observations of Farwell J. in *Kisch* v. *Hawes Brothers Ltd.* (above, p. 284) suggested that section 110 could only be relied on if the only defect was the insufficiency of rent. But Romer L.J. in *Davies* v. *Hall* (above, p. 283), did not think that Farwell J. was suggesting this as a general proposition and Ungoed-Thomas J. decided that the section was not so limited.

Note: In *Mogridge* v. *Clapp* [1892] 3 Ch. 382, C.A., a tenant for life, believing himself to be the absolute owner of property, purported to grant a building lease. The lessee assumed that the lessor was the absolute owner. The lessee later contracted to sell the lease and the purchaser objected that the lease was bad, the land having belonged to the lessor's deceased wife and the lessor being merely tenant by the courtesy. Such a tenant had all the powers of a tenant for life under the S.L.A. 1882 but the lease was defective in so far as it contained no reference to the Act and no notice of the lease had been given to S.L.A. trustees and, in any event, there were none. It was held that the lessee having acted in good faith was protected by section 54 of the S.L.A. 1882 (now S.L.A. 1925, s.110(1)).

Note: Cf. the position where land is held on trust for sale (see above, p. 106).

Restrictions on Powers

Settled Land Act 1925, s.108(1)(2)

"(1) Nothing in this Act shall take away, abridge or prejudicially affect any power for the time being subsisting under a settlement, or by statute or otherwise, exercisable by a tenant for life, or (save as hereinafter provided) by trustees with his consent, or on his request, or by his direction, or otherwise, and the powers given by this Act are cumulative.

(2) In case of conflict between the provisions of a settlement and the provisions of this Act, relative to any matter in respect whereof the tenant for life or statutory owner exercises or contracts or intends to exercise any power under this Act, the provisions of this Act shall prevail; and, notwithstanding anything in the settlement, any power . . . relating to the settled land thereby conferred on the trustees of the settlement or other persons exercisable for any purpose, whether or not provided for in this Act, shall . . . be exercisable by the tenant for life. . . . "

Re Jefferys [1939] Ch. 205

A testator who died before January 1, 1926, left his real estate and the residue of his personal estate to trustees in trust to pay an annuity of £150 to Mr. Martin, to accumulate the balance during M.'s life and after his death to hold the property on trust for sale and to divide the proceeds of sale and the accumulations amongst certain hospitals. The trustees were empowered to sell the property with M.'s consent and pay the proceeds immediately to the hospitals. No vesting deed was made after 1925. Certain sales were made after 1925 with M.'s consent and the question arose whether the proceeds of sale were capital moneys to be retained by the trustees or to be distributed to the hospitals, as provided for in the will. The accumulation period permitted by section 164 of the L.P.A. 1925 (see below, p. 328), expired in 1933 and the surplus income over £150 would be payable to the testator's next-of-kin as undisposed of property. Farwell J. held that there was no tenant for life and the trustees were the statutory owners. The requirement for M.'s consent was inconsistent with section 108(1), which preserved powers exercisable by trustees with the consent only of the tenant for life and not a person other than the tenant for life and accordingly the power to sell with M.'s consent was not preserved. The power was in conflict with the statutory power of sale for which no consent was required and therefore the statutory power prevailed by virtue of section 108(2).

Settled Land Act 1925, s.106(1)

"If in a settlement . . . or other instrument . . . a provision is inserted—

(*a*) purporting or attempting, by way of direction, declaration, or otherwise, to forbid a tenant for life or statutory owner to exercise any power under this Act, or his right to require the settled land to be vested in him; or

(*b*) attempting, or tending, or intended, by a limitation, gift, or disposition over of settled land, or by limitation, gift, or disposition of other real or any personal property, or by the imposition of any condition, or by forfeiture, or in any other manner whatever, to prohibit or prevent him from exercising, or to induce him to abstain from exercising, or to put him into a position inconsistent with his exercising, any power under this Act, or his right to require the settled land to be vested in him;

that provision, as far as it purports, or attempts, or tends, or is intended to have, or would or might have, the operation aforesaid, shall be deemed to be void."

Re Acklom [1929] 1 Ch. 195

A testator who died in 1918 bequeathed his leasehold house, Wiseton Court, and effects to trustees upon trust to permit his sister to reside there and he directed the trustees to sell the house if she should not wish to reside or continue to reside there, and divide the proceeds amongst certain charities. The sister lived there for some years, but in 1925 went abroad temporarily for her health, leaving her servants in the house. In 1926 she was unable to return to England because of her health. In 1927 she sold the house as tenant for life and the question arose what interest (if any) she had in the proceeds. Maugham J. held that the sister had properly exercised the statutory power of sale. The power of sale in the trustees never arose, nor did the trustees purport to exercise it. Accordingly the sister had not forfeited her interest in the proceeds of sale.

Re Patten [1929] 2 Ch. 276

A testator who died in 1928 directed his trustees to set aside a sum of £3,000 and apply the income thereof in payment of the rates, taxes and repairs of his freehold house and expressed a desire that his aunt should have the use of the house and furniture for her life or as long as she required but "without power to sub-let" the house or any part. The gift to the aunt made her tenant for life of the house. On the termination of the aunt's occupation the house was to be sold and the testator's nephew was to have the furniture. The question arose as to the effect of the provision against sub-letting and the gift over on the aunt ceasing to use the house. Romer J. held that the prohibition on sub-letting was void under section 106 of the S.L.A. 1925 and the gift over would not take effect if the aunt ceased to occupy the house by reason of her exercising her statutory powers, though it would be effective if she ceased to occupy for some other reason. If the aunt sold the house she would be entitled to the income of the proceeds, but not to the income of the £3,000, though if she let the house, the trust to apply the income in paying rates, etc., would still continue. After exercising her statutory powers, she would still be entitled to the furniture.

Re Herbert [1946] 1 All E.R. 421, Ch.D.

A testator settled the Boyton Manor Estate by his will. He also gave his trustees a fund of £50,000 defined as the maintenance fund on trust to apply the income thereof towards the payment of certain outgoings of the Estate and to pay the balance to the tenant for life. On the sale of Boyton Manor House or on the expiration of a perpetuity period, whichever happened sooner, the maintenance fund fell into residue. The tenant for life sold the house under his statutory powers and the question arose whether the income of the maintenance fund should be paid to the tenant for life by reason of section 106 or whether the fund fell into residue. Vaisey J. held that since the provision for the fund to fall into residue tended to induce the tenant for life not to exercise his statutory power of sale section 106 applied and the income of the fund would continue to be payable to the tenant for life.

Re Burden [1948] Ch. 160

A testatrix settled two houses on respective tenants for life, with gifts over in each case to the same charity. She directed that if the tenant for life should cease to reside in the house, the life interest should determine and the gift to the charity should be accelerated. The testatrix also directed her trustees to set aside two sums of £1,000 each and to hold the same during the respective lives of the tenants for life to pay rates, property tax and the cost of all necessary repairs to the houses and after their deaths for the charity. The question arose whether on a sale the life-tenant would continue to be entitled to the income of the £1,000 fund. Romer J. held that the £1,000 fund was not provided for the personal profit of the tenant for life but solely to enable her to reside in the house free from the expense of outgoings. Therefore if the tenant for life exercised her statutory power of sale she did not lose any benefit the retention of which would be an inducement not to exercise that power.

Note: In *Re Aberconway's Settlement Trusts* [1953] Ch. 647, C.A., where funds were given to trustees on trust to apply the income at their discretion towards the maintenance of Bodnant Gardens in North Wales, it was held that section 106(1)(*b*) did not operate to render void directions which determined provisions which were neither for the benefit of any *cestui que trust* nor in strictness ancillary to the enjoyment by the *cestui que trust* of the trust property.

Assignment of Powers

Settled Land Act 1925, ss.104, 105(1)

"104. (1) The powers under this Act of a tenant for life are not capable of assignment or release, and do not pass to a person as being, by operation of law or otherwise, an assignee of a tenant for life, and remain exercisable by the tenant for life after and notwithstanding any assignment, by operation of law or otherwise, of his estate or interest under the settlement. . . .

(2) A contract by a tenant for life not to exercise his powers under this Act or any of them shall be void.

105. (1) Where the estate or interest of a tenant for life under the settlement has been or is absolutely assured with intent to extinguish the same . . . to the person next entitled in remainder or reversion under the settlement, then the statutory powers of the tenant for life under this Act shall, in reference to the property affected by the assurance, and notwithstanding the provisions of the last preceding section, cease to be exercisable by him, and the statutory powers shall thenceforth become exercisable as if he were dead, but without prejudice to any incumbrance affecting the estate or interest assured, and to the rights to which any incumbrancer would have been entitled if those powers had remained exercisable by the tenant for life. . . . "

Re Shawdon Estates Settlement [1930] 2 Ch. 1, C.A.

A tenant for life was bankrupt. His trustee in bankruptcy sold the bankrupt's life interest to the tenant in tail in remainder. The remainderman required the tenant for life to execute a vesting deed in his favour but the tenant for life refused. The remainderman sought a vesting order under section 12(1)(*a*) of the S.L.A. 1925. It was held that the powers of the tenant for life had ceased under section 105. That section was not confined to cases where the tenant for life had himself assured his interest, but extended to an assurance by any person in whom the tenant for life's interest was vested. The tenant for life therefore ought to execute a vesting deed under section 7(4) of the S.L.A. 1925 and as he had refused to do so the court made a vesting order.

Re Maryon-Wilson's Instruments [1971] Ch. 789

By his will Sir Spencer Maryon-Wilson had settled his Middlesex Estates on Sir Percy for life and then for Sir Percy's sons in tail male with remainders to Sir Hubert in tail male. He directed that the trustees of the will and of various settlements made by him should as far as possible be the same persons and that the tenant for life for the time being of the Middlesex Estates should have the power of appointing new trustees of the will. In 1959 Sir Percy, a bachelor, disentailed and exercised a power of appointment resettling the Estates in effect for (i) himself for life; (ii) his sons in tail; (iii) Sir Hubert for life; (iv) his sons in tail male; (v) Lord Gough for life; and (vi) his sons in tail. By another deed in 1959 Sir Hubert, aged 74 and without issue, assigned his life interest in the Estates expectant on the death of Sir Percy without sons to trustees for the benefit of those entitled as if he were dead. Sir Percy died in 1965 without having married or having any children, so that by virtue of Sir Hubert's 1959 deed Lord Gough became tenant for life in possession subject to defeasance in the unlikely event of Sir Hubert having a son. The question arose, who had the powers of tenant for life, Sir Hubert or Lord Gough? Foster J. held that on the true construction of the words "to the person next entitled in remainder," etc., in section 105(1) of the S.L.A. 1925 Lord Gough did not qualify as the person next entitled because the subsection did not apply where there was an intervening limitation which might still take effect. The power in the will to appoint new trustees did not fall within the terms of "any power . . . relating to the settled land" within section 108(2) of the S.L.A. 1925 so as to vest the power in Sir Hubert and accordingly the power was vested in Lord Gough as the person at the present time entitled to the receipt of the rents and profits.

Settled Land Act 1925, s.24

"(1) If it is shown to the satisfaction of the court that a tenant for life, who has by reason of bankruptcy, assignment, incumbrance, or otherwise ceased in the opinion of the court to have a substantial interest in his estate or interest in the settled land or any part thereof, has unreasonably refused to exercise any of the powers conferred on him by this Act, or consents to an order under this section, the court may, on the application of any person interested in the settled land or the part thereof affected, make an order authorising the trustees of the settlement, to exercise, in the name and on behalf of the tenant for life, any of the powers of a tenant for life under this Act, in relation to the settled land or the part thereof affected, either generally and in such manner and for such period as the court may think fit, or in a particular instance, and the court may by the order direct that any documents of title in the possession of the tenant for life relating to the settled land be delivered to the trustees of the settlement.

(2) While any such order is in force, the tenant for life shall not, in relation to the settled land or the part thereof affected, exercise any of the powers thereby authorised to be exercised in his name and on his behalf, but no person dealing with the tenant for life shall be affected by any such order, unless the order is for the time being registered as an order affecting land.

(3) An order may be made under this section at any time after the estate or interest of the tenant for life under the settlement has taken effect in possession, and notwithstanding that he disposed thereof when it was an estate or interest in remainder or reversion."

Re Thornhill's Settlement [1941] Ch. 24, C.A.

The tenant for life of an agricultural estate became bankrupt and ceased to have any substantial interest in the land. He repudiated his title as tenant for life and neglected the management of the farms. He also refused to sell or let land requisitioned by the War Office. It was held, affirming Bennett J., in five lines, that the tenant for life had unreasonably refused to exercise his powers of leasing and sale and the court could therefore make an order under section 24 vesting all powers of sale and leasing in the Public Trustee, who was the trustee of the settlement, and for delivery to the trustee by the tenant for life of all documents of title relating to the land. The mere fact that the estate had been allowed to fall into a deplorable condition was not in itself a ground for exercising the jurisdiction under section 24. The court had to be satisfied by evidence that the tenant for life had unreasonably refused to exercise his statutory powers.

Liability for Repairs

Re Cartwright (1889) 41 Ch.D. 532

By his will John Cartwright devised land unto and to the use of his daughter Mary Anne Cartwright and her assigns for and during the term of her natural life, then to her children and in default of her having children to the defendant. The will contained provisions dealing with the daughter's liability for waste. The daughter died a spinster. Buildings, gates and fences on the land were in a dilapidated condition owing to the necessary repairs not having been done by her. The defendant claimed the cost of repairs from the daughter's estate. Kay J. held that the daughter's estate was not liable for permissive waste in the absence of an express duty to repair.

Note: Accordingly where a widow or another is given a right of residence in the testator's house (see *e.g. Re Herklot's W.T.*, below, p. 294) it is usual to provide either that the beneficiary be responsible for repairs, etc., or to provide a fund for that purpose (see *e.g. Re Patten*, above, p. 288).

II. TRUSTS FOR SALE

1. Nature of Trust for Sale

Trust not Power

Re White's Settlement [1930] 1 Ch.179

By a marriage settlement made in 1882 and a partition in 1906 realty was settled upon trust either to retain the same in its present condition or with the consent of the life tenant to sell and after her death to sell at the discretion of the trustees. There was no power in the settlement to postpone conversion. On a summons to determine whether the land remaining subject to the settlement was settled land or held on trust for sale, Eve J. held that having regard to the trusts and the powers in the settlement relating to the management of the property as a real estate it was settled land. The primary trust was to retain. There was no duty on the trustees to sell, with a discretion as to the manner and time of the sale, but rather a trust to retain with a power giving the trustees an uncontrolled discretion whether to sell or not.

Note: Section 25(4) of the Law of Property Act 1925 (below) applies only to dispositions coming into operation after the commencement of the Act. Note also that a trust to sell in limited cases will not create a trust for sale: see *Re Smith and Lonsdale's Contract* (below, p. 302).

Law of Property Act 1925, s.25(4)

"Where a disposition or settlement coming into operation after the commencement of this Act contains a trust either to retain or sell land the same shall be construed as a trust to sell the land with power to postpone the sale."

Statutory Definition

Law of Property Act 1925, s.205(1)(xxix)

" 'Trust for sale,' in relation to land, means an immediate binding trust for sale, whether or not exercisable at the request or with the consent of any person, and with or without a power at discretion to postpone the sale; 'trustees for sale' mean the persons (including a personal representative) holding land on trust for sale; . . . "

Immediate

Law of Property Act 1925, s.32(1)

"Where a settlement of personal property or of land held upon trust for sale contains a power to invest money in the purchase of land, such land shall, unless the settlement otherwise provides, be held by the trustees on trust for sale; . . . "

Re Hanson [1928] Ch. 96

A personalty settlement directed under the trustees to purchase a house as a residence for the testator's wife until his son David attained 25, if she so long continued the testator's widow. After D. attained 25 or the wife remarried (whichever happened first) the house was to fall into residue on trust for sale and conversion. A house was purchased by the trustees. Later they wanted to sell it and the question arose whether title would be made under a trust for sale imposed by section 32 of the L.P.A. 1925 or as settled land under the Settled Land Act 1925. Astbury J. held that the direction to purchase a house for the wife's residence was inconsistent with an immediate trust for sale and excluded section 32. It was doubted whether, in any event, section 32 applied to a trust to purchase land. Accordingly the house was settled land and the widow tenant for life.

Re Herklot's Will Trusts [1964] 1 W.L.R. 583, Ch.D.

A testatrix left the residue of her estate, including her house, to trustees on trust for sale with a subsequent direction that the income be paid to Miss G. for life and that Miss G. should be permitted to reside in the house during her life so long as she wished. The plaintiff was given a share of the residue after Miss G.'s death. By a codicil the plaintiff was given the option of taking the house instead of his share of residue. Miss G. proposed to sell the house as tenant for life of settled land and the plaintiff claimed an injunction to stop Miss G. selling, contending that the house was subject to a trust for sale. Ungoed-Thomas J. held that the house was subject to a trust for sale with a prohibition against sale in the lifetime of Miss G. without the plaintiff's consent. There was undoubtedly a trust for sale of the house and the question was whether the permission for Miss G. to reside in the house was inconsistent with the trust for sale. It was held that it was not.

Binding

Settled Land Act 1925, s.3

"Land not held upon trust for sale which has been subject to a settlement shall be deemed for the purposes of this Act to remain and be settled land, and the settlement shall be deemed to be a subsisting settlement for the purposes of this Act so long as:—

(*a*) any limitation, charge, or power of charging under the settlement subsists, or is capable of being exercised; or
(*b*) the person who, if of full age, would be entitled as beneficial owner to have that land vested in him for a legal estate is an infant."

Re Leigh's Settled Estates (No. 1) [1926] Ch. 852

Mrs. T. was tenant for life of settled land under L.'s will subject only to a jointure rentcharge created by a deceased tenant for life in favour of his widow. In 1923 Mrs. T. disentailed and conveyed the settled land subject to the jointure rentcharge to trustees for sale upon the trusts of a new settlement whereunder specified annuities were payable to certain beneficiaries and the balance payable to Mrs. T. The question arose whether the trust for sale created by the 1923 resettlement was an immediate binding trust for sale " . . . : immediate is used as distinct from future. . . . The expression 'Unless the land is subject to an immediate binding trust for sale' must . . . mean unless the land that is the total subject-matter of the settlement is subject to a trust for sale which operates in relation to the whole subject-matter of the settlement and is immediately exercisable . . . where the subject-matter of the settlement is the whole unincumbered fee simple, there is no immediate binding trust for sale so long as there is not a trust for sale capable of overriding all charges having under the settlement priority to the trust for sale." (*Per* Tomlin J.) In the present case the trust for sale in the 1923 deed was not capable of overriding the prior equitable jointure rentcharge. Accordingly there was no immediate binding trust for sale and the land remained settled land. There was a compound settlement consisting of the original will, the disentailing deed and the 1923 documents and Mrs. T. was tenant for life notwithstanding the fact that her right to receive the income was subject to the prior annuities.

Re Leigh's Settled Estate (No. 2) [1927] 2 Ch. 13

After the earlier case the Law of Property (Amendment) Act 1926 had been passed. This amended, *inter alia* section 2(2) of the L.P.A. 1925 dealing with overreaching by *ad hoc* trusts for sale. An *ad hoc* trust for sale was not defined as an immediate binding trust for sale, indeed there would be no point in section 2(2) otherwise. Tomlin J. held that as the trustees of the trust for sale could overreach the jointure rentcharge under this section the land was held subject to an immediate binding trust for sale. The trusts of the 1923 deeds had been approved by the court because Mrs. T. was then an infant. This approval of the trustees sufficed for section 2(2).

Re Parker's Settled Estates [1928] Ch. 247

A. was tenant for life of settled land. In 1901, on his marriage, he charged the land with a jointure rentcharge in favour of his wife and created portions terms to secure portions in favour of his future children. In 1924 A.'s elder child B. disentailed and the land was conveyed to trustees for sale on certain trusts for the benefit of A., B., A.'s wife and his younger children. Romer J. held that the land was settled land subject to a compound settlement and A. was sole tenant for life. He disagreed with Tomlin J.'s definition of immediate binding trust for sale in *Re Leigh's Settled Estate* (*No. 1*). He did not think that a trust for sale was confined to cases where the equitable interest could be overreached by the trustees. He preferred to treat the word "binding" as mere surplusage rather than to give it a meaning which would exclude trusts for sale as that expression had always been understood by lawyers. His test was whether the whole legal estate which is the subject-matter of the settlement is subjected to a trust for sale. Owing to the outstanding *legal* term (the portions term) the whole legal estate was not vested in the trustees for sale and the land was therefore not held on trust for sale.

Re Norton [1929] 1 Ch. 84

On December 31, 1925, certain lands were settled under a compound settlement consisting of various documents on trust for Lord Norton for life and after his death, subject to certain equitable jointure rent charges and portions, for trustees on trust for sale. The legal estate in the land was vested in Lord Norton by a vesting deed. On Lord Norton's death in 1926 probate limited to settled land was granted to the trustees of the compound settlement as special representatives on the footing that the land remained settled land. The trustees for sale claimed to have the lands vested in them on the ground that they were subject to a trust for sale. Romer J. held that there was no immediate binding trust for sale. The judge referred to his previous explanation of trust for sale in *Re Parker's S.E.* (above). The legal estate was not in the trustees for sale but the special representatives nor did the trustees for sale have the right to compel a conveyance. He referred to section 7(5) of the S.L.A. 1925 (above, p. 277). The trustees for sale had not become absolutely entitled to the settled land "free from all charges taking effect under the settlement" because the jointure rentcharges and portions terms had priority to the trust for sale. Therefore not only was the property not held upon trust for sale at Lord Norton's death but also the trustees did not have a right to call for the legal estate.

Re Sharpe's Deed of Release [1939] Ch. 51

Under the will of William Henry Sharpe Sharpe the Hoxton Estate passed to his grandson James William Sharpe subject to two equitable jointures and an annuity. By his will J.W.S. gave the estate, subject to the jointures and annuity, to trustees for sale to hold on the trusts set out in the will. The question arose whether the land was settled land (*cf. Re Norton* where the prior charges had originally been legal but had become equitable on the execution of the vesting deed; here the prior interests were equitable in origin). The trustees of W.H.S.S.'s will and the trustees for sale under J.W.S.'s will were the same persons. The legal estate was vested in the trustees but *qua* trustees of W.H.S.S.'s will. Morton J. considered *Re Parker's S.E.* and *Re Norton* and accepted Romer J.'s test. Accordingly in the present case the land was settled land. The whole legal estate in the land was held by the trustees of W.H.S.S.'s will upon trusts which did not include a trust for sale; the trustees of J.W.S.'s will held upon trust for sale only the beneficial interest in the land which was given to J.W.S. by W.H.S.S.'s will.

Postponing the Sale

Law of Property Act 1925, s.25(1)

"A power to postpone sale shall, in the case of every trust for sale of land, be implied unless a contrary intention appears."

Re Rooke [1953] Ch. 716

A testator directed his executors and trustees to sell his farm as soon as possible after his death and that the proceeds should form part of his residuary estate. He gave his residuary estate to the trustees upon trust to permit and allow his widow to receive and enjoy the net income during her life and on her death to sell, call in and convert the same into money and pay the proceeds between his brothers and sisters. The trustees allowed the widow to carry on the farm but the remaindermen objected and claimed that it was the duty of the trustees to sell. Harman J. held that the direction to sell was sufficiently imperative to be inconsistent with a discretionary power to postponement and therefore a contrary intention within section 25(1) of the L.P.A. 1925. Accordingly if the remaindermen insisted on a sale the trustees must sell as soon as they conveniently could.

Tying up Land by Trust for Sale

Re Inns [1947] Ch. 576

A testator devised his house upon trust for sale (but only with the consent of his widow and the local district council) on trust if the house was unsold to allow his widow to reside there, subject to her keeping the house in good repair and condition and insured. After the widow's death or remarriage the house was to be offered to the council for use as a hospital and, if accepted, the testator bequeathed £10,000 to the council as an endowment. If not accepted the house fell into residue. The case was really concerned with the widow's claim for further maintenance under the Inheritance (Family Provision) Act 1938 as she could not afford to keep the house up. But the effect of the limitations was that in the circumstances the house could not be sold during the widow's lifetime. If the council consented to a sale there would be no house to be offered to it on the widow's death and it would lose both the house and the endowment. This case, therefore, illustrates that a judicious use of consents and gifts over contingent on consent not being given may enable the land to be made temporarily inalienable.

Note: It is rather paradoxical that, whereas before the S.L.A. 1882 the strict settlement was the method of tying up land, the trust for sale, formerly used by persons not especially keen on keeping the land in the family, should become the better method of retaining land.

Conversion

Note: The moment the trust for sale arises any land subject to the trust is treated as personalty (see above, p. 75). However a beneficial interest in land subject to a trust for sale will be treated as an interest in land for some purposes (see above, pp. 50, 75).

2. Commencement and Determination

Note: A trust for sale may be created expressly (see *Re Rooke*, above) and no special documentation is required (*cf.* strict settlements, above, p. 276) or arise by operation of law, *e.g.* under the L.P.A. or the S.L.A. in cases of co-ownership (above, pp. 82-83) or under the Administration of Estates Act 1925, s.33 on intestacy.

The Statutory Trusts

Law of Property Act 1925, s.35

"For the purposes of this Act land held upon the 'statutory trusts' shall be held upon the trusts and subject to the provisions following, namely, upon trust to sell the same and to stand possessed of the net proceeds of sale, after payment of costs, and of the net rents and profits until sale after payment of rates, taxes, costs of insurance, repairs and other outgoings, upon such trusts, and subject to such powers and provisions, as may be requisite for giving effect to the rights of the persons (including an incumbrancer of a former undivided share or whose incumbrance is not secured by a legal mortgage) interested in the land . . . "

Note: A trust for sale will come to an end when either (a) all the land subject to the trust is sold (see *Re Wakeman*, below, p. 300) or (b) the entire beneficial interest in the land is vested in one person (see *e.g. Re Cook*, above, p. 77).

Law of Property Act 1925, s.23

"Where land has, either before or after the commencement of this Act, become subject to an express or implied trust for sale, such trust shall, so far as regards the safety and protection of any purchaser thereunder, be deemed to be subsisting until the land has been conveyed to or under the direction of the persons interested in the proceeds of sale.

This section applies to sales whether made before or after the commencement of this Act, but operates without prejudice to an order of any court restraining a sale."

3. Powers and Duties of Trustees for Sale

Powers

Law of Property Act 1925, s.28(1)

"Trustees for sale shall, in relation to land and to the proceeds of sale, have all the powers of a tenant for life and the trustees of a settlement under the Settled Land Act 1925, including in relation to the land the powers of management conferred by that Act during a minority (and where by statute settled land is or becomes vested in the trustees of the settlement upon the statutory trusts, such trustees and their successors in office shall also have all the additional or larger powers (if any) conferred by the settlement on the tenant for life, statutory owner, or trustees of the settlement): and (subject to any express trust to the contrary) all capital money arising under the said powers shall, unless paid or applied for any purpose authorised by the S.L.A. 1925, be applicable in the same manner as if the money represented proceeds of sale arising under the trust for sale.

All land acquired under this subsection shall be conveyed to the trustees on trust for sale.

The powers conferred by this subjection shall be exercised with such consents (if any) as would have been required on a sale under the trust for sale, and when exercised shall operate to overreach any equitable interests or powers which are by virtue of this Act or otherwise made to attach to the net proceeds of sale as if created by a trust affecting those proceeds."

Investment in Land

Re Wakeman [1945] Ch. 177

A testator appointed a bank his executor and trustee and gave it his residuary real and personal property on trust for sale in trust for his daughter for life. In the course of administration the bank sold the only land in the residuary estate. The daughter claimed that the trustees could invest part of the proceeds in the purchase of a house for her occupation. The bank could only do this (if at all: see *Re Power*, below) if it was a trustee for sale under section 28 of the L.P.A. 1925. Section 205(1)(xxix) (above, p. 293) defines trustees for sale as persons holding *land* on trust for sale. There being no land subject to the trusts of the testator's will there was no trust for sale (Uthwatt J.).

Note: In *Re Power* [1947] 1 Ch. 572, Jenkins J. held that unless expressly authorised by the trust deed (or by the court under section 57 of the Trustee Act 1925) trustees of a personalty settlement cannot purchase a house as a residence for a beneficiary because this is not an investment.

Re Wellsted's Will Trusts [1949] Ch. 296, C.A.

Trustees for sale wanted to invest the proceeds of sale of land and investments in the purchase of land. They claimed to do this by virtue of section 73 of the S.L.A. 1925 and section 28 of the L.P.A. 1925. Vaisey J. had held that section 73 had two aspects—investment powers and administrative powers—and only the latter applied to trustees for sale by virtue of section 28. This interpretation was rejected by the C.A. The powers of application and investment in section 73 apply to capital money raised by the exercise of both Settled Land Act powers and a trust for sale. Cohen L.J. reserved his opinion on the correctness of *Re Wakeman* (above), where trustees for sale have held and then subsequently sold land.

Restrictions on Powers

Re Davies' Will Trusts [1932] 1 Ch. 530

Under the will the net income of a farm and lands was payable to the plaintiff and the testator's nephew equally until the testator's youngest daughter attained 21, and, thereafter, equally between the plaintiff for life or until marriage, the nephew for life or so long as he should reside upon and assist in the management of the farm, and the testator's two daughters. On January 1, 1926, the farm became held upon the statutory trusts for sale. The question arose whether if the farm was sold under the statutory trusts or leased under the powers in the will or the statutory powers, the nephew, being no longer able to reside on the farm, would lose his interest in the farm. Maugham J. held that the nephew's life interest would not be forfeited by any exercise of the statutory trusts. The powers and provisions mentioned in section 35 of the L.P.A. 1925 were to be construed as including a provision that the exercise of the statutory powers should not occasion a forfeiture. It was argued that section 28 of the L.P.A. 1928 incorporated section 106 of the S.L.A. 1925 (prohibiting restrictions on the statutory powers (above, p. 287)), but it was not necessary to decide that point.

Re Flint [1927] 1 Ch. 570

In 1926 land became vested in trustees for sale upon the statutory trusts subject to a right of pre-emption in favour of the testator's son, A. Astbury J. held that the right of pre-emption was not effective against the statutory trusts of section 35 of the L.P.A. 1925 which displaced the trust for sale in the will. A. therefore lost his right of pre-emption.

Note: In *Re House* [1929] 2 Ch. 166, Clauson J., a testator conferred on trustees a future power of sale by public auction and not by private treaty. Nevertheless it was held that the land was subject to a trust for sale and the provision as to the manner of sale void. But in *Re Smith and Lonsdale's Contract* [1934] W.N. 36, Ch.D., where the testator directed his trustees to sell land in building plots for building purposes . . . but not otherwise, Crossman J. held that a trust to sell in limited cases did not create a trust for sale except for that particular purpose and in that particular way.

Consultation

Law of Property Act 1925, s.26(3)

"Trustees for sale shall so far as practicable consult the persons of full age for the time being beneficially interested in possession in the rents and profits of the land until sale, and shall, so far as consistent with the general interest of the trust, give effect to the wishes of such persons, or, in the case of dispute, of the majority (according to the value of their combined interests) of such persons, but a purchaser shall not be concerned to see that the provisions of this subsection have been complied with."

4. Sale by Trustees

Protection of Purchaser

Law of Property Act 1925, s.27

"(1) A purchaser of a legal estate from trustees for sale shall not be concerned with the trusts affecting the proceeds of sale of land subject to a trust for sale (whether made to attach to such proceeds by virtue of this Act or otherwise), or affecting the rents and profits of the land until sale, whether or not those trusts are declared by the same instrument by which the trust for sale is created.

(2) Notwithstanding anything to the contrary in the instrument (if any) creating a trust for sale of land or in the settlement of the net proceeds, the proceeds of sale or other capital money shall not be paid to or applied by the direction of fewer than two persons as trustees for sale, except where the trustee is a trust corporation, but this subsection does not affect the right of a sole personal representative as such to give valid receipts for, or direct the application of, proceeds of sale or other capital money, nor, except where capital money arises on the transaction, render it necessary to have more than one trustee."

Law of Property Act 1925, s.26

"(1) If the consent of more than two persons is by the disposition made requisite to the execution of a trust for sale of land, then, in favour of a purchaser, the consent of any two of such persons to the execution of the trust or to the exercise of any statutory or other powers vested in the trustees for sale shall be deemed sufficient.

(2) Where the person whose consent to the execution of any such trust or power is expressed to be required in a disposition is not *sui juris* or becomes subject to disability, his consent shall not, in favour of a purchaser, be deemed to be requisite to the execution of the trust or the exercise of the power; but the trustees shall, in any such case, obtain the separate consent of the parent or testamentary or other guardian of an infant or of the . . . receiver (if any) of a person suffering from mental disorder."

Overreaching

Note: Beneficial interests in land under a trust for sale are automatically overreached by the doctrine of conversion (above, p. 75) and converted from interests in land to interests in the proceeds of sale thereof. And see the L.P.A. 1925, s.27(1), above, p. 302, and pp. 52, 106, above.

Law of Property Act 1925, s.2

"(1) A conveyance to a purchaser of a legal estate in land shall overreach any equitable interest or power affecting that estate, whether or not he has notice thereof, if:–

. . .

(ii) The conveyance is made by trustees for sale and the equitable interest or power is at the date of the conveyance capable of being overreached by such trustees under the provisions of subsection (2) of this section or independently of that subsection and the statutory requirements respecting the payment of capital money arising under a disposition upon trust for sale are complied with; . . .

(2) Where the legal estate affected is subject to a trust for sale, then if at the date of a conveyance made after the commencement of this Act under the trust for sale or the powers conferred on the trustees for sale, the trustees (whether original or substituted) are either:–

(*a*) two or more individuals approved or appointed by the court or the successors in office of the individuals so approved or appointed; or

(*b*) a trust corporation,

such equitable interest or power shall, notwithstanding any stipulation to the contrary, be overreached by the conveyance, and shall, according to its priority, take effect as if created or arising by means of a primary trust affecting the proceeds of sale and the income of the land until sale."

Note: And see above, p. 25. *Cf.* the S.L.A. provisions, above, p. 282 and the cases thereon.

Forcing a Sale

See the Law of Property Act 1925, s.30 (above, p. 100).

III. PERPETUITIES

1. Specified Perpetuity Period

(i) *Perpetuities and Accumulations Act 1964, s.1*

"(1) Subject to section 9(2) of this Act (see below, p. 323) and subsection (2) below, where the instrument by which any disposition is made so provides, the perpetuity period applicable to the disposition under the rule against perpetuities, instead of being of any other duration, shall be of a duration equal to such number of years not exceeding eighty as is specified in that behalf in the instrument.

(2) Subsection (1) above shall not have effect where the disposition is made in exercise of a special power of appointment, but where a period is specified under that subsection in the instrument creating such a power the period shall apply in relation to any disposition under the power as it applies in

relation to the power itself."

Note: The 1964 Act came into force on July 16, 1964, and applies only to instruments coming into effect on or after that date (s.15(5)). The 80 years, or less, period must be specified as a perpetuity period, *e.g.* " 'the perpetuity period' means the period of 80 years commencing on the date hereof." In a gift to such of the issue of X as may be living at the expiration of 80 years from his death, the 80 years is not specified as a perpetuity period and the perpetuity period will be statutory lives in being (see section 3(5), below, p. 310) plus 21 years, but effect is given to the words of the gift by the fact that those issue born within the perpetuity period *and* alive 80 years from the donor's death (assuming the perpetuity period lasts so long) will take. The introduction of a fixed period not exceeding 80 years was intended to encourage drafters away from the commonly used royal lives clause.

(ii) *Royal Lives Clause*

Re Villar [1929] 1 Ch. 243, C.A.

A will provided that interests should not vest until "the expiration of twenty years from the day of the death of the last survivor of all the lineal descendants of Her late Majesty Queen Victoria who shall be living at the time of my death." The will was made in 1921 and the testator died in 1926. Evidence was brought that in 1922 the number of Queen Victoria's descendants then living was about 120, scattered across the globe. Astbury J. remarked that he felt "the gravest doubt" as to the validity of the gift in view of the difficulty in locating the persons whose lives were to delimit the period, prior to vesting. Nevertheless, he regretfully contended that the ascertainment of these lives was not "beyond the scope of legal testimony in the ordinary sense," whilst hoping (unsuccessfully) that such an inquiry would be rendered unnecessary by the reversal of his decision on appeal.

Re Leverhulme [1943] 2 All E.R. 274, Ch.D.

The first Viscount Leverhulme died in 1925 (one year before Villar) leaving a will which contained a similar provision. The validity of the limitation came before the court in 1943 on the death of the life tenant. Morton J. upheld the gift but he said of the "Queen Victoria" clause: "When that formula was first adopted there was, no doubt, little difficulty in ascertaining who those persons [*i.e.* the descendants] were, and it was not, I think, apprehended that there would be any difficulty in ascertaining when the last of them died. As a result of my decision the clause in question can still be validly employed in the case of a testator dying in 1925; but I do not at all encourage anyone to use the formula in the case of a testator who dies in the year 1943 or at any later date."

Note: In *Re Warren's Will Trusts* (1961) 105 S.J. 511, Cross J. upheld a will made in 1944 containing a "Queen Victoria" clause, despite the above warning. In this case evidence was forthcoming as to the number of descendants at the time of the testatrix's death. Apparently there were 194 legitimate issue and three other persons who might claim to be included. Subject to those, "there would apparently be no other difficulty in ascertaining the descendants." The descendants of King George V are now used as the measuring lines where a fixed period not exceeding 80 years is not employed.

2. At Common Law Possible, not Actual Events

(i) *The Fertile Octogenarian*

Re Dawson (1888) 39 Ch.D. 155

The testator gave his estate to trustees on trust to pay the plaintiff, his daughter, an annuity for life and after her death for such of the plaintiff's children as should attain 21 and also for the children of any child of the plaintiff who should have died under 21 leaving children who did attain 21. In the latter event, such a child of the plaintiff's child should take the share its parent would have received had that parent survived to 21. (This is an example of a substitutionary clause commonly contained in wills.) It is not a gift to two separate classes of children and grandchildren, but a gift to a composite class comprising both children and grandchildren (see below, p. 315). For the gift to vest beyond the perpetuity period, the following events would have had to occur: (1) the plaintiff (who was aged 60 on the death of the testator) must give birth to another child. This would give rise to a life that was not "in being" at the testator's death; (2) that child must die under the age of 21, but more than 21 years after the death of the testator; (3) that same child must be survived by a child of its own which would attain 21 more than 21 years after the death of the plaintiff. Nevertheless, Chitty J. felt obliged to assume that this improbable sequence of events could occur: "with regard to the rule against perpetuities a high degree of probability or improbability will not do." Accordingly he held the gift void. Nor could it be saved by the fact that on the testator's death the plaintiff already had several children, *all of them over 21.* Under the class-closing rules (see below, p. 314) the class would close on the plaintiff's death, but by that time another, later, child might have been borne to the plaintiff who was under 21 when the plaintiff died. That child might die under 21 leaving children who would not attain 21 within 21 years of the plaintiff's death.

Ward v. Van der Loeff [1924] A.C. 653, H.L.

Under a will and codicil, property was left on trust for the testator's wife until her death or remarriage to a non-British subject, then for such of the children of his brothers and sisters as should attain 21 or (being a female child) should marry. The testator died without issue survived by both parents (aged 66) and two brothers and two sisters. Each of these was over 30 at the time of his death, the youngest being 32. Each had infant children, the eldest of these being 14. The widow remarried, her new husband being a Dutchman, and the question arose whether the gift to the testator's nephews and nieces was void for perpetuity. The House of Lords (upholding the Court of Appeal) held that it was. They pointed out the possibility (albeit slender) that the testator's parents might have further children after his death, that these posthumous brothers and sisters might produce children of their own who might attain 21 or marry beyond the perpetuity period. In fact, however, those nephews and nieces who *were* born before the testator's death shared the gift between them, the gift in the will, though prima facie void for perpetuity, being saved by the class-closing rules (see below, p. 314). All children of nephews and nieces alive at the widow's death (the original will providing for the widow for life, then children, then children of brothers and sisters) formed the class. The original will had simply left the property to the children of the testator's brothers and sisters: the qualification as to attaining 21 or marrying had been added by the codicil. Given the codicil was now void for remoteness, *and had not purported to revoke the entire will*, the gift in the will remained valid by the reason of the doctrine of dependent relative revocation.

(ii) *The Precocious Toddler*

Re Gaite's Will Trusts [1949] 1 All E.R. 459, Ch.D.

A testatrix bequeathed a legacy of £5,000 to trustees in trust for Mrs. Gaite for life and then to such of the grandchildren of Mrs. Gaite "as shall be living at my death or born within five years therefrom who shall attain the age of 21 years or being female marry under that age in equal shares." When the testatrix died Mrs. Gaite was a widow of 55 who had two children living and one grandchild (aged eight). The gift to the grandchildren was valid.

The only events which could invalidate the gift were, first, Mrs. Gaite having another child and then that child marrying and having a child, both events happening within five years after the testatrix's death. It was in legal theory physically possible for this to happen. Roxburgh J. felt obliged to assume that Mrs. Gaite *might* have another child; but he regarded the prospect of her offspring's doing so as "legally impossible as it is not lawful to marry under the age of 16 years."

Note: In Morris and Leach, *Perpetuities* (2nd ed.), p. 85, n. 27, there is reference to the case of a Peruvian girl who in 1939 seems to have given birth to a child at the age of either four-and-a-half or five-and-a-half years. The learned authors remark that such offspring (being inevitably illegitimate) could not (before the Family Law Reform Act 1969) qualify as a "child" under an English will or deed. The *Guinness Book of Records* (30th ed.), p. 16, mentions several undocumented instances of septuagenarian mothers: the oldest *recorded* case appears to be that of a woman in her 58th year.

(iii) *Presumptions under the 1964 Act*

Perpetuities and Accumulations Act 1964, s.2(1)

"Where in any proceedings there arises on the rule against perpetuities a question which turns on the ability of a person to have a child at some future time, then—

(*a*) subject to paragraph (*b*) below, it shall be presumed that a male can have a child at the age of fourteen years or over, but not under that age, and that a female can have a child at the age of twelve year or over, but not under that age or over the age of fifty-five years; but

(*b*) in the case of a living person evidence may be given to show that he or she will or will not be able to have a child at the time in question."

(iv) *The Unborn Widow/Widower*

Re Frost (1889) 43 Ch.D. 246

The testator left property in trust for his unmarried daughter for life; and then to any husband she might have for his life; and then for such of her children as she should appoint and in default of appointment for such of her children as should be living at the death of the survivor of the daughter and her husband. Finally, there were gifts over which were dependent (see below, p. 316) on the earlier limitations. Upon the death of the unmarried daughter and her husband without issue, the question arose whether the gifts over were valid. Kay J. held that they were not. The gifts to the daughter and her husband were unexceptionable, but the daughter might have married after the death of the testator a person *not born in the testator's lifetime.* The possibility could therefore arise of the estate being tied up not only during the lifetime of the daughter (who was, of course, herself in existence when the testator died) but also during the life of her husband (who might not be a life "in being" at that time): in other words, it might turn into a limitation "for a life in being, with remainders to a life not in being, with a contingent gift over."

Note: The difficulty exemplified above was not confined to limitations dependent upon *unmarried* children of the testator. Even if the testator's daughter in the above case were married at the time of his death (or, indeed, at the time the will was made) the possibility would still exist of her remarrying a man who was not alive in the testator's lifetime. The gift might be saved, however, by construing "husband" as the husband at the date of the gift.

If T. leaves property on trust for A. for life and then for any widow/widower who may survive A. for life and then for the children of A. at 21 with remainders over, the gift to the children is valid, because all A.'s children are ascertained at A.'s death and they must reach 21, if at all, within 21 years of A.'s death (see *Re Garnham* [1916] 2 Ch. 413, Neville J.).

Perpetuities and Accumulations Act 1964, s.5

"Where a disposition is limited by reference to the time of death of the survivor of a person in being at the commencement of the perpetuity period and any spouse of that person, and that time has not arrived at the end of the perpetuity period, the disposition shall be treated for all purposes, where to do so would save it from being void for remoteness, as if it had instead been limited by reference to the time immediately before the end of that period."

3. Wait and See

Perpetuities and Accumulations Act 1964, s.3(1)(2)(3)

"(1) Where, apart from the provisions of this section and sections 4 and 5 of this Act, a disposition would be void on the ground that the interest disposed of might not become vested until too remote a time, the disposition shall be treated, until such time (if any) as it becomes established that the vesting must occur, if at all, after the end of the perpetuity period, as if the disposition were not subject to the rule against perpetuities; and its becoming so established shall not affect the validity of anything previously done in relation to the interest disposed of by way of advancement, application of intermediate income or otherwise.

(2) Where, apart from the said provisions, a disposition consisting of the conferring of a general power of appointment would be void on the ground that the power might not become exercisable until too remote a time, the disposition shall be treated, until such time (if any) as it becomes established that the power will not be exercisable within the perpetuity period, as if the disposition were not subject to the rule against perpetuities.

(3) Where, apart from the said provisions, a disposition consisting of the conferring of any power, option or other right would be void on the ground that the right might be exercised at too remote a time, the disposition shall be treated as regards any exercise of the right within the perpetuity period as if it were not subject to the rule against perpetuities and, subject to the said provisions, shall be treated as void for remoteness only if, and so far as, the right is not fully exercised within that period."

4. Lives in Being Under the Act

Perpetuities and Accumulations Act 1964, s.3(4)(5)

"(4) Where this section applies to a disposition and the duration of the perpetuity period is not determined by virtue of section 1 or 9(2) of this Act, it shall be determined as follows:–

(*a*) where any persons falling within subsection (5) below are individuals in being and ascertainable at the commencement of the perpetuity period the duration of the period shall be determined by reference to their lives and no others, but so that the lives of any description of persons falling within paragraph (*b*) or (*c*) of that subsection shall be disregarded if the number of persons of that description is such as to render it impracticable to ascertain the date of death of the survivor;

(*b*) where there are no lives under paragraph (*a*) above the period shall be twenty-one years.

(5) The said persons are as follows:–

(*a*) the person by whom the disposition was made;

(*b*) a person to whom or in whose favour the disposition was made, that is to say–

(i) in the case of a disposition to a class of persons, any member or potential member of the class;
(ii) in the case of an individual disposition to a person taking only on certain conditions being satisfied, any person as to whom some of the conditions are satisfied and the remainder may in time be satisfied;
(iii) in the case of a special power of appointment exercisable in favour of members of a class, any member or potential member of the class;
(iv) in the case of a special power of appointment exercisable in favour of one person only, that person or, where the object of the power is ascertainable only on certain conditions being satisfied, any person as to whom some of the conditions are satisfied and the remainder may in time be satisfied;
(v) in the case of any power, option or other right, the person on whom the right is conferred;

(*c*) a person having a child or grandchild within sub-paragraphs (i) to (iv) of paragraph (*b*) above, or any of whose children or grandchildren, if subsequently born, would by virtue of his or her descent fall within those sub-paragraphs;
(*d*) any person on the failure or determination of whose prior interest the disposition is limited to take effect."

5. Reduction of Age Contingencies

(i) *Before 1964 Act*

Law of Property Act 1925, s.163(1)

"Where in a will, settlement or other instrument the absolute vesting either of capital or income of property, or the ascertainment of a beneficiary or class of beneficiaries, is made to depend on the attainment by the beneficiary or members of the class of an age exceeding twenty-one years, and thereby the gift to that beneficiary or class or any member thereof, or any gift over, remainder, executory limitation, or trust arising on the total or partial failure of the original gift, is, or but for this section would be, rendered void for remoteness, the will, settlement, or other instrument shall take effect for the purposes of such gift, gift over, remainder, executory limitation, or trust as if the absolute vesting or ascertainment aforesaid had been made to depend on the beneficiary or member of the class attaining the age of twenty-one years, and that age shall be substituted for the age stated in the will, settlement, or other instrument."

Note: This provision applies where the instrument took effect after December 31, 1925, and before July 16, 1964.

(ii) *After 1964 Act*

Perpetuities and Accumulations Act 1964, s.4(1)(2)

"(1) Where a disposition is limited by reference to the attainment by any person or persons of a specified age exceeding twenty-one years, and it is apparent at the time the disposition is made or becomes apparent at a subsequent time—

(*a*) that the disposition would, apart from this section, be void for remoteness, but
(*b*) that it would not be so void if the specified age had been twenty-one years,

the disposition shall be treated for all purposes as if, instead of being limited by reference to the age in fact specified, it had been limited by reference to the age nearest to that age which would, if specified instead, have prevented the disposition from being so void.

(2) Where in the case of any disposition different ages exceeding twenty-one years are specified in relation to different persons—

(*a*) the reference in paragraph (*b*) of subsection (1) above to the specified age shall be construed as a reference to all the specified ages, and
(*b*) that subsection shall operate to reduce each such age so far as is necessary to save the disposition from being void for remoteness."

6. CLASS GIFTS

Leake v. Robinson (1817) 2 Mer. 363, Ct. of Ch.

A fund was bequeathed, *inter alia*, to W. for life and then for such of W.'s children as should attain 25. There was a gift over in default of W. having issue who attained 25 to W.'s brothers and sisters (see *Ward* v. *Van der Loeff*, above). At the testator's death W. had four children living. The gift to the children was held void because the possibility existed of a fifth child subsequently being born who might not attain 25 until more than 21 years after the death of persons in being at the testator's death. Accordingly the gift failed completely and the four children alive at the testator's death could not take under his will. A class gift is valid only if the interest of *every possible member* of that class must vest within the perpetuity period. Even if only one possible member's interest stands a chance (however slender) of vesting outside that period the *entire* class gift fails.

Note: Subject to the class-closing rules (below) which were not applied in the case, it makes no difference that (a) there is never a fifth child, all the children of the prepositus being born in the testator's lifetime; and (b) some of the prepositus' children attain 25 before the testator's death. In fact, in *Leake* v. *Robinson* there was a fifth child born after the testator's death. In an instrument taking effect after 1925 section 163 of the L.P.A. 1925 would save the gift and after July 15, 1964, a combination of sections 3 and 4 of the 1964 Act would save it.

General note. The rule in *Andrews* v. *Partington* (1791) 3 Bro.C.C. 402, L.C.: "The general principle behind the rule . . . is that if a settlor or testator directs that a fund shall be divided among the members of a class at a time when the class is still capable of increase, the class closes if at that time any member of the class is entitled to call for a distribution of his share. The rule includes all members born before the period of distribution, so as to let in as many members as possible consistent with convenience; but it excludes all those born after the period of distribution. . . .

If there is an immediate gift, *i.e.* one not preceded by any life or other interest, so that the time of distribution is the death of the testator, the rule is that the class closes at the testator's death: all children coming into existence after that time are excluded [see *Picken* v. *Matthews*, below]. . . .

If there is an immediate gift, but the time of payment is postponed until the members of the class attain a specified age, the class closes when the first child attains that age. . . .

If there is a future gift, *e.g.* to A. for life and then to the children of B., the class closes at A.'s death [see the gift in the original will in *Ward* v. *Van der Loeff*, above]. . . .

If there is a future gift, and the time of payment is postponed until the members of the class attain a specified age, the class closes when the life interest determines, or when the first child attains the specified age, whichever is the later."

The rule is one of convenience and yields to a contrary intention.

Picken v. Matthews (1878) 10 Ch.D. 264

A testator called Hooff gave real and personal property on trust for those of the children of his daughters, Helen and Charlotte, who should attain 25. When the testator died Helen had three children (one of whom was 25) and Charlotte had two, both infants. Malins V.-C. held that the existence of a child who had attained 25 on the testator's death caused the class to close at that date under the class-closing rules and so saved the gift from invalidity: "the maximum number to take was, therefore, then ascertained." The class thus closed would include all those children of Helen and Charlotte who were in existence at the time of the testator's death but not any who were born later. Malins V.-C. stated the relevant rules as: " . . . First, that a gift to a class not preceded by any life estate is a gift to such of the class as are living at the death of the testator . . . "; and secondly, "that when you have a gift for such of the children of A. as shall attain a specified age, only those who are *in esse* when the first of the class attains the specified age can take." Given all the five children then alive were lives in being, the rule was satisfied: clearly they could not attain 25 otherwise than during their own lives.

Perpetuities and Accumulations Act 1964, s.4(3)(4)

"(3) Where the inclusion of any persons, being potential members of a class or unborn persons who at birth would become members or potential members of the class, prevents the foregoing provisions of this section from operating to save a disposition from being void for remoteness, those persons shall thenceforth be deemed for all the purposes of the disposition to be excluded from the class, and the said provisions shall thereupon have effect accordingly.

(4) Where, in the case of a disposition to which subsection (3) above does not apply it is apparent at the time the disposition is made or becomes apparent at a subsequent time that, apart from this subsection, the inclusion of any persons, being potential members of a class or unborn persons who at birth would become members or potential members of the class, would cause the disposition to be treated as void for remoteness, those persons shall, unless their exclusion would exhaust the class, thenceforth be deemed for all the purposes of the disposition to be excluded from the class."

7. COMPOSITE CLASS

Pearks v. Moseley (1880) 5 App.Cas. 714, H.L.

A testator gave property to his son, William, for life, then for such of William's children as should attain 21 and the children of such of them as should die under that age leaving children as should attain that age, such children to take the share their parent would have taken had the parent survived. The question was whether there were two classes or one class compounded of persons answering one or other of alternative descriptions. The gift to William's children if it stood alone would be valid. The substitutionary gift to the grandchildren would be invalid. It was held to be a gift to a composite class and was void. The maximum size of the children's shares was not ascertainable until the children of a deceased child attained or failed to attain 21 and that event might happen more than 21 years after the death of lives in being at the testator's death.

Note: And see *Re Dawson*, above, p. 306.

8. EXPECTANT AND DEPENDENT LIMITATIONS

Re Abbott [1893] 1 Ch. 54

The testator left property to his unmarried daughter for life, then to her husband (if any) for his life, then to such of their children as the parents or the survivor of them should appoint, and in default of appointment to the children at 21 or, if female, on earlier marriage. The testator's daughter subsequently married and became Mrs. Frigout. Stirling J. held, on the assumption that the power given to the husband was void for perpetuity (as an unborn widower, see above, p. 309), that the gift over in default was valid. The judge remarked that if a prior limitation under a settlement is void for remoteness then any interest expectant upon that limitation is also, inevitably, invalid: the reason being that one can only take under a *subsequent limitation* if the prior limitation is exhausted, and in a case where that prior limitation is void for perpetuity it does not have a chance to be exhausted because it never comes into operation at all. Thus the testator's intentions are bound in any event to be frustrated. However: "This reason does not necessarily apply to limitations in default of appointment. In many, perhaps I ought to say in most, cases of such limitations the intention is that they should take effect unless displaced by a valid exercise of the preceding power of appointment."

Re Coleman [1936] Ch. 528

The testator left a share of his residuary estate for his son W. for life on discretionary trusts, and thereafter on similar trusts for any widow W. might leave and for all or any of W.'s children and, after the death of the widow, on trust in equal shares for the children of W. on attaining 21 or marriage. Clauson J. held that although the discretionary trust in the widow's favour offended the perpetuity rule (by virtue of the possibility that W. might marry a woman born after the testator's death) the ultimate gift on trust to the children was valid. These children would naturally be ascertained on the death of their father, W. Their interests were vested at that time and were subject to no such contingency as that they should survive the widow in order to qualify. The case thus demonstrates that (to quote Buckley J. in *Re Hubbard's Will Trusts* (below)) "the mere fact that a trust is ulterior to another which is invalid for remoteness, in the sense that the benefit under the former trust can only fall into possession when any possible benefit under the latter, had it been valid, would have ceased, is not sufficient to render the ulterior trust invalid."

Note: And see Re Vaux, below p. 317.

Re Hubbard's Will Trusts [1963] Ch. 275

A testator divided his residuary estate into four equal shares and in the event two parts of it (the sisters' fund) was subject to trusts each for a sister for life, then for her children and then on certain discretionary trusts which were void for perpetuity (the discretion not being limited to the perpetuity period). The will then provided: "on the failure or determination of the trusts hereinbefore declared of any share of my sister's fund" that share was to accrue to the other shares and be held on the same trusts as those other shares. "Subject as aforesaid" the fund was to be held on trust for certain charities. The question arose as to the validity of the accruer clause and the ultimate gift over. Buckley J. held that the accruer provision was dependent upon the prior void trusts and expectant on their failure and was therefore itself invalid. The judge analysed the cases into three classes: (1) where there is a series of successive interests each intended to take effect on, and only on, the exhaustion or termination of all antecedent interests in the chain, so that is one of those interests failed all ulterior interests would fail. The ulterior interest is said to fail by reason of contagion with or dependency on the void prior interest; (2) where there is an interest which will not take effect in possession until a future date but vests in interest within the perpetuity period and the enjoyment of that interest in possession is not dependent on the prior exhaustion of the prior interests (see *e.g. Re Coleman*, above); and (3) where property is given to A. either immediately or at some future date which is not too remote, but A.'s interest may be displaced by the exercise of some power or discretion, A.'s interest will be unaffected by any invalidity of that power or discretion on the ground of remoteness (see *e.g. Re Abbott*, above). In the present case the accruer clause fell into class (1). But the ultimate gift fell into class (2) and was valid. It was the only disposition of the capital of the fund and vested in interest on the testator's death. The enjoyment by the charities of that interest in possession was merely postponed because for a limited time the income was to go elsewhere.

Note: In the above case it was assumed that the failure or determination of the trusts referred to in the will did not include failure for perpetuity. It has been held that "failure or determination" covers failure for perpetuity (see *Re Robinson's Will Trusts* [1963] 1 W.L.R. 628, Ch.D., Plowman J.), but "failure" by itself did not (see *Re Buckton's S.T.*[1964] Ch. 497, Pennycuick J.).

Perpetuities and Accumulations Act 1964, s.6

"A disposition shall not be treated as void for remoteness by reason only that the interest disposed of is ulterior to and dependent upon an interest under a disposition which is so void, and the vesting of an interest shall not be prevented from being accelerated on the failure of a prior interest by reason only that the failure arises because of remoteness."

9. Alternative Contingencies

Proctor v. Bishop of Bath and Wells
(1974) 2 Hy.Bl. 358, C.C.P.

Mary Proctor devised an advowson to the first or other son of her grandson, Thomas Proctor, that should be bred a clergyman and be in holy orders, "but in case Thomas should have no such son" then to another grandson, Thomas Moore, in fee. Thomas Proctor died without ever having a son and Thomas Moore claimed to be entitled to the advowson. Obviously, the first or other son of Thomas Proctor to take to the cloth might do so more than 21 years after Thomas Proctor's death. Furthermore, no son might ever have done so, whereupon one would not have known whether or not Thomas Moore was entitled until all possibility of a son of Thomas Proctor becoming a clergyman had vanished. That might only be after many decades. It was held that the gift to the son of Thomas Proctor was void, and so was the gift over to Thomas Moore, which was contingent upon the failure of the earlier demise.

Note: Where a gift states two alternative contingencies upon which vesting depends and one is too remote but the other is not, the gift is good if the valid contingency occurs (see *Re Curryer's W.T*, below). One could "wait and see" (even at common law) if the valid contingency occurred. But the alternatives must be expressed. In the above case there were two alternatives, *i.e.* (1) Thomas Proctor might have had no son (as was the case) which must be known at his death and therefore within the perpetuity period; and (2) he might have had a son who became a clergyman outside the period. Had the gift been worded "to the first son of Thomas Proctor to become a clergyman, but, if he should have no such son, to Thomas Moore" the gift to Thomas Moore would have been valid if Thomas Proctor died leaving no son.

Re Curryer's Will Trusts [1938] 1 Ch. 952

A testator provided that "on the decease of my last surviving child or on the death of the last surviving widow or widower of my children as the case may be whichever shall last happen" his trustees should stand possessed of the trust fund in trust for his grandchild or grandchildren living at the period of distribution and the issue then living of his grandchild or grandchildren dying before that period. Morton J. held that the gift was not completely void. It was of course possible that one of the testator's children might marry a person not born in the testator's lifetime and such a spouse might survive the child of the testator to whom it was married for more than 21 years. However, in the judge's view the two contingencies (death of last surviving child and death of last surviving widow or widower) were expressed as separate and alternative events. He conceded that the words "as the case may be whichever shall last happen" tended against this construction of the settlement, but he considered that this factor alone was not enough to displace his construction of the provision as encompassing two distinct events. Accordingly, the ultimate gift of the capital was held to be valid "if the death of the testator's last surviving child happens after the death of the last surviving widow or widower of a child of the testator."

Powers of Appointment

Re De Sommery [1912] 2 Ch. 622

A testatrix left two-thirteenths of her residuary estate " . . . upon trust to pay the capital or income thereof to my nephew Eugene . . . or for his benefit or for the benefit of his wife or any child or children of his as my trustees may in their absolute and uncontrolled discretion consider desirable." Parker J. held that " . . . where the settlor has used language from which the court may fairly infer that he contemplated the creation, not of a single power, but of two distinct powers, one of which only is open to objection because of the rule against perpetuities, the court will avoid the latter only and give effect to the power which is not open to this objection." Since the present power was capable of being split up in this way, the power in favour of Eugene (which could only be exercised in his lifetime) would be upheld. However, that in relation to Eugene *or* his wife *or* his children (which was capable of being exercised beyond the period, because they were not necessarily lives in being) was void. "A special power which . . . is capable of being exercised beyond lives in being and 21 years afterwards is . . . absolutely void; but if it can only be exercised within the period allowed by the rule against perpetuities it is a good power, even although some particular exercise of it might be void because of the rule. . . . If a power be given to a person alive at the date of the instrument creating it it must . . . if exercised at all, be executed during his life, and is therefore valid. Again, if a power can be exercised only in favour of a person living at the date of the instrument creating it, it must, if exercised at all, be exercised during the life of such person, and is therefore unobjectionable. Further, the instrument itself may expressly limit a period, not exceeding the legal limits, for the exercise of the power."

Re Vaux [1939] Ch. 465, C.A.

A testator directed the trustees of his will for the time being to hold his residuary estate on trust "to pay and apply both the income and capital thereof in such shares and proportions as they may in their absolute and uncontrolled discretion think fit to or for the benefit of all or any one or more of my children or the issue of any deceased child of mine." This clause was void because an appointment might be made more than 21 years after any life in being at the testator's death. The definition of trustees was not limited to the original trustees, but included their successors in office. However, a subsequent clause of the will provided that the trustees should deal with the residuary estate "for the benefit and provision of my children or grandchildren . . . save only that all such dealings . . . shall be within the limitations prescribed by law." It was held that this clause was independent of, and additional to, the prior discretionary trust and valid, being limited to the period prescribed by law, which, in this case, was held to mean for the lives of the primary beneficiaries, *i.e.* the children and grandchildren of the testator alive at his death and 21 years thereafter.

Re Brown and Sibley's Contract (1876) 3 Ch.D. 156

Under a marriage settlement land was held on trust for the settlor, William Metford, for life and after his death for such of his issue (to be born before the appointment was made) as he should appoint with a gift over in default. By his will W.M. appointed to his son W.E.M. in fee, but in the event of W.E.M. having no child who attained 21, then to his grandson, W.M.B. (who was not born when the settlement was executed). Could W.E.M. (who had sold part of the land to Brown, who in turn had sub-sold to Sibley) give Brown a good title or did he need the concurrence of his nephew W.M.B.? Malins V.-C. held that the gift over to W.M.B. was void for remoteness and W.E.M. could give a good title. Where a person takes property by virtue of the execution of a special power . . . he takes directly under the instrument creating the power. The appointment is, as it were, read back into the settlement. Here the effect was as if the settlement had been for W.M. for life, then his unborn son in fee with a gift over in the event of the son having no child who should attain 21 to this unborn grandson. This was an attempt to make the property inalienable for a period which might extend to 21 years after the determination of the life of a person not in being at the date of the settlement.

Re Paul [1921] 2 Ch. 1

A testator who died in 1895 left part of his residuary estate to his daughter for life and gave her a power to appoint the fund amongst her children by will. The daughter in her will appointed to her son A. upon his attaining 25. When she died in 1919 he was 18 or 19 years old. Sargant J. held that this was a valid exercise of the power. The gift to the named son was good since his interest must vest, if at all, within six or seven years of his mother's death.

Note: The case thus exemplifies what is sometimes called the "second look" doctrine. Although the appointment must, in the case of a special power, be read back into the settlement, the facts existing at the date of the appointment may be examined when considering whether its exercise offends the rule against perpetuities.

Perpetuities and Accumulations Act 1964, ss.1(2), 3(2)(3), 7

1. (2) (above, p. 304).
3. (2) and (3) (above, p. 309).

"7. For the purposes of the rule against perpetuities, a power of appointment shall be treated as a special power unless–

(*a*) in the instrument creating the power it is expressed to be exercisable by one person only, and

(*b*) it could, at all times during its currency when that person is of full age and capacity, be exercised by him so as immediately to transfer to himself the whole of the interest governed by the power without the consent of any other person or compliance with any other condition, not being a formal condition relating only to the mode of exercise of the power:

Provided that for the purpose of determining whether a disposition made under a power of appointment exercisable by will only is void for remoteness, the power shall be treated as a general power where it would have fallen to be so treated if exercisable by deed."

10. Options

Woodall v. Clifton [1905] 2 Ch. 257, C.A.

In a lease for 99 years granted in 1867 the lessor (and through him his heirs and assigns) covenanted that in the event of the lessee (or his heirs and assigns) desiring to purchase the freehold and paying over the purchase money (£500 per acre) he would execute the appropriate conveyance in favour of the purchaser. An assignee of the term sought to enforce this covenant against the assignee of the reversion. Warrington J. held that the covenant was void for perpetuity. Accordingly the option could not be enforced. The judge thought that it was clearly established that the rule against perpetuities did not apply to options to *renew* a lease. But as to options to purchase he said: "If the grant creates an interest in land [which in the present case it did] then it seems to me that the effect of it is to render it something more than a mere covenant, and to create an interest in land which does not vest at the moment at which it is granted, but requires for its vesting the happening of another event, namely, the exercise of the option and the payment of the purchase-money. Which event may happen beyond the limit." The Court of Appeal upheld the decision on the ground that the option did not run with the reversion (above, p. 161) and therefore did not bind the defendant. But it has been suggested that the option would run in equity as a contract to create a legal estate.

Note: On options to renew, see also *Weg Motors Ltd.* v. *Hales* (above, p. 129).

The rule against perpetuities has already been held to apply to an option to repurchase in *L. & S.W. Ry.* v. *Gomm* (1882) 20 Ch.D. 562, C.A., where the purchaser of the land had promised to re-convey it to the vendor if the land should ever again be required for the railway run by the vendor, and the railway company was then trying (unsuccessfully, because the interest created was too remote) to enforce this covenant against the purchaser's assignee. However, in *Worthing Corporation* v. *Heather* [1906] 2 Ch. 532, Warrington J. held that even though an option to purchase *was* void for remoteness and could not, in his view, be specifically enforced by the covenantee, nevertheless this did not debar that covenantee from recovering damages against the estate of the covenantor who had purported to grant him the option and whose devisees were claiming it to be unenforceable. Moreover, these devisees themselves (being heirs and assigns of the covenantor) were also liable. And in *Hutton* v. *Watling* [1948] Ch. 26 ([1948] Ch. 398, C.A.) Jenkins J. refused to allow the fact that an option was void for perpetuity to prevent the grantee of the option from obtaining a decree of specific performance against the grantor. He regarded the House of Lords decision in *S.E. Ry.* v. *Associated Portland Cement Manufacturers Ltd.* [1910] 1 Ch. 12 as binding upon him, and clear authority for the principle that "an option to purchase land without limit as regards time is specifically enforceable as a matter of personal contract against the original grantor of the option, and . . . the rule against perpetuities has no relevance to such a case, as distinct from [one where] such an option is sought to be enforced against some successor in title of the original grantor, not by virtue of any contractual obligation on the part of the successor in title, but by virtue of the equitable interest in the land conferred on the grantee by the option agreement." In the *S.E. Ry.* case a railway company agreed to grant the owner of adjoining land the right to construct a tunnel under the railway line. Sixty-two years later it was held that the company could not restrain a successor in title of the original landowner from making the tunnel, on the ground that his right was a matter of personal obligation to which the rule against perpetuities did not apply. For the avoidance of contractual and other rights in cases of remoteness, see Perpetuities and Accumulations Act 1964, s.10, below.

Perpetuities and Accumulations Act 1964, ss.9, 10

"9. (1) The rule against perpetuities shall not apply to a disposition consisting of the conferring of an option to acquire for valuable consideration an interest reversionary (whether directly or indirectly) on the term of a lease if—

(*a*) the option is exercisable only by the lessee or his successors in title, and
(*b*) it ceases to be exercisable at or before the expiration of one year following the determination of the lease.

This subsection shall apply in relation to an agreement for a lease as it applies in relation to a lease, and "lessee" shall be construed accordingly.

(2) In the case of a disposition consisting of the conferring of an option to acquire for valuable consideration any interest in land, the perpetuity period under the rule against perpetuities shall be twenty-one years, and section 1 of this Act shall not apply:

Provided that this subsection shall not apply to a right of pre-emption conferred on a public or local authority in respect of land used or to be used for religious purposes where the right becomes exercisable only if the land ceases to be used for such purposes."

10. Where a disposition inter vivos would fall to be treated as void for remoteness if the rights and duties thereunder were capable of transmission to persons other than the original parties and had been so transmitted, it shall be treated as void as between the person by whom it was made and the person to whom or in whose favour it was made or any successor of his, and no remedy shall lie in contract or otherwise for giving effect to it or making restitution for its lack of effect.

11. Rights of Entry and Possibilities of Reverter

Re Trustees of Hollis' Hospital and Hague's Contract
[1899] 2 Ch. 540

A grant in 1726 to the trustees of the hospital provided that if at any time thereafter the premises should be employed otherwise than for the purposes of a hospital, they should revert to the grantor's heirs. When the trustees came to sell the premises the effect of the grant was raised. Byrne J. held that the grant was to be construed as the grant of a fee simple subject to a condition subsequent with a right of entry for the grantor and his heirs. The rule against perpetuities applied to rights of entry. The right of entry in the present case was too remote and the original grantees took a fee simple absolute on trust for the hospital.

Note: And see *Shiloh Spinners Ltd.* v. *Harding*, above, p. 24.

Law of Property Act 1925, s.4(3)

"All rights of entry affecting a legal estate which are exercisable on condition broken or for any other reason may, after the commencement of this Act, be made exercisable by any person and the persons deriving title under him, but, in regard to an estate in fee simple (not being as rentcharge held for a legal estate) only within the period authorised by the rule relating to perpetuities."

Hopper v. Liverpool Corporation

(1944) 88 S.J. 213, Lancaster Palatine Court

In 1805 the Corporation conveyed the freehold reversion in the building called the Lyceum to certain members of the Liverpool Library and their heirs "during such time as the building called the Lyceum or any other building to be erected on the site thereof shall be used and enjoyed for the purposes of the said institution called the Lyceum" in trust for the subscribers to the Library. The Library already held the leasehold interest in the premises. The effect of the conveyance was to create a determinable fee simple with a possibility of reverter in the grantor. In 1941 the Library was discontinued and the lease having long since expired the question arose whether the premises reverted to the Corporation. Bennett V.-C. held that the rule against perpetuities applied to possibilities of reverter. The possibility of reverter in the present case was too remote and the original grantees took a fee simple absolute.

Note: Notwithstanding this case other cases had decided that the rule did not apply to possibilities of reverter. The conflict is resolved for dispositions made after July 15, 1964, by section 12 of the Perpetuities and Accumulations Act 1964 which applies the rule to possibilities of reverter.

Perpetuities and Accumulations Act 1964, s.12(1)

"In the case of–

(*a*) a possibility of reverter on the determination of a determinable fee simple, or

(*b*) a possibility of a resulting trust on the determination of any other determinable interest in property, the rule against perpetuities shall apply in relation to the provision causing the interest to be determinable as it would apply if that provision were expressed in the form of a condition subsequent giving rise, on breach thereof, to a right of re-entry or an equivalent right in the case of property other than land, and where the provision falls to be treated as void for remoteness the determinable interest shall become an absolute interest."

12. Administrative Powers of Trustees

Re Allott [1924] 2 Ch. 498, C.A.

A testator directed the trustees of his will to stand possessed of the mines and minerals beneath his residuary realty and the rents and profits thereof on trust to pay annuities to his daughters. The terms of the will were subsequently varied by a deed of family arrangement whereby a surviving husband of any daughter was entitled for his life to his wife's annuity and the trustees were given power to lease the mines to provide the annuities, *inter alia*, during the life of a surviving husband. A husband was not necessarily a person alive at the date of the deed. It was held that because the trustees might have exercised the leasing power after the period of the lives of the daughters and 21 years, the power was void.

Note: Administrative powers like the one in this case *exercised* after July 15, 1964 (even though *created* before that date), are excluded from the rule against perpetuities by section 8(1) of the 1964 Act.

Perpetuities and Accumulations Act 1964, s.8

"(1) The rule against perpetuities shall not operate to invalidate a power conferred on trustees or other persons to sell, lease, exchange or otherwise dispose of any property for full consideration, or to do any other act in the administration (as opposed to the distribution) of any property, and shall not prevent the payment to trustees or other persons of reasonable remuneration for their services.

(2) Subsection (1) above shall apply for the purpose of enabling a power to be exercised at any time after the commencement of this Act notwithstanding that the power is conferred by an instrument which took effect before that commencement."

13. EASEMENTS

Dunn v. Blackdown Properties Ltd. [1961] Ch. 433

Two conveyances made in 1926 and 1938 respectively to the plaintiff's predecessors in title were expressed to contain a grant of a right of way over a private road owned by the defendant's predecessors in title and a right of drainage in the following terms "to use the sewers and drains then passing or thereafter to pass under the road or any part thereof." There were no sewers or drains in existence at the dates of the conveyances. Subsequently drains were constructed by the defendant and the plaintiff claimed a right to connect with these drains when she built on her lands. It was held that the purported grant of a right of drainage was a future easement which was subject to the rule against perpetuities and therefore void for remoteness. The grant was not saved by section 162(1)(*d*)(iv) of the L.P.A. 1925 (which excludes certain ancillary rights of constructing, repairing, etc., drains, etc.), as this provision was merely to make it clear that if a person had a valid right of drainage certain ancillary rights to make the basic right effective were not to be treated as void for perpetuity because they might be exercised outside the period.

Note: For mortgages, see above, p. 165.

14. ACCUMULATIONS

Law of Property Act 1925, s.164(1)

"No person may by any instrument or otherwise settle or dispose of any property in such manner that the income thereof shall, save as hereinafter mentioned, be wholly or partially accumulated for any longer period than one of the following, namely:—

(*a*) the life of the grantor or settlor; or

(*b*) a term of twenty-one years from the death of the grantor, settlor or testator; or

(*c*) the duration of the minority or respective minorities of any person or persons living or *en ventre sa mère* at the death of the grantor, settlor or testator; or

(*d*) the duration of the minority or respective minorities only of any person or persons who under the limitations of the instrument directing the accumulations would, for the time being, if of full age, be entitled to the income directed to be accumulated.

In every case where any accumulation is directed otherwise than as aforesaid, the direction shall (save as hereinafter mentioned) be void; and the income of the property directed to be accumulated shall, so long as the same is directed to be accumulated contrary to this section, go to and be received by the person or persons who would have been entitled thereto if such accumulation had not been directed."

Trustee Act 1925, s.31(2)
(as amended by Family Law Reform Act 1969)

"During the infancy of any such person, if his interest so long continues, the trustees shall accumulate all the residue of that income in the way of compound interest by investing the same and the resulting income thereof from time to time in authorised investments, and shall hold those accumulations as follows:–

(i) If any such person–
  (*a*) attains the age of eighteen years or marries under that age, and his interest in such income during his infancy or until his marriage is a vested interest; or
  (*b*) on attaining the age of eighteen years or on marriage under that age becomes entitled to the property from which such income arose in fee simple, absolute or determinable, or absolutely, or for an entailed interest;

  the trustees shall hold the accumulations in trust for such person absolutely, but without prejudice to any provision with respect thereto contained in any settlement by him made under any statutory powers during his infancy, and so that the receipt of such person after marriage, and though still an infant, shall be a good discharge; and

(ii) in any other case the trustees shall, notwithstanding that such person had a vested interest in such income, hold the accumulations as an accretion to the capital of the property from which such accumulations arose, and as one fund with such capital for all purposes, and so that, if such property is settled and, such accumulations shall be held upon the same trusts as if the same were capital money arising therefrom;

but the trustees may, at any time during the infancy of such person if his interest so long continues, apply those accumulations, or any part thereof, as if they were income arising in the then current year."

Perpetuities and Accumulations Act 1964, s.13

"(1) The periods for which accumulations of income under a settlement or other disposition are permitted by section 164 of the Law of Property Act 1925 shall include–

(*a*) a term of twenty-one years from the date of the making of the disposition, and
(*b*) the duration of the minority or respective minorities of any person or persons in being at that date.

(2) It is hereby declared that the restrictions imposed by the said section 164 apply in relation to a power to accumulate income whether or not there is a duty to exercise that power, and that they apply whether or not the power to accumulate extends to income produced by the investment of income previously accumulated."

Re Ransome [1957] Ch. 348

A testatrix directed that income of a fund should be accumulated until the youngest child of her grandson Robert should attain 21. The testatrix died in 1935. R. had a son by his first marriage who attained 21 in 1951. In 1953 R. had remarried. There were no children of this marriage at the date of the proceedings. The direction for accumulation was excessive and the question was which of the statutory periods was more suitable. The choice was between section 164(1)(*b*) or (*c*)–(*b*) would bring the period of accumulation to an end in 1956, 21 years from the testatrix's death; (*c*) in 1951, when the son attained 21. Neither fitted in with the testatrix's directions but it had to be one or the other. By directing accumulations until R.'s *youngest* child attained 21, the testatrix could hardly have contemplated accumulations until R.'s *eldest* child was 21 and therefore Upjohn J. held that (*b*) was the appropriate paragraph.

Re Watt's Will Trusts [1936] 2 All E.R. 1555, Ch.D.

A testator directed that the share he had previously in the will given to his son G. should be held by his trustees upon trusts, subject to certain provisions for the maintenance of G.'s children, to accumulate the surplus income during the minority of G.'s children. The capital of the G. fund and the accumulations thereof were given to the children of G. at 21 in equal shares. The testator died in 1928, survived by G., G.'s wife and G.'s three children born in 1914, 1917 and 1928 respectively. When G.'s eldest child attained 21 proceedings were taken to determine the validity of the direction for accumulation. Bennett J. held that the period specified by section 164(1)(*d*) was not appropriate here because the income of the *whole* fund had to be accumulated even after one or more of the children had attained 21. The period specified in section 164(1)(*c*) was therefore the appropriate period. But the direction exceeded the statute because the testator had not restricted this period for accumulation to the minority of G.'s *children living at his (T.'s) death*. The accumulation period directed by the will must therefore be restricted to the minorities of the three children of G. who were alive at the testator's death but it could not continue during the minority of any after-born child.

Re Jefferys [1939] Ch. 205

(See above, p. 286.)

The appropriate period for accumulation was under paragraph (*b*), *i.e.* 21 years from the death of the testator. Accordingly the period for accumulation expired in 1933. Thereafter the income from the property must be applied in paying Mr. Martin's annuity but any surplus could no longer be accumulated. It was held that the surplus during the remainder of Mr. Martin's life was undisposed of and passed as on intestacy.

INDEX